Jonah Barrington

Rise And Fall of the Irish Nation

Jonah Barrington

Rise And Fall of the Irish Nation

ISBN/EAN: 9783744734080

Printed in Europe, USA, Canada, Australia, Japan

Cover: Foto ©ninafisch / pixelio.de

More available books at **www.hansebooks.com**

RISE AND FALL

OF

THE IRISH NATION.

BY

SIR JONAH BARRINGTON, LL. D. K. C.

Member in the late Irish Parliament for the Cities of Tuam and Clogher

> The nations have fallen, and thou still art young,
> Thy sun is but rising, when others are set;
> And, though slavery's cloud o'er thy morning hath hung,
> The full noon of freedom shall beam round them yet.
> Erin! oh Erin, though long in the shade,
> Thy star will shine out when the proudest shall fade.
>   MOORE

TWELFTH THOUSAND.

NEW YORK:
D. & J. SADLIER & CO., 31 BARCLAY STREET.
BOSTON:—128 FEDERAL STREET.
MONTREAL, C. E.:—COR. OF NOTRE DAME & ST. FRANCIS XAVIER STS.
1863.

TO

THE BARON PLUNKET,

LORD CHANCELLOR OF IRELAND

My dear Lord,

Even whilst the twilight of life is rapidly descending into that mysterious night, by which the whole human race must inevitably be enveloped, there yet remains one gratification, which, whilst intellect survives, age cannot deprive us of, the recollection of past pleasures.

To me none afford more happy recollections than the splendid days of my variegated life, spent in the society of those great and gifted characters, who once adorned that talented and happy island, we were then proud to call the place of our nativity.

From that society all distinctions of party were banished, and politics were forgotten; all merged in the general glow of private friendship; there were no contests save those of wit, no emulation but in the animated sallies of classic conviviality, there your talents were conspicuous, and your elevation was predicted. In those societies our intimacy commenced, and generated a friendship, from which my heart and my actions have never for one moment deviated.

No man knew me better than your Lordship, no man knows better the sacrifices I made to uphold our country. Once I was formidable to its enemies; but I have lost my sting, and it required the strength of more than ordinary philosophy to bear up against that overwhelming weight of injustice, illegality, haughty and irresistible oppression, which, through unconstitutional proceedings, and for a palpably corrupt purpose, were heaped upon one of the oldest and most proven friends of the British Monarchy. I trust, however, to the justice and liberality of a reformed representation to afford me a full opportunity of bringing before their eyes, that unprecedented scene of injustice, and of convincing the Empire, that real culprits, of the higher orders, were at the same moment, not only screened, but elevated.

On the most important subject that ever agitated (and has not ceased to agitate) the British Empire, our sentiments, my Lord, were congenial: we fought side by side in the cause of Ireland, upon that vital point I yielded my warmest friends, and acquired most inveterate enemies, you broke from no connexion, talent, patriotism, eloquence and integrity stamped your character; I feel, therefore, that, as the intimate of my society, the comrade of my battles, and, I believe, the friend of my declining years, I should pay to you this tribute of regard, by presenting to you a volume, which fills up the chasm of events for twenty of the most momentous years of Irish History; and, if God gives me health to complete what I am undertaking, *the reigns of the seven Viceroys which have succeeded the Union* shall be given to the public, as an irrefragable proof of the truth of the predictions, which, in 1800, were urged in vain against the adoption of that disastrous measure.

As some novel points of view in which I have in this volume placed the present state of the Union question, spring solely from myself, they are only to be considered as the isolated opinion of a worn-out public man; full perhaps of those national prejudices, which are inseparable from his nature, but excusable when they are genuine, and founded on the purest principles of equity and constitution.

One of the proudest days of my life was that when, a candidate for the Metropolis of Ireland, the five first names found on my tally, were those of *the Grattan*, G. Ponsonby, Plunket, Curran, and Ball; you, my Lord, are the only survivor of that illustrious group, who has lived to see the fulfilment of their prophecies, and in that point of view, I feel that not only my private friendship, but almost public duty, commands me to present to you a work, which, whilst narrating the glorious, but unsuccessful struggles of our common country, for its Independence, offers a feeble and melancholy tribute to the patriotism of those illustrious characters, whose memory will ever be revered by a generous and grateful people.

Believe me, my dear Lord, to be,
With the utmost sincerity,
Yours most faithfully,
JONAH BARRINGTON.

Paris, 1st of May, 1833.

PREFATORY OBSERVATIONS.

More than thirty summers have now passed by, since that disastrous measure, called a "legislative Union" extinguished at one blow, the pride, the prosperity, and the Independence of the Irish Nation.

A measure which, under the false colours of guarding for ever against a disunion of the Empire, has taken the longest and surest stride to lead it to dismemberment.

A measure which, instead of "*consolidating the strength and resource of the Empire,*" as treacherously expressed from the Throne of the Viceroy, has, through its morbid operation, paralyzed the resources of Ireland; whilst England is exhausting her own strength, squandering her own treasures, and clipping her own constitution, to uphold a measure, effected by corruption, and maintained by oppression.

A measure which, pretending to tranquillize, has in fact excited more hostile, and I fear, interminable disgust, than had ever before existed between the two nations, and has banished from both, that mutual and invigorating attachment, which was daily augmenting, under the continuance of the federative connexion.

The protecting body of the country gentlemen have evacuated Ireland, and in their stead, we now find official clerks, griping agents, haughty functionaries, and proud Clergy; the resident Aristocracy of Ireland, if not quite extinguished, is hourly diminishing; and it is a political truism, that the coexistence of an oligarchy, without a cabinet, a resident executive, and an absent legislation, tenants without landlords, and magistrates without legal knowledge, must be, from its nature, a form of constitution at once incongruous, inefficient, and dangerous. The present is a state which cannot exist; it is a struggle, that cannot continue, there is "a tide" in the affairs of Empires, as well as of individuals; every fever has a crisis: Ireland is in one now, I am no fanatic, I am the partisan only of tranquillity, in the country where I drew my first breath.

The people of England, and also of some continental kingdoms, are fully aware of the distracted state of Ireland, but are at a loss to account for it; it is now however in proof, that thirty-three years of Union have been thirty-three years of beggary and disturbance, and this result, I may fairly say, I always foresaw.

And when my humble sentiments as to the susceptibility of Ireland, and the misrule that seems entailed on her generations, have the honor of coinciding with those of the highest authority in England, on that subject, I feel myself invincible in the position, that "If Ireland was well governed she would be the brightest jewel in the King's Crown. The proof that the people are not bad is that during two rebellions in **1715** and **1745** that raged in Scotland and England, the Irish people were quite quiet. But she has been badly governed, and has not and does not improve with the rest of the Empire."

In fact the world has now become not only enlightened, but illuminated, by the progress of political information; and it is clear as day that there are but two ways, through which eight millions of Irish population can ever be governed with security: either through the re-enjoyment of her own constitution, and voluntary affection to her rulers, or by physical force of arms, and the temporary right of conquest, the former even now requires only the will of England, and the word reconciliation; but both ancient and modern examples fully prove, that the whole physical force and power of Great Britain might find itself dangerously deceived in trying to establish by the sword, a system so repugnant to the very nature of the English people.

During the short reign of Earl Fitzwilliam with a resident legislature, five thousand men were sufficient to garrison every spot of Ireland, under the protracted reign of the present Viceroy, more than thirty thousand soldiers are found necessary, to enforce obedience even to a single statute of the Imperial legislature.

These are proofs and matters of fact, they carry conviction to the reason of every man susceptible of conviction, and of every party not hurried away by prejudice, and great Britain herself must now perceive that above a third of her military are employed in Ireland, by her minister, to keep down the exuberant spirit of that people, and that army paid out of the English purse, by taxes levied on the English people, is solely maintained to extinguish that very spirit which they have themselves so triumphantly exercised to obtain a reform of their own corrupt legislature.

The subjects of this volume, and some novel suggestions and doctrines it embodies, will of course excite many different opinions, as to the object of its author, in producing such a work, at so critical an epocha of the British Empire. I therefore hesitate not a moment in avowing my reasons; they are just, true, and conciliatory; one is to dispel that profound ignorance of the real state of Ireland, its claims and its deprivations, which appears to have pervaded every class of the British people, and in which lack of information, so great a proportion even of the present Parliament appears to participate.

But above all to convince the British people, that they are the very worst friends of the connexion, who raise up a "repeal of the Union" as a sprite to terrify the English people, into a false belief that it would be only a certain prelude to a separation of the countries.

Never yet was a more mischievous or false position forced on the credulity of an uninformed people; whoever reads this volume will detect that falsehood; there they will find, by comparing times and incidents, that, so far from a resident legislature being a ground of separation, it was the knot that indissolubly united them, whilst the increasing miseries of Ireland, arising from this Union, are only the prelude to a convulsive separation of the two countries.

In the body of this volume (page 391,) I have given my suggestion as to the term "Repeal of the Union" and my opinion, that no power of the Irish representatives or trustees, could enact a line of it, that as a constitutional measure, it is a nullity unqualified, and that no such Union *de jure*, is at present in existence.

I must here observe in reply to the ingenious verbiage of my able friend Baron Smith of the Irish Exchequer Bench, that of all the feeble attempts to uphold the affirmative of that untenable position, his alone is worthy of the most trivial animadversion.

When simply a member of the extinguished legislature, he might, like many others, have supported that vicious doctrine for his temporary purposes; but it is to be lamented, that being a judge he still supports the same doctrine, as to the competence of Parliament, though so distinctly and palpably repugnant to the eternal principles of Justice, and Equity, which form the very essence, and the practice of his jurisdiction.

It is impossible to reconcile such pertinacious retention of that doctrine, save through a supposition, that the subtlety of sophistry and metaphysics, have suggested to his fancy, some imaginary distinction between that equity to which private property, and public right, have been invariably and equally entitled; and that an individual may be entitled to a justice, which a people can be deprived of; and a constitution betrayed by the very trustees, who were delegated for its protection.

The case of England and Ireland is not merely a question of law, or even simply of constitution; it is a question actually embracing the law of nations, commercial treaties existed between them as independent countries, and Ireland enjoyed for eighteen years all the rights which the law of nations confers on independent states.

The difficulties of dissolving the union are exaggerated, the situation of both countries presented far greater obstacles for their arrangement in 1782, than are at this moment existing.

England at that period had usurped a dominion over the Irish legislature; policy and justice, called on her to relinquish that dominion; she obeyed the call, and the epeal of her own statute (sixth George I.) by inference admitted the usurpation of centuries.

Still the power of re-enactment remained; Ireland claimed a statutable renunciation of such a power, and a guarantee for the *entire and unqualified* Independence of the Irish legislature, and realm, *for ever.*

England saw, and admitted, the policy and justice of the demand; she again obeyed the call, and voluntarily did guarantee *for ever,* the independence and integrity of Ireland.

The experiment succeeded, and both countries prospered. The Union was enacted, and both countries feel the ruin of it.

England, therefore, has only to act upon the very same

principle of honour, policy, and justice, as in 1782, and follow her former precedent, which conferred such benefits on both—Ireland has nothing to repeal; her Parliament was incompetent, and her statute was a nullity. The English Act of Union was a statute *de jure*, and may be renounced as in 1782.

I cannot terminate these observations, without expressing how much the arrangement and the correctness of this volume, owe to the research, and revision, of my zealous and talented friend, Doctor Halliday of Paris. That congeniality of sentiment which generated our mutual friendship, excited that exertion, and gives me the pleasing opportunity, of saying, how much my esteem has been encreased, by a more intimate knowledge of his mind and of his principles.

Paris, 1st May, 1833.

CONTENTS.

CHAPTER I.

Ireland at an early period—Misgoverment and oppression of England—Irish statistics—Climate—Geographical advantages—Internal resources—Population—Her depressed condition in 1779—Causes of it—Poyning's law—Usurpation by England to bind Ireland by British Statutes—The Penal Statutes against Catholics—Fatal consequences to Ireland—Ireland roused by the example of America—Success of America—Its Effect on the Irish people—Origin of the Irish Volunteers—Character of Lord Clare—His intolerance—His political inconsistency—His fall, - - - - - p. 23

CHAPTER II.

State of the Irish Parliament previous to 1779—Previous to 1780, occasional contests arose in the Irish Parliaments—The absentees—The Irish Bar—Its influence and Independence—Mr. Burgh Prime-Sergeant—The Attorney-general—France assists America against England—France the champion of Liberty ; England of Slavery—France threatens to invade Ireland—England prostrate and incapable of assisting Ireland—Moderation and patriotism of the Catholics—Character of the Irish people misrepresented and misunderstood in England—Irish character defamed by English writers—Character of the Irish peasant—Their undaunted courage—Attachment to their country—The Gentry—Romantic Chivalry of the Irish gentry—Suicide unknown in Ireland—Irish Peerage—Protestant Clergy—Catholic Clergy—Their conduct and manners, - - - - p. 37

CHAPTER III.

Ireland awakened to a sense of her slavery—The Irish Parliament totally independent of England—The King acknowledged in Ireland through his Irish crown, and not through the crown of England—Perilous position of England—Moderation and attachment of Ireland—Ireland determined to demand her just rights—Conspiracy against the manufactures of Ireland—The non-consumption agreement adopted throughout all Ireland—Progress of the Volunteers—Their principal Leaders—Sir John Parnell—His character—General effects of volunteering upon the people of Ireland, - - - p. 57

CHAPTER IV.

Unexpected events in the Irish House of Commons—Mr. Grattan's Amendment to the Address—His public character and vicissitudes—The Amendment—Its effects—Sir Henry Cavendish—His character—Mr. Hussey Burgh (the Prime-Sergeant) secedes from Government and substitutes an Amendment for Mr. Grattan's—the Amendment passed—First step towards Irish independence—The English Parliament callous to the wrongs of Ireland—Lord Shelburne and Lord Ossory propose resolutions—The Irish nation determined to assert its rights—Resolution for a free trade carried unanimously—This circumstance one of the remote causes of the Union—Rapid progress of the Volunteers—Extraordinary military honours paid to the Duke of Leinster—Attempts to seduce the Volunteers—Earl of Charlemont—His character, - - - - - p. 71

CHAPTER V.

Spirit of the Irish and humiliation of the English Government—Preparation for hostilities—Lord North's embarrassment—King's conciliatory speech and the consequent proceedings—Duplicity of Ministers—The people alarmed—Volunteer Organization proceeds—Mutiny Bill—Alarming rencontre of the Volunteers and Regular Army—Intolerance of England—Further Grievances of Ireland—Proceedings in the Irish Parliament—O'Neill of Shane's Castle—His character and influence—Address to the Volunteers—Its results, - - p. 90

CHAPTER VI.

Observations as to the strength of a people—German mercenaries—Further subject of discontent in Ireland—Dispute between Ireland and Portugal—Portugal encouraged in her hostility towards Ireland by the British Minister—Perseverance of Portugal—Mr. Fitzgibbon's motion—Sir Lucius O'Brien—Proposes that Ireland in her own right should declare war against Portugal—Sir J. Blaquiere—Effects of Sir Lucius O'Brien's amendment—Distinctness of Ireland proved—Federative compact—Arguments for and against prompt proceedings—Spirited reasoning of the Irish—No Habeas Corpus Act in Ireland—Determination of the Volunteers—Origin and progress of delegated assemblies—The Northern Irish—Dungannon meeting—Mr. Dobbs—Extraordinary mind—His eccentricity—Theories—Colonel Irwin—Account of the Dungannon meeting continued—Dungannon resolutions, p. 104

CHAPTER VII.

The Earl of Bristol, Bishop of Derry, declares for Irish Independence—Sketch of his character—Resistance to English Laws unanimously decided on—Declaration of the Irish Volunteers disclaiming all British authority—The Irish Judges dependent on the English Government—Numerical force of the Irish Volunteers—Dissenting Clergymen—Their Leaders—State of the Irish Parliament—Members divided into Classes—The leading members—Mr. Thomas Connolly—Mr. Yelverton—His character, - - - - p. 123

CHAPTER VIII.

The alarm in England increases—The Earl of Carlisle recalled—The Duke of Portland appointed Lord Lieutenant—Duke of Portland's character—He attempts to procrastinate—Remarks on the policy of an Union at that juncture—Mr. Grattan refuses to delay his proceedings—Especial call of the house—Comparison of the English and Irish Houses of Parliament—Character of Mr. Sexton Perry—Embarrassment of the Patriots—Mr. Hutchinson Secretary of State, unexpectedly declares the assent of Government—Mr. Ponsonby moves an address considered insufficient—Dangerous dilemma of Parliament, - - . - - - - p. 142

CHAPTER IX.

Mr. Grattan moves a declaration of rights and grievances in Parliament —Mr. Brownlow—Mr. George Ponsonby—Mr. Flood—Mr. Fitzgibbon's conduct—His Declaration of Independence—Enthusiastic rejoicings, - - - - - - p. 160

CHAPTER X.

Design of the British Goverment to recall the independence of Ireland— Singular conduct of the Attorney General—His speech—Its powerful effect—Palpable dread of an Insurrection—Effect on England—Duke of Portland's duplicity—Attains an ascendency over Earl Charlemont —Embarrassment of the English Cabinet—The Volunteers prepare for actual service—Imbecility of England—Insidious designs of the English Government—Mr. Fox—Mr. Pitt—Important meeting of Parliament—The Volunteer Regiments occupy the avenues to the House of Commons—Designs of the Duke of Portland—Duke of Portland's speech — Mr. Grattan — Mr. Brownlow — The Recorder and Mr. Walshe oppose Mr. Grattan's address — Mr. Flood neutral — Mr. Walshe—Mr. Yelverton—The Secretary—Division—Consequent embarrassment, - - - - - p. 176

CHAPTER XI.

Temporary credulity of the Irish Parliament—Country Gentlemen— Singular character of Mr. Bagenal—His Exploits—Popularity—His patriotism—Commanded many Volunteer Corps—Gives notice of a motion to reward Mr. Grattan — Anti-prophetic observation —Mr. Grattan's increasing popularity—Hasty repeal of the declaratory act 6th Geo. III.—And transmitted by the Viceroy to the Volunteers— Doctrine of Blackstone declared unconstitutional—Mr. Bagenal's motion to grant £100,000, to Mr. Grattan—Mistaken pride of his friends— Extraordinary occurrence—Insidious conduct of Government—Mr. Thomas Connolly makes a most unprecedented motion—Viceroy offers the Palace to Mr. Grattan and his heirs as a reward for his services— Objects of the Government in making the offer—Discovered by the indiscretion of the Secretary, Col. Fitzpatrick—His character—Real objects developed—Mr. Grattan's friends de line so large a grant—

Their mistaken principle—Effects of the calumnies against Ireland—False arguments—Comparison of the conduct of England and Ireland—Comparative loyalty, - - - - p. 190

CHAPTER XII.

Epitome of Irish History—Treacherous system of the English Government—First Irish Union—Second Union compared with the first—King Henry's Acts in Ireland—His plan to decimate the nation—He relinquished his dominion over Ireland—Abortive attempts to colonize—Totally failed, - - - - - p. 202

CHAPTER XIII.

Ireland kept in a state of oppression and turbulence—Elizabeth becomes Queen—Character public and private of Queen Elizabeth—Henry the VIII.—Fanaticism of the English—True principles of tolerance—Union of religion and political fanaticism—Religious schisms excited through Luther—Violent dissensions—The Irish roused—Cruel tyranny of Elizabeth—Earl of Tyrone excites the Irish—Extract from his speech—General rising of the Irish and old English colonists—Immense slaughter—Confiscation of whole provinces to Elizabeth—Accession of James the First—Comparison with Elizabeth—His wise maxims—Conciliatory principles—Its full success—Charles the First—Disloyalty of the English—Ireland desolated by Cromwell, p. 207

CHAPTER XIV.

Restoration of the Stuart dynasty—Usurpation of William—Ireland remained loyal—Comparison of the people—The revolutionary principle undefined—The Irish treated as rebels by William for their loyalty to their King—Character of William the Third—Continued oppression and malgovernment of Ireland—The Scotch and English rebelled—Ireland remained tranquil—Comparison of the English and Irish as to their kings—Ireland first infected by the Scotch and English rebellions—Mr. Pitt suppressed the spirit of insurrection in England promptly—Suffered it to increase in Ireland, - - p. 219

CHAPTER XV.

Catholic relaxation Bills opposed by Mr. Rowley—Sir Edward Newenenham—Doctor Patrick Duigenam—His Character—Mr. Ogle—Bills passed—Unjust doctrine—Change in the Irish Parliament—Mr. Fox's candour—His speech—Deception of the British Government developed—Marquis of Rockingham—Total absence of energy—Mr. Burke—Inactive as to Ireland—New debates—Embarrassing consequences of Mr. Grattan's address—Mr. Grattan's motion objectionable—Mr. Flood's reply—Unfortunate collision of Grattan and Flood—Mr. Grattan's fallacious motion—Mr. Flood's reply—Mr. Montgomery moves to build an Irish navy—Negatived—Parliament prorogued—Most important session—Moderation of Ireland—Duke of Portland's hypocritical speech, - - - - p. 230

CHAPTER XVI.

Insufficiency of Mr. Grattan's measures—Death of the Marquis of Rockingham and its consequences—Earl Temple Lord Lieutenant—Mr. Grenville Secretary—His Character—Lord Temple—Not unpopular—Mr. Corry a principal instrument of Lord Temple—Proceedings of the Volunteers—Strong resolutions to oppose English Laws—Bad effects of the dissension between Grattan and Flood—Sir George Young—Effect of Sir George Young's speech—Lord Mansfield's conduct accounted for—Consequence of these speeches—British Parliament belie their own Act—Lord Abingdon denies the King's right to pass the Bill—England by Statute admitted her usurpation, and relinquished for ever her right to legislate for Ireland—Renunciation Act—Mr. Grattan still perversely opposes Mr. Flood—The renunciation Act confirmed Mr. Flood's doctrine, - - - p. 245

CHAPTER XVII.

Lord Charlemont's courtly propensities—Comparison of Grattan and Flood—Consequences of their jealousy to the country—The people enlightened, learn the true state of their situation—Discussion—And Arguments—Inefficiency of the measures as a future security—A Reform of Parliament indispensable to public security—Mr. Pitt—His duplicity and corruption—Constitutional reasons for a Reform of Parliament—Deduction—Conclusion drawn by the Volunteers—Proved by incontrovertible fact—State of Electors and Representatives compared—Mr. Curran—His character, - - - p. 261

CHAPTER XVIII.

Volunteers received by the King—Happy state of Ireland—Progressively prosperous—Untoward consequences of the collision between Flood and Grattan—A second Dungannon meeting of delegated Volunteers—Mr. Flood gains ground—Arguments—A National Convention decided on—Their first meeting — Interesting procession of the Delegates described—Entrance of the Delegates—Extraordinary coincidence of localities—Embarrassing situation—The Delegates meet at the Rotunda, - - - - - - p. 276

CHAPTER XIX.

The Bishop of Derry takes his seat at the Convention—His splendour—And pageantry—Procession—Popularity—Extraordinary Visit to the House of Lords—A Guard of Honour mounted at his house—Entirely devoted to the Irish people—His great qualities and acquirements—Opposes Charlemont and Grattan—First treacherous Scheme of the British Government again to enslave Ireland—The spirit of the Irish Parliament declines—Reasons for Reform in Parliament—Absolutely essential to her prosperity—Further traits of Lord Charlemont's Character—His inefficiency—His views—Opposes the Bishop of Derry's Election for the Presidency of the National Convention—Many Members of Parliament attend the Convention also—Earl Charlemont's dilemma—Proceedings of the Convention—The Bishop and Mr. Flood acquired the ascendency—The Parliament and Convention—Desperate step of Government—Fitzgibbon's Philippic—Most violent Debates—Bill rejected—Extraordinary coincidence of facts—Mr. Connolly's motion—Feeble and insidious resolution of Lord Charlemont—Fatal adjournment—Called a meeting of his partisans—Breaks his trust—Inexcusable conduct—False statement—Virtually dissolves the Convention before the full meeting—Lord Charlemont justly reprobated—Volunteers beat to arms—Lord Charlemont's intolerance—Opposed by the Bishop of Derry, - - - p. 289

CHAPTER XX.

Celebrated Address of the Volunteers to the Bishop—Reply of the Bishop—Some thought the Bishop's answer too strong—A new Bill suggested—New measures of Earl Charlemont—Decline of the Volunteers—Insincerity of the concessions—Cupidity of English traders—Sordid interest absorbed her justice—Commercial treaty and tariff proposed—Commercial propositions—Mr. Pitt's duplicity—Magnificence of the Irish Court—The Propositions rejected—Mr. Brownlow opposes the eleven propositions—Passed the Commons—Mr. Pitt proposes twenty propositions—Embarrassment of the Secretary—Most violent debates in the Irish Parliament—The Minister virtually defeated—The treaty ended—Defeat of the treaty effected by the country gentlemen—Mr. Forbes a leading member of the House of Commons—Mr. Hardy—Mr. Carleton, Solicitor General—His singular character, - - - - - - p. 305

CHAPTER XXI.

Death of the Duke of Rutland—Marquis of Buckingham's second Government—The question of a Regency—Mr. Pitt's conduct—The Prince submitted to the restraints—The Irish resisted, and refused to restrain him—Unprecedented case—Collision between the two Parliaments—Round Robin—Irish address to the Prince—Sketch of the Arguments on the Regency question in Ireland—Constitutional state of both nations—Conduct of the nations contrasted—Reasons for the Irish Parliament proceeding by Address, and not by Statute, to appoint a Regent—Question whether the Parliaments of England or Ireland had committed a breach of the Constitution—Threats of the Viceroy—The Round Robin—Viceroy determined to retire—Reception of the Irish delegates by the Prince—Address of the Irish Parliament to the Prince—Reply of the Prince, eulogizing the Irish legislature—Afterwards neglected, - - - - - p. 319

CHAPTER XXII.

Ireland acted on her independence—Prosperous state of Ireland at that Period—The Rise of the Irish Nation consummated by the withdrawal of the Viceroy—Particularly important observation—Lord Westmoreland—Major Hobart—His character—State of Ireland on his accession to office—Concessions by Government—Delusion and negligence of the

Opposition—Catholic emancipation commenced—Arguments of the Catholics—Catholic petition rejected by a great majority—Deep designs of Mr. Pitt—Mr. Pitt proceeds with his measures to promote a union—Lord Fitzwilliam appointed Lord Lieutenant—His character—Deceived and calumniated by Mr. Pitt—Great popularity of the Lord Lieutenant—Earl Fitzwilliam recalled—Fatal consequences—Ireland given up to Lord Clare, and insurrection excited—Lord Camden—United Irishmen—Unprecedented Organization—Lord Camden's character—Despotic conduct of Lord Clare—Earl Carhampton commander-in-chief—Disobeys Lord Camden—Again disobeys—The King's sign-manuel commands him to obey—He resigns, - - p. 330

CHAPTER XXIII.

Insurrection—Topography of Wexford County—Persecutions and cruelties of the Wexford Gentry—Commencement of Hostilities—State of the Insurgents—And their number—Expected attack on Dublin—Excellent plan of the Insurgents—Executions in cold blood, and barbarous exhibition in the Castle yard—Major Bacon executed without trial—Major Foot defeated—Col. Walpole defeated and killed—General Fawcett defeated—General Dundas and the Cavalry defeated by the Pikemen—Captain Armstrong's treachery—Henry and John Shears—The execution of the two brothers—Progress of the insurrection—Different Battles—Important Battle of Arklow—Spirited reply of Colonel Skerrit—Battle of Ross—Bagenal Harvey—Death of Lord Mountjoy—Unprecedented instance of Heroism in a Boy—The Royal Army driven out of the town—Description of Vinegar Hill—Details of the Engagement—General Lake's horse shot under him—Enniscorthy twice stormed—Wounded peasants burned—Mr. Grogan tried by Court Martial—His witness shot by the military—Bill of attainder—Ten thousand pounds costs to the Attorney General—Barbarous execution of Sir Edward Crosby and Mr. Grogan, under colour of a Court Martial, - - - - - p. 345

CHAPTER XXIV.

Appointment of Lord Cornwallis—His crafty conduct—French invade Ireland in a small number—British troops totally defeated, their artillery all taken—Races of Castlebar—Ninety militia men hanged by Lord Cornwallis—French outwit Lord Cornwallis—Lord Jocelyn taken prisoner—French surrendered—Mr. Pitt proceeds in his projects of a Union—The subserviency of the Lords—The Bishops—Bishops of Waterford and Down—Political characters of Lord Cornwallis and Lord Castlereagh—Unfortunate results of Lord Cornwallis's conduct in every quarter of the world—Lord Castlereagh—Union proposed—Great splendour of the Chancellor—Celebrated Bar Meeting—Mr. Saurin—Mr. Saint George Daly—Mr. Thomas Grady—Mr. Grady's curious harangue—Mr. Thomas Goold's speech—Thirty-two County Judges appointed by Lord Clare—Lord Clare opposes the Bar—Opening of the session of 1799—Lord Clare's great power—Lord Tyrone's character—Seconded by Mr. Fitzgerald—Mr. John Ball—His character, - - - - - - 367

CHAPTER XXV

The three leading arguments used in Parliament in favour of a Union—Arguments of the Anti-Unionists—Not England which quelled the insurrection—English militia never acted in Ireland—Mr. William Smith supports the Union—Corrupt conduct of Mr. Trench and Mr. Fox—Mr. Trench palpably gained over—Mr. Trench recanted what he had a few moments before declared—The Place Bill and its unfortunate effects—Mr. Fox created a Judge of the Common Pleas for his tergiversation—Originally a Whig—Made a false declaration to avoid being counted—Effect of the Place Bill—His second deception—Conduct of Mr. Cooke and Admiral Pakenham—Mr. Marshall's disgraceful conduct—Debate commenced—Great popularity of the Speaker—Lord Castlereagh's policy—Sir John Parnell denied the competence of both the King and the Parliament to enact a Union—Mr. Tighe the same—Great effect of Mr. Ponsonby's speech—Remarkable agitation—Description of the scene—Lord Castlereagh's violent speech—Attack on Mr. Ponsonby—Mr. Ponsonby's sarcastic reply—Lord Castlereagh's desperation—Mr. John Egan attacks Mr. William Smith—Sir Laurence Parsons made a most able and eloquent speech—Mr. Frederick Falkiner nothing could corrupt—Prime Sergeant Fitzgerald dismissed—Mr. Plunket's speech—Spirited speech of Col. O'Donnell—Second shameful tergiversation of Mr. Trench, created Lord Ashtown—Most important incident in the annals of Ireland—State of the House of Commons—Mr. Fortescue's fatal speech—Mr. French and Lord Cole seceded—John Claudius Beresford—Extraordinary change in the feelings of the House—Sarcastic remark of Sir Henry Cavendish—Great popularity of the Speaker—Joy and exultation of the people—Singular anecdote of Mr. Martin—Meeting of the Lords—Their infatuation—Conduct of Lord Clare—Unpopularity of the Irish Peers—Two Bishops, Down and Limerick, opposed him—Character of the Bishop of Down—Commission of Compensation—Subsequent proceedings of the Viceroy and Lord Castlereagh—Ruinous consequence of Mr. Fortescue's conduct—Mistaken conduct of the Anti-Unionists—Their embarrassment—Bad effects of Mr. Fortescue's conduct—The Catholics—State of parties, - - p. 383

CHAPTER XXVI.

The different views of the Opposition—Opposition not sufficiently organized or connected—Disunion in consequence of the Catholic question—Catholics duped—Alternately oppressed and fostered—Lord Clare's great influence—Very important despatch from Mr. Pitt, to Lord Cornwallis—Unprecedented plan of Lord Castlereagh—Remarkable dinner—The plan or conspiracy—Acceded to—Rewards in Perspective—Meeting of Anti-Unionists at Lord Charlemont's—Opposition Lords meet—Lord Castlereagh's Plan laid before them—Counterplan proposed—Rejected—Earl Belmore—His motion to the same effect as Mr. Ponsonby's—Rejected—Very numerous addresses against the Union—Particularly Dublin—A Privy Council—Lord Clare's violence—Military execution—People killed and wounded—Inefficiently brought before Parliament—Anti-Union dinner—Mr. Handcock of Athlone, a conspicuous patriot—Corrupt state of the British Parliament—Compared with that of Ireland at the Union—Mr. Handcock bribed, - - - - - - p. 420

CHAPTER XXVII.

Felons in the gaols induced, by promise of pardon, to sign petitions in favour of the Union—Every means of corruption resorted to by the Viceroy—Viceroy doubtful of future support—Resorted to Place Bill—Unparalleled measure of public bribery avowed by Lord Castlereagh—Bill to raise £1,500,000, for bribes—Grave reflection on the King's assenting to an avowed act of corruption—A few bribes called Compensation—The British Parliament had anticipated the proposal—Lord Cornwallis's speech peculiarly artful—Lord Loftus moves the address—Lord Castlereagh's reason—Sir Laurence Parson's important motion and speech—Debate continued all night—Lord Castlereagh's plan put into execution—Mr. Bushe—Mr. Plunket—Mr. St. George Daly—His character—His attack on Mr. Bushe—On Mr. Plunket—Replied to by Mr. Barrington—Mr. Peter Burrows—Affecting appearance of Mr. Grattan in the House of Commons—Returned for Wicklow the preceding evening—The impediment laid by Government—Returned at midnight—Entered the house at seven in the morning in a debilitated state—Description of his entry—Powerful sensation caused by his splendid oration—Mr. Corry induced to reply—No effect on the House—The three Bagwells seceded from Government—Lord Ormond changed to the minister—Mr. Arthur Browne's tergiversation—Division—Mr. Foster's speech—Important incident—Bad conduct of the clergy—Very singular circumstance—Mr. Annesley chairman of the committee on the Union—Bishop of Clogher returns Mr. Annesley to Parliament—Messrs. Ball and King petition—Succeed—Mr. Annesley declared not duly elected—Left the chair and quitted the House—Not a legal chairman—Shameful and palpable act of corruption by Sir William Gladowe Newcomen—Bribe proved—Bribery of Mr. Knox and Mr. Crowe—Their speeches against the Union—The Earl of Belvidere most palpably bribed to change sides—His resolutions—Mr. Knox and Mr. Crowe bribed—Mr. Usher bribed to secrecy—The corrupt agreement of Mr. Crowe and Mr. Knox to vacate their seats for Union members, in presence of Mr. Usher, a Parson—The terms with Lord Castlereagh—Mr. Charles Ball's affecting conduct—The Anti-Union members, despairing, withdraw in a body—Last sitting of the Irish Parliament—The House surrounded by military—Most affecting scene—Bad consequences to England—Unhappiness of the Speaker—Ireland extinguished, - - - p. **432**

RISE AND FALL

OF

THE IRISH NATION.

CHAPTER I.

Ireland at an early period—Misgovernment and oppression of England—Irish statistics—Climate—Geographical advantages—Internal resources—Population—Her depressed condition in 1779—Causes of it—Poyning's law—Usurpation by England to bind Ireland by British Statutes—The Penal Statutes against Catholics—Fatal consequences to Ireland—Ireland roused by the example of America—Success of America—Its effect on the Irish people—Origin of the Irish Volunteers—Character of Lord Clare—His intolerance—His political inconsistency—His fall.

I. More than six centuries had passed away, since Ireland had first acknowledged a subordinate connexion with the English Monarchy—her voluntary but partial submission to the sceptres of Henry and of Richard had been construed by their successors into the right of conquest—and the same spirit of turbulence and discord, which had generated the treachery and treasons of M'Morrough, was carfully cultivated by every English potentate, as the most effectual barrier against the struggles of a restless and semi-conquered people—and Ireland, helpless and distracted, groaned for ages in obscurity, under the accumulated pressure of internal strife and external tyranny.

The apathy produced by this habitual oppression had long benumbed the best energies of Ireland;—her national spirit, depressed by the heavy hand of arbitrary restraint, almost forgot its own existence; and the proudest language of her constitution could only boast, that she was the annexed dependant of a greater and a freer country.

It was not until an advanced stage of the American revolt had attracted the attention of enlightened Europe to the first principles of civil liberty, that Ireland began steadily to reflect on her own deprivations. Commerce and constitution had been withdrawn from her grasp, and the usurped supremacy* of the British Parliament gave a death-blow to every struggle of Irish independence.

II. But in whatever relative situation the two nations really stood, the same jealous and narrow principle might be perceived uniformly attending every measure enacted as to the Irish people. If at any time a cheering ray of commercial advantage chanced for a moment to illuminate the dreary prospects of Ireland, the sordid spirit of monopoly instantly arose in England, and rendered every effort to promote a beneficial trade, or advance a rival manufacture, vain and abortive.

Commercial jealousy and arbitrary government united, therefore, to suppress every struggle of the Irish nation, and root up every seed of prosperity and civilization.

Alarmed at the increasing population, the unsubdued spirit, and the inexhaustible resources of that strong and fertile island; a dread of her growing power excited a fallacious jealousy of her future importance. In her timidity or her avarice, England lost sight of her truest interests, and of her nobler feelings; and kings, usurpers, and viceroys, as they respectively exercised the powers of government, all acted towards Ireland upon the same blind and arbitary principles, which they had imbibed from their education, or inherited from their predecessors.

This desperate policy, so repugnant to the attachment, and fatal to the repose of the two countries, excited the spirit of eternal warfare:—an enthusiastic love of na-

* The claim of the British Parliament to bind Ireland by *British* statutes was at length most ably refuted by Mr. William Molyneux, representative for Dublin University, in his celebrated work, published in 1693, entitled " *The Case of Ireland.*"

tional independence sharpened the sword, and the zealots of religious fanaticism threw away the scabbard—the septs fought against each other, the English against all—the population was thinned, but the survivors became inveterate; and though the wars and the massacres of Elizabeth and of Cromwell, by depopulating, appeared to have subjugated the nation—the triumph was not glorious—and the conquest was not complete.

Direct persecution against principles only adds fuel to a conflagration—the persons of men may be coerced—but it is beyond the reach of human power to subdue the rooted, hereditary passions and prejudices of a persevering, ardent, and patriotic people:—such a nation may be gained over by address, or seduced by dissimulation, but can never be reclaimed by force, or overcome by persecution—yet from the very first intercourse between the two countries, that destructive system of force and of dissension, which so palpably led to the miseries of Ireland, had been sedulously cultivated, and unremittingly persevered in.

Thus grievously oppressed, and ruinously disunited, Ireland struggled often, but she struggled in vain: the weight of her chains was too heavy for the feebleness of her constitution, and every effort to enlarge her liberty only gave a new pretext to the conqueror, to circumscribe it within a still narrower compass.

On the same false principle of government this oppressed nation was also systematically retained in a state of the utmost obscurity, and represented to the world as an insignificant and remote island, remarkable only for her turbulence and sterility: and so perfectly did this misrepresentation succeed, that, while every republic and minor nation of Europe had become the theme of travellers, and the subject of historians, Ireland was visited only to be despised, and spoken of only to be calumniated. In truth, she is as yet but little known by the rest of Europe, and but partially even to the people of England. But when the extraordinary capabilities, the resources, and the powers of Ireland are fully developed, an interest must arise in every breast, which reflects on her misfortunes. It is time that the curtain, which has been so long interposed between Ireland and the rest of

Europe, should be drawn aside for ever, and a just judgment formed of the impolicy of measures, which have been adopted nominally to govern, but substantially to suppress her power and prosperity.

III. The position of Ireland upon the face of the globe peculiarly formed her for universal intercourse, and adapted her in every respect for legislative independence. Separated by a great sea from England—the Irish people, dissimilar in customs, more than equal in talent, and vastly superior in energy, possess an island about 900 miles in circumference; with a climate, for the general mildness of temperature and moderation of seasons, unrivalled in the universe—the parching heats, or piercing colds, the deep snows, the torrent, and the hurricane, which other countries so fatally experience, are here unknown. Though her great exposure to the spray of the Atlantic increases the humidity of the atmosphere, it adds to the fecundity of the soil, and distinguishes her fertile fields by the productions of an almost perpetual vegetation.

The geographical situation of Ireland is not less favorable to commerce, than her climate is to agriculture. Her position on the western extremity of Europe would enable her to intercept the trade of the new world from all other nations—the merchandise of London, of Bristol, and of Liverpool, skirt her shores, before it arrives at its own destination; and some of the finest harbours in the world invite the inhabitants of this gifted island to accept the trade of India, and form the emporium of Europe.

The internal and natural advantages of Ireland are great and inexhaustible. Rich mines are found in almost every quarter of the island; gold is discovered in the beds of streams, and washed from the sands of rivulets—the mountains are generally arable to their summits—the vallies exceed in fertility the most prolific soils of England—the rivulets, which flow along the declivities, adapt the country most peculiarly to the improvement of irrigation; and the bogs and mosses of Ireland, utterly unlike the fens and marshes of England, emit no damp or noxious exhalations; and give a plentiful and cheering fuel to the surrounding peasantry; or, when reclaimed, become the most luxuriant pastures.

The population of Ireland is great and progressive. Above five* millions of a brave and hardy race of men are seen scattered through the fields, or swarming in the villages—a vast redundancy of grain, and innumerable flocks and herds, should furnish to them not only the source of trade, but every means of comfort.

Dublin, the second city in the British empire, though it yields in extent, yields not in architectural beauties to the metropolis of England. For some years *previous* to the Union, its progress was excessive—the locality of the parliament—the constant residence of the nobility and commons—the magnificent establishments of the viceregal court—the indefatigable hospitality of the people—and the increasing commerce of the port, all together gave a brilliant prosperity to that splendid and luxurious capital.

Ireland,† possessing the strongest features of a powerful state, though labouring under every disadvantage which a restricted commerce and a jealous ally could inflict upon her prosperity, might still have regarded with contempt the comparatively unequal resources and inferior powers of half the monarchies of Europe. Her insular situation—her great fertility—the character of her people—the amount of her revenues—and the extent of her population, gave her a decided superiority over other nations, and rendered her crown, if accompanied by her affections, not only‡ a brilliant but a most substantial ornament to the British empire.

However, though gifted, and enriched by the hand of Nature, the fomented dissensions of her own natives had wedded Ireland to poverty, and adapted her to subjuga-

* *Now upwards of eight millions.*
† The relative size of Ireland, compared to England and Wales, is about 18 to 30. It contains about eighteen millions of acres; is about 285 miles long, and above 160 broad. In time of war she lends more than one hundred thousand soldiers and sailors to the English fleet and army, and retains at home above one million of hardy men, from 17 to 47 years of age, fit to bear arms.
‡ In the very words of the highest authority in Great Britain this day, "*If well governed*, Ireland would be the brightest jewel in the king's crown."

tion—her innate capacities lay dormant and inactive—her dearest interests were forgotten by herself, or resisted by her ally; and the gifts and bounties of a favouring Providence, though lavished, were lost on a divided people.

IV. By the paralyzing system thus adopted towards Ireland, she was at length reduced to the lowest ebb—her poverty and distresses, almost at their extent, were advancing fast to their final consummation—her commerce had almost ceased—her manufactures extinguished—her constitution withdrawn—the people absolutely desponding—while public and individual bankruptcy finished a picture of the deepest misery;* and the year 1779 found Ireland almost every thing but what such a country and such a people ought to have been.

This lamentable state of the Irish nation was not the result of any one distinct cause: a combination of depressing circumstances united to bear down every progressive effort of that injured people. Immured in a labyrinth of difficulties and embarrassments, no clew was found to lead them through the mazes of their prison; and, helpless and desponding, they sunk into a dose of torpid inactivity, while their humiliated and inefficient parliaments, restrained by foreign and arbitrary laws, subjected to the dictation of the British Council, and obstructed in the performance of its constitutional functions, retained scarcely the shadow of an independent legislature.

A statute of Henry the Seventh of England, framed

* This wretched period cannot be more pathetically described, than by a most able and just statement of Irish grievances, published in the year 1779, by Mr. Hely Hutchinson, (father of the present Lords Donoughmore and Hutchinson,) then Provost of the Dublin University, an eloquent and very distinguished member of the Irish Parliament. In his book entitled " *Commercial Restraints*," Mr. Hutchinson gives a pathetic description of the state to which Ireland was reduced by the jealous and narrow policy of England.

This book acquired so much character, and spoke so many plain truths, that for many years it was quoted as an authority in the Irish Parliament. Mr. Flood often declared, that, if there were but two copies of it in print, he would give a thousand pounds for one of them. It will be interesting to compare the miserable state of Ireland in 1779 with her prosperity in 1794, when she had enjoyed only twelve years of constitutional independence and unrestricted commerce.

by his Attorney-General, Sir Edward Poyning, restrained the Irish Parliament from originating any law whatever, either in the Lords or Commons. Before any statute could be finally discussed, it was previously to be submitted to the Lord Lieutenant of Ireland and his Privy Council, for their consideration, who might at their pleasure reject it, or transmit it to England. If transmitted to England, the British Attorney General and Privy Council were invested with a power either to suppress it altogether, or model it at their own will, and then return it to Ireland, with *permission* to the Irish Parliament to pass it into a law, but without any alteration, though it frequently returned from England so changed, as to retain hardly a trace of its original features, or a point of its original object.

Yet, as if this arbitrary law were insufficient to secure Great Britain from the effect of those rival advantages, which Ireland might in process of time eventually acquire; and as if that counteracting power, with which England had invested herself by the law of Poyning, were unequal to the task of effectually suppressing all rivalship of the Irish people, and independence of the Irish Parliament; it was thought advisable by Great Britain, to usurp a *positive* right to *legislate* for Ireland, without her own consent, or the interference of her Parliament: and a law was accordingly enacted at Westminster, in the sixth year of the reign of George the First, by one sweeping clause of which England assumed a *despotic* power, and declared her inherent right to bind Ireland by every *British statute*, in which she should be *expressly* designated: and thus, by the authority of the British Council on the one hand, and the positive right assumed by the British Parliament upon the other, Ireland retained no more the attributes of an independent nation, than a monarch, attended in a dungeon with all the state and trappings of royalty, and bound hand and foot in golden shackles, could be justly styled an independent potentate.

The effect of this tyrannical and ruinous system fell most heavily on the trade of Ireland. Its influence was experienced not merely by any particular branch of commerce, but in every stage of manufacture, of arts, of trade, and of agriculture. In every struggle of the Irish Parliament to promote the commerce or the manufactures of their country, the British monopolizers were perpetually victorious; and even the speculative jealousy of a manufacturing village of Great Britain was of sufficient weight to negative any measure, however beneficial to the general prosperity of the sister country.

The same jealousy and the same system, which operated so fatally against the advancement of her commerce, operated as strongly against the improvement of her constitution. England was well aware, that the acquirement of an independent Parliament would be the sure forerunner of commercial liberty; and, possessed of the means to counteract these objects, she seemed determined never to relax the strength of that power, by the despotic exercise of which Ireland had been so long continued in a state of thraldom.

But exclusive of these slavish restraints (the necessary consequence of a dependent legislature,) another system, not less adverse to the general prosperity of the whole island, than repugnant to the principles of natural justice and of sound policy, had been long acted upon with every severity, that bigotry could suggest, or intolerance could dictate.

V. The penal statutes, under the tyrannical pressure of which the Catholics had so long and so grievously laboured, though in some instances softened down, still bore heavily upon four-fifths of the Irish population—a code, which would have dishonoured even the sanguinary pen of Draco, had inflicted every pain and penalty, every restriction and oppression, under which a people could linger out a miserable existence. By these statutes, the exercise of religion had been held a crime, the education of children a high misdemeanour—the son was encouraged to betray his father—the child rewarded for the ruin of his parent—the house of God declared a public nuisance—the officiating pastor proclaimed an outlaw—the acquirement of property absolutely prohibited—the exercise of trades restrained—plunder legalized in courts of law, and breach of trust rewarded in courts of equity—the Irish Catholic excluded from the possession of any office or occupation in the state, the law, the army, the navy, the municipal bodies, and the chartered corporations—and the mild doctrines of the Christian faith perverted, even in the pulpit, to the worst purposes of religious persecution.

Yet under this galling yoke the Irish, for near eighty years remained tranquil and submissive. The ignorance, into which poverty and wretchedness had plunged that people, prevented them from perceiving the whole extent of the oppression; and these penal laws, while they operated as an insuperable bar to the advancement of the Catholic, deeply affected the general interest of the Protestant. The impoverished tenant—the needy landlord—the unenterprising merchant—the idle artisan, could all trace the origin of their wants to the enactment of these statutes. Profession was not permitted to engage the mind of youth, or education to cultivate his understanding. Dissolute habits, the certain result of idleness and illiterateness, were consequently making a rapid progress in almost every class of society. The gentry were not exempt from the habits of the peasant; the spirit of industry took her flight altogether from the island; and, as the loss of commerce and constitution had no counteracting advantages, every thing combined to reduce Ireland to a state of the most general and unqualified depression.

VI. It was about this period, when the short-sighted policy of the British Government had by its own arbitrary proceedings planted the seeds of that political philosophy, afterwards so fatal to the most powerful monarchies of Europe, that Ireland began to feel herself affected by the struggles of America. The spirit of independence had crossed the Atlantic, and the Irish people, awakened from a trance, beheld with anxiety the contest, in which they now began to feel an interest. They regarded with admiration the exertions of a colony combating for the first principles of civil liberty, and giving to the world an instructive lesson of fortitude and perseverance.

Spread over a vast expanse of region, America, without wealth—without resources—without population—without fortresses—without allies—had every thing to contend with, and every thing to conquer. But freedom was her call, and as if she had been designated by Providence for an example to the universe of what even powerless states can achieve by enthusiasm and *unanimity*, her strength increased with her deprivations, and the firmness of one great and good man converted the feebleness of a colony into the power of an empire. The defeats of Washington augmented his armies—his wants and necessities called forth his intellect—while his wisdom, firmness, and moderation, procured him powerful friends, and secured him ultimate victory. The strength of Great Britain at length yielded to the vigor of his mind, and the unflinching fortitude of his people; and Lord Cornwallis, (the chosen instrument for oppressing heroic nations,) by his defeat and his captivity, established the independence of America. The arrogance of England bowed its proud head to the shrine of liberty, and her favorite general led back the relics of his conquered army, to commemorate in the mother country the impotence of her power, and emancipation of her colonies.

While these great events were gradually proceeding towards their final completion; Ireland became every day a more anxious spectator of the arduous conflict—every incident in America began to communicate a sympathetic impulse to the Irish people:—the moment was critical:—the nation became enlightened—a patriotic ardor took possession of her whole frame, and, before she had well considered the object of her solicitude, the spark of constitutional liberty had found its way into her bosom.

The disposition of Ireland to avail herself of the circumstances of those times, so favourable to the attainment of her rights, now openly avowed itself. Her determination to claim her constitution from the British Government became unequivocal, and she began to assume the attitude and language of a nation *" entitled to independence."*—The sound of arms and the voice of freedom echoed from every quarter of the Island—distinctions were forgotten, or disregarded—every rank, every religion, alike caught the general feeling,—but firmness and *discretion* characterised her proceedings:—she gradually arose from torpor and obscurity—her native spirit drew aside the curtain, that had so long concealed her from the world; and exhibited an armed and animated people, claiming their natural rights, and demanding their constitutional liberty.

When the dawn of political liberty begins to diffuse itself over a nation, great and gifted characters suddenly spring up from among the people—animated by new subjects, their various talents and principles become developed—they interweave themselves with the events of their country, become inseparable from its misfortunes, or identified with its prosperity.

Ireland, at this era, possessed many men of superior capacities—some distinguished by their pure attachment to constitutional liberty—others by their slavish deference to ruling powers and patronizing authorities. Among those whom the spirit of these times called forth to public notice was seen one of the most bold and energetic leaders of modern days an anticipated knowledge of whose marked and restless character is a necessary preface to a recital of Irish recurrences, in which the effects of his passions will be every where traced, and the mischievous errors of his judgment be perceived and lamented.

VII. This person was John Fitzgibbon, afterwards Earl of Clare—Attorney General, and Lord High Chancellor of Ireland. His ascertained pedigree was short, though his name bespoke an early respectability. His grandfather was obscure—his father, intended for the profession of a Catholic pastor, but possessing a mind superior to the habits of monkish seclusion, procured himself to be called to the Irish bar, where his talents raised him to the highest estimation, and finally established him in fame and fortune.

John Fitzgibbon, the second son of this man, was called to the bar in 1772. Naturally dissipated, he for some time attended but little to the duties of his profession; but on the death of his elder brother and his father, he found himself in possession of all those advantages, which led him rapidly forward to the extremity of his objects. Considerable fortune—professional talents—extensive connexions—and undismayed confidence, elevated him to those stations, on which he afterwards appeared so conspicuously seated; while the historic eye, as it follows his career, perceives him lightly bounding over every obstacle, which checked his course, to that goal where all the trophies and thorns of power were collected for his reception.

In the Earl of Clare we find a man eminently gifted with talents adapted either for a blessing or a curse to the nation he inhabited; but early enveloped in high and dazzling authority, he lost his way; and considering his power as a victory, he ruled his country as a conquest:—indiscriminate in his friendships—and implacable in his animosities—he carried to the grave all the passions of his childhood.

He hated powerful talents, because he feared them; and trampled on modest merit, because it was incapable of resistance. Authoritative and peremptory in his address; commanding, able, and arrogant, in his language, a daring contempt for public opinion was the fatal principle which misguided his conduct; and Ireland became divided between the friends of his patronage—the slaves of his power—and the enemies to his tyranny.

His character had no medium, his manners no mediocrity—the example of his extremes was adopted by his intimates, and excited in those who knew him feelings either of warm attachment, or of rivetted aversion.

While he held the seals in Ireland, he united a vigorous capacity with the most striking errors: as a judge, he collected facts with a rapid precision, and decided on them with a prompt asperity: but he hated precedent, and despised the highest judicial authorities, because they were not his own.

As a politician and a statesman, the character of Lord Clare is too well known, and its effects too generally experienced, to be mistaken or misrepresented—the era of his reign was the downfall of his country—his councils accelerated what his policy might have suppressed, and have marked the annals of Ireland with stains and miseries unequalled and indelible.

In council,—rapid, peremptory, and overbearing—he regarded promptness of execution, rather than discretion of arrangement, and piqued himself more on expertness of thought than sobriety of judgment. Through all the calamities of Ireland, the mild voice of conciliation never escaped his lips; and when the torrent of civil war had subsided in his country, he held out no olive, to show that the deluge had receded.

Acting upon a conviction, that his power was but coexistent with the order of public establishments, and the tenure of his office limited to the continuance of administration, he supported both with less prudence, and more desperation, than sound policy or an enlightened mind should permit or dictate; his extravagant doctrines of religious intolerance created the most mischievous pretexts for his intemperance in upholding them; and, under colour of defending the principles of one revolution, he had nearly plunged the nation into all the miseries of another.

His political conduct has been accounted uniform, but in detail it will be found to have been miserably inconsistent. In 1781, he took up arms to obtain a declaration of Irish independence; in 1800, he recommended the introduction of a military force to assist in its extinguishment, he proclaimed Ireland a free nation in 1783, and argued that it should be a province in 1799; in 1782 he called the acts of the British Legislature towards Ireland " *a daring usurpation on the rights of a free people*,"* and in 1800 he transferred Ireland to the usurper. On all ocasions his ambition as despotically governed his politics, as his reason invariably sunk before his prejudice.

Though he intrinsically hated a Legislative Union, his lust for power induced him to support it; the preservation of office overcame the impulse of conviction, and he strenuously supported that measure, after having openly avowed himself its enemy: its completion, however, blasted his hopes, and hastened his dissolution. The restlessness of his habit, and the obtrusiveness of his disposition, became insupportably embarrassing to the British cabinet—the danger of his talents as a minister, and the inadequacy of his judgment as a statesman, had been proved in Ireland: he had been a useful instrument in that country, but the same line of services which he per

---

* In his Lordship's answer to the address of Dublin University, on the 14th of April 1782, upon the declaration of rights, he used these words: and added, that " he had uniformly expressed that opinion both in public and in private."

formed in Ireland, would have been ruinous to **Great** Britain, and Lord Clare was no longer consulted.

The union at length effected through his friends, what Ireland could never accomplish through his enemies—his total overthrow. Unaccustomed to control, and unable to submit, he returned to his country, weary, drooping, and disappointed; regretting what he had done, yet miserable that he could do no more: his importance had expired with the Irish Parliament, his patronage ceased to supply food for his ambition, the mind and the body became too sympathetic for existence, and he sunk into the grave, a conspicuous example of human talent and human frailty.

In his person he was about the middle size, slight, and not graceful, his eyes, large, dark, and penetrating, betrayed some of the boldest traits of his uncommon character, his countenance, though expressive and manly, yet discovered nothing, which could deceive the physiognomist into an opinion of his magnanimity, or, call forth a eulogium on his virtues.

During twenty momentous and eventful years, the life of Lord Clare is in fact the history of Ireland—as in romance some puissant and doughty chieftain appears prominent in every feat of chivalry—the champion in every strife—the hero of every encounter, and, after a life of toil and of battle, falls surrounded by a host of foes, a victim to his own ambition and temerity.

Thus Earl Clare, throughout those eventful periods, will be seen bold, active and desperate, engaging fiercely in every important conflict of the Irish nation and at length after having sacrificed his country to his passions and his ambition, endeavouring to atone for his errors, by **sacrificing himself.**

CHAPTER II.

State of the Irish Parliament previous to 1779—Previous to 1780, occasional contests arose in the Irish Parliaments—The absentees—The Irish Bar—Its influence and Independence—Mr. Burgh Prime-Sergeant—The Attorney-general—France assists America against England—France the champion of Liberty; England of Slavery—France threatens to invade Ireland—England prostrate and incapable of assisting Ireland—Moderation and patriotism of the Catholics—Character of the Irish people misrepresented and misunderstood in England—Irish character defamed by English writers—Character of the Irish peasant—Their undaunted courage—Attachment to their country—The Gentry—Romantic Chivalry of the Irish gentry—Suicide unknown in Ireland—Irish Peerage—Protestant Clergy—Catholic Clergy—Their conduct and manners

I. The habits of commerce and the pursuits of avarice had not, at this period, absorbed the spirit or contracted the intellect of the Irish people. That vigorous comprehensive, and pathetic eloquence, so peculiar to Ireland, which grasped at once the reason and the passions, still retained its ascendency at the bar, and its pre-eminence in the Senate: and the Commons' House of Parliament, about the period of Lord Clare's first introduction into public notice, contained as much character, as much eloquence, and as much sincerity, as any popular assembly since the most brilliant era of the Roman republic.

II. It might be reasonable to infer that a nation so long retained in the trammels of dependence, so habituated through successive generations, to control and to subjection would have lost much of its natural energy, and more of its national feeling. But, though the Irish Parliament, previous to 1779, in general manifested strong indications of a declining and a subservient body, yet, even after centuries of depression, when roused by the sting of accumulating usurpation, its latent spirit occasionally burst forth, and should have convinced the British Government, that though the flame of liberty may be smothered, the spark is unextinguishable.

Although, by the operation of Poyning's Law, the parliamentary discussions were generally restricted to local subjects and domestic arrangements, yet constitutional questions of a vital tendency incidentally occurred; and the exercise of controling powers, assumed by the British Cabinet over the concerns of Ireland often afforded matter of serious controversy between the viceroy and the nation and had, in some instances, been resisted by the Parliament with a warmth and a pertinacity which foretold a certainty of more important contests.*

These struggles, however, although frequent, were fruitless. The country was not yet ripe for independence, constitutional freedom had been so long obsolete, that even its first principles were nearly forgotten, and the people were again to learn the rudiments, before they could speak the language of liberty. But the fortitude, the wisdom, and the perseverance of the Anglo-American colonies, the feebleness, the impolicy, and the divisions

* On many occasions previous to 1779, the Irish Commons asserted their independent rights and privileges with great warmth, though sometimes without success. In 1749, a redundancy of £53,000 remaining in the Irish treasury—an unappropriated balance in favour of the nation, after paying all the establishments—the King sent over his letter to draw that sum to England, as a part of his hereditary revenue. But the Irish Parliament resisted the authority of his Majesty's letter, as an encroachment on the distinctness and independence of Ireland; a part of that sum having arisen from additional duties imposed by her Parliament. The King consulted the English judges, who were of opinion that the King's *previous consent* was necessary to its appropriation; but the Irish Commons insisted on their right of appropriation, and asserted that his Majesty's *subsequent assent* only was necessary. This contest was warmly maintained until the year 1753, when the Irish Commons succeeded in establishing their principle.

The principles of Mr. Molyneux's "*Case of Ireland,*" published in 1698, had never ceased to make a strong impression on the minds of the Irish people. The *British* Parliament ordered it to be burned by the hands of the common executioner; but that measure defeated its own object, by greatly increasing its celebrity and circulation. The same principles were strongly inculcated, in several publications, by a very able writer, Doctor Charles Lucas, member for Dublin. For those writings, he was expelled from the house; but he afterwards resumed his seat with increased character and influence; and, to this day, his statue, in white marble, stands eminently conspicuous in the Royal Exchange at Dublin, as a monument of his steady patriotism. Before him, Dean Swift, whose name is still adored by the Irish, had employed his masterly pen with powerful effect in fostering the spirit of independence.

of Great Britain, soon taught Ireland the importance of the crisis; and by a firmness, a moderation, and an unanimity, unparalleled in the annals of revolution, the Irish Volunteers acquired for their country a civic crown, which nothing but the insanity of rebellion and the artifices and frauds of Union, could ever have torn from the brow of the Irish people.

III. Absentees* who have ever been and ever will remain an obstacle to the substantial prosperity of Ireland exerted themselves more particularly at this period, in giving a strenuous and weighty opposition to every measure of innovation, they knew their Irish demesnes only by name and by income, they felt no interest but for their rents, and no patriotism but for the territory, alarmed at any legislative measure originating in Ireland. They showed themselves equally ignorant and regardless of her constitution, and ever proved themselves the steady adherents of the Minister for the time being; their proxies in the Lords, and their influence in the Commons, were transferred to him on a card or in a letter, and, on every division in both houses, almost invariably formed a phalanx against the true and genuine interest of the country.

IV. However zealous and determined the incipient exertions of the Irish nation might have been, they would probably have been crushed and extinguished, had not a class of men, possessing the first talents in the senate and the highest confidence of the country, stepped boldly forward to support the people. In those days the Irish Bar, a body equally formidable to the Government by their character and their capacity, too independent to be restrained, and too proud to be corrupted, comprised many sons of the resident noblemen and commoners of Ireland. The legal science was at that time considered as part of an Irish gentleman's education: the practice was then not a trade, but a profession. Eloquence was cultivated by its votaries, as a preparation for the higher duties of the senate, and, as almost every peer and every

* The absentees of the present day annually draw from Ireland above three millions sterling, to be expended in Great Britain. Some of the law offices of the greatest emolument, connected with the Irish courts of justice, are now held by constant absentees.

commoner had a relative enrolled among their number, so they had no interest in the conduct and honor of that department of society. The influence therefore of the bar as a body, increased by the general respect for the connexions and cultivated talents of its members, gave them an ascendency both in and out of Parliament, which could scarcely be counteracted, and, on certain trying occasions the conduct of some of the law-officers afforded experimental proof, that even they considered their offices as no longer tenable with advantage to the King, if the Minister should attempt to use them as instruments against the people.

The rank and station of the law-officers of Ireland in those days were peculiarly dignified, and conveyed an impression of importance, which the *modern* degeneracy of talent and relaxation of wholesome forms and of distinctions has altogether done away with.—The office of Prime Sergeant, then the first law-officer of Ireland, was filled at this period by one of the most amiable and eloquent men that ever appeared on the stage of politics—Walter Hussey Burgh, whose conduct in a subsequent transaction rendered him justly celebrated and illustrious. This gentleman was then representative for Dublin University ; in which office, he and M. Fitzgibbon were colleagues—men in whose public characters, scarcely a trait of similarity can be discovered. Mild, moderate, and patriotic, Mr. Burgh was proud without arrogance, and dignified without effort : equally attentive to public concerns and careless of his own, he had neither avarice to acquire wealth, nor parsimony to hoard it :—liberal, even to profusion—friendly, to a fault—and disinterested, to a weakness—he was honest without affluence, and ambitious without corruption :—his eloquence was of the highest order—figurative, splendid, and convincing :—at the bar, in the Parliament, and among the people he was equally admired, and universally respected.

But, when we compare Mr. Burgh with the then Attorney General of Ireland, who had been selected by Lord Townsend to bear down, if possible, the spirit of the country, the contrast may give a strong view of that policy, which falling ministers frequently and perhaps judiciously adopt, of endeavouring, if practicable, to enlist

and seat upon their benches some popular and elevated personage of opposition, who, by his character, may give strength to the party which surrounds him, or at least may for ever prostrate his own reputation by the unpopularity of the connection.

Mr. John Scott, then Attorney General, and afterwards created Earl of Clonmel, and Chief Justice of Ireland, exhibited the most striking contrast to the character of the Prime Sergeant. Sprung from the humbler order of society, he adventured upon the world without any advantage, save the strength of his intellect and the versatility of his talents. He held his head high, his boldness was his first introduction, his policy, his ultimate preferment. Courageous,* humorous, artificial, he knew the world well, and he profited by that knowledge; he cultivated the powerful; he bullied the timid, he fought the brave, he flattered the vain, he duped the credulous, and he amused the convivial. Half liked, half reprobated, he was too high to be despised, and too low to be respected. His language was coarse, and his principles arbitrary: but his passions were his slaves, and his cunning was his instrument. He recollected favors received in his obscurity, and, in some instances, had gratitude to requite the obligation: but his avarice and his ostentation contended for the ascendency: their strife was perpetual, and their victories alternate. In public and in private, he was the same character; and, though a most fortunate man and a successful courtier, he had scarcely a sincere friend, or a disinterested adherent.

This marked contrariety in character and disposition, which distinguished those chief law-officers of government, was equally discernible in almost every other department: the virtues and the talents of Grattan, of Flood, of Yelverton, of Daly, found their contrasts on the same benches; and these two distinguished characters are thus brought forward, by anticipation to show in the strongest point of view how powerful and insinuating the public feeling of that day must have been, that could finally draw together, in one common cause, personages so

* His Lordship fought several duels before he was Chief Justice of the King's Bench. The late Earl of Landaff, and the present Lord Tyrawly, were two of his antagonists.

opposite and so adverse on almost every political object, and in every national principal.

The crisis, however, now approached, when Ireland was for a moment to rear her head among imperial nations: strange and unforseen events began to crowd the annals of the world,—the established axioms of general polity began to lose their weight among nations; and governments, widely wandering from the fundamental principles of their own constitutions, seemed carelessly travelling the road to anarchy and revolution.

The rival powers of England and of France—ever jealous ever insincere—concluding deceptious negotiations by fallacious treaties—doubtful of each other's honor, and dreading each other's prowess—had long stood cautiously at bay—each watching for an unguarded open to give a mortal wound to her adversary—yet each dreading the consequences of an unsuccessful effort.

However, the perseverance and successes of America communicated a stimulating impulse to the councils of the French King; and that ill-fated monarch, urged on to his destiny, determined to strike a deadly blow at the pride and the commerce of England, by giving an effectual aid to her revolted colonies.

The question soon came to a speedy issue; an undecisive engagement with the French fleet in the Channel alarmed and irritated England; every prospect of accommodation vanished; and a declaration of war was issued by the French Government, with a pompous manifesto proclaiming the wanton injuries they had sustained from Great Britain.

Plunged into destructive warfare, each nation used their utmost efforts to accomplish their respective purposes. France, determined to establish the independence of America; while England, sought to reduce her colonies to the most decisive slavery. A transposition of national principles seemed to have been adopted by the Governments of both countries—despotic France combating, to establish the rights of civil liberty—and England exerting all her energies, to enforce a system of tyrannic government—the one marshalling the slaves of her arbitrary power to battle in the cause of pure democracy—the other rallying round an English standard the hired mercenaries of German avarice, to suppress the principles of British freedom—and both Governments soliciting the aid of sanguinary savages, to aggravate the horrors of a Christian war by the scalping-knife and the tomahawk of heathen murderers.

Europe beheld with amazement a combat so unnatural and disgusting: but it would have required a prophetic spirit, to have then foretold that the French throne would be eventually overturned by the principles of those new allies, and would, by the mighty shock of its fall, shake even the foundations of the British constitution; though the total prostration of the one, and the ministerial inroads upon the other, would since have fully justified the hazard of that prediction.

V. Amidst the confusion incident to those great events, Ireland yet remained unheeded and unthought of: her miseries and her oppressions had hardly engaged the consideration of the British minister. Meanwhile, the Irish people, with a dignified anxiety, contemplated the probable termination of a contest, by the result of which their own destiny must be determined. The subjugation of America might confirm the dependence of Ireland; and she was soon convinced,—that she could obtain her own constitutional rights from Great Britain only by the complete success and triumph of her colony.

Awaiting therefore the decrees of Providence, Ireland steadily surveyed the distant prospect of great and rival empires wantonly lavishing the blood and treasures of their people in a contest fundamentally repugnant to their established principles: but—cautious, moderate, and firm in her conduct—though she wisely determined to avail herself of the crisis to promote the establishment of her independence,—she fed the flame of liberty, she kindled not the blaze of licentiousness: while America fought to obtain a separation from Great Britain, Ireland took up arms only to obtain a just participation of her constitution.

To embarrass the offensive measures of England, and make a formidable diversion in favor of America, France manifested an intention of invading Ireland.—In this alarming emergency, Great Britain, from the dispersions of her military force, scattered into many distant stations of the world, and so numerously employed on the continent of America, found it impossible to afford a body of regular troops sufficient to protect Ireland in case of such invasion. Here let us for a moment pause, and dispassionately reflect upon the situation of Great Britain and the conduct of Ireland at this most trying moment: let us survey the increasing imbecility of the one, and the rising enemies of the other; and we must—do justice to the moderation and generosity of a people, whose long and grievous oppressions, if they could not have justified, would at least have palliated, a very different proceeding.

The state of England during this war became every day more difficult and distressing. A discontented people, and an unpopular ministry—an empty treasury, and a grievous taxation—a continental war, and a colonial rebellion—together formed an accumulation of embarrassment, such as Great Britain had never before experienced. Her forces in America were captured or defeated: her fleets, had not yet attained that irresistible superiority which has since proved the only protection of the British Islands.—Ireland, without money, militia, or standing army—without ordinance or fortifications—almost abandoned by England, had to depend solely on the spirit and resources of her own natives; and this critical state of Ireland, which the misconduct of Great Britain herself had occasioned, gave the first rise to those celebrated associations, the immediate means of obtaining Irish independence.

Many inducements prevailed, to fill the ranks of these associations. The warlike propensities of the Irish people, so long restrained—and personal attachment to their chiefs and leaders, were with them the first excitements: but the blending of ranks, and more intimate connexion of the people, which was the immediate consequence of a general military system, quickly effected an extensive and marked revolution in the minds and manners of the entire nation—an important and extraordinary change, of which the gradations became every day more conspicuously discernible. The primary stimulus of the Irish farmer was only that which he felt in common with every other animated being—the desire of self preservation:— he associated against invasion, because he heard that it would be his ruin: but his intercourse with the higher ranks opened the road to better information. Thus he soon learned that the Irish people were deprived of political rights, and that his country had endured political injuries: his ideas became enlarged, and quickly embraced more numerous and prouder objects; he began, for the first time, to know his own importance to the state; and, as knowledge advanced, the principles of constitutional independence were better understood, and more sedulously cultivated. The Irish peasant now assumed a different rank, and a higher character:—familiarised with arms, and more intimate with his superiors, he every day felt his love of liberty increased: the spirit at length became general enthusiastic; and, in less time than could have been supposed from the commencement of these associations, the whole surface of the island was seen covered with a self-raised host of patriot soldiers.

VI. In the formation of those armed associations, the long-established distinctions between the Protestant and the Catholic could not be altogether forgotten. Many of the penal laws were still in full force; Catholics were prohibited by statute from bearing arms in Ireland; and, from the rooted prejudices against allowing to that body any civil or military power whatever, strong objections arose to their admission into those armed bodies. The Catholics, however, neither took offence nor even showed any jealousy at this want of confidence, on the contrary, with their money and their exhortations, they zealously assisted in forwarding those very associations into which they themselves had not admission. Their calmness and their patriotism gained them many friends, and a relaxation of intolerance appeared rapidly to be gaining ground but it was not until the volunteers had assumed a deliberative capacity, and met as armed citizens, to discuss political questions, that the necessity of uniting the whole population of the country in the cause of independence became distinctly obvious. Those who foresaw that a general association of the Irish people was essential to the attainment of their constitutional objects, endeavoured to reconcile the schisms of sectarian jealousy by calm and rational observations; they argued, that religious feuds had, in all countries, proved subversive of national prosperity, but to none more decidedly fatal than to modern

Ireland;—that the true interest of the Catholic and of the Protestant was substantially the same, they breathed the same air, tilled the same soil, and had equal rights and claims to the participation of liberty, that they were endowed by nature with equal powers and faculties, intellectual and corporeal, that they worshipped the same God, the truths and doctrines of revealed religion equally constituting the basis of their social duties, and the foundation of their religious tenets, and the principles of virtue and of morality being equally inculcated from their pulpits, and propagated at their altars. "Why, then," they asked, "should a few theological subtilties, whose mysterious uncertainties lay far beyond the reach of human determination, and were altogether unnecessary to the arrangements of municipal institutions, why should they distract a nation which, to become *free* should become *unanimous?* why should they excite controversies so strongly tainted with fanatic phrenzy, that no personal insult or aggravated injury, no breach of moral tie or of honorable contract, could rouse rancor more acrimonious, or animosity more unrelenting, than that which originated solely from theoretic distinctions upon inexplicable subjects? as if Irishmen were bound to promote the happiness of their neighbours in a future state, by destroying their comforts and disturbing their tranquillity in the present!"

It was also observed, that, although this strange insanity might have existed in remote and dark ages, when the disciples of every new sect proclaimed themselves the meritorious murderers of the old, when Christian chiefs assailed the pagan power, only to make new proselytes to their own errors, and victims to their own intolerance, and though, in such unhappy times, Ireland might have partaken of the general madness, and, without peculiar disgrace, have participated in the infirmities of Europe, yet, when the progress of civilization had opened the eyes and enlarged the understanding of the people, when the voice of rational liberty loudly called for the unanimous exertion of every sect in the common cause of independence, it was full time to discard those destructive prejudices, which had so long and so effectually restrained the rights and retarded the prosperity of the Irish nation.

Nor can any historic incident more clearly illustrate

the inestimable value of unanimity to an oppressed people, than a contrasted exhibition of the independent spirit displayed by the Catholics in 1782, when they acquired a constitution by their firmness, and of their degenerate conduct in 1800, when they lost that constitution through their divisions and their servility.

VII. Before the progress of the Irish Volunteers is particularly detailed, or the ultimate objects which they had in view, the genuine character of the people among whom so extraordinary an association originated, should be clearly developed and perfectly understood; as many important events in Irish history would appear obscure and unaccountable, without a due knowledge of the national character—a character, ever misconceived or misrepresented in England, because the persons by whom the picture was drawn were generally either too ignorant or two interested to draw it with fidelity, and so little of intimate intercourse had subsisted between the two countries, that the people of England were in general as unacquainted with the real dispositions and habits of the Irish, as with those of any nation upon the European continent.

It was therefore impossible that England should judiciously govern a people with whose feelings she was wont to trifle, and with whose natural character she was so imperfectly acquainted, nor can she ever effectually acquire that knowledge, until she is convinced *that Ireland though formed by nature for her sister, was never intended for her servant*—and that, within her own bosom, she possesses powers, treasures, and resources, yet unexplored by England, but which, if kindly cultivated and liberally encouraged, would contribute more strength and benefit to both than Great Britain has ever heretofore derived, or ever yet merited from the connexion.

To attain a just conception of the remote causes of two great and repugnant revolutions in Ireland within eighteen years, we must view the ranks of which society is there composed, as well as their proportions and their influence on each other; and, in the peculiarities and ardency of that character, will be clearly discovered the true sources of many extraordinary events; it will evidently appear, that, to the foibles of that unfortunate nation, worked upon by art, and imposed upon by policy, and **not to** native crimes or peculiar views, are attributable the frequency of her miseries and the consummation of her misfortune.

VIII. The Irish people have been as little known, as they have been grossly defamed to the rest of Europe.

The lengths to which English writers have proceeded in pursuit of this object would surpass all belief, were not the facts proved by histories written under the immediate eye and sanction of Irish Governments, histories replete with falsehood, which, combined with the still more mischievous misrepresentations of modern writers, form all together a mass of the most cruel calumnies that ever weighed down the character of a meritorious people.

This system, however, was not without its meaning. From the reign of Elizabeth, the policy of England has been to keep Ireland in a state of internal division perfect unanimity among her inhabitants has been considered as likely to give her a population and a power incompatible with subjection, and there are not wanting natives of Ireland, who, impressed with that erroneous idea zealously plunge into the same doctrine, as if they could best prove their loyalty to the King by vilifying their country.

IX. The Irish peasantry, who necessarily composed the great body of the population, combined in their character many of those singular and repugnant qualities which peculiarly designate the people of different nations; and this remarkable contrariety of characteristic traits pervaded almost the whole current of their natural dispositions. Laborious, domestic, accustomed to wants in the midst of plenty, they submit to hardships without repining, and bear the severest privations with stoic fortitude. The sharpest wit, and the shrewdest subtilty, which abound in the character of the Irish peasant, generally lie concealed under the semblance of dulness, or the appearance of simplicity; and his language, replete with the keenest humour, possesses an idiom of equivocation, which never fails successfully to evade a direct answer to an unwelcome question.

Inquisitive, artful, and penetrating, the Irish peas**ant** learns mankind without extensive intercourse, and has **an** instinctive knowledge of the world, without mingling in its societies, and never, in any other instance did there exist a people who could display so much address and so much talent in the ordinary transactions of life as the Irish peasantry.'

The Irish peasant has, at all periods, been peculiarly distinguished for unbounded but indiscriminate hospitality, which, though naturally devoted to the necessities of a friend, is never denied by him even to the distresses of an enemy.* To be in want or misery, is the best recommendation to his disinterested protection; his food, his bed, his raiment are equally the strangers and his own; and the deeper the distress, the more welcome is the sufferer to the peasant's cottage.

His attachments to his kindred are of the strongest nature. The social duties are intimately blended with the natural disposition of an Irish peasant though covered with rags, oppressed with poverty, and perhaps with hunger, the finest specimens of generosity and heroism are to be found in his unequalled character.

A martial spirit and a love of desultory warfare is indigenous to the Irish people. Battle is their pastime; whole parishes and districts form themselves into parties, which they denominate factions; they meet by appointment at their country fairs, there they quarrel without a cause, and fight without an object, and having indulged their propensity and bound up their wounds, they return satisfied to their own homes, generally without anger, and frequently in perfect friendship with each other.† It is a

* It has been remarked that the English and Irish people form their judgment of strangers very differently:—an Englishman suspects a stranger to be a rogue, till he finds that he is an honest man; the Irishman conceives every person to be an honest man, till he finds him out to be a rogue; and this accounts for the very striking difference in their conduct and hospitality to strangers.

† Natural cruelty has been imputed to the Irish peasant by persons who either are unacquainted with his character, or wish to misrepresent it. National character can never be drawn with justice from incidents which take place amidst all the rage and violence of civil war or religious phrensy. The barbarities, committed in Ireland during the insurrection of 1798, were not all on the one side: and at least as many persons were sacrificed in cold blood by the musket or sabre of the soldiery, as by the pike or blunderbuss of the insurgent. But all those enormities are incidental to civil wars, and should never be brought up as a criterion, whereby to judge of the national character of any people. In Eng-

melancholy reflection, that the successive Governments of Ireland should have been so long and so obstinately blind to the real interest of the country, as to conceive it more expedient to attempt the fruitless task of suppressing the national spirit by legal severity, and penal enactments than to adopt a system of national instruction and general industry which, by affording employment to their faculties, might give to the minds of the people a proper tendency, and a useful and peaceable direction.

In general, the Irish are rather impetuously brave, than steadily persevering: their onsets are furious, and their retreats precipitate: but even death has for them no terrors, when they firmly believe that their cause is meritorious. Though exquisitely artful in the stratagems of warfare, yet, when actually in battle, their discretion vanishes before their impetuosity; and—the most gregarious people under heaven—they rush forward in a crowd with tumultuous ardor, and without foresight or reflexion whether they are advancing to destruction or to victory.

An enthusiastic attachment to the place of their nativity is another striking trait of the Irish character, which neither time nor absence, prosperity nor adversity, can obliterate or diminish. Wherever an Irish peasant was born, there he wishes to die; and, however successful in acquiring wealth or rank in distant places, he returns with fond affection to renew his intercourse with the friends and companions of his youth and his obscurity.

An innate spirit of insubordination to the laws has been strongly charged upon the Irish peasantry: but a people—to whom the punishment of crimes appears rather as a sacrifice to revenge than a measure of prevention—can never have the same deference to the law, as those who are instructed in the principles of justice, and taught to

---

land, during a peaceable year (1794,) two hundred and eighteen persons received sentence of death, of whom forty-four were for *murder*. In Ireland, during a troublesome year (1797,) eighty-seven received sentence of death, of whom only eighteen were for murder: so that England committed her full proportion of crimes and more than her proportion of murders; which does not substantiate the charge of cruelty, with which the Irish character has been exclusively aspersed. The murders in Ireland, moreover, are very different from those in England: many murders in Ireland occur in the heat of their battles: most of those in England are perpetrated in cold blood and on *women*.

recognise its equality. It has, however, been uniformly admitted by every impartial writer on the affairs of Ireland, that a spirit of strict justice has ever characterised the Irish peasant.* Convince him, by plain and impartial reasoning, that he is wrong; and he withdraws from the judgment-seat, if not with cheerfulness, at least with submission: but, to make him respect the laws, he must be satisfied that they are impartial; and, with that conviction on his mind, the Irish peasant is as perfectly tractable, as the native of any other country in the world.

An attachment to, and a respect for females is another marked characteristic of the Irish peasant. The wife partakes of all her husband's vicissitudes: she shares his labor and his miseries, with constancy and with affection. At all the sports and meetings of the Irish peasantry, the women are always of the company: they have a great influence; and, in his smoky cottage, the Irish peasant, surrounded by his family, seems to forget all his privations. The natural cheerfulness of his disposition banishes reflexion; and he experiences a simple happiness, which even the highest ranks of society might justly envy.

X. The middle class of gentry, interspersed throughout the country parts of the kingdom, possessed as much of the peasant character as accorded with more liberal minds and superior society. With less necessity for exertion than the peasant, and an equal inclination for the indulgence of indolence, their habits were altogether devoid of industry, and adverse to reflexion:—the morning chase and evening conviviality composed the diary of their lives, cherished the thoughtlessness of their nature, and banished the cares and solicitudes of foresight. They uniformly lived beyond their means, and aspired beyond their resources: pecuniary embarrassment only gave a new zest to the dissipation which created it; and the gentry of Ireland at this period had more troubles and fewer cares than any gentry in the universe.

These habits, however, while they contracted the dis-

* Sir John Davis, Attorney General of Ireland, who, in the reign of James the First, was employed by the King to establish the English laws throughout Ireland, and who made himself perfectly acquainted with the character of the inhabitants, admits that "there were no people under heaven, who loved equal and impartial justice better than the Irish."

tance between the lower and the superior order, had also the effect of promoting their mutual good-will and attachment to each other. The peasant looked up to and admired, in the country gentleman, those propensities which he himself possessed:—actuated by a native sympathy of disposition, he loved old customs; he liked to follow the track and example of his forefathers, and adhered to the fortunes of some ancient family, with a zealous sincerity; and, in every matter of party or of faction, he obeyed the orders of his landlord, and even anticipated his wishes, with cheerfulness and humility.

The Irish country gentleman, without either the ties of blood or the weight of feudal authority, found himself surrounded by followers and adherents ever ready to adopt his cause, and risk their lives for his purposes, with as warm devotion as those of the Scottish laird or the highland chieftain; and this disposition, cultivated by family pride on the one side, and confirmed by immemorial habit on the other, greatly promoted the formation, the progress, and the zeal, of those armed associations which soon afterwards covered the face of the country, and for a moment placed the name of Ireland on the very highest pinnacle of affective patriotism.

It was the fashion of those days to cast upon the Irish gentry an imputation, it would be uncandid not to admit that there was some partial ground for it, that they showed a disposition to decide petty differences by the sword, and too fastidious a construction of what they termed the "point of honor." This practice certainly continued to prevail in many parts of Ireland, where time and general intercourse had not yet succeeded in extinguishing the romantic but honorable spirit of Milesian chivalry: and, when we reflect on the natural warlike disposition of the Irish people, that indigenous impetuosity and love of battle which so eminently distinguished their aboriginal character, it is not surprising that hasty and unnecessary encounters should occasionally occur among a people perpetually actuated by the pride of ancestry and the theories of honor. But, even in these contests, the Irish gentleman forgave his adversary with as much readiness as he fought him: he respected the courage which aimed at his own life; and the strongest friendships were sometimes formed, and frequently regenerated, on the field of battle. It is natural to suppose that this practice should have been exaggerated, by the English people, whom nature had endowed with less punctilious and much more discreet propensities.

The cowardly crime of suicide, which prevailed and prevails in England, was scarcely ever known among the Irish. Circumstances, which would plunge an Englishman into a state of mortal despodency, would only rouse the energies of an Irishman to bound over his misfortunes:*—under every pressure, in every station, and in every climate, a lightness of heart and openness of disposition distinguishes him from the inhabitants of every other country.

On the whole of their characters, the Irish gentry, though far from being faultless, had many noble qualities: —generous, hospitable, friendly, brave—but careless, prodigal, and indiscreet—they possessed the materials of distinguished men with the propensities of obscure ones, and, by their openness and sincerity, too frequently became the dupes of artifice, and the victims of dissimulation.

Among the highest orders of the Irish people, the distinguishing features of national character had been long wearing away, and becoming less prominent and remarkable. The manners of the nobility, in almost every European country, verge to one common centre: by the similarity of their education and society, they acquire similar habits; and a constant intercourse with courts clothes their address and language, as it does their persons, in one peculiar garb—disguising the strong points, and concealing the native traits, of their original characters.

The unprecedented expenses of the American war, which first familiarised the English people to empty their purses for the support of unnecessary and inglorious warfare (in which they have since become such extraordinary proficients,) called every day for new resources;

* The Irish people have been accused of frequently committing what are termed *blunders*, or perverted phraseology: but many sayings, which have acquired that name, are in fact the aphorisms of sound sense, and strongwitted observation. The Irishman's remark, that "he would rather commit *suicide* on *any one* than *himself*," would puzzle the ingenuity of a moral casuist, and places the crime of self-murder in a very uncertain rank of homicide.

and the minister conceived and executed the artful project of increasing his financial means and parliamentary power by erecting a banking and commercial interest on the site and ruins of the landed representation. Money brokers—began to constitute a new order in the state, and to form, if not an integral part, at least a necessary appendage to every subsequent administration of Great Britain.

Experience has proved the mischiefs of that fatal policy to the whole of the empire.

Though the greater number of the Irish noblemen had been of remote creations—a few had not been long enough removed from the mass of the community to have acquired very high ideas of hereditary pride, or to have emblazoned the shield of very ancient or illustrious pedigrees.

As a body, the Irish lords were not peculiarly prominent in the affairs of their country: but they were dignified. Their debates (until the accession of Lord Clare) were calm and temperate; and, though, like the members of all other political assemblies, they were individually various in talent and in character, the appearance of the whole was grand; and their conduct, if not spirited, was firm, respectable and decorous.

The Protestant church had great weight in the community: the hierarchy, participating in the dignity of an independent parliament, possessed the united influence of spiritual rank and legislative importance: the parochial clergy, though well affected to the state, still adhered to the interests of their country, and, assuming a deportment decorous and characteristic, were, at that time, generally esteemed, and deservedly respected.

The provision of the inferior Protestant clergy was then (as at present) quite disproportioned to their duties and their profession. Many of that meritorious class of men, the officiating curates, whose precepts and example were to direct the morals and guide the conduct of the people, had become grey in poverty, and, labouring under the pressure of severe necessities, effectually preached up to their congregations the exercise of that charity, which would have been aptly and benevolently applied to their own persons.

The general conduct of these men had at all times remained unexceptionable. From them the character of the Irish clergy was best to be collected; the luxurious possessor of sinecure and plurality, enjoying ease and abundance without care or solicitude, must form a very inferior criterion of experienced merit, when compared to the distressed pastor, whose conduct remains exemplary, while his indigence and necessities might have tempted him into errors. The extremes of income among the Protestant clergy were too distant, their wealth and their poverty formed too strong a contrast.

The Catholic clergy had then an unlimited influence over the people of their own persuasion. Though the cruel impolicy of the penal statutes had not been altogether set aside, they remained dutiful and obedient to the sovereign power, cheerfully submissive to the existing laws, and friendly and affectionate to their Protestant fellow-subjects.

Candidates for Catholic ordination were sent to France for spiritual instruction, and returned to their own country though learned, still retaining many of the propensities of their origin, they showed that their respect to superior rank, and submission to the constituted authorities, were rather increased than diminished by their foreign education.

The monarchy of France, despotic, splendid, and powerful, was at that time regarded with devotion by the French people, as a structure which neither time could destroy, nor tempests endanger. Its broad base covered every portion of the people; its stupendous height was surveyed with awe, and its colossal strength beheld with admiration. The ecclesiastical communities, fostered under its shelter, experienced the protection of despotic power, and, by their doctrines and their practice endeavoured to increase its strength, and secure its permanence.

The Irish student, early imbibing those monastic principles was taught at Saint Omer the advantages of undefined power in a king, and of passive obedience in a subject; he was there instructed to worship a throne, and to mingle his devotion to heaven and to monarchy. The restoration of a Catholic king over Ireland had long ceased to be practicable, such projects, therefore, were hopeless, and relinquished; and the Irish Catholic clergyman, however he might naturally have wished for the regal supremacy of his own sect, had long since abandoned every view of an object altogether unattainable.

British supremacy had then no overt enemies, save its own ministers, nor any conspiracies against its power, but the arbitrary determinations of its own cabinet.

Thus returning from his noviciate, and educated with all the dispositions of a submissive subject he found his native country in a state of profound tranquillity. His views were contracted; his ambition extended no further than the affections of his flock, and the enjoyments of society. The closest intimacy subsisted between him and his parishioners, he mingled in all their pastimes, and consoled them in their miseries; but the most convivial among them knew how to distinguish clearly between the occasional familiarities of personal intercourse, and a dutiful respect for his religious functions; and, even though their companion might have been condemned, their priest was always sure to be respected.

The Catholic and the Protestant at the same time lived in habits of great harmony; they harboured no animosities or indisposition toward each other; the one governed without opposition, the other submitted without resistance; and the Catholic clergy had every inclination to retain their flock within proper limits and found no difficulty in effecting that object.

The severity with which the agents of the Protestant clergy in some parishes collected their tithes, and the exactions and oppressions, which the middle-man exercised over the occupant of the land, occasionally excited partial disturbances; but, in these, there was nothing of a revolutionary nature; they were only the nocturnal riots of some oppressed and mismanaged districts which the civil power in general found no difficulty in suppressing.

CHAPTER III.

Ireland awakened to a sense of her slavery—The Irish Parliament totally independent of England—The King acknowledged in Ireland through his Irish crown, and not through the crown of England—Perilous position of England—Moderation and attachment of Ireland—Ireland determined to demand her just rights—Conspiracy against the manufactures of Ireland—The non-consumption agreement adopted throughout all Ireland—Progress of the Volunteers—Their principal Leaders—Sir John Parnell—His character—General effects of volunteering upon the people of Ireland.

I. THE population of Ireland, distributed into those classes, endowed with those qualities, and borne down by an accumulation of impolitic and ungenerous restraints, at length awakened as it were from a deep trance. The pulse of that nation, torpid through habitual oppression, began to throb; her blood, stimulated by the stings of injustice, which she had so long and so patiently endured, circulated with a new rapidity; her heart, re-animated, sent motion and energy through her whole frame; and from a cold and almost lifeless corse, Ireland was seen majestically arising from the tomb of obscurity, and paying the first tribute of her devotion at the shrine of liberty.

Roused to a sense of her miserable situation, she cast her eyes around on the independent States of Europe, and compared their strength, their capacity, and their resources with her own. Encouraged by the view of her comparative superiority, she soon perceived that she had strength, and means, and opportunity to redress herself from the wrongs and degradations she was suffering; and that so long as she tolerated the authority of the British Legislature over her concerns, so long her commerce, her constitution, and her liberties, must lie prostrate at the foot of every British minister.

The political situations of both nations at that critical period, afforded a more than common scope for political contemplation: even the coldest politicians of that day were led involuntarily to reflect on the nature of the federative compact between the two countries, and could not avoid perceiving the total absence of that reciprocal good faith and confidence which alone could ensure the integrity of the empire, or the permanence of the connexion. In theory, the two nations were linked together by the strongest ties of mutual interest and mutual security; but in practice those interests were separated, and that *conjunction* of strength, on which the security of empires must at all times depend was too frequently disregarded, as if England had forgotten that she owed a great proportion of stability to the co-operation of the Irish people, and that if one hundred thousand Irish subjects, who fought her battles in her armies and in her navy, became even neutralized, by insults or by injuries, to their country, the English nation might too late discover the fatal impolicy of her system.

II. The fundamental principles upon which the connexion between the two nations was intrinsically founded, soon became a subject of general inquiry and universal discussion amongst every rank and class of society; and it required but little difficulty to convey to the quick conception of a naturally acute and intelligent people, a comprehensive view of their rights and of their deprivations. Nor was Ireland, at this period, destitute of able and active partisans, anxious and competent to instruct her people in language best adapted to impress upon the poignancy of their national feelings, and enlarge the scope of their political understandings.

They were told by those instructors, that Ireland was constitutionally connected with Great Britain, upon the basis of a complete equality of rights, that she possessed *a resident Parliament* of her own, competent, in all points, to legislate on her own concerns, *in no point connected with, or subordinate to, that of Great Britain.*

That their king was bound to govern Ireland, not through his *crown of England, but through his crown of Ireland*—conferred upon him by the Irish nation, and worn by him, in *conjunction* with that of Great Britain, as the chief magistrate of both—but to govern each country severally by their respective laws and their *dis tinct legislatures,* and not the one through the other; and though the Irish crown was, by the constitution of that country, placed for ever on the head of the same legitimate monarch who should wear that of England; yet the Irish people were not legally bound to obey any laws but those enacted by their own legislature, to transfer the sceptre of their realm to any usurped authority, or submit to the hostile or corrupt policy of any minister who might occasionally occupy the seat of power in England; that their oath of allegiance was taken to the king of *Ireland,* and not to the Parliament of Great Britain; that the establishment of this principle was indispensable to their existence as a nation, and that every violation of it was a direct deviation from the duty of the Irish crown, and a virtual dereliction of the compact between the two countries; and that the king's ministers of either country advising unconstitutional measures, to violate the constitutional independence of Ireland, must be considered as traitors to the Irish crown, and enemies to the British empire.

It was also observed, that this assumption of authority to legislate for Ireland, whatever colouring it might have received by the dissimulation or ingenuity of its supporters, had, in fact, for its real object the restraint of her commerce and the suppression of her manufactures, so far as they might interfere with the interests of England; because the management of the mere local concerns of Ireland by her own parliament was altogether immaterial to Great Britain, unless where a commercial rivalship might be the probable consequence of successful industry and legislative encouragement.

From this reasoning, it was obvious that the redress of these grievances could not depend solely upon any exertions of the Irish legislature. The Peers—from the causes herein before assigned—were influenced at that time by a very small portion of public feeling; the measures of the Commons might be suppressed by an act of the Privy Council; and it became manifest, that an universal and determined co-operation of the whole people with their representatives, to rescue their representation by vigorous measures, could alone operate with sufficient effect upon the policy and fears of England; and that a general appeal to the people would be justified by the soundest axioms of civil government—as long experience had fully ascertained, that nothing was to be gained by the forbearance of the one nation, or to be expected from the voluntary justice of the other.

The Irish people being thus apprised of the real source of all their grievances, the subject quickly engrossed their whole thoughts, and became familiar to their understandings. A new and broad field of reflection was opened to the middle orders; political discussions necessarily followed from day to day; at every public and private meeting, and in every district, these discussions turned on the principles of liberty: and as the subject expanded, their ideas became enlarged; those who could read, liberally instructed the illiterate as to the rudiments of their history and the rights of the constitution; and by familiar deductions, the misery of the peasant was without difficulty brought home to the corruption of the ministers. All ranks of the community began to mingle and converse at their public meetings; the influence of that general communication diffused itself rapidly amongst every class of society; and the people, after having perfectly ascertained the hardships of their situation, naturally proceeded to discuss the most decisive means of redressing their grievances.

III. The circumstances of public affairs in America and on the continent of Europe, but more especially in England herself, were every moment becoming more and more propitious to the political emancipation of Ireland. A dark cloud appeared collecting over the head of Great Britain—the rays of her setting sun could scarcely penetrate the obscurity of the gloom which surrounded her—and though she faced the impending hurricane with magnanimity and perseverance, she experienced a most anxious solicitude at the awful crisis which was rapidly approaching her.

Her situation was terrific. The States of America, colonised by her industry, and peopled by her convicts, tearing themselves away from the mother country, and appealing to the whole world against the tyranny which at once *had caused and justified her disobedience;* British armies wandering through boundless deserts, and associating with the savage tribes for savage purposes, dwindling by their victories, and diminishing by their conquests, surrendering their swords to those whom they had recently vanquished, and lowering the flag of England, with all the courtesies of continental warfare, to those very men whom the preceding moment they had proclaimed as traitors to their king and to their country.*

However, the wise and deliberate measures which Ireland on this occasion adopted, proved not only her unshaken fidelity, but her moderation and her unaffected attachment to Great Britain. She saw the perilous situation of her sister country; and though she determined to profit by the crisis, in justly reclaiming her commerce and her constitution, she also determined to stand or fall with the British empire, and to share the fate of England in the tremendous confederacies which were formed and were forming against her.

* The very different line of conduct adopted by England towards America and Ireland, when respectively in a state of insurrection, is very remarkable. The Americans (a mere *colony*) united with French troops, stood in open rebellion, for the avowed purpose of final separation from the mother country, and were proclaimed *traitors* and *rebels* by the King and Parliament; yet they uniformly experienced from the British military commanders the most decorous and respectful treatment. Their generals were addressed by their appropriate official titles—their military rank was recognized by the British army—their officers, when taken, were admitted on their parol of honour—and their prisoners were treated with humanity and attention.

The Irish experienced a very different conduct in 1798, when immediate *execution* was generally the gentlest punishment inflicted upon the insurgents of every rank, office, and description, and the laws of retaliation giving rise to a competition of barbarities, deluged the whole country in blood, extinguished its spirit, divided its people, and destroyed its reputation.

To persons unacquainted with the true history of those transactions, and the project of the British minister, the ambiguous conduct of Lord Cornwallis will appear altogether inconsistent and unaccountable. But the difficulty will be solved, when it becomes evident, from historic facts, that, without that general horror, depression, and dismay which the extent and continuance of those mutual barbarities had excited throughout all ranks and classes of people, the measure of a Legislative Union never *durst* have been proposed to Ireland, and that this terrific sensation was critically made use of, as the strongest instrument, to impose that measure on a people sunk under the lassitude of civil war, and while in search of peace, forgetting liberty.

The Irish people felt that they had a double duty to perform—to themselves, and to their posterity. England herself had given them a precedent. She had proved by the experience of centuries, that when she had an object to achieve in Ireland, she had never been restrained by the punctilious dictates either of honour or humanity, and had never failed to take advantage of the feebleness of Ireland to impose the grievous weight of her arbitrary restrictions; she had, at all periods, systematically encouraged the internal dissensions of that people, the better to humble them for the yoke which she had always been ready to place upon their country. Ireland, therefore, felt that she would be justified by British precedent to take advantage of this important crisis, and that even the practical principles of the British constitution had declared and justified the right of popular resistance. England had, upon the same principle of resistance to arbitrary power, attempted to justify the murder of one king, and the deposition of another, whilst Ireland, preferring her allegiance to her policy, remained faithful to both, and was rewarded for her loyalty by massacre and confiscation.

However, a hasty or impetuous resistance of the Irish people, even to the most arbitrary acts of their King or of their Government, was by no means a principle congenial to their political character; whilst it was obvious to the whole world that England had adopted those violent and outrageous proceedings against her own monarchs, upon principles and pretences far less constitutional, and more inconsistent with her liberties, than the measures and conduct which had been wantonly and systematically practised by British ministers against Irish freedom. With this useful and awful lesson before her eyes, Ireland wisely considered that she would best raise and establish her national character, and effect her just objects, by a gradual reassumption of her rights, and a temperate and fair demand of constitutional liberty; that her moderation would form an edifying contrast to the violence and intemperance of England, whenever her liberties were invaded, and that the advantage which the embarrassed state of Great Britain had now thrown into the hands of Ireland, would be most honourably exercised by a calm and loyal, but resolute and effectual proceeding. She perceived, however, that the moment most favourable to her objects had arrived; which, if suffered to pass by without effort, might never recur; and it therefore only remained to Ireland to ascertain the means most moderate but most likely to call Great Britain to a sense of reason and of justice, and to secure to herself the attainment of her rights, without the danger of hostile convulsion, or the horrors of civil conflict.

England, notwithstanding she had in some instances suspended, and in others prohibited, the exportation of Irish manufactures, inundated the Irish markets with every species of her own; and with a view effectually to destroy all power of competition in Ireland, the great capitalists of England determined, even at any loss, to undersell the Irish in their own markets—a loss, however which they thought would be eventually and amply repaid by the monopoly which must necessarily succeed the utter destruction of the Irish manufacture.

This system it was impossible for the Irish manufacturer to resist or counteract; his capital was too small to bear the losses of competition; resistance would have been vain; he had therefore no alternative but to change his trade, or submit, and famish.

It depended on the exertions of the people at large to resist every vicious and destructive project; and they lost no time in adopting incipient measures of resistance. With this view, they resolutely determined to adopt a non-importation and non-consumption agreement throughout the whole kingdom; and by excluding not only the importation, but the consumption of any British manufacture in Ireland, visited back upon the English combinators the ruin of their own treachery. No sooner was this measure publicly proposed, than it was universally adopted; it flew quicker than the wind throughout the whole nation: the manufacturing bodies, the corporate towns, the small retailers, the general merchants, at once universally adopted this vigorous determination, and the great body of the people, by general resolutions, and universal acclamations, avowed their *firm* determination to support the measure, till they should acquire a restoration of their political rights.

IV. Meanwhile, the armed associations hourly gained strength in numbers; they began to acquire the appendages and establishments of a regular army—discipline and confidence; and gradually consolidated themselves into regiments and brigades; some procured cannon and field equipages, and formed companies of artillery; the completion of one corps stimulated the formation of another, and at length almost every independent Protestant of Ireland was enrolled as a patriot soldier; and the whole body of the Catholics declared themselves the decided auxiliaries of their armed countrymen.

This extraordinary armament—the recollections of which will for ever excite in Ireland a devotion to the cause of liberty, which neither time can efface nor misfortunes extinguish—actuated solely by the pure spirit of incorruptible patriotism, and signalized by a conduct more temperate and more judicious, than had ever controlled the acts and objects of any military body in the history of the world.

The modern military corps, which have been skilfully, and perhaps wisely, imbodied, to preclude any recurrence to the measure of volunteering, possess no analogy to these celebrated associations, save that the loyalty of the Volunteers was to their *country* and *their King*—the loyalty of the Yeomen, to the *King of England* and *to his Ministers*.

Self-formed, and self-governed, the Volunteers accepted no commissions whatever from the Crown, and acknowledged no connection whatever with the Government; the private men appointed their own officers, and occasionally cashiered them for misconduct or incapacity; they accepted no pay, the more wealthy soldier cheerfully shared his funds with his poorer comrade—and the officers contributed their proportions to the general stock purse.

Yet notwithstanding this perverted state of all military establishments, their subordination was complete: the soldier obeyed, from the instinctive impulse of honour to himself and duty to his country; the officer commanded upon the same principle, and very few instances occurred where either were found to deviate from the straightest line of military rectitude. The rules of discipline were adopted by general assent, and that passive obedience which, in regular armies, is enforced by punishment, amongst the Volunteers of Ireland was effected by honour.

They assumed various uniforms; green, white, scarlet, or blue, were the prevailing colours.* Their line, therefore, appeared variegated, and peculiarly striking. Their arms were at first provided by themselves; but the extraordinary increase of their numbers rendered them at length unable to procure a sufficient supply by purchase: they had then but one course—they confidently required arms from the Government; the Government, whatever reluctance they might have felt to arm men who acknowledged no supremacy, yet did not think it safe to refuse their demand; and with an averted eye handed out to the Volunteers twenty thousand stand of arms from the Castle of Dublin.

V. Being completely equipped, the acquirement of persons capable of instructing so large a body in military tactics, appeared a matter of the greatest difficulty; but the same events which had at first inspired the Irish with a determination to arm, furnished them with the means not only of acquiring discipline, but of increasing their ardour.

The disasters of the American war had restored to the bosom of Ireland many brave men, whose health had sunk under the consequences of wounds and sufferings, and who, having witnessed the successful struggles of America for liberty, had returned to Ireland at that moment when she was critically preparing to assert her own. The association of these experienced veterans was sedulously courted by the Irish Volunteers; their orders

* The Lawyer's regiment of Volunteers adopted exactly the uniform of the King's Guards—their motto, "*Pro aris et focis.*" The Kilkenny regiment (the late Earl of Ormond's,) and the regiments of *Irish Brigades*, &c., wore green; the motto of the latter, "*Vox populi suprema lex est.*" During the continuance of the Volunteer corps, no other *police* whatever was necessary throughout the whole nation—no public delinquent could possibly escape apprehension—and the most perfect peace and tranquillity prevailed throughout every county and district in Ireland; the Volunteers exerted themselves in every department, as the preservers of public peace, and with an effect never known at any former or later period in that country.

were obeyed with confidence and alacrity, and amongst the country corps the effect of their instructions became suddenly conspicuous; and, under their experience, discipline advanced with rapid progress.

The intercourse and conversation of those persons also had a powerful effect, by transfusing into their pupils that military mind which a veteran soldier can never relinquish. In their convivial hours, the serjeant, surrounded by his company, expatiating on the events of actual service, and introducing episodes of individual bravery, perhaps of his own undauntedness and sagacity, gradually banished every other topic from their conversation at those meetings. The successful perseverance of America had impressed even the soldier himself who had fought against her, with an involuntary respect for the principles of his enemies; a constant intercourse with his Irish associates soon excited in him congenial feelings, and he began to listen with pleasure to their interesting question, "Why should not his own brave countrymen possess as much constitutional liberty as those foreign colonists who had conquered him?"

It is difficult to conceive the fascination which seized upon the heretofore contracted intellect of the military farmer, by a repetition of these novel and warlike subjects; the martial propensity of his innate character had already rendered him peculiarly susceptible of these animating impressions, and he now almost imperceptibly imbibed a military mind, and acquired a soldier's feeling. In a word, the whole nation became enamoured of arms; and those who were not permitted to bear them, considered themselves as honoured by being employed to carry the food and ammunition of the soldier.

The chief commanders of these armed bodies were men of the highest and most distinguished characters, and each corps was in general headed by persons of the first respectability in their respective districts, selected generally for their popularity and independence; but all these corps were, for a considerable time, totally distinct and unconnected; nor was it until they had formed into a consolidated column, under the command of the amiable and the illustrious Charlemont, that they acquired the irresistible impulse of a co-operating power. The mild, but determined patriotism of that respected nobleman, gave a new tint of character to the whole army which he commanded, and chased away the tongue of slander from their objects and their conduct.

In the number of those who, at this moment were launched, for the first time, into public observation, there appeared a person, who, without possessing the highest reputation for public talent, or the most undeviating line of public principle, by the honest and spirited termination of his political life, has been justly raised upon the elevated pedestal of national gratitude; a person, whose early appointment to the first financial department of Ireland, and whose official conduct, from that day to the catastrophe of Irish Parliaments, will necessarily be the subject of frequent and important observations, and authorizes an introduction of his name and character, at an earlier stage of this history, than would otherwise be consistent with the regular detail of a progressive narrative.

VI. Sir John Parnel, the commandant of a Volunteer association,* was the son of a crafty and prudent minor politician (Sir John Parnel, of Rathlegue, in the Queen's County.) and was educated with a view to a diplomatic situation; but on his return from the Continent, was found by his father too deficient in the necessary attainments of evasion and duplicity, to qualify him for the high departments of foreign diplomacy: his talents, therefore, became destined for home consumption, and by the intrigues of his father, and a forced exertion of his own abilities, he was soon noticed in the Irish Parliament as a person of more than ordinary capacity—and after a veering course of local politics, he was appointed Chancellor of the Exchequer. In that situation he continued, till the project of a union called forth the public virtues of every man who possessed any, and too late opened the eyes of the nation to its steady friends, and to its temporizing enemies.

Sir John Parnel had an eminent capacity for public business, but a lamentable deficiency of system in its arrangement. His strong mind and cultivated understanding lost much of their effect by the flurry of his

* The Maryborough Volunteers.

manner, which frequently impeded the perspicuity of his language.

His intellect was clear, his memory retentive, and his conception just; he possessed esteem, without an effort to obtain it, and preserved his friends, without exercising his patronage; he supported the Ministry without offending the opposition, and all parties united in calling him an honourable man.

Plain, frank, cheerful and convivial, he generally preferred society to trouble, and seemed to have rid himself of a weight when he had executed a duty. As a financier, he was not perfect—as a statesman, he was not deep—as a courtier, he was not polished—but as an officer, he was not corrupt; and though many years in possession of high office, and extensive patronage, he showed a disinterestedness almost unparalleled; and the name of a relative, or of a dependent, of his own, scarcely in a single instance increased the place or the pension lists of Ireland.

Though his education and habits were ministerial, his mind was intrinsically patriotic, and a sentiment of independent spirit not unfrequently burst out from under the pressure of that official restriction which the duties of his station had necessarily imposed upon him; but his appointment as a minister never induced him to forget his birth as an Irishman; and his attachment to the sovereign, never diminished his philanthropy to the subject.

After an honest, faithful, and zealous service of his king, for seventeen years—as Chancellor of the Irish Exchequer—he was called upon by the minister to sacrifice his principles, and betray his country—to efface the impressions of his youth, and tarnish the honour of his maturity—to violate his faith, and falsify his conviction; but the fetters of office could not restrain the spirit of its captive: he lost his station, but he retained his integrity, and was compensated for the consequences of an undeserved dismissal, by the approbation of his conscience and the affection of his country.

The Volunteer corps which he commanded, early and zealously adopted the cause of Irish independence—a cause he strenuously adhered to, to the last moment of his existence—and in that noble firmness with which he resisted a legislative union, and disobeyed the mandates of a crafty and vindictive viceroy; he has left to the present age a brilliant and a rare example of a minister, honest enough to prefer his character to his office, and proud enough to postpone his interest to his honour.

VII. The Volunteer system now becoming universal in Ireland, effected an important and visible change in the minds and manners of the middle and lower orders of the people; by the occurrence of new events, and the promulgation of novel principles, their natural character became affected in all its bearings, and acquired, or rather disclosed, new points, which at that period tended to promote their prosperity, but eventually formed the grand pretence for the extinguishment of their independence.

The familiar association of all ranks, which the nature of their new military connection necessarily occasioned, every day lessened that wide distinction, which had theretofore separated the higher and lower orders of society—the landlord and the tenant—the nobleman and the artisan—the general and the soldier—now, for the first time, sat down at the same board—shared the same fare—and enjoyed the same conviviality. The lower order learned their own weight in the community—the higher were taught their dependance upon the people—and those whose illiterate minds had never before conceived or thought on the nature of political constitutions, or the fundamental principles of civil government, now learned from the intercourse and conversation of their superiors, the rudiments of that complicated but noble science; the misconception and the abuse of which, has since become the severest scourge that ever afflicted the states of Europe.

A visible alteration was also soon observable in the general appearance of the people; the squalid garb and careless dress of the Irish farmer was now exchanged for the minute cleanliness and regularity of the soldier. A striking revolution took place not only in the minds, but also in the external appearance of the Irish; their intellect acquired strength by exercise and information—their address was improved by intercourse and discipline—and their general appearance by dress and regularity; and had not the same causes, which led to the concessions of 1782, induced the British Government to recall that constitution which had been wrested from its feebleness, these unparalleled associations would have conferred advantages on the country, beyond all measures which human wisdom could have suggested, for its improvement.

CHAPTER IV.

Unexpected events in the Irish House of Commons—Mr. Grattan's Amendment to the Address—His public character and vicissitudes—The Amendment—Its effects—Sir Henry Cavendish—His character—Mr. Hussey Burgh (the Prime-Sergeant) secedes from Government and substitutes an Amendment for Mr. Grattan's—the Amendment passed—First step towards Irish independence—The English Parliament callous to the wrongs of Ireland—Lord Shelburne and Lord Ossory propose resolutions—The Irish nation determined to assert its rights—Resolution for a free trade carried unanimously—This circumstance one of the remote causes of the Union—Rapid progress of the Volunteers—Extraordinary military honours paid to the Duke of Leinster—Attempts to seduce the Volunteers—Earl of Charlemont—His character.

I. WHILE those transactions were taking place throughout the country, a memorable and unexpected event occurred in the Irish Parliament.

The sessions of 1779-80 commenced with a scene which while it elevated the Irish people to the height of expectation, and inspired them with a new confidence, paralyzed the British Government, and for the first moment, made known decidedly to the councils of that country, that they had no longer to deal with a timid, dispirited, and unprotected nation.

The adoption of non-importation and non-consumption agreements had already created considerable anxiety in the British Minister as to the probable result of the ensuing Session, and the Lord Lieutenant was directed to open the Parliament with a speech, remotely alluding to his Majesty's sentiments of liberality, but without specifying any measure of concession, and so cautiously guarded, as neither to alarm the Public, nor commit the Government, but the days of insipidity had now passed away; the Viceroy's speeches from the throne, for almost a century, had been composed nearly in the same commonplace language and trite observation, and the addresses of both Houses, in reply to those speeches, had been almost invariably mere echoes of the speech itself, with general assurances of liberal supplies and increasing loyalty.

On the opening of this Session, however, there appeared a more than common sensation amongst the leading members of Parliament, the strong and animated declarations of public sentiment which had been published during the prorogation, made an extraordinary impression, but the extent or consequences of that impression could not be ascertained, until the proceedings of the House of Commons gave an opportunity of observing what effect the new spirit of the people would now have upon the conduct of their representatives.

At length the Parliament assembled; the anxious and inquisitive eye of the Secretary and of the steady partisans of Government passed rapidly throughout the whole House alarmed by the appearance of some unusual resistance, they endeavoured, from the looks, the suggestions, the manner of the members, to prejudge the result of the first night's debate, which had generally decided the complexion of the ensuing session, but no sagacity could have anticipated the turn which Irish affairs were to receive on that night—no human foresight could have predicted that blow which the system of the British Cabinet was about to receive by one single sentence—or have foreseen that that single sentence would be the composition of the first law-officer of the Irish Government.

The Lord Lieutenant's speech was delivered by him, in the House of Lord's in the accustomed tone of confidence, ambiguity, and frivolous recommendations; and in the Commons, the usual echo and adulatory address was moved by Sir Robert Deane, a person completely devoted to the views of Government. A pause succeeded and an unusual communication was perceivable between several members on the Government and Opposition sides of the House. A decided resistance to the usual qualified address now became certain; the Secretary, moving irresolutely from place to place, was seen endeavouring to collect the individual opinions of the members —and the law-officers of the Crown evinced a diffidence never before observable in their department; throughout the whole House a new sense of expectation and anxiety was evident.

II. At length Mr. Henry Grattan arose, with a somewhat more than usual solemnity;—he seemed labouring with his own thoughts, and preparing his mind for a more than ordinary exertion. The address and the language of this extraordinary man were perfectly original; from his first essay in Parliament, a strong sensation had been excited by the point and eccentricity of his powerful eloquence;—nor was it long until those transcendent talents, which afterwards distinguished this celebrated personage—were perceived rising above ordinary capacities, and, as a charm, communicating to his countrymen that energy, that patriotism, and that perseverance, for which he himself became so eminently distinguished; his action, his tone, his elocution in public speaking, bore no resemblance to that of any other person; the flights of genius, the arrangements of composition, and the solid strength of connected reasoning, were singularly blended in his fiery, yet deliberative language; he thought in logic and he spoke in antithesis; his irony and his satire, rapid and epigrammatic, bore down all opposition, and left him no rival in the broad field of eloquent invective; his ungraceful action, however, and the hesitating tardiness of his first sentences, conveyed no favourable impression to those who listened only to his exordium, but the progress of his brilliant and manly eloquence soon absorbed every idea, but that of admiration at the overpowering extent of his intellectual faculties.

This was Mr. Henry Grattan of 1779—in the vicissitudes of whose subsequent life will be remarked three dictinct eras of public character, and disgusting proofs of popular inconsistency—the era of his glory, the era of his calumny, and the era of his resurrection; in the first, elevated to a pitch of unbounded gratification, by the attachment, the gratitude, and the munificence of his countrymen;—in the second, despoiled of health, of happiness, and of character, by the artifices of a powerful enemy, and in the third rising from the bed of sickness, re-embarking a shattered frame in the service of his country. In Parliament he taught the doctrines of Molyneux and of Lucas—he drew the true constitutional distinctions between the Crown and the Government—the magistrate and the function—the individual and the sceptre. But the partiality of the friend may possibly bias the pen of the historian ;—his public principles will be best ascertained by tracing the undeviating line of his public conduct.

The career of this extraordinary man is finished. But he survived his country, he lived to view the demolition of that noble fabric raised by the exertion of his own virtue and perseverance, and the catastrophe of that constitution, which, " as he watched over it in its cradle, so he attended it to its grave."

III. After an oration, replete with the most luminous reasoning, the severest censure, pathetic and irresistible eloquence, Mr. Grattan moved an amendment to the address, viz. " That we beseech your Majesty to believe, that it is with the utmost reluctance we are constrained to approach you on the present occasion ; but the constant drain to supply absentees, and the unfortunate prohibition of our trade, have caused such calamity, that the natural support of our country has decayed, and our manufacturers are dying for want ; famine stalks hand in hand with hopeless wretchedness ; and the only means left to support the expiring trade of this miserable part of your Majesty's dominions, is to open a free export trade, and let your Irish subjects enjoy their natural birthright."

His arguments had been so conclusive, his position so self-evident, his language so vigorous and determined, his predictions so alarming, and the impression which those combined qualities made upon the House was so deep, and so extensive, that the supporters of Government, paralyzed and passive, seemed almost ready to resign the victory, before they had even attempted a resistance.

The confusion which now appeared on the Treasury bench was very remarkable, because very unusual. The Secretary (Sir Richard Heron,) for the first time, showed a painful mistrust in the steadiness of his followers ; he perceived that the spirit of the House was rising into a storm, which all the influence of his office would not be able to allay, direct opposition would be injudicious, if not fatal, palpable evasion would be altogether impracticable, the temporizing system was almost worn out, and procrastination seemed to yield no better prospect of a favourable issue; the officers of Government sat sullenly on their benches, awaiting their customary cue from the lips of the Minister, but he was too skilful to commit himself to a labyrinth, from whence return was so diffi cult and precarious, and all was silent. At length ԝir Henry Cavendish hesitatingly arose, to declare his dissent to this first decided effort of the Irish Parliament to assert its liberties.

IV. Sir Henry Cavendish was one of those persons who are generally found in the front of a popular assembly, and acquire notoriety by becoming the oracle of some insulated department. Though possessed of a plain, shrewd understanding, abundance of craft, a convenient temper, and imposing plausibility; after unavailing effort to acquire the fame of a rhetorician, Sir Henry contented himself with the reputation of profound knowledge in parliamentary precedents and points of order.

He was ever prepared with a string of parliamentary precedents, appropriate to every question, and adapted to every circumstance, which he skilfully contrived to substitute for reasoning, and oppose to argument, and should his prolific memory chance to fail him in the quotation of his documents, his inventive genius never let the subject fail for want of an auxiliary.

On points of order he was at least as garrulous as orthodox, and peculiarly expert at critical interruption; under colour of keeping order, he assumed a licence for transgressing it,—and in affecting to check the digression of others, he frequently made it the first figure of his own rhetoric;—he was admirably calculated for desultory debate—when he was right, he was concise—when he was wrong, he was pertinacious, sarcastic, obstinate, plausible, persevering—he gained time when he could not make proselytes, and became the very essence and soul of procrastination. Sir Henry was well aware that he durst not venture an unqualified negative, and endeavoured craftily to administer his panacea of precedents, and to propose what he termed "something more orderly in the House, and more gracious to the Sovereign." He said he would vote against the amendment—that the business would be better effected by following a precedent in the year 1661, when the Lords and Commons of Ireland appointed commissioners to attend the King—to " supplicate the redress of grievances."

V. The die was now cast—and a resistance to the measure was announced and proceeded on. Mr. Scott (Attorney General) affected to support Sir Henry—but as if conscious of his ultimate failure, he appeared almost a new character;—the bold audacity of his address degenerated into an insidious plausibility—his arrogance fled without an effort—and for once in his life he was tame, vapid, and equivocal;—an ardent spirit now burst forth from every quarter of the House. Mr. Henry Flood, a most prominent personage in Irish history, whose endowments were great, and whose character was distinguished, the Provost—Mr. Ogle—Sir Edward Newnham—and many others—declared their coincidence with the amendment. But though it stated, in true and pathetic language, the miseries Ireland was subject to, by reason of her absentees, if pressed too strongly on the tenderest spot of the interest of Britons, to admit of their concurrence; while, on the other side, it was conceived not to be thoroughly explicit—and not sufficiently peremptory;—the object was most important—the moment was most critical —and the amendment was exceptionable. These difficulties had been foreseen.

VI. Mr. Hussey Burgh (the Prime Sergeant) at length arose from the Treasury bench, with that proud dignity so congenial to his character, and declared, that he never would support any Government, in fraudulently concealing from the King the right of his people;—that the high office which he possessed could hold no competition with his principles and his conscience, and he should consider the relinquishment of his gown only as a just sacrifice upon the altar of his country;—that strong statement, rather than pathetic supplication, was adapted to the crisis; and he proposed to Mr. Grattan to substitute for his amendment the following words—" That it is not by *temporary expedients*, that this nation is now to be saved from impending ruin."

The effect of his speech* was altogether indescribable, nor is it easily to be conceived by those who were not witnesses of that remarkable transaction; the House, quick in its conception, and rapidly susceptible of every impression, felt the whole force of this unexpected and important secession. The character—the talents—the eloquence of this great man, bore down every symptom of further resistance;—many of the usual supporters of Government, and some of the Viceroy's immediate connections, instantly followed his example, and in a moment the victory was decisive,—not a single negative could the Minister procure,—and Mr. Burgh's amendment passed unanimously, amidst a tumult of joy and exultation.

This triumph of Irish patriotism, made an instantaneous and powerful impression on the minds of the people;—it was their first victory, and the ministers' first discomfiture. The volunteers attributed this unexpected success to the impressions which their spirit had diffused throughout the country, and they determined to adopt this measure, as if it had been their own offspring—and thereby identify the virtues of the Parliament with the energies of the people. On the circumstance being announced, the drums beat to arms—the Volunteer associations collected in every part of the metropolis—and they resolved to line the streets, and accompany to the gates of the Castle that part of the legislative body which moved in solemn procession, to present their wholesome warning into the hands of the Viceroy.

The secession of Mr. Burgh from the Government, was not more important than that of M. Connolly, brother-in-law to the Viceroy, and Mr. Burton Cuningham, a constant supporter of ministerial measures—men

* The author of this memoir was present at that memorable debate (if debate it can be called,) and the impression it then made upon his mind can never be effaced. The depression on the one side—the exultation on the other—the new sensation on both—the obvious feeling which this unexpected event excited in the galleries, crowded by six or seven hundred of the most respectable persons out of Parliament, and a great number of ladies of high rank—the general congratulation on the spirit of the Parliament, was a scene so remarkable, as never to be forgotten; but is attended by the sad reflection, that Mr. Burgh did not long survive the service he did his country—nor did his country long survive the service which he rendered it.

in high estimation and of large fortunes—which gave **Mr.** Grattan an opportunity for observing, that " the people were thus getting *landed security* for the attainment of their liberties."

The effect of this measure, though in its nature inconclusive, appeared to lay the first stone of Irish independence, and greatly increased both the numbers and confidence in Volunteer associations.*

Several attempts had been previously made to fix the attention of the British legislature on the distressed and dangerous situation of Ireland; but every such effort had proved totally abortive. Although the critical state of that country had been discussed in both houses of Parliament, and addresses had been voted to the King requesting his immediate attention to the affairs of Ireland, to which favorable answers had been returned by his Majesty; and though the Irish Commons had also framed a resolution, in the language of more than common expostulation; yet the subject passed away from the

* The secret history of this celebrated amendment is worthy of recording; it proves that the measures adopted by Ireland, at that period, were not the work of party or of faction, but the result of the secret and deliberate consideration of the most able and virtuous men of the Irish nation.

Mr. Dennis Daly, a man of great abilities, large fortune, exquisite eloquence, and high character, together with Mr. Grattan, withdrew themselves to Bray (a village ten miles from the metropolis,) there to deliberate privately on the most effectual means of attaining the just rights of their country;—previous confidential communications had taken place between them and Mr. Perry, then Speaker of the House of Commons, who recommended a strong and comprehensive amendment to the address of the ensuing session, as the first step to be taken on the occasion. Mr. Grattan drew up one amendment—Mr. Daly another—and Mr. Daly's, in his own hand-writing, formed that which Mr. Grattan moved in the Commons.

At the same time similar communications had taken place between Mr. Hussey Burgh and Mr. Henry Flood, which gave rise to the amendment moved by Mr Burgh.

That proposed by Mr. Grattan leaning heavily on *absentees*, the friends of that body did not, from the complexion of the House, wish to hazard any division respecting them; and therefore, to avoid such discussion, acceded to Mr. Burgh's ammendment, which did *not* allude to absentees, to avoid Mr. Grattan's which did;—and to this circumstance is to be attributed the unaccountable unanimity with which the measure passed both Houses of Parliament—and the extraordinary secession of Mr. Connolly, and other weighty supporters of Administration.

attention of the Ministers, and even this session closed, affording only further and decided proofs of their temporizing duplicity.

VII. Great Britain was not as yet sufficiently alarmed, to become just;—she could not as yet be persuaded that the Irish people were competent to the redress of their own grievances; and she considered the warmth of their public declarations only as the brilliant flashes of a temporary patriotism.

Her egotism blinded her to her state and she fancied that the same *revolution* which had confirmed *her* liberties, had subjected to her power the liberties of her sister; and still paramount to justice and to policy, she felt too proud as yet to bend her attention to the grievances which she had herself inflicted.

Some powerful friends of Ireland at length began zealously to espouse her interests. The good Earl Nugent, whose memory and character are still revered by those who recollect the sincerity of his attachment to that country in 1778, made an effort in the British Lords to call their attention to the distresses of Ireland: but his efforts were ineffectual. The same nobleman soon after repeated the same effort; but his weight and abilities were not equal to his zeal and integrity. His motion was treated with an unbecoming superciliousness by Lord North, and death unfortunately, soon after, deprived his country of one of its truest friends and most dignified and honest advocates.

VIII. The Earl of Shelburne, in the Lords, and the Earl of Upper Ossory, in the Commons, also proposed strong resolutions in both Houses, declaratory of the dangerous state of that country.* But though the mo-

* The following resolution was moved, by the Earl of Shelburne, in the British House of Lords, on the 1st day of December, 1779:—

"Resolved—That it is highly criminal in his Majesty's Ministers to have neglected taking effectual measures for the relief of the kingdom of Ireland, and to have suffered the discontents of that country to rise to such a height, as evidently to endanger the constitutional connection between the two kingdoms, and to create new embarrassments to the public councils, through division and diffidence, in a moment when real unanimity, grounded upon mutual *confidence and affection*, is confessedly essential to the *preservation* of the British empire."

After a short debate, this motion was rejected. For the motion—37 Lords. Against it—82.

tion was well-timed, the motives of the noble movers did not proceed from the same feeling which actuated the resident inhabitants of Ireland. Neither of those noblemen had been habitual friends to the general interests of that country. Both of them were total absentees—they possessed large estates in Ireland, and trembled for their properties—they acted in general opposition to the Government, and wished to register the culpability of their adversaries. Their motions were, after very sharp debates, rejected in both Houses, and Ireland became fully and finally convinced, that it was not through the occasional exertion of Irish emigrants, in a foreign legislature, that she was to seek for the recovery of her rights, and alleviation of her miseries.

Applications to the Government—petitions to the Parliament—and supplications to the Crown, had all been tried in vain: neither the bold remonstrances of right, nor the piercing cries of necessity, could reach the royal ear, or penetrate the circle of Ministers which surrounded the British throne, and concealed from the Irish king a distinct view of his Irish people. Humble and pathetic language had failed—the voice of the nation was exhausted by unevailing supplication—and it now became full time to act in the cause of liberty.

Such being the ascertained disposition of the whole body of the people, not a moment was to be lost in the adoption of some measure, too strong to be despised by ministers, and too moderate to be dangerous to the connection. Delay might now terminate all the hopes of Ireland—the crisis might pass away—the public spirit might cool—and the moment so auspicious to the interests of the nation might be lost for ever. Though this determination quickly circulated throughout the whole country, the people still acted with that deliberate firmness, which, of all conduct, is the most fatal to a political adversary, and adds most strength and character to popular proceedings.

IX. The personages who then led Ireland forward to her bloodless victory, well knew the inestimable value of that prudent principle. They were men of great abilities—profound wisdom—and that effective patriotism, which considers activity its necessary friend, but precipitation its most dangerous enemy. They instructed the people, that while they acted with undeviating firmness, they should also act with prudential moderation—that the suspended liberties of a people were most likely to be recovered from a powerful oppressor, by a determined but cool and progressive perseverance—that by deliberate system none would be alarmed—wise men would be attended to—the impetuous be restrained—the wavering confirmed—and the people steadied: patriotism and confidence would grow up together and become more intimately blended, and the whole nation, without alarm, be imperceptibly led to one common centre, and become competent to achieve the strongest measures, before they were well aware that they had commenced the preparation for them.

They were instructed, that on the other hand, undigested and impetuous proceedings, if not successful, by the first rapidity of their execution, in general defeat their own object, and rivet the chains of that country which they were intended to emancipate—that it is more practicable to advance on gradual claims than recede from extravagant determinations—and that the inevitable miseries of civil war, however justifiable upon the principles and precedent of constitutional resistance, established at the revolution, should be the last resource even of an enslaved people—and, that though the Irish were armed, and might demand concession in the attitude and tone of confidence, it would be much wiser to give their *incipient* proceedings the weight and character of citizens, and reserve for the last extremity the threat of soldiers—that England, by this means, would be sufficiently informed of the determination of Ireland, without feeling her pride too much hurt, to propose a negotiation, or so much alarmed as to prepare for resistance.

This discreet reasoning had its full effect upon the generality of the nation; and though the ebullitions of public feeling occasionally broke forth in ardent resolutions of the Volunteer associations—the temperate system was generally adopted; and it was only upon fully experiencing its final failure, that the exhilarating shouts of an embattled people were heard reverberating from every quarter of a military country.

X. As before mentioned, public resolutions neither to import, purchase, or consume any British manufacture, or commodity whatever, had been universally but peaceably adopted, throughout the whole island—a measure at all times justifiable by any people, who may have been deprived of their commerce and their constitution by the power or the machinations of an insidious neighbour.

Inundated as Ireland had been with every species of British manufacture, there could be no step so just, so moderate, or which promised so many beneficial consequences, as the total exclusion from the Irish markets of every commodity which she was herself competent to manufacture, or of which she could possibly dispense with the immediate consumption. However, it was not until after the grievances of Ireland could be no longer endured, and she found that nothing but propositions, without sufficient latitude to be beneficial, or security to be permanent, were offered for her acceptance, that these resolutions became almost universal—spread themselves like a rapid flame, throughout every village of the island—and were zealously promoted by almost every individual in the country. At length, a general meeting was convened by the High Sheriffs of the city of Dublin, and resolutions* then entered into by the whole

---

* THOLSEL, DUBLIN.
At a general meeting of the Freemen and Freeholders of the City of Dublin, convened by public notice,

William James, and John Exshaw, *High Sheriffs*, in the chair.

The following Resolutions, amongst others, were unanimously agreed to:

"That we will not, from the date hereof, until the *grievances of this country* shall be *removed*, directly or indirectly import or consume ANY of the manufactures of *Great Britain*; nor will we *deal* with any merchant, or shopkeeper, who shall *import* such manufactures; and that we recommend an adoption of a similar agreement to *all* our countrymen who regard the commerce and constitution of this country.

"Resolved unanimously, That we highly applaud the manly and patriotic sentiments of the several corps of Merchants, Independent Dublin, Liberty, and Goldsmiths' Volunteers, and heartily thank them for their demonstration of zeal and ardour in the cause of their country—and that we shall ever be ready to join with them in defending our rights and constitution, and gladly and cheerfully contribute to PROTECT them from PROSECUTION or PERSECUTION.

Signed, JOHN EXSHAW, Sheriff."

metropolis, which finally confirmed and consummated that judicious measure, and at length convinced Great Britain, that Ireland would no longer submit to insult and domination, and had commenced a gradation of active proceedings, of which the climax might ultimately, though unfortunately, produce a rupture of the connection.

These resolutions were enforced with rigor and strictness. Few men, however their interest might be affected, would wantonly risk the imputation of being traitors to their country, and encounter the dangers of popular retribution, which was, in some few instances, actually inflicted.

The nation now paused for a moment: it found itself prepared to commence its great work of constitutional regeneration, and stood steadily and firmly watching with an anxious eye, for the operation of this first overt act of determined patriotism. The people had now ascended an eminence sufficiently elevated to give them a full view of their friends and of their enemies—they had peaceably hoisted the first standard, and made the first proclamation of liberty. A mutual compact of the citizen to support the soldier, and the soldier to defend the citizen, formed a very remarkable feature in all their resolutions—and though the military associations had not (as such) yet assumed a deliberative capacity, it was obvious that their discretion alone had continued the distinction—and, that though they spoke by two tongues, there was in fact but one heart amongst the people.

This bold measure, however it may have been eclipsed by the more striking importance of events which succeeded each other in a rapid progression, yet had a momentous influence on the subsequent fate and policy of Ireland, and must be considered as the commencement of that interesting course of political transactions, which suddenly raised her to the highest pitch of national pride and prosperity, and afterwards hurled her down the destructive precipice of misery and degradation.

The spirited adoption and obstinate adherence of the

N. B.—This resolution had been preceded, some months before, by similar resolutions in Galway and other parts of Ireland; but the nation could not be considered as having generally adopted those sentiments, till they were sanctioned by the metropolis.

Irish people to these resolutions, now flashed as a new light in the eyes of the British Administration. The power of the English statutes, which bound the commerce of Ireland, was, by these resolutions, almost at the same moment denied and demolished, without the aid of arms, or tumult of insurrection, and the pride and power of Great Britain received that warning blow, which taught her what she had reason to expect from a further perseverance in her favorite system. The Ministry were astonished : the arm of usurpation, which had so long wielded alternately the sword and commanded the coffer, fell paralyzed and lifeless by the side of the usurpers. But the fate of empires is governed by the same fatality as the chequered life of individuals; and this very measure, which so auspiciously and proudly asserted, and the events which afterwards so completely acquired the constitutional independence and commercial freedom of Ireland, will be found the ulterior pretence for revoking those great acquirements. England, compelled to concede was determined to reclaim, and from the first hours of reluctant concession, pursued that deep and insidious system, which will be fully traced and developed in the course of Irish transactions, and will be found conspicuously active, from the commercial tariff of 1784, through every stage of the regency, and the rebellion, to the completion of that measure, entitled a legislative Union between the two countries.

XI. The Volunteer associations of the metropolis soon perceived, that however numerous their force and extensive their popularity, it required some strong link of connection to unite military bodies, so entirely distinct and independent of each other—who acknowledged no superior to their respective commanders, and no control but voluntary obedience.

To secure their unanimity, perhaps even their permanence, it required some consolidating authority, whose weight might restrain within proper limits the uncontrolled spirits of a body, assuming the double capacity of a soldier and of a citizen.

This essential object could only be attained by the selection of some high and dignified personage, whose rank and character, rising beyond the reach of common competition, might unite together, under one common chief, that diversity of views and objects which must ever distract the proceedings of detached associations.

The Volunteers of Dublin saw clearly, that military bodies, however laudable their views, must be more than commonly subject to the fallibility of human institutions, and that to have the effect and impetus of an army, they must submit themselves fully to its control and organization.

They did not, however, long hesitate in their choice of a commander. Every eye seemed to turn, by general instinct, on William, Duke of Leinster. His family, from the earliest periods, had been favorites of the people—he had himself, when Marquis of Kildare, been the popular representative for Dublin—he was the only Duke of Ireland—his disposition and his address combined almost every quality which could endear him to the nation. The honesty of his heart might occasionally mislead the accuracy of his judgment; but he always intended right, and his political errors usually sprung from the principle of moderation.

This amiable Nobleman was therefore unanimously elected, by the armed bodies of the metropolis, their General, and was immediately invested with all the honours of so high a situation; a guard of Volunteers was mounted at his door—a body guard appointed to attend him on public occasions—and sentinels placed on his box when he honoured the theatre; he was followed with acclamations whenever he appeared; and something approaching to regal honours attended his investiture.*

* A whimsical circumstance took place on this occasion, which shows the extreme credulity with which every intelligence respecting Ireland was then swallowed in Great Britain. The appointment of the Duke, as General in Chief, was celebrated by the Volunteers in College-green, with great solemnity. Their artillery was ordered out, and a vast concourse of people were assembled. The captain of a Whitehaven collier, who had just landed, and come unexpectedly to the spot, on inquiring the reason of such rejoicing, was jocularly informed, that the people were crowning the Duke King of Ireland. He waited for no further information—got back with all expedition to his vessel in the bay, and sailed instantly for Liverpool; where he made an affidavit before the Mayor, that he was present and saw the Duke of Leinster crowned King of Ireland the preceding day. An express was instantly despatched to London with the affidavit to the British Ministers—a cabinet council

This was the first measure of the Volunteers towards the formation of a regular army; its novelty and splendor added greatly to its importance, and led the way to the subsequent appointments which soon after completed their organization. The mild and unassuming disposition of the Duke, tending, by its example, to restrain the over zeal of an armed and irritated nation, did not contribute much to increase the energy of their proceedings and at no distant period deprived him, for a moment, of a portion of that popularity which his conduct (with but little deviation) entitled him to, down to the last moments of his existence.

A new scene now presented itself to the view of the British Minister, and embarrassed, to an unparalleled degree, every measure of the Irish administration. A regular army, composed of every rank of society, raised, armed, and disciplined in the midst of the metropolis, independent of the Crown, and unconnected with the Government, disdaining all authority of either over their military concerns, and, under the eye of the Viceroy, appointing a commander in chief, and avowing their determination to free their country or perish in its ruins,* the standing army tame spectators of this extraordinary spectacle, and almost participating the flame which they might be called upon to extinguish; the Government, irresolute, and shrinking within the Castle, not only tolerated, but even affected to countenance, this unparalleled procedure. The new commander of the Volunteers was received and recognized by the public authorities, and the regular soldiery at length involuntarily paid him the same military attentions as their own commanders.

But though the Government, from policy, affected to bear the sight with complacency and patience, they reflected, with the deepest solicitude, on the situation of the country, and secretly made every effort to divide or weaken the military associations. Every device was

was immediately summoned, to deliberate on this alarming intelligence, when the arrival of the regular mail dissipated their consternation, by stating the real causes of the rejoicing.

* The following label was affixed to the mouth of the Volunteer cannon—"*A Free Trade or- -*"

used to seduce the soldier from his officers, or to detach the most popular officers from the command of the soldiers. The one was offered commissions and pay from the Crown, the other offices in the public departments. No scheme was left untried—no means were forgotten, to achieve this object ; but it was all in vain—the spirit of the people was then too high, and their patriotism too ardent to admit of such negociation—and every attempt became not only futile, but also gave an additional strength to the measures and declarations of the people.

The appointment of the Duke of Leinster to the command of the Volunteers of the metropolis, was quickly followed by that of other district generals; and the organization of four provincial armies was regularly proceeded on ; the country gentlemen, of the highest consideration and largest fortune, vied with each other in their efforts to promote it ; many leading members of the Irish parliament were individually active in promoting the common object—and from single corps were soon collected county regiments and provincial armies ready to take the field at the command of their officers, and to sacrifice their lives and their properties for the emancipation of their country.

Still, however, something was wanting to complete their organization ; provincial armies had been formed and disciplined, but still these armies were independent of each other—there was no general head, to put the whole in motion—no individual to whom all would own obedience, and such an appointment seemed indispensably essential to secure their co-operation.

But this was a task more serious and more difficult than had yet occurred. Where could be found the man, whose integrity was incorruptible—whose wisdom was profound, whose courage was invincible, yet whose moderation was conspicuous, and whose popularity was extensive? Ireland could not boast a Washington, yet so critical was her situation at that moment, that a combination of all these qualities seemed to be requisite in the person to whom should be entrusted the guidance of eighty thousand patriot soldiers. Such a personage was not to be discovered ; and it was only left to the Volunteers to select the purest character of that day, and leave his guidance to the councils less of the concurring than of the counteracting qualities of the inferior commanders.

XII. Public affairs in Ireland now began to wear a serious and alarming aspect. The Leinster army appointed the Earl of Charlemont its commander in chief, the other armies proceeded rapidly in their organization. Provincial reviews were adopted; and every thing assumed the appearance of systematic movement.

The elevation of Lord Charlemont to that high command, though it formed a more decided military establishment for the Volunteer army, was probably the very means of preserving the connection between the two countries; had the same confidence and command been entrusted to a more ardent or ambitious character, it might have been difficult to calculate on the result of combining an intemperate leader with an impatient army, but the moderation of Lord Charlemont gave a tone and a steadiness to the proceedings of the people, which might otherwise have pointed to a distinct independence. His character had long preceded his elevation; in the North, his influence was unlimited, and though the Southern and Western Volunteers had not as yet consolidated their force with the other provinces, they were in a high state of discipline and preparation, and soon adopted the same principles, which the appointment of the Earl of Charlemont had now diffused through the other parts of the Nation.

From the first moment that James Earl of Charlemont embarked in Irish politics, he proved himself to be one of the most honest and dignified personages that can be traced in the annals of Irish history; the love of his country was interwoven with his existence—their union was complete, their separation impossible; but his talents were rather of the conducting class, and his wisdom of a deliberative nature—his mind was more pure than vigorous—more elegant than powerful—and his capacity seemed better adapted to counsel in peace, than to command in war.

Though he was not devoid of ambition, and was proud of his popularity, his principles were calm, and his moderation predominant;—for some years at the head of a great army in the heart of a powerful people—in the hand of an injured nation—during the most critical epoch that a kingdom ever experienced—he conducted the Irish nation with incredible temperance—and, in the midst of tempests, he flowed on, in an unruffled stream, fertilizing the plain of liberty, and enlarging the channel of independence—but too smooth and too gentle to turn the vast machinery of revolution.

His view of political objects, though always honest was frequently erroneous;—small objects sometimes appeared too important, and great ones too hazardous;—though he would not actually temporize, he could be seduced to hesitate—yet even when his decision was found wandering from the point of its destination, it was invariably discoverable that discretion was the seducer.

Had the unwise pertinacity of England persisted in her errors, and plunged his country into more active contest, his mildness—his constitution—and his love of order—would have unadapted him to the vicissitudes of civil commotion, or the energetic promptitude of military tactics;—but fortunately the adoption of his counsels rendered his sword unnecessary; and by the selection of one man, to combat for the liberties of Ireland, he raised a youthful champion for his country, whose sling soon levelled the giant of usurpation, and he wound a laurel round the bust of the deliverer, which will remain unfaded, till the very name of Ireland shall be obliterated from amongst nations.

His indisposition to the extent of Catholic liberty—nourished by the prejudice of the times—was diminished by the patriotism of the people;—the Catholics of 1780 preferred their country to the claims, as those of 1800 preferred their claims to their country—and amongst that people he gained by his honesty, what he lost by his intolerance, and lived just long enough to experience and to mourn the fallibility of his predictions.

Around this Nobleman the Irish Volunteers flocked as around a fortress;—the standard of liberty was supported by his character—the unity of the Empire was protected by his wisdom; and as if Providence had attached him to the destinies of Ireland, he arose—he flourished—and he sunk with his country.

CHAPTER V.

Spirit of the Irish and humiliation of the English Government—Preparation for hostilities—Lord North's embarrassment—King's conciliatory speech and the consequent proceedings—Duplicity of Ministers—The people alarmed—Volunteer Organization proceeds—Mutiny Bill—Alarming rencontre of the Volunteers and Regular Army—Intolerance of England—Further Grievances of Ireland—Proceedings in the Irish Parliament—O'Neill of Shane's Castle—His character and influence—Address to the Volunteers—Its results.

I. The British Government at length awakened from their slumbers—their dreams of power and security now vanished before the view of their increasing dangers;—a reliance on the omnipotence of English power—at all times chimerical—would now have been presumptuous;—the Irish nation, to whose bravery and whose blood the victories and conquests of Britain had been so eminently indebted, now called imperatively for their own rights, and demanded a full participation of that constitution, in support of which they had daily sacrificed so great a proportion of their treasure and their population.

The Irish soldier and the Irish seaman could never be supposed to remain unfeeling spectators, whilst their own country was struggling for its dearest liberties, or become the mercenary instruments of their own subjugation. Even their indisposition to the British service would have reduced the armies and navy to debility; but their defections would have been fatal to the power of Great Britain, and have enabled Ireland irresistibly to effect her total independence. The balance of Europe was likely to undergo a great change;—the improvident attachment to continental politics—almost exclusively engrossed the attention of England; and the completion of a mercenary league with a petty potentate of a Germanic principality, inferior even to one Irish county was considered of more importance by the British Cabinet, than all the miseries, the dangers, and oppressions of

Ireland. But the British Government now perceived their error, when it was too late to temporize—and that arrogance, which, for centuries, had hardly condescended to hear her groans, was now started into attention.

II. Affairs now approached fast towards a crisis; the freedom of commerce being the subject most familiar and comprehensible to the ideas of the people, was the first object of their solicitude. "A Free Trade" became the watchword of the Volunteers, and the cry of the Nation; —the Dublin Volunteer Artillery appeared on parade, commanded by James Napper Tandy, with labels on the mouths of their cannon, "*Free Trade or speedy Revolution;* placards were pasted up in every part of the city, to the same effect, until the determined proceedings of all ranks and classes of the people, connected with the operation of the non-importation agreements, left no further room for ministerial procrastination.

The British Minister now became alarmed, and trembled for the consequences of his political intolerance; he had no passage to retreat by, and after every struggle which circumstances could admit of, the British Cabinet at length came to a resolution, that "something must be done to tranquilize Ireland." The King was informed of their determination, and was prevailed upon to accede to it. His Majesty had received a severe shock, by the unexpected events of the American contest, and the additional mortification of compulsory concessions to Ireland, was little calculated to tranquilize his feelings; however, absolute necessity required his acquiescence; and it was finally determined, by the executive Power of Great Britain, to adopt means, if not altogether to satisfy, at least to conciliate and to concede considerably to Ireland.

From this determination, the affairs in the British Empire began to wear a new aspect; the day was fast approaching when England, for the first time, must condescend to acknowledge her own errors, and, in the face of Europe, to humble herself before a people, who had, for six centuries, been the slaves of her power rather than the subjects of her affection.

Lord North had now a more difficult task to perform than he at first conceived, to recant his avowed principles, to humble the pride of his own country, and submit to the justice of another, and above all, to justify his own conduct, which had reduced both countries to that state which required those concessions : an awful lesson to all Governments, how cautiously they should arrogate to themselves a dominion, of which the basis was power and the superstructure injustice.

III. But all subterfuge had ended, and on the 24th of November, 1782, his Majesty ascended the throne, to proclaim his first substantial act of grace to the Irish nation, and to call the immediate attention of his British Parliament to the situation of that country,[*] but his Majesty obviously insinuated, that his attention to Ireland was attracted by a consideration for the safety of Great Britain—and that the benefits to be extended to Ireland should be only such as would be for the common interest, not of Ireland abstractedly, but of *all* his dominions— and by that very act of conceding to Ireland, he virtually asserted the supremacy of the British Parliament.

This speech was immediately attended to by the British Parliament ; the opposition received it as a triumph over the Minister, and gladly acceded to a declaration which proclaimed the imbecility and misconduct of the Cabinet. An actual insurrection in Ireland—the certain consequence of further inattention—would have certainly deprived the Minister of his station, and perhaps eventually of his head.

A coincidence of events thus united two hostile inter-

---

[*] That clause of his Majesty's speech, which related to Ireland, ran as follows:

"In the midst of my care and solicitude for the *safety* and welfare of THIS country, I have not been inattentive to the state of my *loyal* and *faithful* kingdom of Ireland. I have (in consequence of your addresses, presented to me in the *last* session) ordered such papers to be collected and laid before you, as may assist your deliberations on this important business; and I recommend it to you to consider what FURTHER benefits and advantages may be *extended* to that kingdom, by such regulations and such *methods*, as may most effectually promote the COMMON strength, wealth, and interests of ALL my dominions."

This was quickly followed up by resolutions—giving the lie direct to King William, and to the assertions of their own ancestors—and by passing bills, distinctly repealing all the acts which their predecessors had declared absolutely *essential* to secure the *prosperity* of England from the *dangerous industry* of the Irish.

ests in one honest object ; and Ireland was destined to receive, through the ambition of one party, and the terror of another, those rights which she had so long in vain solicited from their justice.

This speech was immediately followed by the measures recommended by his Majesty, and the same Parliament which had so repeatedly withheld the just rights of Ireland, now thought they could not too hastily accede to her claims ; and hardly a day was omitted, till the proposed arrangement was proceeded on.*

Messages were sent over to Ireland, to announce the happy tidings to the people, and emissaries were dispersed over every part of the kingdom, to blazon the liberality and justice of Great Britain.

IV. The Minister, however, justly suspecting, that so soon as the paroxysms of Irish gratitude, for this unaccustomed condescension, should subside, and give way to calm reflection, that nation could not avoid perceiving, that until their *constitution* became independent, and the *usurpation of England should be altogether acknowledged*, these favours could have no stability, and might be revoked, at a more favourable opportunity, by the same authority which originally conceded them.

To obviate these feelings, the Minister continued the Committee on Irish affairs open from time to time, now and then passing a resolution in favour of that country, and thus endeavouring to wear out the session, which he, no doubt, intended should terminate his favours.

The whole nation at length perceived the duplicity of proceedings which, while they purported to extend benefits to Ireland, asserted the paramount authority of Great Britain, and converted its acts of *concession* into declaratory statutes of its own *supremacy.*

Reasoning of this nature soon made a deep impression on the public mind, and meetings were held throughout the kingdom, to declare the *national feeling on this important subject ;* fourteen counties at once avowed their determination to tear down these barriers which excluded them from a full participation of the British constitution,

* The British Parliament met the 25th of November, and the first bills of concession received the royal assent the 21st December.

and to establish, at the risk of their lives and fortunes, the independence of the Irish legislature, beyond the power of British re-assumption.*

This spirit and this determination spread themselves universally amongst the people; the cry of "Free Trade" was now accompanied with that of "*Free Parliament,*" and that patriotic enthusiasm which had so effectually asserted the commerce of Ireland, now arose with double vigour to assert its constitution.

V. The Volunteer army, in the mean time, rapidly advanced in discipline and numbers: the success which had attended this first effort of their steadiness acted as a powerful incitement to the continuation of their exertion; they felt, with exultation, that at the very time they were in arms, *without* the authority of the Crown, or *control* of their Sovereign, his Majesty, from his throne, condescended to pass unqualified eulogiums on *the loyalty and fidelity of the people*—expressions, which, if considered with reference to the King, were gracious— but with reference to the Government, which framed them, were clearly intended as an anodyne to lull that spirit which durst not be encountered.

Provincial reviews of the Volunteer armies were now

* As the genius and disposition of a people are often discoverable, not only by trivial but ludicrous circumstances, so their national poetry and music have a very considerable effect in rousing the spirit, and disclosing the character. At this period the press teemed with publications of every quality, in prose and verse, on the subject of fresh grievances. A stanza from one of the popular songs of that day, shows the pointed humour and whimsical lightness which characterize that people even upon the most important subjects.

In alluding to the Irish being deprived of the woollen trade by *England*, and the military associations of Ireland to assert her liberty, the stanza runs thus:

" Was she not a fool,
When she took of our *wool*,
To leave us so much of the
    leather, the *leather?*
It ne'er entered her pate,
That a *sheep's skin, well beat,*
Would draw a whole nation
    TOGETHER, TOGETHER."

These words were adapted to a popular air, and became a favourite march of the Volunteers, and a patriotic song amongst the peasantry throughout the kingdom.

adopted, and a more regular staff appointed to the general officers; new trains of artillery were formed—that of Belfast was brought to considerable perfection. Earl Charlemont was called on to review the Northern army; on his tour he was attended by many persons of the highest distinction, and his suit had all the appearance of military dignity and national importance. His Lordship returned to review the Leinster corps in Dublin. His aid-de-camps were men of the highest character and of the first ability. Barry Yelverton, Hussey Burgh (both of whom were afterwards Chief Barons of the Exchequer,) and Mr. Grattan, were on his staff.

The Volunteer army had acquired the discipline of an efficient force, and at that period amounted to above eighty thousand soldiers, ready for actual service, aided by the zeal, the prayers, and the co-operation, of nearly five millions unarmed inhabitants.

The British Government, which had vainly supposed that enough had been done, if not to satisfy, at least somewhat to disunite the Irish people, now perceived how ill they had calculated on the character of that nation, and felt, with pain and disappointment, the futility of their designs, and the feebleness of their authority.

The dilemma of the Minister was difficult and distressing; any effort to seduce the Volunteers would have roused—any attempt to dupe them would but inflame, and to resist them would have been impossible: distracted, therefore, by every species of embarrassment, he suffered the Irish nation to pursue its course without direct opposition, and trusted to the chance of events for the preservation of the empire.

Grave and most important circumstances now opened to the public view, and imperatively concurred to put the constitutional claims of Ireland directly in issue with the British legislature.

The army in Ireland had been under the regulations of a British statute; and the hereditary revenue of the Crown, with the aid of a perpetual mutiny bill, enabled the British Government to command at all times a standing army in Ireland, without the authority or the control of its Parliament.

This unconstitutional power, hitherto almost unnoticed

in Ireland, now that the principles of liberty had been disseminated amongst the people, and that an independent army of Irishmen had been organized, became a subject of general dissatisfaction. Some patriotic magistrates determined to make a stand upon that point, and to bring the legality of British statutes, as operating in Ireland, into issue, through the medium of their own conduct, in refusing to obey them.

To effect this measure, they determined to resist the authority of the British mutiny act, and by refusing to billet soldiers, under the provisions of that statute, solicited complaints against themselves, for the purpose of trying the question.

This measure would at once have put Ireland and the usurpation of Great Britain in direct issue; but the Irish judges were then dependent upon the Crown; they held their offices during pleasure only; judges might differ with the juries—the people with both—and the result of a trial of such a question, in such a way, was considered by all parties as too precarious, to hazard the experiment.

The career of independence however proceeded with irresistible impetuosity; a general feeling arose that a crisis was fast approaching, when the true principles of the Irish constitution must be decisively determined.

Though the regular forces and the Volunteer army were on the most amicable terms, yet jealousies might eventually be widened into a breach, pregnant with the most disastrous consequences. This was an extremity the Viceroy determined to avoid; and orders were issued to the army, to show every possible mark of respect to the Volunteers; their officers received the usual military salute from the regular soldiers, and at the request of the Volunteers a few troops of cavalry were ordered by the Lord Lieutenant to assist in keeping the Volunteer lines at a review in the Phœnix Park. But an accidental circumstance some time afterwards occurred, which showed the necessity for cultivating that cordiality, on the continuation of which the tranquillity of the nation so entirely depended.

VI. Lieutenant Doyne, of the second regiment of Horse, marching to relieve the guards in Dublin Castle, at the head of the cavalry, came accidentally, on Essex Bridge, directly at right angles with a line of Volunteer infantry commanded by Lord Altamont. An instant embarrassment took place—one party must halt, or the other could not pass: neither would recede—etiquette seemed likely to get the better of prudence—the cavalry advanced—the Volunteers continued their progress, till they were nearly in contact; never did a more critical moment exist in Ireland. Had one drop of blood been shed, through the impetuosity of either officer, even in that silly question of precedence, the Irish Volunteers would have beat to arms, from north to south, in every part of the kingdom, and British connection would certainly been shaken to its very foundation.

As the cavalry advanced, Lord Altamont commanded his corps to continue their march, and incline their bayonets, so as to be ready to defend their line. The cavalry officer, wisely reflecting, that by the pause even of a single moment, every possibility of disagreement would be obviated, halted his men for an instant—the Volunteers passed on—and the affair ended without further difficulty.

This circumstance, however trivial, was quickly circulated, and increased the public clamour. Resolutions were entered into by almost every military corps, and every corporate body, that they would no longer obey any laws, save those enacted by the King, Lords, and Commons of Ireland; and this spirit gradually embraced the whole population, till at length it ended in the celebrated resolutions of Dungannon, which established the short lived independence of that nation.

VII. William Duke of Leinster had long been the favourite and the patron of the Irish people, and never did the physiognomist enjoy a more fortunate elucidation of his science: the softness of philanthropy—the placidity of temper—the openness of sincerity—the sympathy of friendship—and the ease of integrity—stamped corresponding impressions on his artless countenance, and left but little to conjecture as to the composition of his character.

His elevated rank and extensive connections gave him a paramount lead in Irish politics, which his naked talents would not otherwise have justified; though his capacity was respectable, it was not brilliant, and his abilities were not adapted to the highest class of political pre-eminence.* On public subjects, his conduct sometimes wanted energy, and his pursuits perseverance; in some points he was weak, and in some instances erroneous, but in all he was honest: from the day of his maturity to the moment of his dissolution he was the undeviating friend of the Irish nation—he considered its interests and his own indissolubly connected—alive to the oppressions and miseries of the people, his feeling heart participated in their misfortunes, and felt the smart of every lash which the scourge of power inflicted on his country. As a soldier, and as a patriot, he performed his duties; and in his plain and honourable disposition, was found collected a happy specimen of those qualities which best compose the character of an Irish gentleman.

He took an early and active part in promoting the formation and discipline of the Volunteer associations, he raised many corps and commanded the Dublin Army. The ancient celebrity of his family, the vast extent of his possessions, and his affability in private intercourse, co-operated with his own popularity in extending his influence and few persons ever enjoyed a more general and merited influence amongst the Irish people.

The Irish Catholics, at this period, were much attached to the Geraldines, and pursued a conduct so meritorious, that even the bitterest enemies of that body acknowledged the uncommon merit of their conduct: their open friends multiplied, their secret enemies diminished, and they gradually worked themselves into the favour and confidence of their Protestant countrymen, though loaded with severe restrictions, though put out of the pale of the British constitution, and groaning under the most cruel and unjust oppression, they were active and patriotic, they forgot the tyranny under which they groaned, and only felt the chains which fettered and oppressed their country; a general union of all sects seemed to be cementing—the animosity of ages was sinking into oblivion, and

* The political abilities of his Grace were likened, by a gentleman of great public talent, to "a fair fertile field, without either a *weed* or a *wild* flower in it."

it was reserved for the incendiaries of a ater period to revive that barbarous sectarian discord—a weapon, without which the British Government would have ever found Ireland too proud for the influence of power, and too strong for the grasp of annexation.

The doctrine of pure democracy was then but a weak exotic, to which the heat of civil war in America had given the principle of vegetation. In Ireland, it was uncongenial to the minds, and unadapted to the character of the people; and during the whole progress of those events, which preceded the attainment of Irish independence, its progress was only observable in the intimate association of the distant ranks in military bodies, and the idea of revolution never extended further than to attain the undisturbed enjoyment of a free Parliament, and to remove for ever the ascendency of the British Government over the crown of Ireland.

VIII. Notwithstanding all these occurrences, the British people, in their nature jealous and egotistical, still remained obstinately blind to the true state of Ireland enjoying the blessings of independence, under a resident monarch and an unfettered parliament—they felt interested only in their own aggrandizement—their solicitude extended solely to their own concerns—and without reflecting that the same advantages which they so liberally possessed, were denied to Ireland, they attributed the uneasiness of that nation rather to innate principles of disaffection, than the natural result of misery and oppression.

Every element of a free constitution had been torn away by the rough hand of a foreign legislature, enacting laws, to which the representatives of the Irish people were utter strangers. Yet this usurpation had been sanctioned by the dictum of a British judge, who added to his reputation, by giving an unqualified opinion for Irish slavery.*

---

* It is painful to see a British judge and commentor—whose duty it was at least to respect the vital principles of that constitution under which he acted—giving a decisive opinion for "*legislation without representatives*," and, in the case of Ireland, condemning that sentinel, by whose vigilance alone the property, the liberty, and the lives of *Englishmen* are protected.

IX. The salaries of the Judges of Ireland were then barely sufficient to keep them above want, and they held their offices only during the will of the British Minister, who might remove them at his pleasure: all Irish justice, therefore, was at his control. In all questions between the Crown and the people, the purity of the judge was consequently suspected: if he could not be corrupted, he might be cashiered, the dignity of his office was lost in his dependence, and he was reduced to the sad alternative of poverty or dishonour; nor was this grievance lessened by many of the judges being sent over from England, prejudiced against the Irish, and unacquainted with their customs.

The Irish Parliament, at this period, met but once in two years, and in the British Attorney General was vested the superintendence of their proceedings, and the British Privy Council the alteration and rejection of their statutes; and the declination or ruin of her commerce was at least a matter of indifference, if not of triumph, to the British monopolists.

These grievances, in themselves almost intolerable, were greatly aggravated by the abuses which had been creeping into the executive and legislative department of the British Government, and infected every proceeding adopted as to Ireland.

X. However, the British Government found that resistance had now become impossible, and something more must be done. The Irish Viceroy, therefore, was instructed to act according to the best of his judgment. Accordingly, on the 9th of October, 1781, he, for the first time met the Irish Parliament with a speech from the throne; which, though received with great cordiality by the House, upon a close investigation, appears a composition of the most Jesuitical sophistry; it complimented the country on a prosperity which it never enjoyed—expressed a solicitude for its interest, which was never experienced, and promised future favours, which were never intended to be conceded, and was mingled, at the

His zeal to support this arbitrary principle over Ireland, blinded him to its operation as to the rest of the world, disentitled him rather to the character of a constitutional lawyer, and stamped him with that of a miserable statesman.

same time with recommendations the most vague, and observations the most frivolous. The good temper of the House, however, was so excited by the cordial assurances it contained, it was received with general approbation, and Mr. John O'Neill, of Shane's Castle, the first Commoner of Ireland, was very wisely prevailed upon, by the Secretary, to move an address of thanks to his Majesty, for this gracious communication of his minister with a view that the weight and character of this gentleman might excite that unanimity at the present crisis so very desirable, and which must be so highly advantageous to the Irish Government.

Mr. John O'Neill, descended from the most celebrated chiefs of ancient Ireland, bore in his portly and graceful mien indications of a proud and illustrious pedigree; the generous openness of his countenance, the grandeur of his person, and the affability of his address, marked the dignity of his character, and blending with the benevolence of his disposition, formed him one of the first Commoners of the Irish nation, a rank from which he so unfortunately sunk, by humbling his name to the level of purchased peerages, and descending from the highest bench of the Commons to the lowest among the Nobles.

In public and in private life Mr. O'Neill was equally calculated to command respect, and conciliate affection; high minded, open, and well educated, he clothed the sentiments of a patriot in the language of a gentleman; his abilities were moderate, but his understanding was sound—unsuspecting, because he was himself incapable of deception, he too frequently trusted to the judgment of others that conduct which would have been far more respectably regulated by his own; though he did not shrink from the approbation of the court, he preferred the applauses of his country, and formed one of the most perfect models of an aristocratic patriot.

This step, however, was instantly succeeded by a measure, which did honour to the patriotic spirit of Mr. O'Neill, and preserved his character in that station, from which it might have sunk had he concluded his observations, by the fulsome and indecisive address which he had so injudiciously patronized.

As soon as the address to his Majesty had passed, Mr.

O'Neill moved a resolution of thanks to "all the Volunteers of Ireland, for their exertions and continuance." This motion was received with exultation by the opposition and created a new embarrassment to the Minister. To return thanks to an independent army for their exertions and continuance, which acknowledged no military superiority, and called, with arms in their hands, upon their Irish king to restore their civil rights and plundered constitution, was a step, undoubtedly, not warranted by precedent; but prompt decision was necessary, and the then Mr. John Fitzgibbon, in one of the first efforts of that decided but inconsiderate impetuosity which distinguished him throughout life, harshly opposed Mr. O'Neill's motion, but by endeavouring to support Government he deeply embarrassed it; and Mr. Scott the Attorney General, on that occasion showed, in its strongest colours the advantages of well regulated policy. He instantly acceded to what he could not oppose, and gave an appearance of full approbation on the part of the Government, to an address of thanks to those men, whom nothing but that political duplicity which he so amply possessed, could have induced him to consent to.

All opposition to the motion, therefore, fell to the ground. Mr. Fitzgibbon, who, however, never relinquished an object, from a conviction of its impropriety, though he persisted in his opposition, was reluctantly necessitated to give way, and an address to the armed Volunteers of Ireland was unanimously voted, and directed to be circulated throughout all Ireland, and to be communicated by the Sheriffs of the counties to the corps within their bailiwicks.

Never had a measure been adopted, which gave so sudden and singular a change to the aspect of affairs in Ireland. It seemed to reverse all the maxims of former Governments, and gave to the people an ascendency they had never expected. It legalized a military levy, independent of the Sovereign, and obliged the Ministers to applaud the exertions, and court the continuance of an army, whose dispersion was the leading object of all their councils.

This resolution made a considerable progress towards the actual emancipation of the Irish people; it brought down the British Government to the feet of the Volunteers, and raised the Volunteers above the supremacy of Britain, by a direct Parliamentary approbation of self-armed, self-governed, and self-disciplined associations, whose motto* bespoke the fundamental principle of revolution of which England had given the precedent.

It also taught the people the strength of their own arms and the timidity of their opponents, they perceived, by the unanimous adoption of this resolution, that the people had only to march, and as certainly to conquer. It was, in fact, a flag of truce from the minister, and proved to the world, that unable to contend he was preparing to capitulate.

In reflecting on the circumstances which led the Government to this concession, observations on the moral and physical strength of the nation must naturally occur. The Irish nation saturated with patriotic spirit, by a union of its mental and corporeal energies, had united in its narrow focus all the moral and physical powers of which a people are susceptible.

* The motto of the Barristers' corps of Volunteers, which always took the lead of, and, in most instances, gave the precedent to, all the other corps, was—" *Vox Populi suprema Lex est*"—a maxim which, whilst it gives the widest latitude of construction to 'he first principles of the constitution, would open too wide a door to democratic authority, unless guarded against by the system of *delegated representation*.

CHAPTER VI.

Observations as to the strength of a people—German mercenaries—Further subject of discontent in Ireland—Dispute between Ireland and Portugal—Portugal encouraged in her hostility towards Ireland by the British Minister—Perseverance of Portugal—Mr. Fitzgibbon's motion—Sir Lucius O'Brien—Proposes that Ireland in her own right should declare war against Portugal—Sir J. Blaquiere—Effects of Sir Lucius O'Brien's amendment—Distinctness of Ireland proved—Federative compact—Arguments for and against prompt proceedings—Spirited reasoning of the Irish—No Habeas Corpus Act in Ireland—Determination of the Volunteers—Origin and progress of delegated assemblies—The Northern Irish—Dungannon meeting—Mr. Dobbs—Extraordinary mind—His eccentricity—Theories—Colonel Irwin—Account of the Dungannon meeting continued—Dungannon resolutions.

I. WHEN the physical strength only of a nation is employed in the accomplishment of its objects, however great its bodily force, it loses the advantages of its dead weight, by the absence of that animating fire of intellect, which alone gives real vigour to bodily exertion: clumsy powers, mechanical discipline, and compulsory obedience, must ever yield to the force of an opposing body, where both the *moral* and the *physical* powers of the people are *blended* and *inseparable*.

It is only, therefore, by a union of those qualities, that a limited population becomes invincible. The vigour of the body receives inexhaustible subsistence from the energy of the mind, and bids defiance to any power where these qualities are not united.

Thus circumstanced were the Irish people at the moment of this resolution: and perhaps in no former period of modern history has any nation been discovered in so powerful and commanding a position. It was a triumphant moment.

A population above five millions, whose moral and physical powers were so intimately united, that the whole nation seemed one great and active giant, endowed with all the warlike qualities of the human race—one heart—one soul—and one object.

Though prejudice and intolerance had limited the possession of arms to a comparatively very small proportion of the people, yet it was difficult to determine whether the armed or disarmed were most zealous for their country's liberties. The armed and disciplined Volunteers by this time exceeded in numbers the whole regular military force of the British empire, while those, who, in case of action, would pant to supply the ranks of their fallen countrymen, numerically surpassed the whole organized military power of the European continent. This great force also, from the smallness of the island, was collected in a narrow space, its powers were concentrated, its resources were always within its grasp, the sound of the horn could reach from one village to the other, every man was ready to obey its call, and the whole population was prepared to rush to every station where it would be most likely to attain its liberty and independence.

It was impossible for a reflecting mind not to contrast the noble fire and voluntary spirit which at that time raised, and embodied in patriotic bands, an entire people for the sole purpose of supporting, with their lives and property, the purest principles of constitutional freedom —with these troops of foreign principalities, who, at the same moment, were employed, not as fair auxiliaries by treaty on principles, but as mere mercenary automata, collected to suppress the natural liberties of America, and who, had they been successful there, would have attempted their next triumph over the independence of Ireland—vassals, purchased from the avarice of petty German princes, who filled their narrow treasuries by measuring out the blood of their peasantry to the highest bidder and transporting their wretched subjects to put down the eternal rights of civilized society—men, who had no object but their pay, no enthusiasm but for plunder; bought by mercenary treaty from the potentates of the old world to butcher the inhabitants of the new, sold like the oxen of the field for like profit and like slaughter, and, as the combatants of the brute creation, fighting only through a vicious instinct, and seeking no higher glory than to gore their fellow animals.

II. Notwithstanding the avowed disposition of the

British Legislature to concede full commercial liberty to Ireland, intrigues were soon fomented by monopolists, to render abortive, or diminish as much as possible, the advantages of the concessions: and, amongst other circumstances of that nature, one—of the greatest importance, in every point of view, constitutional as well as commercial—occurred, which excited throughout Ireland well founded suspicions as to the sincerity of Great Britain.

By the resolutions of the British Legislature, Ireland had been admitted to export her linen and woollen manufactures to Portugal, agreeable to the provisions of the treaty of Methuen, from which liberty she had been previously and explicitly prohibited by express statutes. The Irish merchant taking advantage of this concession —liberated from these commercial restrictions, and left freely to wing his way to all the amicable ports of Europe—immediately exported a considerable quantity of Irish manufactures to Portugal; but to the surprise of the Irish people, the Portuguese Ministry peremptorily refused to receive Irish manufactures into their ports, and not only absolutely prohibited their importation, but seized on the property of the Irish merchants!

This strong and unaccountable proceeding being adopted by a nation, not only in profound peace with Great Britain, but by a people always dependent upon her for protection, subservient to her views, and obedient to her wishes, and by a court where a British Minister resided, and in ports where British Consuls were resident, it was palpable, that such a step never durst have been adopted by the Court of Portugal without at least the connivance of the British Cabinet. It was incredible that a nation, almost dependent upon the will of England, would presume to insult a federative portion of the British King's dominions, and it became necessary to investigate the grounds of so unwarrantable a proceeding.

No doubt could exist that the active jealousy of the British manufacturers had been roused by the resolutions in favour of Ireland, and that the trade of England might be somewhat affected by these resolutions. The avarice of the British monopolists would naturally take every secret method of counteracting advantages, the possession of which, by Ireland, would certainly operate somewhat as a drawback upon their own; and the British Minister durst not displease the British trade.

The Irish merchants soon felt the effects of their exclusion. Their new spirit of enterprise was damped, the earliest commercial exertions of Ireland were paralyzed, their speculations extinguished, and the whole transaction appeared to be of the most suspicious character.

The Irish, as a nation, now felt themselves not only aggrieved, but sorely insulted. The merchants of Dublin, through their Recorder, Sir Samuel Broadstreet, presented a petition to parliament, expressive of their sufferings. Mr. Eden, the Chief Secretary for Ireland, who generally affected to be well disposed towards that country, had recourse to the usual diplomatic plausibility—arguing on the impolicy of precipitation, and the disinterested feelings of the British—he resisted any immediate resolution on the subject, but moved that this transaction, and the fair and just petition of the first commercial body in Ireland should lie on the table, and wait for the result of negociations, the commencement of which was uncertain, and the termination of which would certainly be protracted.

This proceeding, however, did not satisfy the Irish nation; and, as is generally the case of impolitic, short-sighted evasion, that line of conduct which was intended to quiet the subject, and evade the investigation, served to raise it into greater notice, and excited a latitude of discussion which the Irish Government had never dreamed of, and which ultimately became highly serviceable to the cause of liberty.

Some negociations were certainly carried on by the British Ministers with the Court of Portugal upon the subject, but without that sincerity which could effect their purposes. Portugal could have no just cause to resist the admission of Irish manufactures into her ports; she had no distinct treaties with Ireland, and no foreign treaties hostile to the interests of the British empire; she relied on the good will of England and of Ireland for the reception of her own wines, on which so great a proportion of her commerce depended; yet yielding to the secret machinations of interested English merchants, she depended on the feebleness and incapacity of Ireland to resist her determination, and on the disposition of England to favour her monopolists. Nor was she deceived in her expectation. The deceptive remonstrances of the British Ministry ended in the perseverance of Portugal; and, at the commencement of the ensuing session, Mr. Eden found Ireland in a state of general agitation, and it became absolutely necessary to retreat from his mean system of procrastination—a line of conduct now too palpable, and which the Irish nation would no longer submit to—and feeling it impossible any further to evade the discussion, Mr. Eden, with an address and skill, highly useful on many occasions to a Minister, determined to anticipate a subject which he knew must come forward, and, as a Minister, unexpectedly snatch from the Opposition the merit of the inquiry.

Mr. Eden, on this occasion, with all the symptoms of sincerity, commenced his statement by representing the strong and unavailing efforts of England to bring the Court of Portugal to a due sense of its impropriety; and concluded by declaring, that notwithstanding every effort, the Minister of Portugal had given a final and adverse answer to the rightful claims of Ireland.

This statement, however plausible, could not escape the sagacious penetration of many members; and it appeared clearly, that Mr. Eden had determined, by this means, to rid himself of responsibility, by employing a person of less compunction than himself.

The person who was thus selected for the purpose of again sacrificing the rights of his country, was the same Mr. J. Fitzgibbon, who, in the arrogant and able manner so peculiar to himself, seemed rather to command than move an address to his Majesty, as if it was of his own composition, though in fact it was the production of the Secretary. In this address, he prayed " His Majesty to take into his consideration the subject (already discussed,) and to apply for a redress" (already decidedly negatived) —and the whole address was couched in terms feeble, fulsome, and indecisive, unbecoming the dignity and the importance of any independent nation.

This rapid and insidious measure was warmly opposed by the real friends of Ireland; and Sir Lucius O'Brien, with a spirit and language which spoke his real attachment to the interests of his country, and a perfect knowledge of its commercial rights, moved an amendment to Mr. Fitzgibbon's address—the terms of which form a very remarkable circumstance in Irish history—and by its peremptory and independent language, led directly to the consideration of national rights and constitutional distinctness, which, till that period, had never been so strongly expressed or so decisively put in issue.

III. Sir Lucius O'Brien was descended from one of the most ancient and illustrious of the aboriginal Irish families, a large part of whose fortune he still retained, and by means of a rational understanding, and very extensive and accurate commercial information, he acquired a considerable degree of public reputation; though his language was bad, his address miserable, and his figure and action unmeaning and whimsical, yet, as his matter was good, his reasoning sound, and his conduct spirited and independent, he was attended to with respect; and, in return, always conveyed considerable information.

Sir Lucius was always strong and decisive; he carried with him at least a portion of that weight which justly appertained to his information, his family, and his character.

Mr. Fitzgibbon's motion was most strongly reprobated by Sir Lucius; but aware that he could not completely defeat the measure, he moved an amendment of a grand and novel nature which, if adopted, would have placed Ireland on a pinnacle. This amendment called upon his Majesty, as King of *Ireland* to assert the rights of *that* kingdom, by *hostility with Portugal*, and concluding with these remarkable expressions—" we doubt not that nation has *vigour* and *resources* sufficient to maintain all her rights, and *astonish all her enemies!*"—at once manfully asserting the constitutional independence, and publishing the military power, of his country, and giving to England herself a wholesome hint of her spirit and determination.

The boldness of this motion, its promptitude, its vigour, its consequences, made an instantaneous and visible impression on the whole House; it was at once a declaration of war, a declaration of rights, and a declaration of superiority; it gave a new character to the Irish Parliament, and a new existence to the Irish people. But they were not yet sufficiently prepared to receive the impression with conclusive effect, their chains were not yet loosened, they had not been enlarged from their prison, and however disposed to adopt this spirited and vigorous proceeding, their keepers were yet too numerous and too strong to permit their liberation.

The motion of Mr. Fitzgibbon was, however, opposed by many of the first characters in Ireland; and even some friends of Government, ashamed of its imbecility, refused to support it. Sir John Blaquiere, an habitual supporter of the Minister, holding offices and pensions, and who had been himself a Minister, spiritedly, amongst others, gave it his decided negative. However, after a warm and animated debate, the Secretary succeeded, and Mr. Fitzgibbon added a new thorn to that goad with which he endeavoured to drive, but which he finally found had only the effect of irritating, his country.

IV. Sir Lucius O'Brien's amendment gave the keenest spur to the cause of national independence. The King of *Ireland*, required by an Irish Parliament, and his Irish subjects, to take hostilities on behalf of *Ireland*, against a foreign nation with which England had no quarrel, exhibited a new scene to an enlightened people, and soon excited thoughts and inquiries, which led to the important discussion that soon followed, and at length attained their emancipation.

An inquiry into the nature of the federative compact between England and Ireland was now excited and occupied every thinking mind throughout the latter country; it was a subject which the depressed state of Ireland had heretofore suspended: so desperate had been its situation—so desponding the people—so hopeless its redress—that the nature of that connection had been hardly considered worthy of discussion: and though its abuses had been frequently resisted, its principles had never been defined.

So soon, however, as the people learned that their connection with England was strictly federative, that the King of Ireland might, in right of his *Irish* crown, make war with a foreign Power, without the King of

England (as such) being a principal in the contest, that Ireland was, in fact, an independent nation, connected with England only by the identity of the Monarch, and that the King governed Ireland only in right of his Irish crown, and not as a part of the *realm* of *Great Britain*, the features of the Irish constitution soon became familiar to the people, a distinctness perfectly apparent and unequivocally proved, by the language and the conduct of the British Ministers themselves, who calmly permitted Portugal to insult and injure Ireland, without treating it with insult to, or aggression against the Crown of Great Britain.

This unanswerable reasoning, and these indisputable facts, now engrossed almost the exclusive consideration of all the armed associations. It was manifest that, in every point of view, Ireland had been denied the rights of a free constitution, though, in every point of view, she was entitled to enjoy it; if she was to be considered merely as a partner of the British empire, she was then entitled to the full rights and advantages of the whole British constitution, but if, on the other hand, she was connected with England solely as a federative state, she was then decidedly entitled to enjoy the distinct rights and advantages of a distinct constitution; but, in fact, she enjoyed neither the one nor the other, and that usurpation of Government, though sanctioned by the statutes of the usurping Power, could never bind the constitutional rights and prerogatives of the suffering Nation, longer than until it could mature the power of resistance.

V. The reason and the justice of these considerations penetrated the understanding of the people, in every quarter of the nation. The Volunteers reflected, that the remedy was with themselves—their grievances were heavy—their means ample—their determination decisive —and their redress attainable. If the Parliament would not act, the people would—if the representatives were corrupt, the constituents were honest. Nothing was necessary but a declaration of the rights of the Nation, and of the will of the People—and England, already humbled, disgraced, and dispirited by America, had lost the means and the spirit of opposition—and would concede, however reluctantly, to the just claims of a free and defined constitution to Ireland.

On the other hand, it was suggested, by those whose irresolution, timidity, or corruption, still endeavoured to damp the spirit and curb the impetuosity of the nation, that, circumstanced as England was, it would be ungenerous to take advantage of her feeble moment—to enforce, by threat, those claims which her late conduct evidently showed a disposition to concede without force or reluctance; that it would be more magnanimous to wait till Great Britain had recovered from her panic, and from her dangers—to give her time to breathe—and receive from her friendship and generosity those certain and amicable concessions, which would be more gratifying and more permanent, than those acquired by humbling her pride, and taking advantage of her weakness. But this reasoning, peculiarly adapted to the open and generous character of the Irish people, was, in this instance, too feeble to be attended to, and recourse was had to another line of argument.

It was stated that Ireland had no navy to protect her commerce—no wealth to support a contest—and, after a destructive effort, might ultimately fall into the trammels of England, with lost claims and diminished importance. But this reasoning only added to the spirit of the nation, its pride was roused, its jealousy excited, arguments ill adapted to a people, who had lately acquired a thorough knowledge of its own powers and resources, who were now unanimously leagued against usurpation, and who, after an inactivity of almost a century, had once more been roused to that *pastime* of arms, which had ever been the favourite and predominant passion of the Irish people, from the moment their island had been peopled. They said, that it was neither ungenerous nor dishonourable to catch the favourable moment of rescuing, from an usurping power, those liberties which had been wrested from the weakness of their ancestors, and therefore retained from them through the feebleness of themselves, *that it is never necessary for the plundered to await the awakening of plunderers to take back their property,* that the favourable moment might never recur, and that the laws of God, of Man, and of Nature, prescribe no peculiar moment to assert the liberties of a people, or arrest the oppression of an usurper.

Those grievances which Irishmen so loudly complained of, and those constitutional rights which they so resolutely demanded, were numerous and indispensable to the liberty not only of the nation, but of the individual. Ireland had then no security for either; the Judges dependant on the Crown, the army independent of the Parliament, her Legislature at the feet of the British Attorney General, and the people bound by the laws of Scotch and English delegates, altogether formed the means and basis of a despotism, which the caprice or displeasure of England might at any time put in practice, if she were strong enough.

VI. The precarious state of personal liberty in Ireland, was one of the most glaring grievances, *the want of a Habeas Corpus* statute gave absolute power to any Government which might venture experiments of a despotic nature, and enabled the Minister to suppress, in the very first instance the liberty of the press—the ablest advocate of reform—the most powerful auxiliary of freedom. But it was now too late, the people were united, and their divisions suspended or forgotten; it would have been desperate to have resorted to the hand of power and in vain to attempt any measure but conciliation. England was reduced to the singular and humiliating situation of stooping to the dictates of an inferior country—and beholding her arrogant and arbitrary Ministers treating, with all the courtesy of fawning courtiers, a people armed in defiance of their authority, and conceding to the peremptory demands of the Irish nation, those rights which had been refused, not only by themselves, but by every former Government of Great Britain.

A repeal of the English statute of the 6th of George the First, was the first and most indispensable measure to be effected—and it required no logical deductions to prove to the armed Volunteers, that the attainment even of all their objects would probably, at a future day, become void and nugatory, unless they tore up by the root that standard of usurpation. The effects and operation of this statute became perfectly understood, and formed one of the insufferable of those grievances, which the Volunteers, at every risk, were determined to abolish.*

VII. An explicit and detailed declaration of the people's rights was now demanded in every part of the nation; the press teemed with publications on the subjects best calculated to call patriotism into activity: the doctrines of Swift, of Molyneux, and of Lucas, were re-published in abstract pamphlets, and placed in the hands of every man who could read them; their principles were recognized and disseminated; the Irish mind became enlightened; and a revolution in literature was made auxiliary to a revolution in liberty.

Delegates from all the armed bodies of the people were regularly appointed by their respective corps, and met, for the purpose of giving additional weight and importance to their resolves, by conjointly declaring their sentiments and their determination. These meetings, first confined to districts, soon multiplied, and extended

* Nothing can more clearly speak the *determined* spirit of the Volunteers—than the following Resolutions, entered into about this time by the Volunteer corps of the city of Dublin, published in all the Newspapers, and circulated throughout every part of the kingdom. The same language was generally adopted by the whole nation—and the Lord Lieutenant, immediately after the publication of these Resolutions, permitted the military bands of the regular army to attend a review of the very same corps in the Phœnix Park—to which they marched, playing the Volunteers march, under the windows of the Castle, and in the view of his Excellency.

"At a meeting of the Corps of Dublin Volunteers, on Friday, the 1st of March, 1782, his Grace the Duke of Leinster in the chair:

"Resolved, that the King, Lords, and Commons of *Ireland* only are competent to make laws, *binding* the subjects of *this* realm; and that we will not OBEY, or give operation to ANY laws, save only those enacted by the King, Lords, and Commons of *Ireland*, whose rights and privileges, jointly and severally, we are determined to support with our lives and fortunes."

"At a meeting of the Corps of Independent Dublin Volunteers, on Thursday, March 5th, 1782:

"Resolved, That we do *not* acknowledge the jurisdiction of any Parliament, save only the King, Lords, and Commons of *Ireland*.

"Resolved, That we will, in every capacity, oppose the execution of any statute, imposed upon us by the pretended authority of a British Parliament."

More than 200 resolutions to the same effect (many stronger) were quickly published by corps and regiments of Volunteers throughout Ireland.

themselves to the counties—thence to provinces—and at length to the united nation; their deliberations became regular and public, and their resolutions decisive—and at length the celebrated convention at Dungannon was convoked, which formed a most remarkable incident of Irish history, and one of the wisest and most temperate measures, that ever signalized the good sense, good conduct, and the spirit of a people.

The northern counties of Ireland, though not more spirited, more regular and more intelligent than the other provinces, took the lead in this celebrated meeting. The armed associations of Ulster first appointed delegates, to declare the sentiments of their province, in a general assembly; and, on the 15th day of February, 1782, one of the most solemn and impressive scenes which Ireland had ever witnessed, took place in the inconsiderable town of Dungannon.

There were comparatively but few Roman Catholics in the northern counties of Ireland, and still fewer of the strictly Protestant religion. The population of Ulster were principally Dissenters, a people differing in character from the aboriginal inhabitants, fond of reform, and not hostile to equality, examining the constitution by its theory and seeking a recurrence to original principles, prone to intolerancy, without being absolutely intolerants, and disposed to republicanism, without being absolutely republicans; of Scottish origen, they partook of many of the peculiarities of that hardy people: penetrating, harsh minded, persevering, selfish, frugal, by their industry they acquired individual, and by individual political independence, as brave, though less impetuous than the western and southern Irish, they are more invariably formidable; less slaves to their passions than to their interest, their habits are generally temperate, their address quaint, blunt, and ungracious, their dialect harsh and disagreeable—their persons hardy and vigorous. With these qualities, the Northern Irish convoked delegates from twenty-five thousand soldiers, to proclaim the sentiments of the Irish people.

This celebrated meeting was conducted with a decorum, firmness, and discretion unknown to the popular meetings of other times and of other countries. Steady, silent, and determined, two hundred delegated Volunteers, clothed in the uniform and armed with the arms of their respective regiments, marched, two and two, to the Church of Dungannon, a place selected for the sanctity of its nature, to give the greater solemnity to this memorable proceeding.

The entrance of the Delegates into that sacred place, was succeeded by an awful silence, which pervaded the whole assembly; the glittering arms of two hundred patriots, for the first time selected by their countrymen, to proclaim the wrongs and grievances of the people, was in itself a scene so uncommon and so interesting, that many of those men, who were ready in a moment to shed the last drop of their blood in the cause of their country, as soldiers were softened into tears, while contemplatively they surveyed that assembly, in which they were about to pledge themselves to measures irrevocably committing Ireland with her sister nation—the result of which must determine the future fate of themselves, their children, and their country.

VIII. This memorable assemblage of patriotism and discretion, whose proceedings soon became a theme of eulogium throughout every nation of Europe, was composed of men not of an ordinary description, they were generally persons of much consideration—selected for character and abilities, many of them persons of high rank and large fortune, some of them members of Parliament, and all of them actuated by one heart, filled with one spirit, and determined upon one procedure.

Amongst those who, at this meeting, first distinguished themselves, was Mr. Francis Dobbs, who afterwards became a person of singular reputation, the mere incidents of whose life have nothing to engage diffusely the pen of an historian; no great transitions of rank, no deep depressions, no unexpected elevation, no blaze of genius, no acts of heroism distinguished his moderate and peaceable progress through the world, but the extraordinary bent of his understanding, and the whimsical, though splendid extravagances of his eccentric mind, introduced him into a notice, which the common exercises of his talent would never have effected.

Francis Dobbs was a gentleman of respectable family,

but of moderate fortune, he had been educated for the bar, where he afterwards acquired some reputation as a constitutional lawyer, and much as a zealous advocate, but his intellect was of an extraordinary description; he seemed to possess two distinct minds, the one adapted to the duties of his profession, and the usual offices of society, the other, diverging from its natural centre, led him through wilds and ways, rarely frequented by the human understanding, entangled him in a maze of contemplative deduction from revelation to futurity, and frequently decoyed his judgment beyond the frontiers of reason. His singularities, however, seemed so separate from his sober judgment, that each followed its appropriate occupation without interruption from the other, and left the theologist and the prophet sufficiently distinct from the lawyer and the gentleman.

There were but few virtues he did not, in some degree, partake of, nor were there any vices discernible in his disposition; though obstinate and headstrong, he was gentle and philanthropic, and, with an ardent temper, he was inoffensive as an infant.

By nature a patriot and an enthusiast, by science a lawyer and an historian, on common topics he was not singular, and on subjects of literature was informed and instructive; but there is sometimes a key in the human mind which cannot be touched without sounding those wild chords which never fail to interrupt the harmony of reason, and when expatiating on the subjects of antichrist and the millennium, his whole nature seemed to undergo a change, his countenance brightened up as if by the complacent dignity of a prophetic spirit, his language became earnest, sometimes sublime, always extraordinary and not unfrequently extravagant.

These doctrines, however, he made auxiliaries to his view of politics, and persuaded himself of its application to Ireland and the infallibility of his reasoning. Mankind has an eternal propensity to be seduced by the lure of new sects, and entangled in the trammels of inexplicable mysteries: and problems of theology, in their nature incapable of demonstration, are received with avidity by the greediness of superstition.

Yet on these mysterious subjects Mr. Dobbs seemed

to feel no difficulties, he devoted a great proportion of his time to the development of revelation, and attempted to throw strange and novel lights on divine prophecy. This was the string on which his reason seemed often to vibrate, and his positions all tended to one extraordinary conclusion.

"That Ireland was decreed by heaven to remain for ever an independent state, and was destined to the supernatural honour of receiving the antichrist;" and this he laboured to prove from passages of Revelation.

At the Dungannon meeting Mr. Dobbs first appeared as a delegate from a northern Volunteer corps, he was afterwards appointed a member of the national convention of Ireland for the province of Ulster, and will be found throughout the whole course of Irish events during his life, a distinguished and ardent advocate for the constitutional rights of his country.

The deliberations of the Dungannon meeting were continued for several days without interruption or intermission; its discussions were calm and dignified, its resolutions firm, moderate, and patriotic. Every member of that assembly, on taking his seat in the awful hall, felt the great importance and novelty of his delegation, as the elected representative of united civil and military bodies, blending the distinct functions of the armed soldier and of the deliberative citizen, to protect his country against the still more unconstitutional coalescence of a mercenary army, and an external legislature.

Colonel Irwin, a northern gentleman of the highest respectability, of a discreet, moderate, and judicious, though active, steady, and spirited character, was called to the chair by the unanimous voice of the assembly, and conducted himself in that most important presidency, throughout the whole of the business, with a moderation and decorum, which aid the cause, and never fail to give weight to the claims of a people.

At length, on the 15th of February 1782, this assembly finally framed and agreed upon that celebrated declaration of rights and of grievances, under which the Irish nation had so long been languishing, and announced to the world the substantial causes by which its commerce had been so long restrained, and every trace of a free constitution almost obliterated.

To give the complexion of constitutional legality to the unprecedented organization of this meeting, it was thought judicious to refer pointedly to the first principle of popular freedom universally admitted, established, and acted upon in England by the Revolution, namely, "the people's right of preparatory resistance to unconstitutional oppression." The assembly therefore plainly recognized that principle by its first resolution: "That citizens, by learning the use of arms, abandon none of their civil rights," thereby asserting the otherwise questionable legality of a self-created military body, exercising also the deliberative functions of a civil delegation, and boldly bottoming the assertion of that right upon the very same principle which the Prince of Orange had used to usurp the throne of England, "the popular expulsion of a tyrannical monarch."

This resolution was also wisely adapted to check all legal proceedings, or even ministerial cavil, as to the constitutionality of their meeting, by putting in direct issue with the British Government a previous question of right, which, if contested, must have drawn into public discussion and controversy the principles of the Revolution, and the very tenure of the crown of England: for the English nation had by that revolution exploded the doctrine of passive obedience, and acting on that ground, had armed against their own sovereign, and put the sword of popular resistance into the hand of William, to cut away the allegiance of the Irish people even to his own father.

The Dungannon meeting next proceeded to denounce, by subsequent resolutions, as altogether unconstitutional, illegal, and grievances, all British legislation over Ireland the law of Poyning, the restraint of Irish commerce, a permanent standing army in Ireland, the dependence of the superior judges on the crown, and consequently on the minister; and the assembly finally resolved to seek a redress of all those grievances, and invited the armed bodies of the other provinces of Ireland to unite with them in the glorious cause of constitutional regeneration.

The most weighty grievances and claims of Ireland

were by these means, in the mildest and simplest language without argument or unnecessary observation, consolidated into one plain and intelligible body of resolutions, entered into by delegates from twenty-five thousand Ulster soldiers, and backed by the voice of above a million of inhabitants of that province, combining together the moral and physical strength of one of the strongest quarters of Ireland, all actuated by a fixed and avowed determination to attain redress at every risk of life and fortune, and headed by the highest and most opulent gentlemen of that province, feeling the claims to be equally just and irresistible, and therefore not speculating on success without substantial grounds, or denouncing grievances without solid and just foundation.

" Whereas it has been asserted that Volunteers, as such, cannot with propriety debate or give their opinions on political subjects, or the conduct of parliaments or public men :

" Resolved unanimously, That a citizen, by learning the use of arms, does not abandon *any* of his *civil* rights.

" That a claim of *any* body of men, other than the KING, LORDS, AND COMMONS OF IRELAND, to make laws to bind *this* kingdom, is *unconstitutional, illegal, and a grievance.*

" That the power exercised by the privy council of both kingdoms, under pretence of the law of *Poyning*, is *unconstitutional and a grievance.*

" That the ports of this country are by *right* open to *all* foreign countries, not at war with the King, and that any burthens thereupon, or obstructions thereto, save only by the parliament of IRELAND, are *unconstitutional, illegal, and grievances.*

" That a mutiny bill, not limited in point of duration from session to session, is *unconstitutional and a grievance.*

" That the independence of judges is equally essential to the impartial administration of justice in Ireland, as in England ; and that the refusal or delay of this right to Ireland, makes a distinction where there should be no distinction ; may excite jealousy where perfect union should prevail ; and is in itself *unconstitutional and a grievance.*

"That it is our *decided* and *unalterable* determination to seek a redress of these grievances; and we pledge ourselves to each other, and to our country, as freeholders, fellow-citizens, and men of honour, that we will, at every ensuing election, support those only who have supported us therein, and that we will use every constitutional means to make such our pursuit of redress, *speedy and effectual.*

" That as men, and as Irishmen, as Christians, and as *Protestants,* we rejoice in the relaxation of the penal laws against our Roman Catholic fellow-subjects; and that we conceive the measure to be fraught with the *happiest consequences* to the union and prosperity of the inhabitants of Ireland.

" That four members from each county of the province of Ulster (eleven to be a quorum) be, and hereby are appointed, a committee till next general meeting, to act for the Volunteer corps here represented, and, as occasion shall require, to call general meetings of the province.

" That the said committee do appoint nine of their members to be a committee in Dublin, in order to communicate with such other Volunteer associations in the other provinces, as may think proper to come to similar resolutions; and to deliberate with them on the most constitutional means of carrying them into effect."

The truth and simplicity of these resolutions, whilst they defied every imputation of party faction or of revolutionary disloyalty, yet convinced the minister that the Irish people would be no longer trifled with. By the firmness that was observed respecting them, the wavering were steadied, the too moderate, roused, and the too ardent, moderated, while the adverse were deterred by an anticipation of their success. Adapted to almost every class, and to the disposition of almost every character, their effect through all Ireland was electric, and the consequence fully answered the most sanguine hopes, nay wishes, of their framers.

Having passed these resolutions, the assembly adjourned, committing the further procedure to the coincidence and zeal of the other provinces of the nation; and, with a discretion almost unparalleled, a body of patriots, who might in one week have collected a military force, which all the power of England could not then have coped with, and, at the head of an irresistible army in a triumphant attitude, might have dictated their own terms to a trembling government, by their wise and temperate conduct avoided the horrors of a civil commotion, proved to the world the genuine attachment of Ireland to her sister country, and deliberately represented to Great Britain the grievances, which, by more hostile proceedings, they could by their own power have redressed in a moment

CHAPTER VII.

The Earl of Bristol, Bishop of Derry, declares for Irish Independence—Sketch of his character—Resistance to English Laws unanimously decided on—Declaration of the Irish Volunteers disclaiming all British authority—The Irish Judges dependent on the English Government—Numerical force of the Irish Volunteers—Dissenting Clergymen—Their Leaders—State of the Irish Parliament—Members divided into Classes—The leading members—Mr. Thomas Connolly—Mr. Yelverton—His character.

THIS transaction, which, with reference to all its circumstances, may be ranked as one of the most extraordinary incidents that have marked the page of modern history, brought into notice a most singular personage—Frederick, Earl of Bristol,—an Englishman by birth, a British peer and bishop of Derry, who altogether adopted the views, and avowed himself a partizan for the rights of Ireland. Like many others of his profession, not content with ecclesiastical authority, he became ambitious of political power, and sought by patriotic professions and decisive conduct to place himself at the head of the Irish nation. Possessed of an immense revenue—by rank a temporal peer—by consecration a spiritual one—with powerful patronage, and extensive connections—he united most of the qualities best calculated to promote his objects,—and in particular, had acquired a vast popularity amongst the Irish, by the phenomenon of an English nobleman identifying himself with the Irish nation, and appearing inferior to none in a zealous assertion of their rights against his own countrymen. It was a circumstance too novel and too important to escape their marked observation, and a conduct too generous and magnanimous not to excite the love, and call forth the admiration, of a grateful people.

The bishop, at one time, assumed nearly a royal state. Dressed in purple, he appeared in the streets of Dublin in a coach drawn by six horses, and attended by a troop of light dragoons as a life-guard, which had been raised and was commanded by his nephew—the unfortunate and guilty George Robert Fitzgerald.

He was a man of elegant erudition, extensive learning, and an enlightened and classical, but eccentric mind. Bold, ardent, and versatile, he dazzled the vulgar by ostentatious state, and worked upon the gentry by ease and condescension; he affected public candour, and practised private cabal; without the profound dissimulation of Becket, or the powerful abilities of Wolsey, he was little inferior to either of them in their minor qualities; and altogether formed an accomplished, active and splendid nobleman, a plausible and powerful prelate, and a seemingly disinterested and zealous patriot. He was admirably calculated to lead on an inflamed and injured people; and had there been no counteracting discretion in the country—at a crisis, too, when almost any measure could have been carried by boldness, popularity, and perseverance—it is more than probable his views might have extended to the total separation of the two nations.

II. But though the voice of the people had decided unanimously upon two points, namely, national independence and a redress of grievances; yet many different shades of opinion existed among some of the leading characters, as to the precise time and modes of proceeding to attain those objects. The moderate and cautious party in general followed the indecisive and feeble counsels of Earl Charlemont; whilst the more bold, decisive, and straight-forward conduct of the Bishop of Derry appeared far more congenial to the critical and proud position of the Irish nation, and better adapted to hasten the attainment of their rights, than the slow and almost courtly approaches of the Charlemont system.

The Duke of Leinster also, as well as Mr. Brownlow, and many of those who had occasionally been in the habit of supporting the Irish government, leaned to the moderate and regular course of proceeding recommended by Earl Charlemont, whilst fewer of the leaders, but more of the people, followed the fascinating boldness of the military prelate, who wished to take instant advantage of a crisis, the continuance of which might be uncertain; and the conduct of those two noblemen becoming decidedly dissimilar, if not altogether adverse, it was soon apparent, that one or the other of them must necessarily sink in public estimation.

This contest for pre-eminence, however, was carried on only at a distance, and in no respect impeded the general cause. The partisans of each never came into decisive collision until a contest for the presidency of the general national convention decided that important point in favor of Earl Charlemont, and the rough dissolution of that assembly through the imbecility of his Lordship, soon after put a final conclusion to the power and controversies of both those personages.

However, on one point no difference of opinion existed between them—all the leading characters were unanimous as to giving immediate and full effect to the Dungannon resolutions by calling upon every military association in the kingdom forthwith to declare their public sentiments on all the important subjects discussed by that assembly. An immense number of publications immediately issued from the press, auxiliary to this determination—an increased activity as well as spirit pervaded the whole kingdom—meetings were called in every county, city, town, and village—the municipal as well as military bodies held public meetings—the determination of all coincided with those of Dungannon—no important difference of opinion existed—all appeared unanimous in the common cause—and Poyning's Law, the true parent of all Irish grievances, became the pass-word of liberty. A particular word has frequently had an extraordinary effect in exciting the enthusiasm and rousing the passions of the Irish people "Poyning's Law," therefore, acquired by repetition almost the power of a talisman—it operated on all occasions as a reviving stimulant against the usurpation of England—and became the most obnoxious and reprobated of all their grievances.

III. The statute of George I., declaratory of the legislative supremacy of the British Parliament over Ireland, though a more modern was a still more decisive grievance; as without its abolition the redress of all other grievances would be vain and precarious.

The statutes had originally been enacted upon principles the most unjust, and for objects the most tyrannical the first to reduce the Irish House of Commons to a mere instrument of the privy council of both nations, and consequently of the British Cabinet—the second, to neutralize the Irish legislature altogether, and to establish an appellant jurisdiction to the British lords, whereby every decree and judgment of the Irish superior courts, which could tend to affect or disturb the questionable or bad titles of the British adventurers and absentees to Irish states or Irish property, might be reversed or rendered abortive in Great Britain by a vote of the Scotch and English nobility.* Many British peers and commoners, through whose influence the latter statute had been enacted, had themselves been deeply interested in effecting that measure, to secure their own grants of Irish estates; and some British judges were led to disgrace their judicial character by giving decisive opinions on the justice of a statute unequivocally illegal and unconstitutional. It was therefore unanimously agreed upon by all the armed associations of Ireland, to publish, on their own behalf, and that of the nation in general, a counter-declaration to that of the British judges, renouncing all future obedience to that statute—by one bold and decisive step to throw off the weight of that usurped authority altogether—and, by actual unanimous resistance to its operation, for ever extinguish the most extravagant and illegal assumption of power, which one free country and limited monarchy ever yet attempted to impose upon a people, supposed to wear even the tattered garb of freedom.

The Volunteers reasoned—and reasoned unanswerably—that an attempt to legislate for a nation not represented in the acting legislature, was the very acme of despotic power—the practical ground of tyrannic polity; and, whether exercised by a king, a parliament, or a privy council, was unnatural to the governed—it was still a subjection to foreign jurisdiction, which nothing but the rights of conquest and the superiority of power could justify or perpetuate.

It was upon the same principle, though differently modified, that Pagan princes had established Christian sla-

* This re-enacted by the union.

very—it was upon the same principle, that so large a portion of the eastern world was subjugated to the domination of a few British merchants—and it was the success of that vicious precedent, the 6th of George III., which had encouraged the British Parliament fatally to attempt to legislate for America: but it was a species of usurpation which the renovating principles of the British constitution itself never could extend to a sister nation, and which the immutable laws of nature gave her the right of resisting, the very first opportunity which occurred to render that resistance effectual.

IV. It was now perfectly understood by the Irish people, that the British statute in question, having passed only in England, could have received the royal assent by George I., only as King of Great Britain—in which distinct capacity the Irish nation altogether denied his power or authority over Ireland—because the federative principle, though it placed the two distinct crowns of the two distinct nations for ever in one dynasty, yet acted in the name of two distinct legislations, and if it authorized the legislature of either nation to counter-legislate for the other—it must have reciprocally authorized both—and would equally have enabled the Irish Parliament, and George I., as King of Ireland, to pass a similar statute, declaratory of their legislative supremacy over the kingdom of Great Britain.

The truth of this position admitted of no argument: but even if it did, the physical strength of Ireland was now too much alive to its own power to admit of any prolonged discussion upon so clear a subject: all diplomatic evasions were now useless—the Irish people were right, and they were peremptory—the British Government was wrong, and it was intimidated—the English fleets and armies, crowded with Irishmen, could not be supposed to remain indifferent spectators to such a contest with their own country—the claim of rights was upon a principle so plain and so comprehensive, that soldiers and sailors could not be supposed to be ignorant of what the simplest peasant was capable of understanding.

The Irish judges (though some of them, as before remarked, were very respectable men) were at this time but little to be trusted on subjects respecting which England appeared to be deeply involved, or the Minister much interested—the precarious tenure of their offices almost obliged them to be partisans for British supremacy—and, being totally dependent on the Government for their bread, were prepared to discountenance, and, if possible, by judicial dictums to put down the military associations. It was therefore obviously necessary, that the public declaration of positive resistance to all British statutes and legislation should be *universal,* proceeding from all ranks, and all bodies, civil and military—magistrates and people—that by its generality every attempt to check it by judicial interference, or individual prosecution, might be rendered impracticable and desperate.

V. The armed associations, therefore, assembled in every quarter of the kingdom, and, by corps and regiments, distinctly adopted the resolutions of the Dungannon meeting, and explicitly declared, " that no earthly authority, save the King, Lords, and Commons of Ireland, had power to make laws for their country—and that they would resist, with their lives and fortunes, the execution of all British statutes, affecting to bind the independent kingdom of Ireland.

These resolutions* were unanimously adopted by the

* The author's father and brothers commanded four Volunteer regiments, viz.,—the Cullenagh Rangers, Durrow Light Dragoons, Kilkenny Horse, and Ballyroom Cavalry. The first essay of the *author's* political pen was the following resolutions, adopted by the first of these corps; and proves that an attachment to the constitutional independence of Ireland had been the earliest, as it was the last, of his political predilections.

" At the meeting of the Cullenagh Rangers, 22d of May, 1802, COLONEL BARRINGTON in the chair, the following Resolutions were unanimously agreed to:—

" Resolved—That as citizens armed in defence of the laws and constitution of our country, and disclaiming every political jurisdiction, save the king, lords, and commons of IRELAND, we are determined to resist, with our lives and fortunes, every statute which the usurped authority of the British parliament have heretofore enacted, or may hereafter attempt to impose on a country determined to be FREE.

" Resolved—That we heartily coincide in all the resolutions of the Dungannon meeting, as the surest step towards redressing those grievances, which it was as impolitic in England to adopt, as it would be pusillanimous in Ireland to submit to.

" *Signed,* by order of the Corps,
" GEORGE REILY, Secretary."

Resolutions to the same effect were entered into by almost every regiment of Ireland.

Volunteer corps in every province of Ireland, some in more cool, others in warmer language, but all to same effect—all in terms equally decisive, explicit, and patriotic.

The necessity of adopting the Dungannon resolutions distinctly as to all their points, was manifest; for they were so congenial in their nature, and so closely allied, as to be inseparable. That respecting the independence of Irish judges seemed quite indispensable to the security of individuals, perhaps to the success of any of their other measures. Unless judges were totally independent of the King and his government, their purity never could be confidently relied on, in any case where the crown and the subject might be at issue on questions of English legislature.

To preserve, in legal decisions, as much as possible the appearance of consistency, judges generally consider themselves as bound to follow the precedents of their predecessors; and when imperative justice and their own conviction oblige them to overrule any of those precedents, they do so delicately, upon some actual or supposed shade of distinction between the cases, authorizing an alteration of rule, without a change of principle—which alteration would otherwise prove that wrong *had* been done to either the former or the latter suitor—and the repugnant decisions would appear to form a code of legal incongruity, changing its rules as often as it changed its interpreters, and exhibiting justice as obscure, and decision as inconclusive.

But as to Ireland, the decided opinion of the celebrated British judge, Blackstone, that " she was by right, as well as law, bound by all British statutes specially naming her," would have been a precedent permanently imperative on dependent Irish judges. The total independence of the Irish judges on the crown was therefore indispensable to the Irish people, and was peremptorily demanded by the whole nation.

VI. The Volunteers also perceived, that, though their exertions for national independence might, by their then power and unanimity, be entirely successful, yet England when she recovered her strength, might re-assume her power, punish the champions of Irish liberty, and again plunge Ireland into its former state of dependence and imbecility.*

They, therefore, saw the necessity of a mutiny bill, enacted by their own parliament, and limited in its duration, as in England, only from session to session; by which the Irish parliaments would constitutionally acquire the power of protecting their national independence, as their refusing to re-enact the mutiny bill would at any time operate as a discharge of the whole standing army of the Irish establishment. This, and nothing less than this could effectually preserve the nation from future shackles, should any minister of Great Britain be bold enough again to attempt the subjugation of the country. Accordingly, this resolution of the Dungannon meeting was also unanimously decided on throughout all Ireland, and formed one of those demands from which the Volunteers determined never to recede, and never to lay down their arms until they had unequivocally obtained it.

Reasons equally cogent and conclusive induced the Volunteers to adopt and peremptorily to insist upon each of the other resolutions of the Dungannon meeting whilst the old habits of domination, the pride of national superiority, the prejudices of a mistaken policy, the avarice of a monopolizing commerce, and the principles of an arbitrary ministry, equally operated against such concessions. But England felt that she had neither pretences to justify, nor means nor strength to support, a direct refusal of the claims of Ireland.

VII. When a people are bold enough to throw off oppression, strong enough to resist it, and wise enough to be unanimous, they must succeed. Oppression, though clothed in all the haughtiness of arbitrary power, is ever accompanied by the timidity of guilt. On the contrary

* The Irish Parliament took the most quiet, constitutional, and effectual means of carrying their point, that could possibly be suggested. Their sessions were biennial, and consequently their grants to government were for two years at once; and till more money was required, their legislative was inactive. They now determined on granting supplies to the crown for six months only, as a hint that they would grant no more till their grievances were redressed: this had its effect.

a just resistance to tyranny, however feeble in its commencement, acquires strength in its progress, the stimulants of rising liberty, like the paroxysms of fever, often communicating a supernatural strength to a debilitated body. Ireland had arrived at that crisis, her natural vigour was rapidly surmounting the malignancy of her disorder, and her dormant powers at once burst forth on an astonished empire, and an embarrassed administration.

By this time the national armed force had greatly increased, not only in numbers, but in respectability, and had improved not only in discipline, but in all the military requisites for a regular and active army.

About that period there were nearly ninety thousand soldiers ready, armed, disciplined, and regimented, burning with impatience for the enjoyment of their liberties, not acting on a wild enthusiastic impulse, but guided by reason and depending upon justice.* The conduct of the British parliament had taught them the necessity of national unanimity, the whole population therefore were ready to be embodied if necessity required it, and in one month five hundred thousand active soldiers might have been enrolled for service. They saw clearly that Great Britain, by the consolidation of her strength, had risen to that height of power, which alone protected her from her ambitious neighbours, and that, whilst she kept all her liberty at home for her own consumption, she was able to exercise despotic authority over every other quarter of the world, which she governed. It was

* It is impossible with precision to compute the number of effective Volunteers who had taken up arms in Ireland, because many were enrolled who were incapable of duty. The number on paper therefore exceeded the effective force; nor is it probable that more than eighty thousand effective disciplined troops could at that time have been brought into the field, until the arming became general, and the numbers increased by the admission of Catholics, when, had there been arms in the kingdom for all who were anxious to bear them, above four hundred thousand effective men certainly would have come forward. In the insurrection of 1798, the county of Kildare alone had more than twenty thousand insurgents in arms and the county of Wexford above thirty thousand, and had the other counties furnished in proportion to their population, the amount would have exceeded a million, but this comprised the Catholics, who were in very scanty numbers enrolled as Volunters in 1782.

therefore only by the same unanimity that Ireland could counteract her; and all the capacities and talents which the Irish people possessed seemed to collect their united strength for the cause of their independence.

They had now, by the constant discussions of political subjects in every rank of society, acquired a capacity of acute reasoning on constitutional controversies, their native eloquence breaking forth at every meeting nourished their native ardour, and almost every peasant became a public orator.* "Kings" (said a private volunteer at one of those provincial assemblies in Leinster) "are, we now perceive but human institutions, Parliaments are but human institutions, Ministers are but human institutions, but Liberty is a right Divine, it is the earliest gift from heaven, the charter of our birth-right, which human institutions can never cancel, without tearing down the first and best decree of the Omnipotent Creator."

The pulpit too from which fanaticism was expelled, did not fail to become auxiliary to the general cause. Some dissenting clergymen in the north of Ireland were particularly eloquent; a passage in one of their sermons deserves to be recorded.

"My brethren and brother soldiers, said the pastor, let us, by prayer and by humiliation supplicate heaven to grant our attainment of that liberty, without which life is but a prison, and society a place of bondage. Our tutelary providence has permitted that blessing to be so long withheld from us by the corrupt and the unworthy only as a punishment for our past offences, and a trial for our future fortitude and perseverance. But the time of our expiation seems now to have been completed, a bright flame

* Eloquence was at that period highly estimated and universally cultivated in Ireland. The number of able men who at that period filled the bar and the senate had never been equalled at any former period. The flame of liberty seemed to communicate a glow to the language even of the humblest orator. The bar was not a trade it was a profession, from which servility was excluded. The senate was not a bank; it was a lyceum; eloquence flourished in both; the students of the university had free access to the gallery of the commons; their young minds became enlarged and enlightened by what they daily heard and admired, and were thus trained by their patriotism and their imitative powers to supply the place of declining veterans. The change has been great and lamentable.

has blazed up amongst the people, and, in the hands of justice, lights them to the plains of Virtue and of Victory. The justice of our cause has drawn down that flame from a superior power, and we may well anticipate, that through its fire, the priests of Baal will soon perish before the altars of the Almighty."

Almost every Irish gentleman had now either raised a military corps, or had enlisted himself in that of his neighbour. Some Roman Catholic gentlemen also took to arms, and raised corps composed solely of persons of that persuasion, whilst many Protestants, relinquishing their prejudices, received their Catholic fellow-subjects into their ranks with cordiality, and the whole nation became almost as a single family. The most profound peace and good conduct signalized the lowest peasantry, the most perfect and effectual police was established, hardly a public crime of any kind was committed without instant detection, and every man of every rank seemed to have adopted one prominent and permanent principle, that of uniting good order, patriotism, and firmness.

The love of liberty, however, is often palled by enjoyment: the miseries of former oppression are sometimes forgotten in the views of avarice, or the pursuits of ambition, and there are two many instances in history, of sanguinary contests for the attainment of independence, and voluntary relapses into the fangs of tyranny. Human nature is subject to inconsistencies, and man cannot counteract the errors of his original formation: but when that inconsistency is the voluntary result of depraved or corrupted principles, the weakness becomes a vice, and the object disgusting. Nor can there be a stronger elucidation of this position, or a more painful comparison of times and persons, than that which will occur in the progress of this Narrative, where we shall discover the very same men, who in 1782 were foremost in offering their lives and fortunes to attain the independence of their country, metamorphosed on the Union, eighteen years afterwards, into the veriest slaves of direct and shameless corruption, and publicly selling themselves, their connections, and their country, for money, for office or for title. The individual proofs of this are numerous, indisputable and easily produced; and the comparison will afford a whole some lesson for states and nations to look with more caution and less confidence on the professions of public men, who too frequently remain no longer honest, than till public opinion may safely be encountered by plausible pretences. The shouts of popularity only gratify the momentary vanity of man, whilst successful ambition rewards more substantially his pride, or fills the measure of his avarice. The instances are rare, and therefore more precious, of perfect purity attending public character, without deviation, through the whole course of its career.

VIII. Of those who led the Volunteer associations in Leinster, Lord Charlemont, the Duke of Leinster, Mr. Grattan, and Mr. Henry Flood, had the greatest weight and authority: their popularity was extreme, and it was merited.

To this list may be added the names of many others, particularly Archdall, Stewart, and Brownlow, names that will forever remain engraved on the tablet of Irish gratitude, as belonging to men who remained steady during all the subsequent ordeals through which their unfortunate country was doomed to pass, and formed a striking and melancholy contrast to Altamont and Belvidere, Shannon and Clanricard, Longfield and Nevil, and the crowd of those, whose apostacy, in 1800, has stained the records of Irish history, and tarnished the character of Irish patriotism. A dereliction of public principle can only be accounted for by reflecting, that the accomplished politician and the polished patriot are no less susceptible of the debasing passions of the human mind, than the most humble and illiterate amongst uncultivated society. High rank and influence oftener expose the dormant errors, than multiply the virtues of a public character.

As soon as the Dungannon Volunteers had received the concurrence of the armed associations, the commons house of parliament assumed a new aspect. Its former submission and unqualified adulation to the minister and the lord lieutenant had departed. The old supporters of the government seemed only solicitous how they could diminish their obedience without sacrificing their connection, and every successive debate showed evident symptoms of an approaching and decisive crisis.

The proceedings of the people without doors, now began to have their due weight on their representatives within: the whole house appeared forming into parties, accordingly as they were operated on by different degrees of caution, of timidity, of patriotism, and of interest, the leaders of each party became more conspicuous, and every question, however trivial, confessed the unsteadiness of the government, and betrayed the embarrassment of its supporters.

Fitzgibbon pursued an unvaried course. His haughty and inflexible mind despised the country which he hoped one day to govern. Her release from British domination might also liberate her from his own grasp, and, so long as he could, he uniformly opposed every measure which might tend to her emancipation, save in a few instances, which, by exposing his duplicity, confirmed his character. Perfectly indifferent as to the public, he every day gave fresh proofs of that arbitrary and impetuous talent, which so strongly contributed to bring the nation to its end, and himself to his conclusion and he often embarrassed the government more by the intemperance of his support than their opponents by the steadiness of their opposition.

A variety of causes contributed to add both numbers and weight to the opposition, and gained it the accession of many country gentlemen, whom the excitation of the moment had aroused from their lethargy, and who found it no longer possible indolently to temporize on those ministerial measures, which even their own tenantry in arms had resolved to resist. Several on this principle united with the opposition.

The flame reached even those, who from office or connection were necessitated to adhere to the measures of government, lowering their usual tone of arrogance and of triumph, they condescended to give reasons for their conduct, and appeared almost to court a supposition, that this adherence was compulsatory, and their conviction open; while the number was small of those who, looking to the possibility of a termination favourable to government, and their future interests, still gave them a support, the more acceptable, because now more necessary. But it was too late, negotiation was at an end, the mine was charged, the train laid, the match was burning the summons was peremptory, and either surrender or explosion was inevitable. At this moment the leading characters all started from their ranks: every party had its chief, and every chief turned his eyes, by almost unanimous assent, to the eloquence and energy of the ardent Grattan. The favourite of the parliament, the terror of the minister, the intimate friend of the ablest men, and the indefatigable advocate of his country, he seemed most peculiarly calculated to bring forward some great or decisive measure, which should at once terminate the dangerous paroxysm to which the minds of the whole nation were now worked up, and by its decision inform them, whether they were to receive their rights from the justice, or to enforce them by the humiliation of Great Britain.

The period, however, had not quite arrived for this step. Extensive as the abilities of Mr. Grattan were, they had many competitors: jealousies intrude themselves even into the highest minds; the spirit of rivalship is inseparable from great talents; Mr. Grattan's importance was merely individual, and he was then only advancing to that pre-eminence, which he soon after acquired over all competitors. Though it was approaching fast, it was evident that it had not indisputably arrived: it was essential that all those parties in the house should be a little more approximated, before a measure was announced on which unanimity was of vital importance.

IX. So much talent never had before appeared in the Irish senate as at that particular moment; rank and fortune also were in higher estimation there than in England, where both are more common, and consequently less imposing. Eloquence and talents have always had their appropriate weight in a popular assembly; but several members of the Irish Parliament, in addition to splendid talents, having great fortune and distinguished rank to recommend them, the commons house was not as yet fully prepared to give so splendid a lead to any individual, who, devoid of these, had nothing to recommend him but his talents and his character.

Those who led their respective parties were all men of eminent abilities or of extensive connections. Flood, Grattan, Brownlow, Burgh, Daly, Yelverton, appeared the most respected or efficient leaders of the opposition;

Scott (the attorney general) and Fitzgibbon were the most active and efficient supporters of government; while Daly, Bagenall, Sir Edward Newenham, Mr. Joseph Dean and a number of country gentlemen, all dissimilar in habits, and heterogeneous in principles, were grouped together without any particular leader, but always paid a marked deference to the opinions of Mr. Brownlow, whose good sense, large fortune, and reasonable efficiency, constantly ensured him a merited attention.

A few of these country gentlemen had a sort of exclusive privilege of speaking without interruption, whether they spoke good sense or folly, with reason or without, as suited their whims, or accorded with their capacities. Of this class was Mr. Thomas Connolly, who appeared to have the largest personal connection of any individual in the commons house of parliament. He took a principal lead amongst the country gentlemen, because he spoke more than any of them, though probably his influence would have been greater, if he had remained totally silent. He was a person of very high family, ample fortune, powerful connections, and splendid establishments; friendly, sincere, honourable, and munificent in disposition, but whimsical, wrongheaded, and positive, his ideas of politics were limited and confused; he mistook obstinacy for independence, and singularity for patriotism, and fancied he was a Whig, because he was not professedly a Tory.

Full of aristocracy, he was used by the patriots, when they could catch him, to give weight to their resolutions, and courted by the government, to take advantage of his whimsicality, and embarrass the opposition. He was bad as a statesman, worse as an orator. In parliament he gave his opinions at the close of a debate, without having listened to its progress; and attacked measures with a sort of blunt point, which generally bruised both his friends and his opponents. His qualities were curiously mixed, and his principles as singularly blended; and if he had not been distinguished by birth and fortune, he certainly would have remained all his life in obscurity.

This gentleman had an extensive circle of adherents. On some questions he was led away by their persuasions, on others, they submitted to his prejudices, as a bait to fix him on more important occasions; and sometimes he differed unexpectedly from all of them. He was nearly allied to the Irish minister at the discussion of the union, and he followed his lordship's fortunes, surrendered his country, lost his own importance, died in comparative obscurity, and in his person ended the pedigree of one of the most respectable English families ever resident in Ireland.

X. Many other persons, who distinguished themselves at this period of public trial, will be subjects of observation in the course of this memoir: but scarcely any of them more justly deserve notice than Mr. Yelverton, who was, perhaps, the only public character of those days, whose every act could be with ease accounted for, his motives for the act being as palpable as the act was public; and whether his conduct was right or wrong made no difference in this respect, its causes could be traced with equal facility, and he generally struggled as little against the propensities of his nature as any man that ever existed. In this narrative of the concerns of Ireland his name will frequently occur; and as so extraordinary a character can never be forgotten in the minds of his countrymen, it may properly be anticipated.

Barry Yelverton, of humble origin, afterwards Lord Avonmore, and successor to Hussey Burgh, as chief baron of the exchequer, had acquired great celebrity as an advocate at the Irish bar, and was at this time rapidly winging his way to the highest pinnacle of honourable notoriety and forensic advancement. He had been elected member of parliament for the town of Carrickfergus, and became a zealous partisan for the claims of Ireland.

It would be difficult to do justice to the lofty and overwhelming elocution of this distinguished man, during the early periods of his political exertions. To the profound, logical, and conclusive reasoning of Flood; the brilliant, stimulating, epigrammatic antithesis of Grattan; the sweet-toned, captivating, convincing rhetoric of Burgh; or the wild fascinating imagery and varied pathos of the extraordinary Curran, he was respectively inferior; but in powerful, nervous language, he excelled them all. A vigorous, commanding, undaunted eloquence burst in rolling torrents from his lips, not a word was lost.

Though fiery, yet weighty and distinct, the authoritative rapidity of his language, relieved by the beauty of his luxuriant fancy, subdued the auditor without the power of resistance, and left him in doubt, whether it was to argument or to eloquence that he surrendered his conviction.

His talents were alike adapted to public purposes, as his private qualities to domestic society. In the common transactions of the world he was an infant; in the varieties of right and wrong, of propriety and error, a frail mortal; in the senate and at the bar, a mighty giant: it was on the bench that, unconscious of his errors, and in his home unconscious of his virtues, both were most conspicuous. That deep-seated vice, which with equal power freezes the miser's heart, and inflames the ruffian's passions, was to him a stranger; he was always rich, and always poor; like his great predecessor, frugality fled before the carelessness of his mind, and left him the victim of his liberality, and of course in many instances a monument of ingratitude. His character was entirely transparent, it had no opaque qualities; his passions were open, his prepossessions palpable, his failings obvious, and he took as little pains to conceal his faults as to publish his perfections.

In politics he was more steady to party, than to principle, but evinced no immutable consistency in either: a patriot by nature, yet susceptible of seduction, a partisan by temper, yet capable of instability, the commencement and the conclusion of his political conduct were as distinct as the poles, and as dissimilar as the elements.

Amply qualified for the bench by profound legal and constitutional learning, extensive professional practice, strong logical powers, a classical and wide ranging capacity, equitable propensities, and a philanthropic disposition, he possessed all the positive qualifications for a great judge: but he could not temporize; the total absence of skilful or even necessary caution, and the indulgence of a few feeble counteracting habits, greatly diminished that high reputation, which a cold phlegmatic mien, or a solemn, imposing, vulgar plausibility, confers on miserably inferior judges.

But even with all his faults Lord Avonmore was vastly superior to all his judicial contemporaries. If he was impetuous, it was an impetuosity in which his heart had no concern; he was never unkind that he was not also repentant; and ever thinking that he acted with rectitude, the cause of his greatest errors seemed to be a careless ignorance of his lesser imperfections.

He had a species of intermitting ambition, which either led him too far, or forsook him altogether. His pursuits, of course, were unequal, and his ways irregular. Elevated solely by his own talents, he acquired new habits without altogether divesting himself of the old ones. A scholar, a poet, a statesman, a lawyer, in elevated society he was a brilliant wit, at lower tables, a vulgar humourist; he had appropriate anecdote and conviviality for all, and whether in the one or in the other, he seldom failed to be either entertaining or instructive.

He was a friend, ardent, but indiscriminate even to blindness, an enemy, warm, but forgiving even to folly; he lost his dignity by the injudiciousness of his selections and sunk his consequence in the pliability of his nature; to the first he was a dupe, to the latter an instrument, on the whole he was a more enlightened than efficient statesman, a more able, than unexceptionable judge, and more honest in the theory, than the practice, of his politics. His rising sun was brilliant, his meridian, cloudy, his setting, obscure: crosses at length ruffled his temper— deceptions abated his confidence, time tore down his talents he became depressed and indifferent, and after a long life of chequered incidents and inconsistent conduct, he died, leaving behind him few men who possessed so much talent, so much heart, or so much weakness.

This distinguished man, at the critical period of Ireland's emancipation, burst forth as a meteor in the Irish senate, his career in the commons was not long, but it was busy and important; he had connected himself with the Duke of Portland, and continued that connection uninterrupted till the day of his dissolution. But through the influence of that nobleman, and the absolute necessity of a family provision, on the question of the Union the radiance of his public character was obscured for ever, the laurels of his early achievements fell withered from his brow, and after having with zeal and sincerity laboured to attain independence for his country in 1782, he became one of its sale-masters in 1800, and mingling in a motley crowd, uncongenial to his native character, and beneath his natural superiority, he surrendered the rights, the franchises, and the honours of that peerage, to which, by his great talents and his early virtues, he had been so justly elevated.

Except upon the bench, his person was devoid of dignity and his appearance ordinary and mean, yet there was something in the strong, marked lines of his rough unfinished features, which bespoke a character of no common description; powerful talent was its first trait, fire and philanthropy contended for the next, his countenance, wrought up and varied by the strong impressions of his labouring mind, could be better termed indicatory, than expressive; and in the midst of his greatest errors and most reprehensible moments, it was difficult not to respect and impossible not to regard him.

CHAPTER VIII.

The alarm in England increases—The Earl of Carlisle recalled—The Duke of Portland appointed Lord Lieutenant—Duke of Portland's character—He attempts to procrastinate—Remarks on the policy of an Union at that juncture—Mr. Grattan refuses to delay his proceedings—Especial call of the house—Comparison of the English and Irish Houses of Parliament—Character of Mr. Sexton Perry—Embarrassment of the Patriots—Mr. Hutchinson Secretary of State, unexpectedly declares the assent of Government—Mr. Ponsonby moves an address considered insufficient—Dangerous dilemma of Parliament.

I. As the proceedings of the Volunteers and municipal bodies became every day more serious and decisive, and the Irish House of Commons, on the subserviency of which the British ministers had been so long accustomed to rely, assumed an unusual tone of independence, and evinced strong symptoms of an approaching revolution of sentiment, the British cabinet were alarmed for the consequences of further neglect, and at length reluctantly gave up all hopes of effectually resisting or evading the demands of Ireland, they now only sought how they could best gain time for deliberation, so as to moderate the extent of their concessions, and adopt a mode of conduct the least likely to humiliate the pride, or alarm the jealousies of Great Britain.

But Lord North's administration had been disgraced, and ruined through their proceedings towards America, and were, of course equally unfit to negociate with Ireland, as they must feel the same repugnance, as in the American case, to concede independence. With these ministers, therefore, it was found impracticable to proceed to such a measure, and they were at length necessarily displaced. But though the administration was changed individually, they were still a British government with the appropriate characteristics of the old leaven, and could not so suddenly and radically alter the fundamental system of their predecessors or conceal from the world the true motives which caused the change of sentiment in the English councils: in other words it was altogether impossible effectually to mask the reluctance with which England must at length retract her favourite political doctrines—and the ill grace with which she must strike the flag of usurpation to what she considered an inferior nation.

In this state of things, as the Earl of Carlisle could not act on measures which had been resisted by his colleagues it became absolutely necessary for the safety of the empire, to change the ministers of both nations, and the appointment of the Marquis of Rockingham and Mr. Fox by calling to his majesty's councils as much honesty and talent as could reasonably be expected, gave a new impulse to the machine of Government, and increased the hopes, as it raised the spirits of the Irish people.

The members of the new cabinet were well aware that the situation of Ireland was too critical to be for a moment neglected, the great responsibility which that critical state imposed on their heads, impressed them with a full sense of the difficulties and the dangers they had undertaken to encounter; and whatever their private opinions might have been on the affairs of Ireland, they wisely adopted a full tone of pacific conciliation, and professing the true Whig doctrines of constitutional liberty, they assumed the eccentric character of patriot-ministers, an attribute but little known, and seldom found in any country.

These ministers were certainly disposed to act liberally, though probably to a narrower extent than what they soon found was indispensable to the integrity of the empire; for even Mr. Fox had never proved himself to be a very attached friend to the interests of Ireland, further than he was led by his general principles of toleration and liberty, and so inattentive had he been to the concerns of that nation in the abstract, that a few days after his appointment, he fairly acknowledged himself ignorant* of its true state, and uninformed as to its real circumstances.

---

* Mr. Fox, on the 4th of April 1782, wrote to Lord Charlemont in these words—" With regard to the particular *points* between the *two* countries, I am *really not master* of them *sufficiently to discuss them;* but I can say in *general*, the new ministry have no other wish than to settle them in the way that may be most for the real advantage of *both* countries, whose interests cannot be *distinct.*"

Their first step, however, was politic and laudable; they determined to send over to Ireland a nobleman of high rank whose character was popular, and whose principles were conciliatory—and thereby skilfully give the colouring of generous consideration to measures, which in fact, were substantially requisite, for there was not a British minister, if his real sentiments had been known, whatever his affected language might have been, who did not consider the intended concessions as the necessary result of an imperious necessity; existing circumstances had left them no choice, and the Duke of Portland was properly selected Lord Lieutenant for Ireland, as a fair, honest, moderate whig, too temperate and discreet to irritate faction, and sufficiently plausible to soften down the asperity of parties, by insinuating on every occasion the friendly views of the new cabinet, and the kind condescension of his majesty himself, in acceding to claims, which, in more prosperous days, his ministers had uniformly and haughtily rejected.

II. On the 14th of April, 1782, the Duke of Portland arrived to take upon himself the government of Ireland to the great satisfaction of that nation, and the Earl of Carlisle departed, leaving behind him strong impressions both of individual respect and popular disapprobation. However friendly and honourable the Earl's disposition towards the Irish nation might have been, his administration had effected nothing permanently advantageous, either to the country, to the minister, or to his own reputation. The Portugal business had lost him the confidence of the people, and he left Ireland alive to all her grievances—completely awakened from her slumber, and no longer amenable to that narrow and mistaken policy, by which she had been so long kept down, rather than governed, and in the exercise of which the Earl's administration had been by no means deficient.

The Duke of Portland, on his arrival found the nation in a state in which neither procrastination nor evasion was any longer practicable. The spirit of independence had arisen to its highest pitch, the parliament, no longer the vassals of the British Government or of their own, stood boldly determined to support the people, to reclaim them to their old subjection was impossible, to corrupt them anew was impracticable, and a dissolution would have increased the numbers, and added tenfold strength to the power of the patriots.

The Duke therefore, had but one course to take, to proceed as calmly, deliberately, and slowly, as circumstances would admit of, and endeavour, if possible, to contract the number of concessions which the Irish nation were disposed to insist on. But to effect this object he was incompetent, he was not a man of talent, and though not altogether deficient in that species of ambiguity and equivocation, which are supposed to constitute a necessary part of a modern minister's education, he had not enough of those qualifications to carry difficult objects by dissimulation, or ingenuity to defeat, by negociation, measures which he had not the power of openly resisting. He was accounted a plain, fair, well-meaning and rather highminded man, and had the peculiar advantage of being the first credible messenger of intended justice from the British Government to the Irish people.

The courtesy of the Irish House of Peers to so elevated a nobleman, combined with their courtly habits to all former chief governors, procured him a considerable strength in that assembly, but he found the House of Commons quite beyond his grasp. The yoke on their part, was completely thrown off, nor could all his influence rally around his government a sufficient number of that house to support him in any one measure of delay or equivocation. He, therefore, pursuant to his instructions from the British cabinet, endeavoured, by personal application and interviews with the leading members of parliament and country gentlemen of the greatest influence, to gain a little time for deliberation, but he found the determination of Ireland already so very general, and so far matured, and the Volunteer determination so unalterably decided on—that there appeared to be hardly an alternative, between immediate acquiescence, or inevitable revolution.

Whilst the Duke remained in this painful dilemma, irresolute as to his conduct, the important crisis was rapidly approaching, and the very first day of the meeting of parliament portended extraordinary events, not likely to diminish the extent of his embarrassment.

Exclusive of the distinguished personages already mentioned, many other eminent men were daily emerging from the general body of the commons whose talents and eloquence, catching the flame which surrounded them, soon added to that brilliant light which illuminated the whole nation. But the public eye still kept steadfastly fixed on Mr. Grattan, as the person best qualified to take the lead in asserting the rights and independence of his country. The style and fire of his eloquence, the integrity of his character, his indefatigable perseverance, and intrepid fortitude of spirit which had always great weight with the Irish, procured him a consideration far above his contemporaries, in none of whom were these grand qualities so generally united, whilst a kind heart, and the mild, unassuming, playful manners of a gentleman, secured to him that sort of private esteem, which banishes the feelings of rivalship even from the most zealous partisans. Thus as if by general assent, at the time of the Duke of Portland's assuming the government, was Mr. Grattan considered by all ranks as the chosen champion for the independence of Ireland, distinguished by the most elevated characters, admired by the parliament and idolized by the people.

III. Immediately before the Duke of Portland's arrival, Mr. Grattan had prepared, and determined to move, a general declaration of rights in the House of Commons; and it must have been an object of the utmost importance to the Duke either to prevent that measure altogether, or obtain at least its postponement until he became better acquainted with the disposition of the principal persons of the country, the full extent of their views, and how far he might be able to assuage the general irritation, without going the full length of their extensive requisitions. It was also of importance to the credit of his administration, that, if possible, he should have the substance of whatever he was authorized to accede to, made known by anticipation, as the liberal act of his government, through his English secretary, rather than brought forward, as the demand of the people, through their Irish advocate. Under these circumstances, an adjournment of parliament was a most desirable object, and he determined to attempt it through the negociation of Mr. Fitzpatrick, who was at least as sincere a man as his noble employer, and had always expressed himself strongly in favour of the interest of Ireland.

The Duke also felt the great importance of a little breathing-time after his arrival; and both Mr. Fox and Lord Rockingham exerted themselves to obtain that object from the Irish patriots ; and under the circumstances in which his Grace stood, it might be supposed that it would have been granted without much hesitation; and in common times and cases it certainly would have been but just, and even in the existing one did not seem altogether unreasonable—for, in fact, did not every thing promise a harvest of benefits from the new administration ? The avowed and proved enemies of Ireland had retired from office. In their stead, at the head of the government, was the Marquis of Rockingham—as a man, most excellent—as a statesman, constitutional, honest, liberal; as Secretary of State, Mr. Fox, on the admirable nature of whose public principles eulogium would be surplusage; and for the management of the affairs of Ireland, the Duke of Portland, accompanied by Colonel Fitzpatrick. A more propitious prospectus could hardly be expected; nor could England furnish many men, on whose tolerating dispositions the Irish nation had more reason to repose. But still it could not be forgotten that they were all Englishmen; and though naturally munificent, honourable, and conciliatory, yet necessarily partaking in some degree of those inherent prejudices, which education favours and habits confirm in English minds, unacquainted with the state of their sister country, and, of course, cautious of committing themselves with the one country, by too precipitate and favourable a change of system towards the other. Men the most enlightened on general principles are frequently found feeble on abstract subjects; and Mr. Fox was excusable in his wariness of adopting sudden determinations, repugnant to the theories and practice of all former ministers and former parliaments of Great Britain.

Every proper preliminary therefore was adopted by the new ministry, to prepare their nation for measures towards Ireland which never were, and never could be popular in England; and with a view to anticipate the expected proceedings of the Irish parliament, a message was delivered from the King to the British parliament, on the 18th of April, 1782, stating, "That mistrusts and jealousies had arisen in Ireland, and that it was highly necessary to take the same into immediate consideration, in order to a *final* adjustment." This message from the King, when coupled with the address of the British parliament to his Majesty in reply, expressive of "their entire and cheerful concurrence in his Majesty's views of a *final* adjustment," if they are to be understood in the plain and unequivocal meaning of words, and construction of sentences, clearly import—the conjoint sentiments of both the British King and British Parliament to proceed to a *final* adjustment of all differences between the two countries; and this message and reply are here more particularly alluded to, because they form one of the principal points, afterwards relied upon in the Irish parliament, as decisive against any agitation of the question of a Union. The words *final adjustment*, so unequivocally expressed by his Majesty, were immediately acted upon by the parliaments of both nations; and the adjustment, which took place in consequence of the message, was considered by the contracting parties as decisively conclusive and *final*—as intended to be an indissoluble compact, mutually and *definitely* ratified by the two nations.

The measure of a Union, therefore, being proposed, and afterwards carried against the will of the people—by the power, and through the corruption of the executive authority—after the complete ratification of that contract, and after it had been acted upon for seventeen years, was clearly a direct infringement of that *final* adjustment—a breach of national faith—an infraction of that constitutional federative compact solemnly enacted by the mutual concurrence of the King, Lords, and Commons of Great Britain, and the King, Lords, and Commons of Ireland, in their joint and several legislative capacities.

This message, therefore, forms a predominant circumstance, as applying to the most important subsequent occurrences between the two nations; and as such, should be kept in mind through every event detailed in this memoir. It also leads to some considerations, which, though they may be considered as a digression from the transactions which immediately took place in consequence of the message, are yet of considerable utility in elucidating the respective situation of the two countries, at the time this final adjustment was proposed by the King, and the sense that his Majesty's ministers, eighteen years afterwards, were pleased to give to the word *final*, when they conceived it necessary to argue that it bore, not a positive, but an inconclusive import, and could only be construed as giving an indefinite scope for future negociation.

IV. Previous to the year 1780, the distressed state of Ireland—the law of Poyning—the 6th of George the First—the standing army under a permanent mutiny bill—the dependence of the judges—the absence of the Habeas Corpus act—the restraints on commerce, and the deprivation of a constitution, had often suggested, to some of the best friends of Ireland, the idea of a complete incorporation of that country with Great Britain, as the only remedy for its accumulated and accumulating grievances and oppressions—as the most advantageous measure which could be obtained for Ireland under its then deplorable circumstances; and about the year 1753, and subsequently several pamphlets of considerable merit were published on the subject, detailing the advantages which Ireland must necessarily have derived from so close and beneficial a connection.

As Ireland was then trampled upon, oppressed, and put down without the power of resistance, or any probable chance of ever obtaining justice—there can be no doubt that almost any change must have been beneficial; and, in that point of view, a complete union of the two nations would then have been, in many respects, extremely fortunate for that ruined country. The British parliament had declared itself paramount to that of Ireland. The Irish parliament, tired of ineffectual struggles for even the name of independence, had become indifferent to its fate, and sunk into a state of lassitude and debility, from which, though it was occasionally roused by the sharp stings of oppression, it soon relapsed into its old apathy, partly through despair and partly through corruption, while the people, kept systematically ignorant, and of course having but little public mind, and less public information, were naturally indifferent to the existence of a representative assembly, of which they neither felt the honour nor experienced the utility.

But at that period England was too powerful, too jealous, and too haughty, to equalize her constitution and her commerce, with what she considered as a conquered country. She had then no object to obtain from a captive, who lay groaning at her feet, picking up the crumbs that fell from the rich man's table. The prejudiced, contracted and fallacious views which England then took of the state of Ireland, deceived her as to her own interests, connected with the general strength and prosperity of the whole empire, and every idea of an incorporate union with Ireland was rejected with disdain by the British nation. England had united herself with Scotland to avoid the chance of a total separation, which it was more than probable might otherwise have been the consequence of distinct dynasties: but the state of Ireland and the nature of her federal connection with England occasioned no risk of such an event, and therefore created no such uneasiness or necessity, and the idea seemed to have been totally relinquished by both countries; by the one, because she was too haughty and avaricious to grant, by the other, because she was too poor and too dejected to obtain so advantageous an arrangement.

But when Ireland, by the causes heretofore detailed, had been awakened to a sense of her own strength, and a knowledge of her own resources; when America had shown her the example of perseverance, and the possibility of obtaining justice, every idea of annexation to England vanished like the passing wind; liberty was attainable, prosperity must follow liberty, and, in 1782, there was scarcely an Irishman, who would not have sooner sunk under the ruins of his country, than submit to a measure, which, a few years before, was an object, at least of indifference. England too late perceived its error, a union in 1753 would have effectually ended all claims of an independent constitution, by Ireland, in 1782, and would have been an object of the highest importance to Great Britain: but now it was a word she durst not even articulate, the very sound of it would have been equal to a declaration of hostility, and however indisposed the new ministers of England might have been to admit all the claims of Ireland, the words "final adjustment," so emphatically used by his majesty, left no room to suppose that a union could be in contemplation, or ever afterwards be insisted on : and yet it is singular, that the very same words, " final adjustment," were repeated, by the Irish minister, when a union was proposed to the Irish parliament in 1800 for its consideration.

So many arguments afterwards arose from that expression, so many sophistical constructions were placed on his majesty's message, so much duplicity did his ministers attribute to his language, that it is impossible to believe that all the ministers of that day were unreservedly sincere, as to the finality of the arrangement made with Ireland under its then commanding attitude, and it reminds us of one very remarkable truism of Irish history, that no compact had ever before been entered into between the two countries, that had not been infringed or attempted to be infringed by England, when her power enabled her, or her interest seduced her, to withdraw from her engagements.

V. Nothing can more clearly elucidate the public conduct of the Duke of Portland. In 1782, he came to Ireland to consummate a *final* adjustment between the two nations, and in pursuance of such proposal, a final adjustment was apparently effected, passed by the parliaments of both nations, confirmed by the honour of Great Britain, and sanctified by the faith of Majesty. The Duke of Portland was the accredited agent of that final adjustment, the responsible minister of both nations, the official voucher of its perpetuity, and therefore should have been the guardian of that independence, which was effected through himself, and declared by him, as viceroy, to be final and conclusive.

Yet, in 1800, the same Duke of Portland is found retracing all his former steps, recanting his Irish creed, demolishing that independence of which he was the guardian, falsifying his own words, and equivocating on those of his sovereign to both parliaments, and arguing upon an incongruity, never yet paralleled, namely, that the words "final" and "inclusive" were synonymous in politics: for upon no other principle could his grace's first and latter conduct be explained or justified.

It is impossible therefore to give the Duke the merit of sincerity towards Ireland in 1782. The altered state of Ireland in 1800, was made the solitary but fallacious pretence for dissolving a solemn bond, breaking the ties of national faith, and diminishing the character of royal integrity.

The Duke was obliged to meet the Irish parliament within two days after his arrival; those days were employed in endeavouring to procure an adjournment of the house, and several confidential communications took place between him, Mr. Grattan, and others, who had determined not to admit the delay of a single hour. The Duke's arrival in Ireland had been preceded by letters from the Marquis of Rockingham and Mr. Fox to the Earl of Charlemont, requesting an adjournment of parliament for three weeks, and expressing their conviction that the request would be immediately acceded to. Nothing could more clearly prove their ignorance of the state of Ireland. All the influence of the crown could not have adjourned the commons for a single day. The people were too impatient for any procrastination. By adjournment, the parliament would have lost its character, and the members their influence, anarchy would have been the inevitable result, and instead of a placid, constitutional, parliamentary declaration of rights, a recess would probably have occasioned popular declarations of a more alarming tendency. For every reason therefore an adjournment, though, superficially considered, seemed an object of importance to government, might have ended in measures greatly to their disadvantage.

The reasons for declining all delay were communicated to the Duke of Portland by Mr. Grattan, and the Duke, though not convinced, having no power of resistance, was passive on a proceeding which he could not encounter.

Mr. Grattan also, previously to proposing his measure to parliament, fairly submitted the intended declaration of rights to the Duke; but it was rather too strong and too peremptory for his grace's approbation. He durst not however say he would oppose, and yet could not say he would support it; but he proposed amendments, which would have effectually destroyed the vigor and narrowed the compass of these resolutions, and recommended modifications, which would have neutralized its firmness. Mr. Grattan declined any alteration whatever, and the Duke remained doubtful, whether his friends would accede to or resist it, and it is more than probable he was himself at the same moment equally irresolute as to his own future conduct: he had no time to communicate with England, and his only resource was that of fishing for the support of eminent persons in both houses of parliament, in the hope of being able, in modifying, to moderate by their means the detailed measures which would follow the declaration.

Whilst the chief governor was thus involved in perplexity and doubt, every step was taken by the advocates of independence to secure the decisive triumph of Mr. Grattan's intended declaration. Whoever has individually experienced the sensations of ardent expectation, trembling suspense, burning impatience, and determined resolution, and can suppose all those sensations possessing an entire nation, may form some, but yet an inadequate idea of the feelings of the Irish people on the 16th of April, 1782, which was the day peremptorily fixed by Mr. Grattan for moving that declaration of rights, which was the proximate cause of Ireland's short-lived prosperity, and the remote one of its final overthrow and annexation. So high were the minds of the public wound up on the eve of that momentous day, that the Volunteers flew to their arms without having an enemy to encounter, and, almost breathless with impatience, inquired eagerly after the probability of events, which the close of the same day must certainly determine.

It is difficult for any persons, but those who have witnessed the awful state of expected revolutions and of popular commotion, to describe the interesting moments which preceded the meeting of the Irish parliament; and it is equally impossible to describe the no less interesting conduct of the Irish Volunteers on that trying occasion. Had the parliament rejected Mr. Grattan's motion, no doubt could exist in the minds of those who were witnesses to the temper of the times, that the connection with

England would have been shaken to its very foundation; yet the most perfect order and decorum were observed by the armed associations, who paraded in every quarter of the city. Though their own ardor and impatience were great, they wisely discouraged any manifestation of the same warm feelings amongst the lower orders of the people, and though they were resolved to lose the last drop of their blood to obtain the independence of their country, they acted as preservers of the peace, and by their exertions effectually prevented the slightest interruption of public tranquillity: the awe of their presence restrained every symptom of popular commotion.

VI. Early on the 16th of April, 1782, the great street before the house of parliament was thronged by a multitude of people, of every class, and of every description, though many hours must elapse before the house would meet, or business proceeded on. As it was a circumstance which seldom takes place on the eve of remarkable events, it becomes a proper subject of remark, that though more than many thousands of people, inflamed by the most ardent zeal, were assembled in a public street, without any guide, restraint, or control, save the example of the Volunteers, not the slightest appearance of tumult was observable, on the contrary, such perfect order prevailed, that not even an angry word or offensive expression escaped their lips. Nothing could more completely prove the good disposition of the Dublin populace, than this correctness of demeanour, at a time when they had been taught that the very existence of their trade and manufactures, and consequently the future subsistence of themselves and their families, was to be decided by the conduct of their representatives that very evening; and it was gratifying to see that those who were supposed or even proved to have been their decided enemies, were permitted to pass through this immense assemblage, without receiving the slightest token of incivility, and with the same ease as those who were known to be their determined friends.

The parliament had been summoned to attend this momentous question by an unusual and special call of the house, and by four o'clock a full meeting took place. The body of the House of Commons was crowded with its members, a great proportion of the peerage attended as auditors, and the capacious gallery, which surrounded the interior magnificent dome of the house, contained above four hundred ladies of the highest distinction, who partook of the same national fire which had enlightened their parents, their husbands, and their relatives, and by the sympathetic influence of their presence and zeal communicated an instinctive chivalrous impulse to eloquence and to patriotism.

Those who have only seen the tumultuous rush of imperial parliaments, scuffling in the antiquated chapel of St. Stephen's, crowded by a gallery of note-takers, anxious to catch the public penny by the earliest reports of good speeches made bad, and bad speeches made better, indifferent as to subjects and careless as to misrepresentation, yet the principal medium of communication between the sentiments of the representative and the curiosity of the represented, can form no idea of the interesting appearance of the Irish House of Commons. The cheerful magnificence of its splendid architecture, the number, the decorum and brilliancy of the anxious auditory, the vital question that night to be determined, and the solemn dignity which clothed the proceedings of that awful moment collectively produced impressions, even on disinterested strangers, which perhaps had never been so strongly, or so justly excited by the appearance and proceedings of any house of legislature.

VII. Mr. Sextus Perry* then occupied the speaker's chair, a person in whose integrity the house, the nation, and the government reposed the greatest confidence; a man in whose pure character, spirit, dignity, independence of mind, and honesty of principle, were eminently conspicuous; decisive, constitutional, patriotic, discreet, he was every thing that became his office, and every thing

* Mr. Perry was the son of a gentleman of business in Limerick, and had been called to the Irish bar where he practised with considerable reputation and success. He was not a distinguished orator in parliament, but few men ever sat in that house more personally respected by all parties. He was chosen speaker on Mr. Ponsonby's resignation, and his brother appointed a bishop some time after. Mr. Perry was uncle to the present Earl of Limerick, on whom his estates have descended; and it has been remarked that there seldom appeared two public personages more dissimilar than the uncle and nephew.

that became himself. He had been a barrister in extensive practice at the time of his elevation, and to the moment of his death he never departed from the line of rectitude, which marked every step of his progress through life, whether in a public or private station. Mr. Perry took the chair at four o'clock. The singular wording of the summonses had its complete effect, and procured the attendance of almost every member resident within the kingdom. A calm but deep solicitude was apparent on almost every countenance, when Mr. Grattan entered, accompanied by Mr. Brownlow and several others, the determined and important advocates for the declaration of Irish independence. Mr. Grattan's preceding exertions and anxiety had manifestly injured his health; his tottering frame seemed barely sufficient to sustain his labouring mind, replete with the unprecedented importance and responsibility of the measure he was about to bring forward. He was unacquainted with the reception it would obtain from the connections of the government, he was that day irretrievably to commit his country with Great Britain, and through him Ireland was either to assert her liberty, or start from the connection. His own situation was tremendous, that of the members attached to the administration embarrassing, that of the people anxious to palpitation. For a short time a profound silence ensued, it was expected that Mr. Grattan would immediately rise when the wisdom and discretion of the government gave a turn to the proceedings, which in a moment eased the parliament of its solicitude, Mr. Grattan of the weight that oppressed him, and the people of their anxiety, Mr. Hely Hutchinson (then secretary of state in Ireland) rose. He said, that his Excellency the Lieutenant had ordered him to deliver a message from the King, importing, that "His Majesty, being concerned to find that discontents and jealousies were prevailing amongst his loyal subjects of Ireland, upon matters of great weight and importance, recommended to the house to take the same into their most serious consideration, in order to effect such a *final* adjustment as might give satisfaction to both kingdoms." And Mr. Hutchinson accompanied this message—and his statement of his own views on the subject with a determination to support a declaration of *Irish rights,* and constitutional *independence.*

VIII. Notwithstanding this official communication, the government members were still greatly perplexed how to act. Mr. Grattan's intended declaration of independence was too strong, decisive, and prompt to be relished as the measure of any government, it could neither be wholly resisted, nor generally approved of, by the viceroy. His secretary Colonel Fitzpatrick, was not yet in parliament, all modification whatsoever had been rejected by Mr. Grattan and his friends; and it is generally believed, that the members of government went to parliament that day without any decided plan or system, but determined to regulate their own individual conduct by the circumstances which might occur, and the general disposition indicated by the majority of the house in the course of the proceedings.

IX. Thus, on the 16th of April, 1782, after nearly 700 years of subjugation, oppression, and misery, after centuries of unavailing complaint, and neglected remonstrance did the King of Ireland, through his Irish secretary of state, at length himself propose to redress those grievances through his Irish parliament; an authority which, as King of England, his minister had never before recognised or admitted. In a moment the whole scene was completely changed; those miserable prospects which had so long disgusted, and at length so completely agitated the Irish people, vanished from their view: the phenomena of such a message had an instantaneous and astonishing effect, and pointed out such a line of conduct to every party and to every individual, as left it almost impossible for any but the most mischievous characters, to obstruct the happy unanimity which now became the gratifying result of this prudent and wise proceeding.

Mr. Hutchinson, however, observed in his speech, that he was not officially authorized to say more, than simply to deliver the message; he was therefore silent as to all details, and pledged the government to none, the parliament would act upon the message as to themselves might seem advisable. Another solemn pause now ensued, Mr. Grattan remained silent, when Mr. George Ponsonby rose and, after eulogising the King, the British Minister, and the Irish Government, simply proposed an humble address in reply, "thanking the King for his goodness and condescension, and assuring his majesty that his faithful commoners would immediately proceed upon the great objects he had recommended to their consideration."

X. This uncircumstantial reply, however, fell very short of the expectation of the house, or the intentions of Mr. Grattan. On common occasions it would have answered the usual purposes of incipient investigation; but the subject of Irish grievances required no committee to investigate, no protracted debates for further discussion. The claims of Ireland were already well known to the King and to his ministers; they had been recorded by the Dungannon convention, and now only required a parliamentary adoption in terms too explicit to be misconstrued, and too peremptory to be rejected. It is true, the good intentions of his majesty were announced—the favourable disposition of his cabinet communicated, a redress of discontents and jealousies suggested, but nothing specific was vouched or even alluded to; the present favourable government might be displaced, and the King's conceding intentions changed by a change of ministers, and Ireland thus be again committed with Great Britain under circumstances of diminished strength, and more difficult adjustment, every man perceived the crisis, but no man could foresee the result, some decisive step appeared inevitable, but without great prudence that step might be destructive, popular impetuosity frequently defeats its own objects, the examples of European history in all ages have proved, that rash or premature efforts to shake off oppression, generally confirmed, or rent the chains of despotism from the grasp of one ruler, only to transfer them with stronger rivets to the power of a successor. It is less difficult to throw off the trammels of an usurping government, than to secure the preservation of a new-gained constitution, and in cold and phlegmatic nations where the sublime principles of political freedom were less investigated or less valued than in Ireland at that enlightened epoch, more comprehensive powers might be entrusted to the prudence of the people or delegated to the guardianship of selected chieftains but in an ardent nation, distinguished more for its talents and its enthusiasm, than for its steadiness or its foresight, where every man fostered his heated feelings, and the appetite for liberty was whetted even to voracity by the slavery of ages, hasty or violent proceedings, however they might for a moment appear to promote a rescue of the country from existing evils, would probably plunge it still deeper into unforeseen and more deplorable misfortunes, visionary men and visionary measures are never absent from such political struggles, but if the phrenzy of Eutopian speculations gets wing amongst a people, it becomes the most plausible pretext to oppressive rulers, and the most destructive enemy to the attainment of constitutional liberty; and at this important crisis, had one *rash* step prematurely committed Ireland and Great Britain in hostile struggle, the contest would have ended in the ruin of one country, if not of both.

These considerations had great weight, and excited great embarrassments amongst the leading members in the Irish Parliament, different characters of course took different views of this intricate subject, strength of intellect, courage, cowardice, interest, ignorance, or information, naturally communicated their correspondent impressions, and but few persons seemed entirely to coincide on the specific limits to which these popular proceedings might advance with safety.

CHAPTER IX.

Mr. Grattan moves a declaration of rights and grievances in Parliament—Mr. Brownlow—Mr. George Ponsonby—Mr. Flood—Mr. Fitzgibbon's conduct—His Declaration of Independence—Enthusiastic rejoicings.

I. Mr. Grattan had long declared the absolute necessity of gratifying the people by a legislative declaration of Irish rights and constitutional independence, marking out by an indelible record that sacred Rubicon past which the British government should never more advance, and beyond which the Irish nation should never wander. On that point the fate of Ireland vibrated as on a pivot, it must rise or it must fall, it could no longer remain stationary, and the great landed proprietors strongly felt that they must necessarily participate in its vicissitudes, the court had totally lost its influence, the people had entirely acquired theirs, the old system of Irish government was annihilated, and the British cabinet had neither the wisdom nor the disposition to take a decisive lead in more popular arrangements, the parliament and the people were gradually drawing together, an instinctive sense of the common difficulty called all men towards some common centre, and as that centre, all parties, all sects, and all factions looked to the talents and the honesty of Mr. Grattan, they knew that he had no object but his country, and no party but its supporters, they knew that his energetic mind could neither be restrained by resistance nor neutralized by subterfuge, he possessed all those intellectual qualities best calculated to lead the Irish people to the true standard of freedom.

II. It is an observation not unworthy of remark, that in describing the events of that important evening, the structure of the Irish House of Commons (as before mentioned) at the period of these debates was particularly adapted to convey to the people an impression of dignity and of splendor in their legislative assembly, the interior of the Commons House was a rotunda of great architectural magnificence; an immense gallery, supported by Tuscan pillars, surrounded the inner base of a grand and lofty dome, in that gallery, on every important debate, nearly seven hundred auditors heard the sentiments and learned the characters of their Irish representatives; the gallery was never cleared on a division; the rising generation acquired a love of eloquence and of liberty, the principles of a just and proud ambition, the details of public business, and the rudiments of constitutional legislation.

The front rows of this gallery were generally occupied by females of the highest rank and fashion, whose presence gave an animating and brilliant splendour to the entire scene, and in a nation such as Ireland then was, from which the gallant principles of chivalry had not been altogether banished, contributed not a little to the preservation of that decorum so indispensable to the dignity and weight of deliberative assemblies.

This entire gallery had been crowded at an early hour by personages of the first respectability of both sexes, it would be difficult to describe the interesting appearance of the whole assemblage at this awful moment; after the speech of Mr. Hutchinson, which in fact decided nothing, a low confidential whisper ran through the house, and every member seemed to court the sentiments of his neighbour without venturing to express his own, the anxious spectators, inquisitively leaning forward, awaited with palpitating expectation the development of some measure likely to decide the fate of their country, themselves, and their posterity, no middle course could possibly be adopted, immediate conciliation and tranquillity, or revolt and revolution, was the dilemma which floated on every thinking mind, a solemn pause ensued, at length Mr. Grattan, slowly rising from his seat, commenced the most luminous, brilliant, and effective oration ever delivered in the Irish parliament.

This speech, ranking in the very first class of effective eloquence, rising in its progress, applied equally to the sense, the pride and the spirit of the nation, every succeeding sentence increased the interest which his exordium had excited, trampling upon the arrogant claims and unconstitutional usurpations of the British government, he reasoned on the enlightened principle of a federative compact, and urged irresistibly the necessity, the justice, and the policy of immediately and unequivocally declaring the constitutional independence of the Irish nation, and the supremacy of the Irish parliament, as the only effectual means of preserving the connection between the two nations. His arguments were powerful and conclusive, but they were not original,* it was the very same course of argument which that great Irish statesman, Molyneux, had published near a century before, the same principles on which Swift, the ablest of Irish patriots, had defended his country, and the same which that less able, but not less sincere and honest friend to Ireland, Dr. Lucas, had continually maintained, frequently in opposition to the doctrines of Mr. Grattan's own father. Some passages of this oration were particularly characteristic of Mr. Grattan's energetic manner. "He admired that steady progressive virtue which had at length awakened Ireland to her rights, and roused her to her liberties, he was not yet old, but he remembered her a child, he had watched her growth, from childhood she grew to arms, from arms she grew to liberty; whenever historic annals tell of great revolutions in favour of freedom, they were owing to the quick feelings of an irritated populace excited

* It is a circumstance worthy of observation, that the principal arguments of Mr. Grattan went to establish the same doctrines, and were expressed partly in the very same words, as those of Mr. Molyneux and Dr. Lucas, and that Mr. Grattan's speech was received with universal approbation by parliament, and these principles of Irish independence acceded to by the King's government, and even supported by his law officers, whilst the celebrated book published by Mr. Molyneux, containing the *same* " claims of Ireland," had been voted a *treasonable* libel by the Irish parliament, *when under the influence of the English government*, and was ordered to be burned by the hands of the common hangman, which sentence was accordingly executed before the door of the House of Lords; and that Dr. Lucas, for publishing the same principles at a later period, had been voted *an enemy to his country*, and necessitated to fly from Ireland for his safety.

Nothing can more strongly exemplify the dreadful vassalage into which the Irish nation had sunk, or prove the inestimable value *of national independence*, than the fact that Mr. Grattan gained immortal honour and substantial rewards for the same acts for which his illustrious predecessors had been declared enemies to their country. Such are the resulting distinctions of slavery and of freedom.

by some strong object presented to their senses, such was the daughter of Virginius sacrificed to virtue, such were the meagre and haggard looks of the seven Bishops sacrificed to liberty. But it was not the sudden impulse of irritated feelings which had animated Ireland, she had calmly mused for centuries on her oppressions, and as deliberately rose to rescue the land from her oppressors.

For a people to acquire liberty they must have a lofty conception of themselves, what sets one nation above another, but the soul that dwells within her? deprive it of its soul, it may still retain a strong arm, but from that moment ceases to be a nation, of what avail the exertions of Lords and Commons if unsupported by the soul and the exertions of the people? the Dungannon meeting had spoken this language with the calm and steady voice of an injured country, that meeting had been considered as an alarming measure, because it was unprecedented but it was an original transaction, and all original transactions must be unprecedented; the attainment of Magna Charta had no precedent, it was a great original transaction, not obtained by votes in parliament, but by Barons in the field, to that great original transaction England owes her liberty, and to the great original transaction at Dungannon, Ireland will be indebted for hers, the Irish Volunteers had associated to support the laws and the constitution, the usurpations of England have violated both, and Ireland has therefore armed to defend the principles of the British constitution against the violations of the British government. Let other nations basely suppose that people were made for governments, Ireland has declared that governments were made for the people, and even crowns, those great luminaries whose brightness they all reflect, can receive their cheering fire only from the pure flame of a free constitution. England has the plea of necessity for acknowledging the independence of America, for admitting Irish *independence* she has the plea of justice ; America has shed much English blood, and America is to be free: Ireland has shed her own blood for England, and is Ireland to remain in fetters? is Ireland to be the only nation whose liberty England will not acknowledge, and whose affections she cannot subdue? we have received the civic crown from our people, and shall we like **slaves** lay it down at the feet of British supremacy ?"

Proceeding in the same glow of language and of reasoning, and amidst an universal cry of approbation, Mr. Grattan went fully into a detail of Irish rights and grievances, and concluded his statement by moving, as an amendment to Mr. Ponsonby's motion—" That an humble address be presented to his Majesty, to return his Majesty the thanks of this house for his most gracious message to this house, delivered by his Grace the Lord Lieutenant.

" To assure his Majesty of our unshaken attachment to his Majesty's person and government, and of our lively sense of his paternal care in thus taking the lead to administer content to his Majesty's subjects of Ireland.

" That thus encouraged by his royal interposition, we shall beg leave, with all duty and submission, to lay before his Majesty the cause of all our discontents and jealousies; to assure his Majesty that his subjects of Ireland are a free people, that the crown of Ireland is an *imperial crown*, inseparably connected with the crown of Great Britain, on which connection the interests and happiness of both nations essentially depend—but that the kingdom of Ireland is a *distinct kingdom*, with a parliament of her *own* the sole legislature thereof—that there is no body of men competent to make laws to bind the nation but the King, Lords, and Commons of Ireland—nor any parliament which hath any authority or power of any sort whatever in this country, save only the parliament of Ireland —to assure his Majesty, that we humbly conceive that in this right the very *essence of our liberty exists*—a right which we, on the part of all the people of Ireland, do claim as their birthright, AND WHICH WE CANNOT YIELD BUT WITH OUR LIVES."

The effect of this speech, and the concluding amendment, was instantaneous and decisive. A legislative declaration of independence at once placed the rights and determinations of Ireland on a footing too high to be relinquished without an exterminating contest; the circumstances of both nations were imperative; Ireland was committed and must persist, and Great Britain had lavished in America her powers of resistance. That haughty government, which in all the arrogance of superior force had for so many centuries lorded over the natural rights and scoffed at the groans of her sister country, at length reached the highest climax of oppression and intolerance, and was necessitated to acknowledge the wrongs and the virtues of that people, and peaceably capitulate to a nation which, by honest means, it might at any time have conciliated. The whole house in a moment caught the patriotic flame, which seemed to issue from every bench of the entire assembly.*

III. Mr. Grattan had selected, to second and support his declaration, a person who gave it as much influence as character and independence could possibly communicate. Well aware of the great importance which was attributed to the accession of the landed interest in parliamentary measures, he judiciously selected Mr. Brownlow, member for the county of Armagh, as one of the first of the country gentlemen in point of wealth and reputation.

No man could be better adapted to obtain the concurrence of the landed interest than Mr. Brownlow. His own stake in the country was too great to be risked on giddy speculations; his interests were entirely identified with those of the country; and having no courtly connections to detract from his independence, or aristocratic taints to trifle with his purity, every thing he said, and every measure he supported, carried a certain portion of influence amongst the country gentlemen, and they often followed his example solely because they could not suspect its honesty.

The great body of the landed proprietors in parliament, though intrinsically honest, were simple, prejudiced, refractory, and gregarious; the Government, on ordinary occasions, found it not difficult to delude or disunite them: and even on this day, without such a leader as Mr. Brownlow, the entire unanimity of their opinion on their conduct could by no means be depended on.

* The author of this work, then a student in the University of Dublin, was present at this important scene as a spectator, and the impression it made on his youthful mind, years have not been able in any degree to efface; and he is therefore enabled to delineate the circumstances attending that important event with more than ordinary accuracy. In truth, time has not left many contemporaries to tell the story.

After Mr. Grattan had concluded, Mr. Brownlow instantly rose—a general symptom of approbation ran through the house at perceiving so weighty an auxiliary to so decisive a declaration—his example gave countenance to many, and confidence to all—his speech was short, but it was decided, and expressed in such terms as at once determined the country gentlemen to adopt the measure in its fullest extent without further delay, and to pledge their lives and fortunes to the support and establishment of Irish independence; he said, "as he had the honour to second the mover in adversity, he could not avoid maintaining the same honour at a moment of triumph. He had long seen that things must come to this; the people had learned their rights, and they *would* have them—an end has been proclaimed to temporizing expedients—to artful delay, and to political junctions—the people have demanded their rights, and the Irish parliament will support them with their lives and fortunes. He would leave the other side of the house to discuss the subject, and if they were anxious to atone for their past conduct, he would not check the ardour of their patriotism, which, after being so long restrained, seemed ready to burst forth, and he should rejoice in the explosion. As to the declaration of rights, the honourable gentleman would have the eternal gratification of having reared this infant child—his (Mr. Brownlow's) only merit would be, that, though he could not maintain it with ability, his utmost zeal should be exerted to support it."

On the conclusion of Mr. Brownlow's speech, another short pause ensued; but it was not a pause of doubt—the measure was obviously decided—the victory was complete—nothing remained in suspense but through whom, and by what species of declaration the Government could submit to so strong a measure; some of the officers of the crown had been the servants of the last administration, and the short period from the arrival of the Duke of Portland had given no time to his cabinet for consideration or concert—the dynasty of diplomatic evasion had ceased to reign—and for the first time in the annals of British history, the officers and ministers of government appeared to be let loose upon the parliament, to recant their principles and capitulate for their characters. The first they performed, the latter they failed in. Men may pity the feelings of a vanquished enemy, but they can never securely trust to his compulsory repentance, and they who had expended every day of their political life in upholding the principle of British supremacy, could hardly expect to receive more confidence from the nation than that which belongs to the character of defeated apostates.

IV. Mr. George Ponsonby, on the part of the Lord Lieutenant, submitted with as good a grace as the circumstance would admit of, to a proceeding which it was impossible could be pleasing to any English ministry. Mr. Ponsonby had been generally in opposition since the time of his father's disagreement with Lord Townsend, and his family being entirely attached to the Whig interests of England, the change of ministry naturally brought to the Marquis of Rockingham's administration and aid, the persons who had been so long in opposition to his predecessor. Mr. Ponsonby's family, of course, connected itself in Ireland with the Duke of Portland, and it was expected that he would have been placed high in confidence under his Grace's administration.

Blending an aristocratic mind with patriotic feelings, and connected with a Viceroy who could himself hardly guess the road he might have to travel, Mr. Ponsonby could not at such a moment be expected to play the full game of popular expectation. Extensive and high family connections, whatever party they espouse in public transactions, ever communicate some tints of their own colouring, and impose some portion of voluntary restraint upon the free agency of public characters—and had Mr. Ponsonby been an isolated man, he would have been a more distinguished personage. A nation may sometimes look with confidence to individuals, but they are a credulous people who look with confidence to party. Individuals may be honest—but gregarious integrity would be a phenomenon in politics. It is the collisions of party, not their visionary virtue, that is advantageous to a people who frequently acquire their rights not through the political purity, but through the rancorous recrimination of ambitious factions.

On this occasion, however, Mr. Ponsonby's steady, judicious, and plausible address, exactly corresponded with the exigencies of the Viceroy, and gave a tinge of generous concession to his Grace's accedence, which the volatile gratitude of the Irish nation, for a moment mistook for genuine sincerity. Mr. Ponsonby sought to be considered at the same moment as faithful to his country and faithful to its government—a union which the bad policy of England had taught the Irish people to consider as incompatible. His manner and his speech, however, had the effect intended. His fair and discreet reputation gave great weight to so gratifying a declaration; and no impression could be more favourable to the Duke of Portland than that which he derived from the short conciliating observations of Mr. Ponsonby. He stated, "that he most willingly consented to the proposed amendment, and would answer that the noble Lord who presided in the government of Ireland, wished to do every thing in his power for the satisfaction of the nation, and he knew that the noble Duke would not lose one moment in forwarding this remonstrance of parliament to the Throne, and he would use his utmost influence in obtaining the *rights* of Ireland, an object on which he had FIXED HIS HEART."*

This declaration was received with the loudest cheers by a great majority of the House; but there existed men whose wise scepticism still retained their doubts of his Excellency's unsophisticated sincerity. They reflected justly, that the *irresistible* position of Ireland alone had at length induced the British government to this magnanimous declaration—past events had indisputably decided, that whether cabinets of Whigs or cabinets of Tories had ruled the British councils, the system of its government had remained invariably adverse to the rights of Ireland; high British supremacy had been the principle and the practice of all its administrations and of

* Mr. Ponsonby soon after this period acquired the highest legal estimation, and in public affairs connected himself with Mr. Grattan, which connection has continued without interruption.

Mr. Ponsonby was one of the leading and distinguished opponents of Lord Castlereagh, on the question of the Irish Union, and always carried a great and just weight in the Irish Parliament.

all its princes; and amidst all the changes and revolutions of England, Ireland had never yet experienced one friendly ministry.

V. On this subject Mr. Flood (one of the ablest men that Ireland ever produced) was this night silent. He saw further, and thought deeper than any of his contemporaries—he knew the world, and of course was sceptical. As a popular orator, he was inferior to Mr. Grattan, but as a deliberate senator he was vastly his superior. He knew that all precedent of British cabinets gave just reason to attribute this sudden transition of English policy, not to the feelings of her liberality, but to the extent of her embarrassments; and that the Duke of Portland's having "*set his heart*" upon obtaining the rights of Ireland, was only giving the gloss of voluntary merit to a concession which was in fact a matter of absolute necessity, and without which his Grace foresaw that all British authority in Ireland, would be extinguished for ever. Mr. Flood's confidence, therefore, never was implicit. Mr. Grattan, on the contrary, was deceived by his own zeal, and duped by his own honesty; and his friend, Lord Charlemont, was too *courtly* a nobleman to suspect his Grace of such consummate insincerity.[*] But

---

[*] The following Resolutions passed immediately before the meeting of parliament, and being followed by the same, or still stronger, from every armed association in Ireland (at that period nearly one hundred thousand disciplined men) taught the Duke of Portland the total impracticability of postponing the claims of Ireland one hour.

The first of these Resolutions were those of the *Irish Bar*—a body at *that time* of the greatest weight in point of *talent, respectability,* and *patriotism*—it gave the tone to the Resolutions of the whole Irish nation.

Those Resolutions were unanimously adopted, some in stronger terms, by all the armed associations.

LAWYER'S CORPS.

At a full meeting of the Lawyer's Corps, the 28th February, 1782, *pursuant to notice,*

Colonel EDWARD WESTBY in the Chair:

Resolved, That the Members of the House of Commons are the representatives of, and derive their power *solely* from, the people; and that a denial of this position by them would be to *abdicate the representation.*

Resolved unanimously, That the people of this country are now *called upon* to declare that the King, Lords, and Commons of *Ireland* are the only power competent to make laws to bind this kingdom.

Resolved unanimously, That we do *expect such declaration* of right

Mr. Flood even at that moment did not stand alone in this ungracious incredulity; and ensuing events have fully confirmed the wisdom of his scepticism.*

from our representatives, and that we will support them with OUR LIVES AND FORTUNES in WATHEVER measures may be necessary to render such declaration an *effectual security.*
Resolved, that the above resolutions oe printed.
Signed by order,
SAMUEL ADAMS, Secretary.

At a Meeting of the Corps of Dublin Volunteers, Friday, 1st *March,* 1782,
His Grace, the Duke of LEINSTER in the chair:
Resolved, That the King, Lords, and Commons of Ireland only are competent to make laws to bind the subjects of this realm, and that we will not *obey* or give operation to *any* laws, save only those enacted by the King, Lords, and Commons of *Ireland,* whose *rights* and *privileges,* jointly and severally, we are determined to support with our *lives and fortunes.*
Signed by order,
JOHN WILLIAMS, Secretary.

* The *doubts* of Mr. Flood, and *the intentions* of the Irish Volunteers, seem to be fully exemplified in the following resolutions, passed THE VERY DAY AFTER this celebrated declaration of rights had passed in parliament.
At a meeting of the delegates from *one hundred and thirty-nine* Corps of the Volunteers of the Province of Leinster, at Dublin, 17th April, 1782,
Colonel HENRY FLOOD in the Chair:
Resolved unanimously, That we feel ourselves *called upon* to declare our satisfaction in the unanimous sense of the *House of Commons* expressed in favour of the rights of Ireland, in their address to the King yesterday, as amended by Colonel Grattan, and that we will support them therein with *our lives and fortunes.*
Resolved unanimously, That the thanks of this meeting be given to Colonel Grattan, for his extraordinary exertions and perseverance in asserting the rights of Ireland.
Resolved unanimously, That the following thirteen Commanders of Corps be appointed a Standing Committee of Delegates from this Province, to correspond and *commune* with all the other provincial Committees or Delegates of Ireland, to wit:

Earl of GRANARD,
Earl of ALDBOROUGH,
Sir W. PARSONS,
Colonel GRATTAN,
Colonel TALBOT,
Lieut.-Colonel LEE,
Colonel FLOOD,

Colonel PARNELL,
Captain R. NEVILLE,
CAPTAIN GORGE,
COLONEL BURTON,
Colonel M. LYONS,
Captain SMYTH.

This speech of Mr. Ponsonby's is the more remarkable, because it was reserved for the same Mr. Ponsonby, seventeen years afterwards, to expose, in the clearest and most able language, this very duplicity of the same Duke of Portland; and the open avowal of his Grace in seventeen hundred and ninety-nine, that he had "*never*" considered that this concession of England, in 1782, should be a "*final*" adjustment between the two nations, leaves no room to doubt his Grace's mental reservation, and the existence of a diplomatic sophistry which the Irish Parliament, gulled by their own credulity, and enveloped in a cloud of gratitude and exultation, were at that moment prevented from suspecting.

VI. Mr. Hussey Burgh, and some other members, shortly but zealously supported this declaration of Irish independence—all was unanimity—not a symptom of opposition was manifested : but on the close of the proceeding, a circumstance not less remarkable than disgusting unexpectedly occurred.

Mr. John Fitzgibbon, whose indigenous hostility to the liberties of his country had never omitted any opportunity of opposing its emancipation, on a sudden became metamorphosed—assumed a strange and novel character, and professed himself not only the warmest advocate of Irish freedom, but a deadly and inveterate foe to that very system of British usurpation, the practice of which, till that moment, he had himself been an undeviating and virulent supporter.

Mr. Fitzgibbon's embarrassment in making this declaration was too strong and too new in him to remain unnoticed—the unanimity of the House had left him no room for cavil—his former conduct had left him no room for consistency—his haughty disposition despised neutrality, and his overbearing mind revolted from submission ; his stubborn heart, though humiliated, was unsubdued. But he saw that he was unsupported by his friends, and felt that he was powerless against his enemies. To such a mind the conflict was most dreadful—a sovereign contempt of public opinion was his only

Resolved unanimously, That an officer's guard from each corps of Volunteers in the city and county of Dublin, be mounted at Lord Charlemont's house, in rotation, at ten o'clock every morning.

solace, and never did he more fully require the aid of that consolation.

This most remarkable, false, and inconsistent of all political recantations ever pronounced by a confirmed courtier, was delivered in the tone of a confirmed patriot. "No man," said Mr. Fitzgibbon, with an affected emphasis, "can say that the Duke of Portland has *power* to grant us that redress which the nation unanimously demands; but as Ireland is committed, no man, I trust, will shrink from her support, but go through, *hand and heart*, in the establishment of *our liberties*. As I was cautious in committing, so I am now firm in asserting the *rights of my country*. My declaration, therefore, is, that as the nation has determined to obtain the restoration of her liberty, it behoves every man in Ireland to STAND FIRM." Yet this was the Fitzgibbon who in a few years trampled on her liberties, and sold her constitution.

The effect produced by this extraordinary speech from a man, the whole tenor of whose public life had been in hotility to its principles, neither added weight to the measure nor gained character for the speaker, disgust was the most prevalent sensation, but had he been a less able man, contempt would have been more prominent. All further debate ceased, the Speaker put the question on Mr. Grattan's amendment; a unanimous "*aye*" burst from every quarter of the house, he repeated the question, the applause was redoubled, a moment of tumultuous exultation followed, and, after centuries of oppression, Ireland at length declared herself an INDEPENDENT NATION.

This important event quickly reached the impatient crowds of every rank of society, who, without doors, awaited the decision of their parliament, a cry of joy and of exultation spread with electric rapidity through the entire city, its echo penetrated to the very interior of the house, every thing gave way to an effusion of happiness and congratulation that had never before been exhibited in that misgoverned country.

VII. Ireland from that moment assumed a new aspect, she rose majestically from her ruins, and surveyed the author of her resurrection with admiration and with gratitude. A young barrister, without professional celebrity, without family connections, possessed of no considerable fortune, nor of any personal influence, save that which talent and virtue involuntarily acquire, leagued with no faction, supported individually by no political party, became the instrument of Providence to liberate his country, and in a single day achieved what the most able statesmen, the most elevated personages, the most powerful and best connected parties never could effect. Aided by the circumstances of the moment, he seized the opportunity with promptitude, vigour and perseverance; but whilst he raised his country to prosperity, and himself to unexpected fortune and never-fading honour, he acquired vindictive enemies by the brilliancy of his success, and afterwards fell a temporary sacrifice to the perseverance of their malice and the dissimulations of their jealousy.

Mr. Connolly and Sir Henry Cavendish also, on this night, as ardently supported the independence of Ireland, as if it was a principle engrafted on their nature, both of them had put their signatures to a "life and fortune" declaration, to uphold the *perpetual* independence of their country, but it will appear in the progress of Irish affairs, how little reliance is to be placed on political declarations, where an alteration of circumstances or connections so frequently operates as a renunciation of principle. On the discussion of the Union in the year eighteen hundred, Sir Henry had exchanged the Duke of Devonshire for an employment in the treasury, and a new planet had arisen to influence Mr. Connolly; in that year both those gentlemen declaimed as *conscientiously against* the independence of the Irish nation, as if they had never pledged their "lives and fortunes" for their *perpetual* support of it.

It was impossible for any uninterested observer of the character and composition of the Irish Parliament to have conceived that the apparent unanimity of this night could have arisen from any one principle of universal action, men were actuated by various motives forming a mixed composition of patriotism and of policy; it was the unanimous *firmness* of the *people*, and not the abstract virtue of their delegates, which achieved this revolution, nor is it possible to read some of the popular resolutions of that day without feeling admiration at the happy union of spirit, of patriotism, and of prudence, which characterized their proceedings.*

VIII. When the intelligence of these events was circulated through the nation, the joy and rejoicings of the people were beyond all description, every city, town, and village, in Ireland, blazed with the emblems of exultation, and resounded with the shouts of triumph, the Volunteers, however, were not dazzled by the sunshine of the moment, they became rather more active than more remiss; much indeed was faithfully promised, but still every thing remained to be actually performed, and it soon appeared, that human life is not more uncertain in its duration than political faith precarious in its sincerity, the fair intentions of one government are generally called at least injudicious by its successors, political honesty has often vegetated in British Councils, but never yet did it survive to the period of maturity, and the short existence of the Duke of Portland's splendid administration warranted the cautious suspicion of the Volunteers, and afforded the succeeding ministry an opportunity for attempting those insidious measures which soon afterwards characterized anew the dispositions of the British Cabinet.

The parliament, and the people, when the paroxysm of their joy had subsided, waited with some solicitude for the King's reply to the Declaration of their independence, and a general suspension of public business took place until its arrival. It was, however, the first pause of confidence and tranquillity that Ireland had experienced since her connection with Great Britain; little could she then foresee that her new prosperity was but the precursor of

* The following address of the Dungannon Convention to the members of parliament who had voted in the minorities in 1781, and the beginning of 1782, is extremely illustrative of their temper and firmness, and made a very deep impression on the public mind.

"My Lords and Gentlemen,

"We thank you for your noble and spirited, though hitherto ineffectual efforts in defence of the great constitutional rights of your country. *Go on, go on,* the almost unanimous voice of your country is with you, and in a free country, the voice of the people must prevail. We know our duty to our Sovereign, and are loyal. We know our duty to ourselves, and are resolved to be free. We seek for our rights, and no more than our rights, and in so just a pursuit we should doubt the being of a Providence, *if we doubted of success.*"

future evils and of scenes as cruel and as destructive as any she had ever before experienced. The seeds of the Irish Union were sown by the very same event which had procured her independence, so early as seventeen hundred and eighty-four that independence was insidiously assailed by a despotic minister under colour of a commercial tariff, in seventeen hundred and eighty-nine events connected with the malady of the Monarch and the firm adherence of the Irish Parliaments to the constitutional rights of the Heir Apparent determined the same minister in the fatal project of extinguishing the Irish legislature, and in seventeen hundred and ninety-eight a rebellion artificially permitted, to terrify the country, and followed by acts and scenes of unparalleled corruption, for a moment warped away the minds of men from the exercise of common reason, and gave power and pretence to the British Cabinet to effect that extinguishment at a moment of national derangement.

CHAPTER X.

Design of the British Government to recall the independence of Ireland—Singular conduct of the Attorney General—His speech—Its powerful effect—Palpable dread of an Insurrection—Effect on England—Duke of Portland's duplicity—Attains an ascendency over Earl Charlemont—Embarrassment of the English Cabinet—The Volunteers prepare for actual service—Imbecility of England—Insidious designs of the English Government—Mr. Fox—Mr. Pitt—Important meeting of Parliament—The Volunteer Regiments occupy the avenues to the House of Commons—Designs of the Duke of Portland—Duke of Portland's speech—Mr. Grattan—Mr. Brownlow—The Recorder and Mr. Walshe oppose Mr. Grattan's address—Mr. Flood neutral—Mr. Walshe—Mr. Yelverton—The Secretary—Division—Consequent embarrassment.

I. THE foundation of Irish independence had now been laid, by the spirit of the Parliament and the unanimity of the people; and the stately structure of Irish liberty seemed likely to rise with solidity and magnificence. The labourers were numerous and indefatigable; and nothing was to be dreaded but contrariety in the plans, or jealousy among the architects; dangers which are proved by the sequel of her history, to be the true and substantial cause of Ireland's annexation. It is demonstrated by facts, beyond the power of refutation, that from the moment the British ministry found it imperatively necessary to submit to this declaration of Irish independence, no consideration was paramount in their councils to the desire of counteracting it. In furtherance of that object, from the period of the Duke of Portland's administration to that of Lord Cornwallis, the old system of dividing the Irish against each other, and profiting by their dissensions, was artfully pursued by the English Ministry, to re-establish their own supremacy, and from that moment they resolved to achieve, at any risk or price, that disastrous measure, which, at one blow, has prostrated the pride, the power, and the legislature of Ireland, and reduced her from the rank *of a nation to the level of a department.* But the people had now no leisure for suspicious forethought, or mature reflection, and the interval between the declaration of independence, and the reply of his Majesty to that declaration, though a period of deep anxiety, neither awakened serious doubts, nor produced implicit confidence.

An adjournment for three weeks was now proposed in the Commons, to give time for the arrival of His Majesty's Answer to their Address and Declaration. This motion, though it gave rise to a conversation rather than a debate, produced one of the most singular political phenomenons that had ever appeared in the history of any nation.

Mr. John Scott, then Attorney General, afterwards Lord Clonmel, whose despotic conduct had previously given rise to many and severe animadversions, took advantage on this occasion to recant his former and favourite political principle, that "might constitutes right." He now declared his firm and unqualified adherence to the claims of Ireland, in terms which, a week before, he would have prosecuted for as a seditious libel; and tendered his large fortune towards a general fund, to enforce from Great Britain the rights of his country, if force should become necessary.

He said, that, "he now felt it indispensable for him to throw off all equivocal and mysterious silence, and declared as his unchangeable opinion, that Great Britain never had any right whatever to bind his country, and that any acts she had ever done for that purpose were decided usurpations. That if the tenure of his office of Attorney General depended upon the maintenance of doctrines injurious to the rights and independence of Ireland, it was an infamous tenure; and if the Parliament of Great Britain were determined to lord it over Ireland, he was resolved not to be their villain in executing their tyranny.*

* It is a very curious fact, that Mr. Attorney General Scott's declaration of resisting the usurpation of England in 1782, was repeated in 1800, by two other successive Attorney Generals of Ireland, though under different circumstances. Mr. William Saurin, in his place in Parliament, declared that he considered the Irish Representatives incompetent to exact a legislative union; and that any statutes, made by a Parliament so constituted, would not be constitutionally binding on the Irish people. That gentleman, some time after, became Attorney General of Ireland himself, and never afterwards repeated his scepticism

That if matters should proceed to the extremity to which he feared they were verging, he should not be an insignificant subscriber to the fund for defending their common rights. That a life of much labour, together with the blessing of Providence, and what is commonly called good luck, had given him a landed property of £5,000 per year, and an office of great emolument, all which should certainly be devoted to the service of his country. That it would be disgraceful, for the paltry emoluments of an office to stand watching the vibrations of the balance, when he had determined to throw his life and fortune into the scale. I know," concluded the Attorney General, " that the public mind is on fire; I know that the determination of the people is to be free; and I adopt their determination."

A speech of so strong and stormy a nature, never having before been uttered by any Minister or Law Officer of the British Empire, nor even by any member of the Irish Parliament, created a sensation which it is scarcely possible to describe.* One sentence conveyed a volume of information.

" If matters proceed to the extremities to which I fear they are verging," was a direct declaration of mistrust in the Government he served; and such a speech, made in Parliament by the first confidential executive Law Officer of the Crown, possessed a character of mystery and great importance.

The dread of an insurrection in Ireland was thus, in

Mr. Plunkett made the same declaration, but in rather stronger terms, as he vouched for his son as well as himself; and soon after became Attorney General. Mr. Forster, and numerous able lawyers, some of them junior judges, and many country magistrates, united in those sentiments.

No Member of the Irish Parliament opposed the Union more strenuously, than the Author of this Work, and he united with those gentlemen in their opinion as to the incompetence of the Irish Parliament.

* The author was present at all these important debates. On Mr. Scott's recantation, the sensation of the House was so striking and singular, that he can never recollect it without emotion. For a moment, there was profound silence, gradually, the murmur of astonishment was heard, spreading from bench to bench, till one loud and general cry of approbation burst from every quarter of the House, and, in rapid and continued plaudits, evinced the enthusiasm of that era, and the importance of that secession.

direct terms, announced by the King's Attorney General; and by his intrepid determination to risk his life and fortune to support its objects, he afforded good reason to apprehend that his Majesty's reply was not likely to be such as would cultivate tranquillity, and left no doubt that the Attorney General foreboded an unwise reluctance in the British Cabinet, to a measure so vital to the peace, perhaps to the integrity, of the British Empire. This conduct of Mr. Scott, coupled with the previous secession of Mr. Fitzgibbon, must be looked on as among the most extraordinary occurrences of these, or any other times in Ireland.

In the history of Nations and of Parliaments, there is not another instance of two such men, publicly professing and practising the principles of arbitrary power, being so humbled, and reduced to the abject condescension of feigning a public virtue they had theretofore but ridiculed, and assuming a fictitious patriotism, the result, at best, of their fears or of their policy.

However, be the motive what it might, that most unprecedented conduct taught the British Government that they could no longer trifle with Ireland. Their power was then extinct; and no course remained but that of instantly relinquishing their long-vaunted supremacy, and surrendering at discretion to the just demands of a determined and potent people: and the splendid, though temporary triumph achieved by Ireland, affords a glorious precedent for oppressed nations, and an instructive lesson for arrogant usurpation.

II. Immediately on this unexpected turn, the Duke of Portland sent off two despatches to England; one to the Cabinet as a public document, and the other, a private and confidential note to Mr. Fox. The latter document explained his reasons for the necessity he felt of acceding, without any appearance of reluctance, to any demands which might at that moment be made by the Irish Parliament; but intimated " that so strong a difference of opinion appeared to exist between some gentlemen of weight that arrangements more favourable to England might possibly be effected through their *controversies*, although he could not venture to propose such, were they perfectly unanimous. He stated, in conclusion, that he would omit no opportunity of *cultivating* his connection with the Earl of Charlemont, who appeared entirely disposed to place confidence in his administration, and to give a *proper tone* to the armed bodies over whom he had the most considerable influence."

So skilfully did he act upon these suggestions, that he inveigled the good but feeble Earl Charlemont entirely into his trammels; and as long as his Grace remained in the Irish Government, he not only much influenced that nobleman, but kept him at arms length from some of the ablest statesmen of the country, without their perceiving the insidious power that caused the separation.

The other Ministers adopted the same principles, and they did not despair, by plausible conduct, according to the Duke of Portland's policy, to temporize with all parties, play off the people and the Parliament imperceptibly against each other; and, by gradually diminishing their mutual confidence, bring both to a dependence upon the good faith of the British Ministry, and so indispose the Irish Parliament from insisting upon any measures which might humble the pride, or alarm the interests of the British nation.

III. The British Cabinet had certainly great embarrassments to encounter. They had the difficult step to take of gratifying the claims of Ireland, without affecting the egotism of Great Britain. But the relative interests of the two countries being in many points fundamentally repugnant, the dilemma of Ministers was extremely embarrassing. It was doubly increased by a declaration of rights, and a positive demand, which anticipated the credit of a spontaneous generosity—an advantage which was now lost to them for ever. Their voluntary favours would now be changed to compulsory grants, the extent of which they could neither foresee nor control.

While the British Cabinet and the Irish Viceroy actively corresponded, the Irish nation was not idle. No relaxation was permitted in the warlike preparations of the Volunteer army. Reviews and discipline were continued with unintermitting ardour and emulation. Their artillery was daily exercised in the Phœnix Park, near Dublin. Camp equipage was preparing for actual service, and on the day to which the parliament adjourned, the whole of the Volunteer force of the metropolis was under arms, and fully prepared for the alternative (which the decision of his Majesty's Cabinet, through the speech of its Viceroy, might impose upon the people) either to return to their homes for the peaceful enjoyment of their rights or instantly to take the field. Musters had been ordered, to ascertain the probable numbers of Volunteers ready for immediate and active service. The returns had increased from the former census to about 124,000 officers and soldiers, of whom upwards of 100,000 effectives, well armed and disciplined, and owning no superior but God and their country, would, on the first sound of an hostile trumpet, have rushed with enthusiasm to the standards of independence. The Volunteer regiments and corps were commanded by gentlemen of rank and consideration in the country, and disciplined by retired officers of the British army; the serjeants being chiefly veteran soldiers who had fought in the American campaigns, and learned from their own defeats, the powers of a people determined to obtain their freedom. The whole disposable military force of Great Britain was at that period inadequate to combat one week with the Volunteers of Ireland, composing an army which could be increased, at a call, by a million of enthusiasts; and which, in case a contest had arisen, would have also been liberally recruited by the desertion of the Irish soldiers from the British army—and nearly one third of that army was composed of Irishmen. The British Navy, too, was then also manned by what were generally denominated British tars;* but a large proportion of whom were in fact sailors of Irish birth and Irish feelings, ready to shed their blood in the service of Great Britain whilst she remained the *friend of Ireland*, but as ready to seize and to steer the British navy into Irish ports, if she declared against their country, and thus it ever will be.

The safety of England was then clearly in the hands of

---

* The mutiny at the Nore, in the channel fleet, confirms this observation. Had the mutineers at that time chosen to carry the British ships into an Irish port, no power could have prevented them; and had there been a strong insurrection in Ireland, it is more than probable they would have delivered one half of the English fleet into the hands of their countrymen.

Ireland, and one hostile step, at that perilous crisis of the two nations, must have terminated their unity, and of course the power of the British empire. But the Cabinet at length considered that resistance to the just demands of Ireland would be unavailing; and that she was *then* too powerful for England to hazard an insurrection, which, if once excited, it would have been impossible to suppress.

Too cautious to risk a danger so imminent, they yielded to existing circumstances, and determined to concede; a system of conduct, which is called perfidy in private life and policy by Governments, has been very generally and very successfully resorted to in important political dilemmas, and they adopted the low and cunning course of yielding with affected candour, and counteracting with deep duplicity.

IV. The Cabinet reflected, also, that times and circumstances cannot always remain unchanged, and that the political vicissitudes to which every State is subject frequently enable conceding powers to re-assume usurpation; and, when restored to strength and vigour, again to forget the law of nations and of justice, and explain away or deny the spirit of those engagements which their feebleness had contracted. The events which have since occurred in Ireland, and the conduct and equivocation of the British Ministers in 1799 and 1800, proved to the world, that such were the premeditated and ulterior views of the British Cabinet, in 1782; and that the Duke of Portland was well aware of its objects, and freely lent himself to their perpetration.

Mr. Fox never had any especial predilection for Ireland. He was ignorant equally of her rights,* and her localities; and he considered her only as the segment of a great circle, which he laboured to encompass. He wielded the grievances of Ireland only as a weapon of offence against the ministry. He was a great man, with a popular ambition, and assumed the hereditary title of Whig, when its purest principles had nearly become obsolete. Mr. Pitt had in view the very same object, *to rule;* and they only differed in the means of affecting it. The one wished to rise upon the shoulders of the people; the other, to be

* See Mr. Fox's Letter to Earl Charlemont, April 1782. Hardy's Life of Charlemont

elevated upon those of the aristocracy. But the ambition of both was to govern the Empire. Their rivalry was of party, and their struggle was for power; but the internal prosperity of Ireland, as a *distinct abstract consideration*, gave not one hour's solicitude to either one or the other of those celebrated Ministers, though its resources were in part an object to both.

The Duke of Portland was not of sufficient talent or weight to lead the Ministry; but he had enough of both to be an efficient accessory. A man of plain, fair, undistinguished reputation, can effect important acts of duplicity, with less suspicion and more facility than more prominent and energetic personages; and when the moment of development arrives, he can plead the honesty of his character, and the error of his judgment: or, at the worst, he may gain a great point, and can only lose a narrow reputation.

These observations may be interesting, as decidedly applicable to the administration of the Duke of Portland. His Grace's conduct and speeches on the question of the Union, in 1800, leave no doubt that the whole tenor of his conduct, in 1782, must have been a premeditated tissue of dissimulation.

V. The Irish House met, pursuant to the adjournment, on the 27th May 1782, a day teeming with importance to the fate of Ireland and the character of Great Britain. It is not easy to imagine the solicitude and impatience with which the people awaited the decision of Great Britain on its claims.

On the morning of that memorable day, the Volunteers were under arms at an early hour. Their artillery, under the orders of James Napper Tandy, was stationed on the quays, and commanded all the bridges leading from the Military Barracks to the House of Parliament. The other corps, horse and foot, were posted at different stations of communication in the city; while some regular troops, formed in treble files, lined the streets for the passage of the Lord Lieutenant. But though neither party knew what would be the result of that day's proceedings, nor whether war or peace would be proclaimed by the British Ministry, not a symptom of hostile feeling appeared on any side. The Volunteers and the regular troops saluted each other as they passed, and reciprocally showed every mark of military courtesy. The strictest order prevailed; and the whole, by a combination most interesting and extraordinary, formed a scene to which history affords no parallel.

The Duke of Portland had not a very dignified demeanour, but, unfortunately, every body then considered him as a man of political integrity. His time, during the recess, had been skilfully employed, to gain upon the country gentlemen by flattering attention and courtly blandishment.

His Grace had learned, from Earl Charlemont, the character of Mr. Grattan, before he saw him. He was fully apprised of his spirit and patriotism, and knew well that neither could be conquered; but he conceived that by operating on the moderation and generous confidence of that virtuous Irishman, he might eventually divide the Parliament; chill the general enthusiasm of the people, and effect the objects of the British Government; and, before the meeting of Parliament, his Grace had made great progress in exciting shades of difference in the opinions of those who should have been unanimous. A premature gratitude, and credulous confidence, had already prepared the House for his reception; and he delivered the speech from the throne, with a well-affected honesty of emphasis, and an imposing appearance of individual gratification.

The Viceroy's speech gave rise to a debate of the very highest importance, not only as affecting the interests and feelings of that day, but as influencing the subsequent events and destiny of the Irish nation.

"My Lords and Gentlemen. It gives me the utmost satisfaction, that the first time I have occasion to address you, I find myself enabled, by the magnanimity of the King, and the wisdom of the Parliament of Great Britain, to assure you that immediate attention has been paid to your representations, and that the British Legislature have concurred in resolution to remove the causes of your discontents and jealousies, and are united in a desire to gratify every wish expressed in your late Addresses to the Throne.

"If any thing could add to the pleasure I feel in giving

you those assurances, it is that I can accompany them with my congratulations on the important and decisive victory gained by the fleets of his Majesty over those of the common enemy in the *West Indies*, and on the signal advantage obtained by his Majesty's *arms in the Island of Ceylon, and on the Coast of Coromandel.*

" By the papers which, in obedience to His Majesty's commands, I have directed to be laid before you, you will receive the most convincing testimony of the cordial reception which your representations have met with from the Legislature of Great Britain; but His Majesty, whose first and most anxious wish is to exercise His Royal Prerogative in such a manner as may be most conducive to the welfare of His faithful subjects, has further given it me in command to assure you of His gracious disposition to give His Royal Assent to Acts to *prevent* the suppression of Bills in the Privy Council of this Kingdom, and the alteration of them any where; and to limit the duration of the Act for the better Regulation and Accommodation of His Majesty's forces in this Kingdom, to the term of two years.

" These benevolent intentions of His Majesty, and the willingness of His Parliament of Great Britain to second his gracious purposes, are unaccompanied by any stipulation or condition whatever.

" The *good faith*, the generosity, and the honour of *this* nation, afford them the surest pledge of a corresponding dispostion, on your part, to promote and perpetuate the harmony, the stability, and the glory of the Empire.

" On my own part, I entertain not the least doubt, but that the same spirit which urged you to share the freedom of Great Britain, will confirm you in your determination to share her fate also, standing and falling with the British Empire."

Mr. Grattan immediately rose. His unsuspecting and grateful mind, though congenial to the honest liberality of a patriot, was quite too conceding and inexperienced to meet the ways and wiles of deceptious statesmen. Misled by the apparent sincerity of that speech, and the plain and plausible demeanour of the Duke of Portland, he lost sight of every thing but confidence and gratitude, and left to deeper politicians to discover the snare that lay concealed amidst the soothing and honourable language of the Viceroy.

He said,—" That as Great Britain had given up every claim to authority over Ireland, he had not the least idea that she should be also bound to make any declaration that she had formerly usurped that power. This would be a foolish caution, a dishonourable condition.* The nation that insists upon the humiliation of another, is a foolish nation ; and Ireland is not a foolish nation. I move you, to assure His Majesty of our unfeigned affection to His Royal Person and Government ; that we feel, most sensibly, the attention our representations have received from the magnanimity of His Majesty, and the wisdom of the Parliament of Great Britain ; to assure His Majesty, that we conceive the resolution for an unqualified, unconditional repeal of the 6th George the First to be a measure of consummate wisdom and justice, suitable to the dignity and eminence of both Nations, exalting the character of both, and furnishing a perpetual pledge of mutual amity ; to assure His Majesty, that we are sensibly affected by his virtuous determination to accede to the wishes of His faithful subjects, and to exercise His Royal prerogative in the manner most conducive to their welfare. That, gratified in those particulars, we do assure His Majesty, that no constitutional question between the *two nations will any longer exist*, to interrupt their harmony ; and that Great Britain, as she approved of our firmness, may rely on our affection ; and that we remember, and do repeat our determination, to stand or fall with the British Nation."

When Mr. Grattan concluded the Address, which was seconded by Mr. Brownlow, a most animated and interesting, though desultory debate, immediately ensued ; a debate too much connected with the subsequent transactions on the Union, not to be particularly noticed in this stage of the history.

The Recorder of, and Member for, Dublin, Sir Samuel Bradstreet, a strong-minded, public-spirited man, an able

* This was a juvenile syllogism, where there were neither premises nor conclusion to support the argument. Credulity and wisdom are nearly incompatible. Ireland was a credulous nation ; ergo, she could not have been a wise one. Had Ireland been more sceptical in **1782, she would have been less unfortunate in 1800**

lawyer, and independent Member of Parliament; of a rough, decisive, firm deportment, was the first who ventured to insinuate his dissent from the Address, and his suspicions of the Duke's sincerity. He entirely objected to that sweeping clause of Mr. Grattan's Address—" That all constitutional questions between the two countries were at an end." He stated that many were not yet touched upon,—many that were vital to Irish independence still remained unnoticed: for he insisted that the Irish Parliament actually sat at that moment under an English Statute: and that the Address, as moved, was in some instances premature—in others too comprehensive—in all, defective. Subsequent events have since proved the soundness and the acuteness of his judgment and his foresight.

Mr. Flood said but a few words, and they were rather insinuating than insisting on his dissent. He started some difficulties on the subject of external legislation— he expressed his opinion, that matters were not yet sufficiently advanced to form a decided judgment upon the extent and modifications of the proposed arrangements; but it was obvious that this great man was neither confident nor satisfied, and that he conceived, that though the chief demand had been made, and that grant acceded to, yet that it would require profound consideration, and a steady comprehensive system, to secure the tenure. He publicly anticipated nothing; but his own want of faith in the British Cabinet was obvious and comprehensive.

Mr. David Walshe, an able, pertinacious lawyer, courageous and not conciliating, was a still more determined sceptic. He had a clear head, a suspicious, perverse mind, and a temper that never would outstretch itself to meet pacific objects. He debated well, but was too intemperate to acquire or maintain a general popularity. A part of his speech on this memorable night is also of great importance. He followed Sir Samuel Bradstreet on the point of external legislation, and concluded with these remarkable expressions :—

"I repeat it, that until England declares unequivocally, by an act of her own legislature, that she had no right, in any instance, to make laws to bind Ireland, the usurped power of English legislation never can be considered by us as relinquished. We want not the concessions of England to restore us our liberties. If we are true to ourselves, we possess the fortitude, we possess the will, and, thank God, we possess the power, to assert our rights as men, and accomplish our independence as a nation."

VI. The gauntlet was now thrown, the vital question was started—England was put on her defence, and Ireland on her trial.

The great point of confirming the Irish independence and constitution being once started, never could be relinquished; it must be decided—the suspicion of English sincerity once raised, must be satisfied; and it appeared in a moment, that Mr. Grattan's address could never be considered either secure or conclusive. But even those who thought so, did not conceive that the moment had as yet arrived when that subject should be so warmly discussed.

Those who feared that a difference at so early a period might defeat all their expectations, chose rather to accede to an address they did not approve of, than hazard a disunion which might never be remedied.

Mr. Yelverton strongly recommended unanimity at that moment. It seemed, for prudential reasons, to be the general wish; and Mr. Walshe had withdrawn his opposition—when Mr. Fitzpatrick, the Viceroy's secretary artfully seized on the moment of inconsiderate gratitude, and threw out a defiance to those who endeavoured to diminish its unanimity. This to such a temper as Mr. Walshe's, had the effect intended, of causing a division—and the skilful secretary succeeded in his object.

On the division, the Recorder and Mr. Walshe alone divided on the minority, and Mr. Grattan's address was triumphantly carried, with all its imperfections; and a short period proved that these imperfections were neither few nor unimportant. The House adjourned amidst the universal acclamations of the ignorant and credulous people; and the constitutional arrangements between the two countries were fatally supposed, from the tenor of the speech and the address, to have been entirely and for ever arranged to their mutual satisfaction.

It is here proper to pause and reflect upon the embarrassing situation into which this day's debate had thrown both nations; an embarrassment which, since that day, has never yet completely terminated, and probably never will.

The transcendent merits of Mr. Grattan, the unparalleled brilliancy of his language, in moving the declaration of rights, his firmness and his patriotism, had raised him above all his countrymen. That declaration, it was believed, had restored the liberties of his country, and given him a just claim to all the rewards and honours which even the glowing gratitude of that country could confer upon him. But, unfortunately, his own honesty led him to a mistaken confidence in that of others. The courtly patriotism of Earl Charlemont, always inclining him to a blind principle of conciliation, had its influence on Mr. Grattan, who was a statesman, great in principle, but inefficient in detail; and the moderation of Lord Charlemont was not ineffective nor merely passive, when restraining the vigour of a mind, that seemed to be created to think greatly and act decidedly, only upon great and decisive occasions.

CHAPTER XI.

Temporary credulity of the Irish Parliament—Country Gentlemen—Singular character of Mr. Bagenal—His Exploits—Popularity—His patriotism—Commanded many Volunteer Corps—Gives notice of a motion to reward Mr. Grattan—Anti-prophetic observation—Mr. Grattan's increasing popularity—Hasty repeal of the declaratory act 6th Geo. III.—And transmitted by the Viceroy to the Volunteers—Doctrine of Blackstone declared unconstitutional—Mr. Bagenal's motion to grant £100,000, to Mr. Grattan—Mistaken pride of his friends—Extraordinary occurrence—Insidious conduct of Government—Mr. Thomas Connolly makes a most unprecedented motion—Viceroy offers the Palace to Mr. Grattan and his heirs as a reward for his services—Objects of the Government in making the offer—Discovered by the indiscretion of the Secretary, Col. Fitzpatrick—His character—Real objects developed—Mr. Grattan's friends decline so large a grant—Their mistaken principle—Effects of the calumnies against Ireland—False arguments—Comparison of the conduct of England and Ireland—Comparative loyalty.

I. It is as extraordinary as it is true, that the weaknesses and foibles of Irish character were more strikingly displayed during this important discussion, than upon any former occasion. A generous, ardent, credulous, unstatesman-like sensibility, appeared to have seized upon the whole assembly; and even the natural quickness of perception, and acuteness of intellect, which the members of that House displayed on ordinary and trivial subjects, seemed totally to have forsaken them during this memorable debate—of more vital importance to the nation than any other that had ever taken place in the Irish Parliament.

II. The country gentlemen of Ireland, at all times bad casuists and worse lawyers, appeared on this occasion to close both their ears and eyes, and to resign, with one accord, all exercise of judgment and discrimination. The word " unanimity" operated as a talisman amonst them, and silenced all objections. The very important observations of Sir Samuel Bradstreet and of Mr. Walshe were hardly listened to with patience. Mr. Flood himself seemed to be overwhelmed and manacled; and those axioms and that reasoning which were ultimately acceded to and adopted even by the British Ministers themselves, were on this night considered as a species of treason against the purity of the British Government, and the sincerity of the Irish Viceroy. No voice but that of congratulation, joy, and confidence, could make itself heard. No suspicions durst be suggested—no murmurs durst be uttered. The scene was new to Ireland; and exultation took precedence for a time of both reason and reflection.

Beauchamp Bagenal, representative for Carlow county, so soon as the flurry of mutual congratulations had a little subsided in the House, proposed a measure well adapted to the circumstances of that moment, and most happily coincident with the sentiments of the people. How far it had been premeditated, or arose from the impulse of the moment, no person acquainted with the character and eccentricities of Mr. Bagenal could possibly determine.

He was one of those persons, who, born to a large inheritance, and having no profession to interrupt their propensities, generally made in those times the grand tour of Europe, as the finishing part of a gentleman's education. Mr. Bagenal followed the general course; and on that tour had made himself very conspicuous. He had visited every capital of Europe, and had exhibited the native original character of the Irish *gentleman* at every place he visited. In the splendour of his travelling establishment, he quite eclipsed the petty potentates with whom Germany was garnished. His person was fine—his manners open and generous—his spirit high, and his liberality profuse. During his tour, he had performed a variety of feats which were emblazoned in Ireland, and endeared him to his countrymen. He had fought a prince—jilted a princess—intoxicated the Doge of Venice—carried off a Duchess from Madrid—scaled the walls of a convent in Italy—narrowly escaped the Inquisition at Lisbon—concluded his exploits by a celebrated fencing match at Paris; and he returned to Ireland with a sovereign contempt for all continental men and manners, and an inveterate antipathy to all despotic kings and arbitrary governments.

Domesticated in his own mansion at Dunleckny—surrounded by a numerous and devoted tenantry—and possessed of a great territory, Mr. Bagenal determined to spend the residue of his days on his native soil, according to the usages and customs of country gentlemen; and he was shortly afterwards returned a representative to Parliament for the county of Carlow, by universal acclamation.

Though Mr. Bagenal did not take any active part in the general business of the Irish Parliament, he at least gave it a good example of public spirit and high-minded independence. His natural talents were far above mediocrity; but his singularities, in themselves extravagant, were increased by the intemperance of those times; and an excellent capacity was neutralized by inordinate dissipation. Prodigally hospitable, irregular, extravagant, uncertain, vivacious; the chase, the turf, the sod, and the bottle, divided a great portion of his intellects between them, and generally left for the use of Parliament, only so much as he could spare from his other occupations.

However, in supporting the independence and prosperity of Ireland, he always stood in the foremost ranks.

Liberal and friendly, but obstinate and refractory, above all his contemporaries, he had a perfect indifference for the opinions of the world, when they at all differed from his own; and he never failed to perform whatever came uppermost in his thoughts, with the most perfect contempt as to the notions which might be formed either of his rectitude or impropriety.

He was one of the first country gentlemen who raised a volunteer regiment in the county Carlow. He commanded several military corps, and was one of the last Volunteer Colonels in Ireland who could be prevailed upon to discontinue the reviews of their regiments, or to relinquish that noble, patriotic, and unprecedented institution. However, he was, on this occasion, as politically short-sighted as he was nationally credulous. He could see nothing but sincerity in the Viceroy, honour in the British Cabinet, and an eternal cordiality between the two nations: and before the constitutional arrangement was well begun, he fancied it was completely concluded. His admiration of Mr. Grattan was unqualified and ex travagant; and it was with an honest zeal and pure sincerity he rose to propose a measure, at that period the most popular and gratifying to the Irish nation.

III. Having passed many eulogiums on Mr. Grattan's services to Ireland, he gave notice of an intended motion, " that a Committee should be appointed, to consider and report what sum the Irish Parliament should grant, to build a suitable mansion and purchase an estate for their great deliverer."

In prefacing this notice, Mr. Bagenal, full of candour and credulity, used some expressions, so unfortunately anti-prophetic, as to render them worthy of marked observation. He said, that Mr. Grattan had saved the country from an iron age, and unequivocally restored a golden one to his own country for ever. " By our affectionate alliance with Great Britain, we shall not only be benefitted ourselves, but shall see a beloved sister revive from her misfortunes. This great man has crowned the work for ever; under his auspices the throne of freedom is fixed on a basis so firm, and which will always be so well supported by the influence the people must acquire under his system, that, with the help of God, there is no danger, even of Parliament itself ever being able to shake it; nor shall any Parliament be ever again profanely styled omnipotent."

Mr. Grattan attempted to make some observations, but his voice was drowned in the general applause; and the house adjourned without further observations.

IV. He alone now occupied the entire hearts of the people.

They had no room for any other individual. Almost frantic with gratitude to their deliverer, they cried out, that the doctrines of Molyneux had triumphed in the same place where they had before been consigned to infamy. But the day of those pure and lofty feelings has passed away. A broken down constitution seldom recovers its pristine elasticity; and that enthusiastic, proud, patriotic spirit which signalized the Irish nation in 1782, driven to its tomb by misrule and by misfortune, can never rise again but on some congenial crisis.

V. The British Ministry and Parliament now began to feel their own weakness. Their intolerance degenerated into fear; and responsibility began to stare them in the face. The loss of America had been got over by their predecessors without an impeachment; but that of Ireland would not have passed over with the same impunity. The British Cabinet had already signed the capitulation, and thought it impossible to carry it too soon into execution. Bills to enact the concessions demanded by Ireland were therefore prepared with an expedition nearly bordering on precipitancy. The 6th of George the First, declaratory of, and establishing the supremacy of England, and the eternal dependence of Ireland on the Parliament and Cabinet of Great Britain, was now hastily repealed, without debate, or any qualification by the British Legislature. This repeal received the royal assent, and a copy was instantly transmitted to the Irish Viceroy, and communicated by circulars to the Volunteer commanders.

CHAP. LIII. An Act, to repeal an Act made in the sixth year of the reign of His late Majesty King George the First, intituled, An Act for the better securing the *dependency* of the kingdom of Ireland upon the *crown of Great Britain*.

Whereas, an act was passed in the sixth year of the reign of His late Majesty King George the First, intituled: An Act for the better securing the *dependency* of the kingdom of Ireland upon the *crown* of Great Britain; may it please your Most Excellent Majesty, that it may be enacted, and be it enacted, by the King's Most Excellent Majesty, by and with the advice and consent of the lords spiritual and temporal, and commons, in this present parliament assembled, and by the authority of the same, that from and after the passing of this Act, *the above mentioned Act, and the several matters and things therein contained, shall be, and is, and are hereby repealed.*

Thus, the doctrine of Blackstone, that venerated Druid of English jurisprudence, who by his dictum had tried to seal the slavery of the Irish people, was surrendered as unconstitutional, and renounced by the very same legislature that had enacted it. As England drooped, Ireland raised her head; and for a moment she was arrayed with all the exterior insignia of an independent nation.

VI. On the 30th of May, 1782, Mr. Bagenal resumed the subject of the reward to Mr. Grattan; and after a short, but animated speech, moved that "£100,000 should be granted by parliament, to purchase an estate, and build a suitable mansion, as the reward of gratitude by the Irish nation, for his eminent services to his country." No member could directly oppose a measure so merited, so popular, and so honourable to the nation. No absolute murmur was heard; but the magnitude of the sum gave rise to many incidental observations; and some friends of Mr. Grattan endeavoured to impress the house with the idea that he was altogether adverse to the measure, and conceived that his honours and gratification would be greater by the feeling of having served his country without other reward than that arising from its pure and unsophisticated enjoyment.

This idea in modern times, and under Mr. Grattan's peculiar circumstances, was considered less the result of a true pride than of a patriotic vanity. Roman precedents were not applicable to Ireland, and his paternal estates were not sufficiently ample to support so distinguished a man in the dignity of his station. And the wisest friends of Mr. Grattan considered such a grant not as a mercenary recompense, but the reward of patriotic virtue, conferred by the gratitude of a nation to elevate a deliverer.

VII. While the House seemed to hesitate as to the wisest course of carrying the proposed grant into immediate execution, a most unexpected circumstance took place, which, though in its results of no important consequence, forms one of the most interesting anecdotes of Irish events, developes the insidious artifices to which the Government resorted, and forms an episode without a precedent in ancient or modern annals.

Mr. Thomas Connolly, who, as a leading member of the Whig party, had entirely connected himself with the Duke of Portland; and though not holding any ministerial office, was a Privy Councillor, and considered to be particularly confidential in the councils of the Viceroy, after many eulogiums upon Mr. Grattan's unparalleled services to Ireland, stated, "That the Duke of Portland felt equally with the Irish people, the high value of those services; and that he was authorized by the Lord Lieutenant to express, in the strongest terms, the sense he entertained of the public virtue of Mr. Grattan, and of his eminent and important services to Ireland: and as the highest proof he could give of his admiration and respect for that distinguished personage, he (the Lord Lieutenant) begged to offer, as a part of the intended grant to Mr. Grattan, *the Viceregal Palace in the Phœnix Park*, to be settled on Mr. Grattan and his heirs for ever, as a suitable residence for so meritorious a person."

VIII. The Viceroy of His Britannic Majesty, offering to a *private individual a grant for ever* of the King's best palace in Ireland, was repugnant to the principle of Monarchical Governments; while Mr. Bagenal's proposal of a grant by the House of Commons, as a reward for the public services of one of their own independent members, appeared to the Viceroy as making the people every thing and the administration nothing. He saw clearly, that the public spirit was irresistible, and that the grant must pass; and the Viceroy determined, at any sacrifice, to give it a tinge of ministerial generosity, and thereby deaden, as much as possible, the brilliancy and effect of a popular proceeding. He knew that if his proposal through Mr. Connolly should be accepted, the grant would have very considerably changed its democratic complexion, the prerogative would be somewhat preserved, and Mr. Grattan no longer considered as deriving his reward *exclusively* from the gratitude of his countrymen: the Crown would have its share in a claim to his acknowledgements; and thus the merit of the favour be divided between the people and the minister.

This magnificent and unexampled offer, at first view, appeared flattering and showy; at the second, it appeared deceptious; and at the third, inadmissible. Delicacy prevented any debate on the subject; and it would have died away without remark or observation, and have been rejected by a judicious silence, had not the indiscretion of Colonel Fitzpatrick betrayed the whole feeling and duplicity of the Government, and opened the eyes of many to the jealousy and designs of His Grace's administration. Though the secretary was extremely disposed to serve Mr. Grattan individually, the entire failure of the plan, and the frigid manner in which the royal offer had been received on every side, hurt his official pride, and affected him extremely. He recollected his ministry, but forgot his discretion; and he could no longer restrain himself from some observations equally ill-timed and injudicious.

Colonel Fitzpatrick was the brother of the Earl of Upper Ossory. Though not an expert diplomatist, he was well selected to make his way amongst the Irish gentry, and consequently carry into effect the objects of the British ministers, and the deceptions of the Duke of Portland. He was ingenuous and convivial; friendly and familiar; and *theoretically* honest, even in politics. His name was musical to the ear of that short-sighted community (the Irish gentry), and his casual indiscretions in Parliament were kindly attributed to his undesigning nature; and of all qualities, an appearance of unguarded openness is most imposing upon the Irish people. But the office of a minister or of a secretary is too well adapted to alter, if not the nature, at least the habits of a private gentleman; and, as a matter of course, he relinquishes his candour when he commences his diplomacy.

Whatever his individual feelings might have been as Colonel Fitzpatrick, it is impossible that in his capacity of secretary, Mr. Bagenal's motion could have given him any gratification. He declared, that "he conceived the power of rewarding eminent men was one of the noblest of the Royal Prerogatives, which were certainly a part of the constitution. He did not wish to be considered as giving a sullen acquiescence, but he conceived that marks of favour of this nature always appertained to the Crown alone, and he should have wished that this grant had come from the Royal hand; but, as the man was unprecedented, so was the grant; and he hoped this would not be considered as a precedent on future occasions."

IX. By these few, but comprehensive observations of the Secretary, the apparently magnificent liberality of the Viceroy appeared in its real character, and dwindled into a narrow subterfuge of ministerial jealousy. Mr. Connolly appeared to have travelled out of his station, and officiously to have assumed the office of a minister, for a deceptive purpose, and lent himself to a little artifice, to trepan the Parliament and humiliate the people.

By this rejected tender the Whig administration gained

no credit; they evinced a disposition to humble the Crown without elevating the people, and to wind the laurels of both around their own temples.

The Viceroy considered a grant by the Commons too democratic; and the Parliament considered the Viceroy's tender too ministerial. Mr. Grattan was a servant of the Irish people, and was utterly unconnected with the British Government. In every point of view, therefore, the Viceroy's offer, at that moment, was improper, and derogatory alike to the Crown and the individual. The Viceroy of Ireland proposing, on behalf of the King of England, to Ireland's great patriot to reward his services for having emancipated his country from the domination of Great Britain, was an incident as extraordinary as had ever occurred in any government, and, emanating from that of England, told, in a single sentence, the whole history of her terrors, her jealousy, her shallow artifice and humbled arrogance.

This proposal was linked with many other insidious objects, but they were too obvious to be successful, and only disclosed that shallow cunning. His Excellency had perceived in Ireland the phenomena of a governing people, without a ruling democracy,—an armed and unrestrained population, possessing, without abusing, the powers of Sovereignty, and turning their authority, not to the purposes of turbulence or sedition, but to those of Constitution, order, and tranquillity. These armed Associations, however irreproachable in their conduct, were unprecedented in their formation, and were fairly considered by His Grace with a lively jealousy, as tending to establish a species of popular aristocracy, dangerous to the very nature of the British Constitution.

X. Many friends of Mr. Grattan, or those who professed to be so, declared he would not accept of so large a sum as that proposed by Mr. Bagenal; but this was a mistaken, or an affected view of that subject. In fact the grant itself, not its amount, was the only point for dignified consideration. However, after a considerable discussion, it was diminished, by Mr. Grattan's friends, to the sum of fifty thousand pounds, which was unanimously voted to him; and never had a reward, more merited or more honourable, been conferred on any patriot by any nation.

The times when civic crowns conferred honours no longer existed; property had become essential for importance in society. The Irish Parliament had before them a sad and recent example of the necessity of such a reward, in the fate of Dr. Lucas, one of the best friends of Ireland, who had sacrificed himself to support his principles: a man who had, so far as his talents admitted, propagated and applied the doctrines of the great Molyneux; and, like him, was banished, and, like him, declared a traitor; who had sat a Representative for the metropolis of Ireland; and whose statue still adorns the Royal Exchange of Dublin: a venerable Senator, sinking under the pressure of years and of infirmity, carried into their House to support its liberties,—sickening in their cause and expiring in their service; a rare example of patriotism and independence; yet suffered to die in indigence, and leave an orphan offspring to become the prey of famine. With such a reproachful warning before the nation, it was for the people, not for the Crown, to take care that they never should be again disgraced by similar ingratitude. In these degenerate times, honours give no sustenance; and in the perverted practices of modern policy, it is not the province of the Monarch to reward the patriot. And this event leads the historian to others still more important.

Upon every important debate on the claims of Ireland, in the British and Imperial Parliaments, the native character and political propensities of the Irish people had been uniformly made a subject of animated discussion; and the loyalty of that Nation to her Kings had been put directly in issue, by both her friends and her enemies; by the latter, as a pretext for having abrogated her Constitution: by the former, as a defence against libel and exaggeration; each party asserting, that the past events of Irish history justify their reasoning, and afford evidence of their respective allegations.

XI. It is, therefore, at this important epoch highly expedient that this controversy of opinions, as to the loyalty of the Irish people, though probably digressive, should be decided by unequivocal historic matters of fact, undeniable by either party; and thereby, that the true principles of a long persecuted and calumniated people, should be no longer mistaken nor misrepresented.

A reference to the authentic Annals and Records of Irish History, indisputably proves that the unrelenting cruelties and misrule of their British Governors in early ages, goading the wretched natives to insurrection, formed the first pretext for afterwards branding them with an imputation of indigenous disloyalty, thereby exciting an inveterate prejudice against the Irish people; which, becoming hereditary, has descended, though with diminished virulence, from father to son throughout the English nation.

These calumnies had their full and fatal operation, as an argument in urging the necessity of a Legislative Union; an argument at once refuted by reference even to the modern events of 1782, and to the unexampled moderation, forbearance, and loyalty of the Irish nation, who sought only a full participation in the British Constitution, though the moral and physical powers of that ardent people were then consolidated by their patriotism, and rendered irresistible by their numbers, their discipline, and their energy.

XII. At that awful crisis of the British Empire, the Irish were an armed and triumphant people; England a defeated and trembling nation. Ireland was in the bloom of energy and of vigour; England on the couch of discomfiture and malady. And if the spirit of indigenous disaffection, so falsely imputated to the Irish Nation, had, in reality, existed, she had then full scope, and ample powers, to pursue and effect all its dispositions for an eternal separation.

It is not, however, by modern or isolated events alone, that a fair judgment can be formed of the characteristic attributes of any nation; still less so of a worried and misgoverned people. It is only by recurring to remoter periods, thence tracing, step by step, the conduct of Ireland throughout all her provocations, her miseries, and her persecutions, and then comparing the extent of her sufferings, her endurance, and her loyalty, with those of her sister countries during the same periods, that the comparative character of both can be justly appreciated, and those calumnies which have weighed so heavily on her reputation be effectually refuted.

It is a matter of indisputable fact, that during the twenty reigns which succeeded the first submission of the

Irish princes, the fidelity of Ireland to the British monarchs was but seldom interrupted, and that Irish soldiers were not unfrequently brought over to England, to defend their English sovereigns against the insurrections of English rebels.

But when we peruse the authenticated facts of British annals during the same twenty reigns, we find an unextinguishable spirit of disaffection to their princes, and that an insatiable thirst for rebellion and disloyalty signalized every reign, and almost every year of British history, during the same period; that above thirty civil wars raged within the English nation; four of their monarchs were dethroned; three of their kings were murdered, and during four centuries, the standard of rebellion scarcely ever ceased to wave over some portion of that distracted island; and so deeply had disloyalty been engrafted in the very nature of the British nobles and British people, that insurrection and regicide, if not the certain, were the expected consequences of every coronation.

Through these observations, the eye of England will at length be directed to these events. They will then be convinced that there lurked within the bosom of Great Britain herself the germs of a disquietude more unremitting, a licentiousness more inflammatory, a fanaticism more intolerant, and a political agitation more dangerous and unjustifiable, than any which even her most inveterate foes can justly extract from an impartial history of the libelled country.

This short digression must have the advantage of illustrating the principles which led to the transactions of 1798 and 1800, those gloomy epochs of Irish calamity; it may enlighten that dark and profound ignorance of Irish History and transactions which still obscure the intellect of the English people, and even leads members of the united Parliament to avow that utter ignorance of the very country and people as to whom they were at the same moment so severely legislating. Those men are surely the most injurious to the general tranquillity of a state, the collected power of united nations, and the safety of the common weal, whose prejudices ignorance and bigotry lead them by wanton irritation to engender uncongenial feelings in eight millions of so powerful, ardent, and generous a portion of the empire.

CHAPTER XII.

Epitome of Irish History—Treacherous system of the English Government—First Irish Union—Second Union compared with the first—King Henry's Acts in Ireland—His plan to decimate the nation—He relinquished his dominion over Ireland—Abortive attempts to colonize—Totally failed.

I. The Irish annals, though more imperfect, can be traced by tradition farther back than those of England. Ancient records, and other evidence also of a most indisputable nature, of the eighth and preceding centuries, prove that in the earliest ages Ireland had been the seat of literature, arts, and refinement; and scarcely a year passes without discovering strong proofs of her former wealth, skill, and magnificence.* She first degenerated under the invasion of northern barbarians; and while England profited by the intercourse of her great and accomplished conquerors, Ireland had retrograded under the ignorance and brutality of hers.

By the great battle of Howth, her Danish tyrants were at length exterminated, and Ireland was gradually recovering her original prosperity, when she found that

* Some English writers, of the best authority, acknowledge the high state of learning and civilization, which existed in Ireland during the early ages; and numerous works and manuscripts now in the Vatican and the Royal Library at Paris, put the truth of that fact beyond all question. The variety and exquisite workmanship of ornaments and weapons of solid gold, still occasionally found buried in the bogs of Ireland, leave no doubt that great metallic wealth and superior skill once existed in that country, and that some of the arts were cultivated there to an almost unexampled perfection. The author has seen a solid piece of virgin gold, found in one of the Wicklow gold mines, about twenty-eight miles from Dublin, larger than a racket ball, and a great quantity of smaller dimensions. The mines extend many miles up the bed of a shallow stream, springing from the cliffs in the mountains. And an Irish statute in the reign of Henry the Fourth, prohibiting the native Irish from using gold stirrups and bridles, is a convincing proof that, even since the English invasion, sumptuary laws were judged proper to restrain the remaining tendency to profuse splendour among the Irish chieftains.

she had only changed the name, not the nature of her slavery.

It was at this commencement of her convalescence, and before the Irish monarch had as yet been able to reform the chiefs or re-establish his authority, that a band of British adventurers, headed by Stiguel Strongbow, a British nobleman, abetted by the subtlety and practices of a vicious native chieftain, the treacherous Mac Murrough, landed in Ireland, with a view to mend their fortunes by conquest, and by plunder.

Earl Strongbow found in Ireland a powerful but a disjointed people, who though they had regained their independence, were still divided by jealous factions,—enfeebled by civil warfare, and dispirited by the dread of recurring contests. He found it a worn down, palsied nation, well adapted to become a prey to the impression of arms, or the wiles of treachery. He was lavish in the use of both. She struggled much with these disciplined adventurers; but her vigour had been exhausted by her civil contests, and, though occasionally victorious, her energy had declined, and her powers were but intermitting. As her strength failed, her terrors augmented; and she was finally induced to listen to the deceptious representations of Strongbow and Mac Murrough; and after an ineffectual resistance she fell beneath the mingled pressure of arms and of seduction. At a conference in 1170, her Chieftains were told nearly in the same words which disgraced her Parliament in 1800, that there could be no remission of her internal feuds, no protection against future massacres, but by a voluntary sacrifice of that mischievous and agitating independence, which she had so uselessly enjoyed, and was so unavailingly contending for, but that, if united to the flourishing and powerful realm of Britain, its benevolent and potent monarch would then find it to be the interest of his empire to arrest all her feuds, and promote her prosperity.

II. Though the spirit of national independence still lingered in the country, her heart was broken; the melancholy recollection of feuds, of defeats, and misfortunes, made a powerful impression on the jealous and divided leaders. Mac Murrough's treachery had destroyed all confidence amongst the Princes—discord had torn the

Royal Standard of the Irish Monarch—the Chieftains had no general rallying station to collect their powers they submitted to the invaders, and each stipulated for himself, and influenced his Kernes* to a reluctant capitulation.

The choice of difficulties and dangers, or of rewards and honours, was held out to the most obdurate opponents of British annexation. Some leaders were gained by specious promises of territory; many were beguiled by the assurance of future protection, and a large portion of the chieftains at length yielded to the sway of a British sceptre..

But this submission *never* was unanimous. Many who would have resisted it to the last extremity, were dismayed and scattered; many who retained the power to resist it, were terrified or corrupted; and though the acquisition of the entire island appeared to have been effected by the adventurers, the appearance was fallacious. However, the English Strongbow gained great honours for his achievement, the Irish Mac Murrough obtained great rewards for his treachery, the adventurers were compensated at the expense of the natives: and the First Union of Ireland with Britain, in the year **1173**, received a royal assent and consummation from the Second Henry.

It is very remarkable, that though the occurrences were so different, the persons so dissimilar, and the periods so remote, the circumstances attending this first annexation of Ireland cannot be reflected on without the memory also recurring to the circumstances of the last. Though

---

* Kernes were a species of followers who attended the Irish Chieftains, ready to execute any business to which their patrons might order them. The Chiefs generally gained importance with the King in proportion to the number of Kernes he could produce, when the King had occasion for their assistance: and when a Chief made *terms* for himself, he generally stipulated for his *Kernes* into the bargain.

They despised any independent mode of livelihood; and often lived in a state of expectation on their Chief, or by the public. This race seems not to have been totally extinct in Ireland, in 1800, though they then existed under the denomination of gentlefolks. See the fac simile of Mr. Robert Crowe's letter, annexed to this volume, respecting Lord Castlereagh's *treaty* with the Earl of Belvidere, to purchase Messrs. Knox and Crowe (two of his Lordship's members): Witnessed by the Rev. Mr. Usher, his Lordship's chaplain.—*Litera scripta manet.*

Cornwallis was *not* Strongbow, though Castlereagh was *not* Mac Murrough, though the Peers were *not* Princes, and the Commons were *not* Kernes; and though nearly seven centuries had intervened between the accomplishment of these unions, it is impossible not to recognize in their features *a strong family resemblance.*

Henry lost no time in repairing to the Irish metropolis, where, in great state he received the allegiance of his new but reluctant subjects; and feasted the Irish Princes in a style of magnificence and splendour unusual in those times. But his banquets were those of policy, his splendours were founded on contempt, and before the games and rejoicings which accompanied those celebrated feasts were yet entirely terminated, the beards of Irish Kings had been pulled by the vassals of the English monarch.*

III. Henry, on his return to England, soon perceived that the submission of such a people, effected by such means, could never be permanent; that his Irish sovereignty, if not actually precarious, must be inevitably embarrassing. He found that his narrow revenues were inadequate to the expenses of perpetual and desultory warfare; and truly conceived, that the most certain, cheap, and feasible mode of retaining his new subjects in due subjection, would be by fomenting the jealousies which had reduced them to his authority, and aggravating those feuds which he had promised to extinguish; and thus, by alternately fostering and depressing the contending factions to embroil them in eternal contests, and leave them no *strength* to regain their independence when they returned to their reason.

This system of misrule, connecting a decrease of their resources with an increase of their ignorance, had then a powerful operation in keeping down the people; and this

* Henry had a temporary palace erected on Hoghill (now St. Andrew Street), Dublin, where he entertained such Irish princes as acknowledged him for their liege lord. The singularity of their dress and manners were subjects of amusement and ridicule to Henry's courtiers. He entertained them on a feast of storks, a bird never eaten in Ireland. These banquets, which lasted nine days ended without any permanent advantage to Henry. Most of the princes and chiefs considered themselves insulted by the familiarity of his followers, and returned home with a full determination to reassert their independence and resist his authority on the first favourable opportunity.

same fundamental and favourite principle of governing Ireland has been effectively adopted by every king, usurper, and minister of England, for seven distracted centuries.

Henry having discovered by experience that his nominal kingdom of Ireland was likely to afford him, in the end, little more than a fertile desert, sprinkled over with inveterate enemies; and that neither peace, nor strength, nor honour, nor what to him was more important, tribute, was likely to be the produce of his newly-acquired territory, became indifferent to its state, and left it to its destiny.

The successors of Henry also perceiving that they possessed but a naked and consuming power, equally unprofitable and precarious, formed the design of colonizing Ireland by English settlers; who, connecting themselves by affinity with the uncultivated natives, would improve their habits and gradually introduce a growing attachment to the English people.

IV. This theory was plausible and meritorious; but the propensities of human nature were not calculated on in the execution; the project was merely abstract, unconnected with any general system of wise or conciliatory government: and the attempt at colonization, instead of producing in the Irish a more congenial feeling only confirmed their hatred, increased their powers, and became one of the keenest thorns that ever pierced the side of British governments.

There is something cordial, open, and joyous, in the native Irish character, which never fails to attract and seldom to attach, strangers who reside amongst that people. Even their errors become contagious by protracted intercourse; and the habits and propensities of the host and of the domiciliated foreigner become quickly and almost imperceptibly assimilated.

This malady became almost epidemic amongst the colonists, whom the policy of England had vainly sent over to improve the people. On all important occasions, the new race evinced a more than ordinary attachment to the place of their settlement, and vied with the Irish in an inveterate hostility to the domination of their own compatriots; and in the direct descendants of those British colonists, England has since found many of the most able, distinguished, and persevering of her political opponents.

CHAPTER XIII.

Irelan 1 kept in a state of oppression and turbulence—Elizabeth becomes Queen—Character public and private of Queen Elizabeth—Henry the VIII.—Fanaticism of the English—True principles of tolerance—Union of religion and political fanaticism—Religious schisms excited through Luther—Violent dissensions—The Irish roused—Cruel tyranny of Elizabeth—Earl of Tyrone excites the Irish—Extract from his speech—General rising of the Irish and old English colonists—Immense slaughter—Confiscation of whole provinces to Elizabeth—Accession of James the First—Comparison with Elizabeth—His wise maxims—Conciliatory principles—Its full success—Charles the First—Disloyalty of the English—Ireland desolated by Cromwell.

I. The English monarchs, disappointed in this plausible project, perceived that colonization was a hopeless expedient, and became more inveterate against "the degenerate English of the Pale," than against the aboriginal natives; and for some centuries in every contest of the two nations, a full proportion of the British settlers, or of their descendants, fell by the executioner, or under the sword of their own countrymen. Through the same vicious policy by which Ireland had been kept in perpetual warfare, it remained in a state of ignorance, misery, and turbulence, when Elizabeth, one of the most sagacious of rulers, and the most unprincipled of women, succeeded to the throne, and to the vices of her father.

Compared with later periods, Elizabeth's sphere of action was contracted. Compared with modern times, her reign was a reign in minature. But at all times it would have been considered a reign of talent, and in all countries a reign of tyranny.

II. She was well adapted to rule over a nation, where, if she governed with success she might govern despotically. The uncontrolled tyranny of her father, had prepared her subjects to admire any thing on their throne superior to a monster. The imbecility of her brother was contrasted with the vigour of her own intellect; and she assumed the British sceptre, with all the advantages which experience and expectation could excite in a worried people.

Her reign is celebrated as the most glorious and admired era of British history; but, with all its merits, it owed much of its celebrity to the darkness of the times, the habitual slavery of the people, the sex of the monarch, and the talents of the ministry. And Charles afterwards lost his head, and James his throne, for assuming a small portion of that despotic rule which is eulogized by the biographers of their female predecessor.

The wisdom of Elizabeth was not the wisdom of philosophy. It was a penetrating sagacity, prompt, vigilant, and inflexible. The energy of her resolution, and her profound dissimulation, surmounted what her physical powers would have been unable to accomplish; at home, she was despotic, abroad, she was victorious; by sea, by land, by negotiation, she was every way successful. The external glory of England arose under her administration. Providence seemed to pardon her disregard of moral principles, and to smile even upon the vices of this celebrated female. The people admired her, because she was a successful queen; and she liked the people, because they were submissive vassals. By the acuteness of her discrimination she chose able ministers. They served her with fidelity, because they feared her anger and they flattered her vanities, because it prolonged her favour. But they served her at their peril; and she selected and sacrificed them with equal policy and indifference.

She affected learning, and she professed religion. In the one she was a pedant without depth; and in the other, she was a bigot without devotion. She plundered her people, to be independent of her parliaments; and she bullied the parliaments to be independent of the people. She was frugal of their money where she had no passion for expending it; and she was generous to her favourites for her own gratification.

Magna Charta had been trampled on by a succession of tyrants. The principles of civil liberty had been forgotten in the country; and, throughout the whole course of her reign, Elizabeth assiduously laboured to retain her people in the most profound ignorance of constitutional freedom.

The word mercy was banished from her vocabulary.

Her administration as to Ireland where she experienced no restraint, gave the strongest proofs that she felt no compunctions. In her nature there was no feminine softness to moderate her cruelties; no moral scruples to arrest her conscience; no elevated generosity to contract her dissimulation. Though she was mistress of the great qualities, she was a slave to the little ones;* and though the strength of her judgment somewhat restrained the progress of her vices, she was intrepid but harsh, treacherous, and decisive; even the spirit of murdered Mary could not appall her fortitude. The eyes of the people were closed by the brilliancy of her successes, and the crimes of the woman were merged in the popularity of

* Mr. Hume's life and character of Queen Elizabeth appear altogether irreconcileable to each other. In his delineation of her *character*, he states her to be a princess of the most " *magnanimous virtues* " In the anecdotes of her life, he states her to have been guilty of as tyrannic, cruel, and treacherous actions as any crowned head (Richard excepted) that ever filled the throne of England. Amongst numerous other examples of her " *magnanimous virtues*," Mr. Hume details her interview with the Lord Chancellor Bacon, when Her Majesty declared with vehemence, that she would order Mr. Hayward, an innocent inoffensive man, to be put upon the rack and *tortured*, solely because he had translated some passages of Tacitus, which Her Majesty's ignorance of that author permitted her to suppose were Hayward's own composition, and were intended to reflect upon herself

Mr. Hume's attempt to apologise for the despotic conduct of Elizabeth certainly requires a very ample apology for himself. He says, " She did not always do what was *best*, but she did what was *usual;*" the most tyrannic political principle ever avowed by any modern historian. What was "*best*" was her imperative duty as a Sovereign, what was " *usual*" (after the reigns of her father and her sister) must be the apology of a tyrant, sheltering the commission of crime under the protection of *precedent*. Mr. Hume might as justly excuse her errors by the precedent of the Emperor of Morocco, who makes the same apology for shooting one of his subjects every morning as a matter of amusement, *because it was usual*. Had some of Mr. Hume's antitheological essays been published in the reign of his favourite Elizabeth, the author certainly would have retracted either on the rack, or among the faggots, every eulogium on her " magnanimous virtues."

As a further exemplification of Elizabeth's " magnanimous virtues," Mr. Hume states also (vol. v. page 449), a letter of that Queen, to the Earl of Sussex, expressing her displeasure, that *proper severity* had not been exercised against some *English* insurgents, although it appeared, that his Lordship had *previously* hanged above *eight hundred* of them to gratify his mistress. However, this was merciful, in comparison with her orders to Carew and Mountjoy, as to the Irish.

the monarch. Such was the British princess, who first projected an extirpation of the aboriginal Irish; and she soon discovered and put into action the most deadly weapon to effect her purposes.

III. Her father, Henry, the Nero of British history, had assumed, as a pastime, the trade of a theologist; and changing his religion as often as he decapitated his consorts, at length settled his veering faith, by declaring himself a Reformist, with the most unqualified intolerance.

Theological disputes, after this important auxiliary to the Reformation, altogether divested the minds of men of the attributes of common reason; and the blackest enormities were considered as the most holy virtues, if they corresponded with the fanaticism of deluded imaginations.

Henry's sectarial versatility had extended not only to his subjects, but to his children. Mary and Elizabeth had embraced adverse tenets with equal pertinacity; and the whole population of England plunged at once, under the cloak of religion, into the commission of the very crimes which were prohibited by its precepts.

One moment of calm unbigotted reflection must convince every man, not only of the folly, but of the impiety of such controversies. The point is plain, the dogma simple, that no human authority should control man, as to his choice of what words he may utter, what language he may adopt, what posture he may choose, or what ceremonies he may practice, in the abstract act of piously supplicating the mercy of his Creator.

Common sense, however, had taken its flight from England; and the doctrines of Martin Luther, not a founder, but a fanatical Reformist, soon became the greatest scourge that had ever been laid in chastisement upon a sinful people.

His doctrines, which professed only to simplify the exercises of Divine worship, to purify religion from the dross with which it had amalgamated through priestcraft, to diminish the mysteries of Revelation, and reconcile the inconsistencies of Christian theories, failed in its professed end, and instantly kindled a fanatic fire which enveloped in its flames the reason of mankind; and which, daily supplied with new fuel, has continued to the present day alternately smothering and blazing, and consuming, with an inextinguishable violence.

IV. The incendiaries of modern times have preserved this destructive fire for their own purposes. They perceived that the return of reason must be the death of fanaticism, and that *discord* amongst a people would not survive the extinction of *religious prejudice*, without the aid of some new excitement; political feuds have been therefore cultivated, as theological ones were losing ground; and a novel and complicated system of discord has been invented which, by artfully entangling the *theory* of politics with the *theories of religion*, and fallaciously affecting to render their *combination inseparable*, has perpetuated animosities which were declining with rapidity. And this culpable and insidious policy appears to have been most sedulously and successfully cultivated in Ireland.

Elizabeth, even in those early times, well knew the efficacy of this species of weapon, to inflame, to divide, and to conquer.

The Reformation (now fully established in England) furnished her with a weapon for the general subjugation of Ireland, more fatal and effective than the keenest sword which had been whetted by any of her predecessors for the same purpose.

V. The later of the English settlers in Ireland had embraced the novel doctrines of Luther. The natives and the old English colonists adhered to the original faith. This portion of the people, therefore, persecuted and stigmatised, sunk into ignorance; and, hunted down as outlaws, finding *no protection* but with their chiefs, and *no instruction* but from their clergy, naturally attached themselves to both with a savage fidelity. Elizabeth took advantage of every circumstance to attain her objects. The reformation was not only proclaimed, but enforced in Ireland with unexampled rigor. A few adopted, most rejected, but none comprehended it. Elizabeth having lighted the firebrand at both ends, tossed it amongst the people. The sects fought around it, and Elizabeth's officers gave out, " Reform," as the watch-word of the combatants, and the pretext for extermination.

The contending factions massacred each other without

mercy or compunction, and without any intelligible reason for their individual animosities.

The famished, harassed people, in the midst of blood and flame, naturally became alive to every feeling, and susceptible to every argument, which could show them the way to even a prospect of alleviation. Their chiefs and their clergy were their only instructors, who in the wild, strong, persuasive language of their country, impressed in glowing figures on the shivering multitude, the excesses of their misery, fired their irritable minds by a distant prospect of deliverance, and harrowed up all the feelings of hatred to their oppressors, which torture and famine had implanted in their bosoms.

Elizabeth proceeded systematically in her projects. She first ordered the performance of the Catholic worship to be forcibly prohibited in Ireland. She ordered *the rack* to be employed, and directed her officers *to torture the suspected Irish*. She ordered free quarters on the peasantry to gratify her soldiers, and rouse the natives to premature insurrections. Her executioners were ordered to butcher them without mercy. Religion was abolished by *martial law*, and Divine worship prohibited under pain of death.

This curious order of Queen Elizabeth remains still on record. By her instructions to the Deputy of Munster (Carew) in 1598-9, on his going over to carry her exterminating schemes into execution in that country, she authorizes her officers to " put *suspected* Irish to the *rack*, and to *torture* " them when they should find it *convenient*." Carew fulfilled her Majesty's instructions to their full extent, and at the conclusion of his government she had the satisfaction of finding that Munster was nearly depopulated.

It is here well worthy of reflection, that the exercise of free quarters and martial law, the suspension of all municipal courts of justice, the *discretional* application of the *torture* to *suspected* persons, executions in cold blood, and the various measures which Mountjoy and Carew, and the other officers of Elizabeth practised in Ireland by her authority in 1598-9, were again judged to be expedient, and were again resorted to with vigour in the years 1798-9, two hundred years after they had been practised by the ministers of Elizabeth. The ruinous misrule of Ireland for nearly two centuries, and the errors of Elizabeth's barbarous policy, are proved beyond all controversy by the extent of improvement in Ireland, and in the habits of the Irish people, in a very few years, under the mild and benevolent administration of James the First, her successor, and the adoption by him of a system of government diametrically the reverse of that which had been practised by Elizabeth, proves that Ireland advanced more in loyalty, prosperity, and civilization, under a temperate and conciliating administration in a few years, than in four centuries of coercion and severity; a precedent which should never have been lost sight of by British ministers, but to which they seemed too long to have been either entirely blind, or criminally inattentive. Ireland never was governed, nor ever can be ruled, by any *coercive* system, and those who think otherwise know little of her character.

Harassed by every mode that the ingenuity of oppression could inflict or dictate, the natives, already barbarised by servitude, became savage by irritation; and at length the whole population, wrought up to frenzy, flew into resistance, and have been libelled as traitors to the British crown for asserting the indefeasible rights of human nature, and claiming the enjoyments of civil liberty, for which their allegiance to Elizabeth was only a "*condition subsequent.*"

IV. The Earl of Tyrone, an Irish chieftain, was a man of great talents, and for those days a powerful leader. Skilful, courageous, and persevering, he raised the standard of insurrection against the government of Elizabeth. He represented to the wretched natives in the animating colours of uncultivated eloquence: "The miseries they had been enduring under the tyranny of their oppressors."

He presented to their view the proclamation of Elizabeth to extinguish for ever the religion of their ancestors. He told them, "that the power of endurance had arrived at its final limits, that an attempt for their liberation

* This principle has since become an acknowledged maxim, and component part of the British constitution: yet was violated in *Ireland* by William, the same prince through whose usurpation it was established.

though unsuccessful, could not even by its failure aggravate their miseries. That death would be the worst they could experience by battle, and that death was preferable to the slow tortures they were enduring, the famine under which they languished, and the desolation of their families."

He impressed upon their heated minds, that "their lands were overrun by foreign soldiers; their homes plundered or enjoyed by the butchering bands of an English female; that their race of princes had become a family of slaves, and their clergy had been executed as the guiltiest felons:" and he invoked them, "in the name of their country, by the memory of their ancestors, and the holiness of their religion, to rise as one man, and liberate all from their tyrants." Nor can an impartial reader of Irish and English history deny that there was great crimes in Elizabeth's government, and much justice in Tyrone's representations.

The event was a general insurrection of the aboriginal natives, aided by a great number of the *English* settlers, who had become connected by affinity with the Irish chieftains. But in all such contests, a multitude of naked insurgents, without arms, without officers, without any discipline or much subordination, without any of the necessary requisites, except courage and numbers, which could resist a trained and accoutred army, must naturally be defeated, and, if defeated, have seldom reason to expect mercy from the conquerors; such was the fate of Tyrone and his followers.

VII. At the conclusion of these dreadful campaigns, though the Irish people had been diminished by nearly a moiety, and though the entire of Ulster, and a great proportion of the other provinces, were confiscated to her Majesty,* Elizabeth had not sated the voracity of her rancour. The chiefs had been reduced to beggary, the clergy had been executed, the people slaughtered, their towns destroyed, their castles razed; yet still she felt that Ireland was not *extinguished*. Though under the weight

---

* A circumstantial account of this most sanguinary insurrection was afterwards published under the immediate authority of the Queen. Though the *Peccata Hibernia*, as a history, cannot be an impartial one, yet there is a species of horrid candour runs through the pages of that work which gives it altogether strong claims to a *partial* authenticity.

of such an enormous pressure, the chiefs still breathed, but it was the breath of vengeance. The clergy were recruited from inveterate sources; and even the very name of England and Reformation was rendered detestable by the savage cruelties of Elizabeth's Reformers.

Similar efforts of that determined and indefatigable Princess to crush the Irish people were renewed, resisted, and persevered in during her long reign. Ireland appeared to Elizabeth as a country of Hydras; every head she severed produced a number of new enemies: she slaughtered and she burned, but she could not exterminate; and, at length, she expired, leaving Ireland to her successor, more depopulated, impoverished, desolated, ignorant, and feeble, but in principle more inveterate and not more *subdued*, than the day on which she received its sceptre.

VIII. James the First, unfortunately for his own fame, succeeded to so gaudy a reign as that of Elizabeth. A great proportion of his better qualities was thrown away upon the English Nation. Intoxicated by the renown and splendour of Elizabeth's successes, they undervalued the advantages of tranquillity and of improvement. An English Queen of powerful talents, and a Scottish King of moderate capacity; a woman of undaunted fortitude, and a man of personal imbecility; a proud, magnificent, and dignified female; an awkward, shambling, unaffected Monarch, drew down the sarcasms of superficial ridicule upon one of the best reigns for the internal and prospective happiness of the people.

James's system of government was as distinct as possible from that of his predecessor's. While the reign of Elizabeth abounded in wars abroad and despotism at home, that of James was tranquillity every where; the rudiments of civil liberty slowly and gradually advancing, at length became very visible in the results of his mild and pacific, though whimsical administration. But it was in Ireland that the government of James was most remarkable and most *fortunate;* for the sword, the torture, the executioner, and desolation, he substituted improvement and well regulated justice. He sent not a Mountjoy nor a Carew to inflame and massacre; he sent Davies and Petty to investigate and to instruct, to reform and tranquilize.

They sought to convince the natives, by examples and by reasoning, that their ancient laws and customs were less just than the laws of England; and by practising, as far as circumstances could admit, those principles of justice which they so earnestly recommended, gave the people the very best proofs of the integrity of their intentions.

James had been taught, by experience, that *loyalty to Monarchs* never can be *compulsory*; it is not loyalty if it be not *principle*, and it cannot be principle if it be not *voluntary*: past events in Scotland and in England had proved to James, that the loyalty of *force* is but the *lucid interval* of insurrection. He therefore sought to persuade, not to subdue, his Irish subjects; and, to moderate their feelings, and to render them susceptible of persuasion, he thought it necessary to give them overt acts of his own moderation.*

Himself a *bigot* of the first order, yet he knew how to make allowances for the same vice in others; he knew that religious persecution is the assassin of morality, and he substituted his pen for his sword to reform his subjects. Thus James, a most bigoted Protestant Monarch, by tranquillity and moderation, by wise measures and wholesome instruction, *conciliated*, and governed in peace and improvement, a nation of rude and *exasperated Catholics*, still bleeding from the scourge and the sword of his predecessor; and by that conduct James laid the basis of whatever civilization that country afterwards attained to.

The reign of James amply demonstrates that Irish *loyalty* was fully commensurate with royal tolerance; and that whilst plots against his life, and conspiracies against his throne, abounded in England, and debased the British character, a *Catholic population* in Ireland remained faithful to a *bigoted Protestant of England;* and by their conduct, during this reign, unequivocally disproved the charge of native disloyalty. Their advance-

* It cannot be controverted that many acts of civil injustice were committed by Chichester and other officers of James in Ireland, under colour of the Commission of Escheats, and of defective titles which can only be palliated by a comparison with the reign he succeeded to, and the times he lived in; at all events the reign of James the first was the only truly paternal Government ever experienced by Ireland, from its first annexation to the present day.

ment in civilization amply repayed both the people and the monarch; and it is deeply to be regretted, that *no* government of England followed the same course, to tranquilize a country, whose turbulence has ever been a theme for their calumnies and their severity.

However, Providence had decreed that, with the exception of James the First, whether kings, or queens, or usurpers, were the rulers of Great Britain, the same destructive and desolating system should be adopted as to Ireland; all nations, save her, *had some intervals* of tranquillity; she had *none;* and the more she suffered in the cause of royalty, the more she was branded with the charge of disaffection.

IX. When Charles the First succeeded to the throne, the doctrines of Luther were yielding fast to new sects in England. The united standard of bigotry and of treason was now elevated by the Puritans far above the sphere of all former sectaries; and the British Constitution (such as it was in those times) was, at once, demolished even to its foundation. Rebellion and hypocrisy marched hand in hand triumphantly over its ruins; and the intolerance of Mary and of Elizabeth only changed its garb, but retained its principles, in the practice of Cromwell.

The English Commons House of Parliament renounced its allegiance, cashiered the Lords, extinguished the episcopacy, and dethroned their King. The English Rebels subdued him; the Scots betrayed him; conjointly they beheaded him; but Ireland upheld him. She combated his murderers, and, as the reward of loyalty, she met the fate of Rebels.* The wrecks of Cromwell's desolation still appear scattered over every part of Ireland; blood that had escaped the massacres of Elizabeth was only reserved to flow under the sword of usurpation; and Cromwell has the credit of having done his business more effectually than any of his predecessors. He cooped up the surviving Irish in a contracted district, confined the clergy nearly to one country, confiscated two thirds of

---

* So great a hatred did the English Parliamentarians entertain against the Irish Royalists, that they ordered " *No quarter* to be given by their troops to *Irish Soldiers.*" This order was, for a short time, strictly adhered to; but Prince Rupert, on the King's part, making retaliation, this most sanguinary measure was quickly rescinded.

Irish territory, and stained his sanguinary career by indiscriminate massacres in every fortress that resisted him.

Never was any Rebel so triumphant as he was in Ireland; yet it is impossible to deny, that perhaps a less decisive or less cruel general than that splendid usurper, might, by lenity have increased the misery, in prolonging the warfare, and have lengthened out the sanguinary scenes of an unavailing resistance. But it is remarkable that Charles, the graceless son of the decapitated monarch, on his restoration, confirmed under his seal the confiscations against the Irish *royalists*, and actually regranted their estates and territories to the heirs and descendants of his father's murderers.

CHAPTER XIV.

Restoration of the Stuart dynasty — Usurpation of William — Ireland remained loyal—Comparison of the people—The revolutionary principle undefined—The Irish treated as rebels by William for their loyalty to their King—Character of William the Third—Continued oppression and malgovernment of Ireland—The Scotch and English rebelled—Ireland remained tranquil—Comparison of the English and Irish as to their kings—Ireland first infected by the Scotch and English rebellions—Mr. Pitt suppressed the spirit of insurrection in England promptly—Suffered it to increase in Ireland.

I. IRELAND had now been weary of bleeding and begging in the cause of legitimate monarchy; however, a new and not less ruinous opportunity soon occurred of again proving the loyalty, the perseverance, the fidelity, but the folly of the Irish people.

The Puritans had got out of fashion, and the Stuarts had been restored to the British sceptre. Charles the Second, after a long and shameless reign, had by his death, ceased to disgrace the throne and stigmatize the nation; and *England* swore *allegiance* to his brother James, as her *legitimate monarch*, so did Ireland. His English subjects soon became disgusted with his administration, and *privately* negociated with a *foreign* prince to invade their country, and dethrone their king. Heedless of their obligation, they renounced their *allegiance*, recanted their *oaths;* and, without a trial, drove James from his palace, and then proclaimed his throne empty, as if vacated by an act of voluntary abdication.

At the head of his foreign guards, William, unequivocally an usurper, marched into the metropolis of Great Britain, seized on the throne, and occupied the royal palaces. The unnatural desertion of Mary and of Anne to the prince who had dethroned their parent, exhibited to the world (whatever might have been the *political* errors of their father) the most disgusting example of filial ingratitude, and nearly of parricide.

Ireland had not as yet learned those deep political refinements, the adoption of which *now* gives constitutional *sanction* to the *principle* of revolution. That great precedent was to come from England herself. Ireland experienced not, or at least had not felt, James's attempts at despotism, which the English Commons had proclaimed to be a forfeiture of his sceptre.

The *pretence* of his *voluntary* abdication, on which England had proceeded to dethrone her king, had not extended its operation to Ireland, *nor even been notified to that people.* On the contrary, James, a monarch *de jure* and *de facto*, expelled from one portion of his empire, threw himself for protection upon the faith and the loyalty of *another;* and Ireland did not shrink from affording that protection. She defended her *legitimate* monarch against the usurpation of a *foreigner;* and whilst a *Dutch* guard possessed themselves of the British capital, the Irish people remained firm and faithful to their king and fought against the invader.

In strict matter of fact, therefore, England became a nation of decided rebels, and Ireland remained a country of decided royalists. Historic records leave that point beyond the power of refutation.

At the period of James's expulsion, even in England the *right* of popular *resistance*, and the deposition of a British monarch, by a simple vote of the Commons House of Parliament, though exemplified by Cromwell, had no acknowledged place in the existing constitution of the British empire. It was then an *unsanctioned* principle of political polity; and though, in *theory*, according with the original nature and essence of the social compact between the *governor* and the *governed*, yet of the utmost difficulty in its constructions, and dangerous in its execution. Even now the quantity or quality of arbitrary acts and unconstitutional practices which may be deemed sufficient to put that revolutionary principle into operation, remains *still undefined*, and must, therefore, be a matter of conflicting opinions, and of most dangerous investigation; but it is an open argument.

II. The representatives of the people in the Commons House of Parliament are incompetent *solely* to enact the most unimportant local statute; it is therefore not easy to designate the cause and crisis which may legally invest that one branch of the Legislature with a dispensing power as to the others, or enable it to erect itself into an arbitrary tribunal, to decide by its sole authority, questions of revolution.*

As to James, this difficulty was exemplified. The British Commons, and the Irish people, *both* subjects of the *same* king, entirely differed in their opinions as to what acts, regal or despotic, could be construed into *voluntary abdication*, a point of great importance as to subsequent events which took place in Ireland.

III. James was the *hereditary* king of both countries, jointly and severally. The *third* constitutional estate, only of *one* of them (England), had deposed him by their own *simple vote:* but Ireland had never been consulted upon that subject; and the deposition of the King of *Ireland* by the *Commons of England* could have *no* paramount *authority* in Ireland, or supersede the rights, and dispense with the *loyalty*, of the Irish Parliament. The Irish people had held no treasonable intercourse with William; they knew him not; they only knew that he was a foreigner, and *not* their *legal* prince; that he was

* Though the English Commons House of Parliament had taken upon themselves to dethrone and decapitate Charles the First, on their own *sole authority*, it will scarcely be contended, that Bradshaw and Cromwell established any *constitutional* precedent for a *similar* proceeding. Yet the proceedings of the Commons, in James's case, though more peaceable, were not more legal.

The *vacancy* of the English throne, and consequently the deposition of James, was strongly contested and negatived by the House of Peers of England. The questions and divisions of the House of *Lords* were as follows,—

For the *election* of a *new* king, . . . 51
Against the election of *any* king, . . . 49

Majority, . . 2

The next debate came more to the *point*—" whether James had *broken* the *original compact*, and *thereby* made the throne *vacant?"*

This was *negatived* by a *majority* of 2.

It therefore appears, that the Irish people and the English *Peers* were of the same way of thinking. Even *after* James had quitted Ireland in despair, the Irish did not relinquish his cause, which was finally terminated by the gallant defence and ultimate capitulation of Limerick for the whole of Ireland.

supported by a *foreign* power, and had succeeded by *foreign* mercenaries. But even if there was a doubt, they conceived that the most commendable conduct was that of preserving entire their *allegiance* to the King, to whom, in conjunction with *England*, they had *sworn* fealty. The British *Peers* had showed them an example, and on that principle they fought William as they had fought Cromwell: and again they bled, and again were ruined by their adherence to *legitimate monarchy*. Massacre and confiscation again desolated their entire country, and they were treated by William as rebels to a throne which they had never sanctioned, and to an usurping prince whom they had always resisted; at length, the contest ended, and Ireland finally submitted, not in the *field*, but by capitulation.

The triumph of William over the Irish Royalists at the Boyne and at Aughrim, and the *deceptious* capitulation of Limerick, finally established William on the throne of both nations. Their results introduced into the *theory* of the British Constitution, certain principles of a *regenerating liberty*, which have given it a solid and *decided superiority* over every *other* system of Government as yet devised by the wisdom of mankind; yet the advantages of that constitution which England has thus raised upon the *loyalty*, and completed upon the *ruins* of Ireland, never were *participated* in by the Irish people.

William, an able captain, a wise and prudent statesman, was yet a gloomy and discontented magistrate; and had in his nature a portion of sulky despotic principle, which nothing but a consideration of the mode in which he had acquired the English crown could have restrained or counteracted. But as to Ireland, the case was different. William had been invited into England, and he felt that she was his mistress; but he had fought for Ireland, and he considered her as his vassal, and he adapted his government to the relative situation in which he stood as to the two countries.

The massacre of Mac John, his family and clan, in the valley of Glenco, perpetrated by the especial order of William, under his sign manual, has, in point of barbarity, treachery and injustice, no parallel in the annals of Europe. Its details cannot be read without exciting horror; and while it develops the cold-blooded nature of William's character, it accounts for much of his conduct towards the Irish royalists, whom he called rebels, but who owed him no allegiance; so far as it bears upon the events of his reign in Ireland.

The result of William's usurpation, in the general establishment of constitutional liberty in England, and the principles of popular revolution which his accession has sanctioned and confirmed, have rendered the memory of his reign glorious in that country. But little did he foresee his restraints and disappointments on the throne of England; there he felt his arbitrary nature unexpectedly curbed and chained down by the principles of that same liberty, which his own usurpation had originated; and mortified by the resistance he experienced in Great Britain, he lavished his redundant rancour on prostrate Ireland. But had William acted in Great Britain as he did in Ireland, he would have lost his throne, upon the very same principles by which he acquired it, and have left his own short reign as an historic supplement to the deposition of his father-in-law.

IV. For nearly a century after the capitulation of Limerick had been signed and violated by William, Ireland exhibited a scene of oppression, suffering and patience, which excited the wonder and commiseration of every people of Europe. The inveterate system of British political and commercial policy invariably practised against her interests, excluded all hopes of progressive prosperity, and if it were possible, she must have entirely retrogaded to the iron age. But even during this state of depression, it was destined that Ireland should have new touchstones and trials to assay her nature; and again be placed in situations where her loyalty should be proved, and again found preponderating in the balance with the loyalty of Great Britain.

In 1715, and in 1745, the British and Scotch people again forgot their oaths and their allegiance, and again revolted in favour of that very prince whom Ireland had been so ruined and stigmatized for defending against themselves.

The Stuarts again claimed the aid of Ireland. But Ireland, in the interval, had sworn fealty to the House of

Brunswick; and Ireland, though groaning under slavery remained faithful to her obligation. Neither oppression no politics, *nor religion*, swayed her from the line of her allegiance. The noblest blood of Scotland was poured upon the scaffold; the heads of Scottish Peers were elevated upon the gates of London; Britons in crowds expiated their disloyalty by the cord of the executioner; the anger of offended Brunswick fell with desolating weight upon Great Britain; but through all those bloody scenes, English ingenuity could not find *a single traitor* to execute in *Ireland*. She preserved her loyalty and her oath, during two rebellions, but she gained neither favour nor character by that preservation; and her laudable fidelity was only rewarded by new oppressions, and by the incessant calumnies of that same people who had seldom lost an opportunity of being *themselves disloyal*. Tranquil and submissive, though in absolute servitude, nearly one hundred years passed over Ireland. The great population of the Irish nation continued to be deprived of every attribute of liberty, civil, political and religious.

A few of the Penal Acts then in force, or since enacted, against Catholics, were—" *By 7th William III*," no *Protestant* in Ireland was allowed to *instruct* any *Papist*. " *By 8th of Anne*," no *Papist* was allowed to *instruct* any *other* Papist. " *By 7th William III*." no Papist was permitted to be sent *out* of Ireland to *receive instructions*.

By these statutes, as the great body of the Irish people were Roman Catholics, more than nine-tenths of the inhabitants of Ireland were legislatively prohibited from receiving *any instruction* whatever, either from a Protestant or a Catholic, either at *home* or *abroad*, or from going *out* of Ireland to be *instructed*; consequently the darkest and most profound ignorance was enforced under the severest penalties in Ireland. How then can the Irish Catholics admire the *memory* of that prince who *debased* them to the level of brutes, that he might *retain* them in a state of slavery?

Even so late as the 12th George I. any Catholic clergyman marrying a Protestant and Catholic was to be *hanged*. " *By 7th George II*." any barrister or attorney marrying a Catholic, to be *disbarred*. " *By 2nd Anne*," Papist clergymen coming into Ireland, and performing religious exercises, to be *hanged.* " *By 8th Anne,*" Fifty pounds reward for all informers against Catholic archbishops and vicars-general.

But the most extraordinary of these Penal Statutes, is that of 7th William III. No Papist to ride any horse worth more than £5. And by *9th George II. Papists* residing in Ireland, shall make *good* to *Protestants* all *losses* sustained by the privateers of *any Catholic king ravaging the coasts of Ireland.*

29th George II. *barristers* and *attorneys* obliged to *waive* their *privilege,* and *betray* their clients, if *Papists.*

Literally outlaws in their own country, labourers on their own territory, they quarried on their own demesnes, to raise palaces for the descendants of those canting hypocrites who had massacred their monarch, or of the foreign soldiers of that gloomy and ambitious prince, who had seduced away the loyalty of the children from their parents, and had occupied the throne of their banished father.

V. If the future is to be judged by the past, it will probably continue to be alleged, that the adherence of Ireland to her kings has rather been the result of her religion than of her loyalty. That observation could not in any degree be applicable to any reign but that of James, an imputation, however, which in its true construction, general or especial, goes to assert, that a connection of loyalty and religion so cultivated and extolled in England under the title of " Church and State," was a crime of the most heinous culpability when found in Ireland. But when historic facts are resorted to, that charge is retorted; and it will hardly be contended, that it was more loyal and meritorious for Protestant subjects to murder their Protestant king, as they did in England, than for Catholic subjects to defend their Catholic king, as they did in Ireland. And it will be as difficult to defend the rebellions of 1715 and 1745, raised by British Protestant subjects against their Protestant king, as it will be to calumniate the undeviating, unshaken loyalty of Catholic Ireland to her Protestant monarchs, and the House of Brunswick, during the same periods. But unfortunately these indisputable facts will form this miserable precedent for future ages, that in *England the reward of rebellion was liberty; while in Ireland, the reward of loyalty was bondage.*

The Irish insurrection of 1798, which afforded to the British minister the fatal and *premeditated* pretext for annihilating the Irish legislature, differed but little in its ordinary events from those numerous civil wars, which the history of England, and of every nation, so liberally abound with; and more especially with those which desolated some of the finest countries of Europe about the same period, the contagion of which had been imported from *England herself*, where the overthrow of the constitution had been planned, and the murder of the King attempted, *before Ireland had been infected.*

But it was reserved for the recorders of that sanguinary contest in Ireland, with motives not less mischievous than those of the insurgents, to raise by their misrepresentation a permanent standard of enmity between the two nations, and endeavour to persuade one portion of the empire, that its safety was altogether incompatible with the independence and prosperity of the other.

Were the leading authors of these absurd and dangerous doctrines, confined solely to the hired traducers or factionists of that country, their histories and their fabrications would sink, together with their names, into obscurity. But when persons of the superior orders in Great Britain lent their weight, their zeal, and their reason to the purposes of their bigotry and their prejudices, and attempted to impose upon the credulity of their countrymen with the same facility that they had been imposed upon themselves, as to the native disloyalty of the Irish people, it becomes just, if not necessary, to recall their recollection to the affairs and records of their own country at the same epoch: a reference to which, if it cannot check the fanaticism, may at least diminish the authority of the fanatics.

Though in fact a digression, it may be here not improper to follow up that subject a little further, by anticipating some observations more connected with a subsequent part of this memoir.

VI. When it pleased Heaven, during the French Revolution, to inflict a temporary derangement on the reason of mankind, a spirit of wild democracy, under the mask of liberty, appeared in fanciful forms to seduce away or destroy the peace, the morality, the order, and the allegiance of every European people. It would have been more than a phenomenon, if too sensitive and ardent Ireland had escaped that general fever, from which the boasted constitution of England, and the steady character of Scotland, had been unable to protect them. The Catholic in the South, the Presbyter in the North, the Protestant in the metropolis of Ireland, and the professors of every religion in England and in Scotland, became more or less infuriated by the general delirium. That contagion which so vitally affected the nations of Europe, originating in France, soon displayed its symptoms in every part of Great Britain; and when in progress to full maturity, *and not before*, was carried into Ireland by collision with the *English and Scots republicans.**

Religion could have but little influence on the projects and politics of that era, for the total extinction of *all* religion was a fundamental principle of that foreign revolution, which gave birth to a democracy that sought to overturn every throne and constitution of Europe. Yet the calumniators of Ireland place that spirit of insurrection almost exclusively to the credit of religion amongst the Irish people, because the population of Ireland, was chiefly composed of Catholics whom they stigmatized.

At that period, Ireland had a resident Legislature and a free constitution. She was in profound tranquillity, and the most progressive state of national prosperity,† when

* See the state trials and the reports of the Secret Committee of England, in the year 1794.

By these reports of the Secret Committee, it appears that Edinburgh, and various other places in England and Scotland, were infected long before Ireland; and Mr. Secretary Dundas Illustrated these reports by annexing accurate drawings of the different forms of *pikes*, battle-axes, &c., which were fabricated in *Scotland*, his own country, for the purposes of treason and murder. Ireland did not appear to Mr. Pitt forward enough in treason with the kingdom under his more immediate management, and therefore sent over Lord Fitzwilliam to Ireland, to ensure tranquillity; and when his Lordship was on the point of doing so, ordered him back again to excite insurrection.—*See Lord Fitzwilliam's letters to Lord Carlisle.*

† When Lord Westmoreland was removed from Ireland, in 1795, Ireland was in a most unexampled and progressive state of general prosperity. In that year, Mr. Curran informed the Author of his intention to

the emissaries of the English and Scotch societies qui҅k҅l҅y҅ proceeded to pervert her reason, as their own had been perverted. The original societies of Ireland had no such principles as designated the latter ones. The Minister, Mr. Pitt, had made his entrance into public life in the domino of a Reformer. The first and most loyal noblemen, and commoners in Ireland were Reformers; but it was through the prospective policy of that great Minister, that the seeds of insurrection were permitted to take root in Ireland: without it a union had never been accomplished.

VII. In England, the Government took prompt and vigorous measures to stop the progress of that dangerous and destructive principle; but in Ireland they coolly saw the weed springing up, and artfully forced it to premature maturity. They watched its growth till it had covered sufficient of the country to bewilder the residue. Its vegetation was cautiously permitted to proceed, whilst there remained within their own reach sufficient means of suppressing it at their discretion; and this deep and treacherous experiment was risked to effect the greatest object of Mr. Pitt's administration, a final extinguishment of Irish independence.

With that view, it was expedient to suffer that country to plunge itself into a state of sanguinary civil warfare, of terrors and of animosities; whilst England should hold the reigns which could check its progress, and might fallaciously induce it, by the hopes of English protection, to exchange a constitutional independence for a speculative tranquillity, or render it so feeble and so divided by a

---

suggest an impeachment against the Earl of Westmoreland, for having permitted a part of 12,000 troops (which, according to stipulation, should always remain in Ireland) to be drafted out of that kingdom for foreign service.

Mr. Curran laughed at his own project, when the Author asked him what plausible *reason* he could give for saying that any troops were *necessary*.

The day Lord Westmoreland departed, *no* army was necessary in Ireland; and if Earl Fitzwilliam had not been removed, doubtless insurrection might have been prevented. But tranquillity would not have effected Mr. Pitt's purposes: and Earl Fitzwilliam, one of the best and honestest of the British peerage, was appointed, duped, and deposed by the policy of the Minister; the reason was obvious.

continuation of internal contests, that it could not be seduced, it might be compelled, to annexation.

And here lies the secret spring which regulated the insurrection of 1798, and the machinery which moved the Union in 1800, a measure which, for the thirty-two years succeeding its accomplishment, has only operated as a ruin to the annexed, and a torment to the annexing nation. Recorded abstracts of Irish and of British history thus form an incontrovertible exposition of Irish principles, and of English misconception. The character of the Irish people has been always calumniated, their independence has been torn away, but their indigenous loyalty is unaffected, their nation is monarchical, they naturally love kings, the tradition of their old monarchs keeps up the attachment; and never was a greater injustice done to any people, than to call them democratic. But immortality of power is not an attribute of nations, like man, they flourish; but like man, they must decay. Rome had her glory and her power, but, subdued by time, she yielded up her empire; and should some Gibbon of future ages record the decline and fall of British greatness, the historian will probably do justice to Ireland; and tell posterity, that when some gigantic foreign power, nurtured by British folly, for British subjugation, had paralyzed her resources, and decolonized her empire, England, in the last struggles of her superiority, had not a faithful ally left to cover her remains, but her calumniated* sister.

* This observation will not be considered altogether visionary, when men reflect upon the modern events of Europe, and the possible consequences of that extravagant and ruinous system which had been adopted, of blindly subsidizing and strengthening every foreign power at the expense of the British treasury. Russia, Prussia, Austria, Portugal; but above all, Spain, owe their present *independent* political existence to the blood and the treasure of Great Britain and of Ireland, levied for their use, and lavished for their protection.

And miserably is England requited for her protection, her money, and her sacrifices: and miserably has Ireland been requited for her participation.

CHAPTER XV.

Catholic relaxation Bills opposed by Mr. Rowley—Sir Edward Newenenham—Doctor Patrick Duigenam—His Character—Mr. Ogle—Bills passed—Unjust doctrine—Change in the Irish Parliament—Mr. Fox's candour—His speech—Deception of the British Government developed — Marquis of Rockingham—Total absence of energy—Mr. Burke—Inactive as to Ireland—New debates—Embarrassing consequences of Mr. Grattan's address—Mr. Grattan's motion objectionable —Mr. Flood's reply—Unfortunate collision of Grattan and Flood— Mr. Grattan's fallacious motion—Mr. Flood's reply—Mr. Montgomery moves to build an Irish navy—Negatived—Parliament prorogued—Most important session—Moderation of Ireland—Duke of Portland's hypocritical speech.

I. WE now return to the measures which were taken to rock Ireland into a slumber more fatal to her existence than the trance she had awakened from. Bills to ameliorate by partial concession the depressed state of the Catholics, as some reward for their zeal and patriotism, were introduced, and had arrived at their last stages in the House of Commons without any effective opposition; intolerance, however, even to the extent of fanaticism, had so identified itself with the minds of some members of both Houses of Parliament, that these Bills of partial relief to their enslaved countrymen were strenuously opposed, in their latter stages, by statements so exaggerated, and language so aggravating, that a cry of "Danger to Church and State!" was raised and circulated, and actually bewildered the intellect of many, who were on other occasions of reasonable judgment.

These Bills were clamorously opposed in Parliament by several country gentlemen of high local consideration, and principally by Mr. Rowley, member for Meath County, one of the best landlords and best men in Ireland, a downright, honest, headstrong country gentleman. His information was scant, and his abilities were less than moderate; but he was of large fortune, splendid establishments, unbounded hospitality, and full of philanthropy;

yet so perverted was his mind by legendary tales, and hereditary prejudices, that though he most generously afforded to his Catholic tenantry, and to individual Catholics, every service and kindness in his power, he considered and represented them, *collectively*, as a body of demons; their chapels, temples of idolatry; their schools, seminaries of rebellion, and their clergy as a gang of necromancers.

So infatuated was he by these prepossessions, that he saw, or rather fancied that he saw, in any relaxation of the penal statutes, nothing but a total overthrow of the entire Protestant establishment, and an immediate revolution in favour of some Popish monarch.

Those Bills were also pertinaciously opposed by Sir Edward Newenham, member for Dublin County, a weak, busy, narrow-minded, but not ill informed, nor ill-intentioned person. He was very defective in talent, but very confident that he possessed much of it; he fancied he was a great patriot, and was disposed to imagine himself a distinguished personage. He had drawn General Washington into a short literary correspondence with himself as to Ireland, on the strength of which, he affected, with great importance, to be an importer of the most early and authentic information from America.

He was an active officer of the Volunteer Artillery, and a good Irishman; but a busy, buzzing, useless, intermeddling member of Parliament, and one of the most credulous, feeble, and fanatical of all the Irish intolerants.

Many inveterate opponents of any concessions to the Catholics made their appearance in the Irish Parliament; and as the concerns of that body must form a prominent topic in the progress of this memoir, it may be interesting and useful to introduce, even by anticipation, the most distinguished of its opponents.

This celebrated antagonist of the Irish Catholics, so far as invective and declamation could affect their interests, was Doctor Patrick Duigenam, Judge of the Prerogative Court of Ireland; a man whose name must survive so long as the feuds of Ireland shall be remembered, and whose singular conduct, on many points, was of a nature so inconsistent and irregular that, even now, when his race is run, and no further traits of his character can ever be developed, it is yet impossible to decide with certainty as to his genuine principles, if such he possessed, upon any one subject, religious or political.

His father was parish-clerk of St. Werburgh's Church, Dublin, but in what part of Ireland he originated, is still uncertain; he was educated in the Parish School, and (as he told the Author himself) was humourously christened *Paddy*, having been born on St. Patrick's day. He signalized himself as a scholar in the University of Dublin, of which he was chosen a fellow; he soon afterwards quarrelled with the Provost, Mr. Hutchinson, and every person who did not coincide with his humours, and wrote a number of severe pamphlets, of which "*Lachrymæ Academicæ*" and "*Pranceriana*," are the most notable; the first, personally against the conduct of the Provost and Sir Sohn Blaquiere; the second, on a proposal of the Provost's to establish a *riding house* for the students. He was always at open war with some person, during the whole course of his public life.

He left the University, retaining the office of Law Professor; was shortly afterwards appointed King's Counsel; Judge of the Prerogative and Consistory Courts; King's Advocate to the High Court of Admiralty; one of Lord Castlereagh's Commissioners for *bribing Members of Parliament;* (Post;) and to many other public offices, most of which he retained to his death. His income was very large, and he must have privately done many liberal and charitable acts, because he was not extravagant, and left no considerable fortune behind him.

Dr. Duigenam having been King's Advocate to the High Court of Admiralty, where the Author presided; and the Author being a Doctor of Laws, and Advocate in the Court of Prerogative, of which Dr. Duigenam was Judge, their intercourse was constant and very intimate for many years, and the Author had daily private opportunities of observing the curious habits of this most eccentric character; the most outrageous, and at the same time one of the best natured men in the world, to those whom he regarded.

This eccentric person, whose celebrity originated from his crusades for Protestant supremacy, would probably have been a conspicuous character in whatever station he might have been placed, or in whatever profession he might have adopted. Incapable of moderation upon any subject, he possessed too much vigorous and active intellect to have passed through life an unsignalized spectator; and if he had not at an early period enlisted as a champion of Luther, it is more than probable he would, with equal zeal and courage, have borne the standard for St. Peter's followers. A hot, rough, intrepid, obstinate mind, strengthened by very considerable erudition, and armed by a memory of the most extraordinary retention, contributed their attributes equally to his pen, and his speeches.

He considered invective as the first, detail as the second, and decorum as the last quality of a public orator; and he never failed to exemplify these principles.

A partisan in his very nature, every act of his life was influenced by invincible prepossessions; a strong guard of inveterate prejudices were sure, on all subjects, to keep moderation at a distance, and occasionally prevented even common reason from obtruding on his dogmas, or interrupting his speeches.

A mingled strain of boisterous invective, unlimited assertion, rhapsody and reasoning, erudition and ignorance, were alike perceptible in his writings and orations; yet there were few of either, from which a dispassionate compiler might not have selected ample materials for an able production.

He persuaded himself that he was a true fanatic; but though the world gave him full credit for his practical intolerance, there were many exceptions to the consistency of his professions, and many who doubted his theoretic sincerity. His intolerance was too outrageous to be honest, and too unreasonable to be sincere; and whenever his Protestant extravagance appeared to have even one moment of a lucid interval, it was immediately predicted that he would die a Catholic.

His politics could not be termed either uniform or coherent. He had a latent spark of independent spirit in his composition, which the minister sometimes found it difficult to extinguish, and dangerous to explode. He had the same respect for a Protestant bishop that he would probably have had for a Catholic cardinal. Episcopacy was his standard; and when he showed symptoms of running restive to the Government, the primate of Ireland was called in to be the pacificator.

He held a multiplicity of public offices at the same time, unconnected with Government.* He was Vicar General to most of the bishops; and whenever he conceived the rights of the Church were threatened, his bristles instantly arose, as it were, by instinct; his tusks were bared for combat; he moved forward for battle; and would have shown no more mercy to the Government than he would have done to the patriots.

He injured the reputation of Protestant ascendency by his extravagant support of the most untenable of its principles. He served the Catholics by the excess of his calumnies, and aided their claims to amelioration, by personifying that virulent sectarian intolerance which was the very subject of their grievances.

He had, however, other traits, which frequently disclosed qualities of a very superior description. His tongue and his actions were constantly at variance; he was hospitable and surly; sour and beneficent; prejudiced and liberal; friendly and inveterate. His bad qualities he exposed without reserve to the public; his good ones he husbanded for private intercourse. Many of the former were fictitious; all the latter were natural. He was an honest man, with an outrageous temper and perverted judgment; and, as if he conceived that right was wrong, he sedulously endeavoured to conceal his philanthropy under the garb of a misanthrope.

In private society, he was often the first in conviviality; and when his memory, his classic reading, and his mis-

* On the Union, he accepted the office of Commissioner for paying the bribes to Members of Parliament (under the name of *compensation* for the loss of their *Seats* or *Patronage*.) (Vide Post.)

The Doctor, the late Lord Annesley, and a Mr. Jameson, an Englishman, under this commission, *distributed*, by Lord Castlereagh's appointment, ONE MILLION FIVE HUNDRED THOUSAND POUNDS of the Irish money, amongst Members of the Houses of Lords and Commons; without which bribes and gifts of peerages, there would be a vast majority *against* the Union. The Doctor told the Author that he accepted that office, solely that he might be able to take care of the *bishops;* and the Author believes at least half his assertion. But the bishops were outwitted.

cellaneous information were turned to the purposes of humour or of anecdote, they gave a quaint, joyous, eccentric cast to his conversation, highly entertaining to strangers, and still more so to those accustomed to the display of his versatilities.

The most striking singularity of this most singular man, was his unaccountable inconsistency in words and actions toward the Catholic community. He alternately fostered and abused, caressed and calumniated, many intimates of that persuasion; an inconsistency, however, which his last matrimonial connection was supposed to have redeemed; and he died at a very advanced age, upon a short notice, retaining all his strength and faculties, and in the full vigour of all his prejudices.

His strong, sturdy person, and coarse, obstinate, dogmatic, intelligent countenance, indicated many of his characteristic qualities. He was too rough and too unaccommodating to have had many partisans; and after the Union which he vigorously supported, his public importance and reputation dwindled away to nothing; and his death afforded no great cause of regret to his friends, or of gratification to his enemies.

Mr. George Ogle, and many other decided opponents of the Catholic claims, were also prominent characters in the general affairs and politics of the country, and will appear in most of the miscellaneous transactions of the Irish Parliament. But the whole bent and efforts of the Doctor's mind and actions were concentrated and publicly arrayed against the Catholic community, some members of which were in private his chief associates, and his nearest connections, and the early introduction of such a personage may tend to illustrate the singular situation of that body, and that inconsistency which from first to last has signalized the conduct both of their friends and their enemies.

Those Bills relaxing the severity of the penal code passed, however, through both Houses, without any considerable difficulty; and, though the concessions were very limited, they afforded great satisfaction to the Catholic body, as the first growth of a tolerating principle, which they vainly imagined was a sure precursor of that general religious and political freedom, without which, in an ardent and divided population, peace and security must ever be precarious.

Some men, however, saw in those incipient concessions the germ of discord and extravagant expectation. The most unrelenting of their opponents, in the full zeal of unqualified fanaticism, used arguments so cruel and unjust in principle, that the distorted mind, or crooked policy of legislators alone could have resorted to.

They argued, that the nearly insupportable oppressions under which the Irish Catholics had so long laboured, were rapidly disgusting them with their own tenets, which had entailed upon them all the attributes of slavery and deprivation; that, worn down by penal codes, under the pressure of which they could neither rise nor prosper, they were daily recanting those disqualifying tenets, and embracing that religion, under which their wants and their ambition could be fully gratified; that noblemen, gentlemen, peasants, and even their priests, were rapidly embracing the Protestant profession; and that if the same propensity to recantation was still kept in progress, by a full and strict continuance of that same penal code, the severity of which had originally caused it, Ireland would gradually acquire a protestant population, if not a majority of the people, at least more than a proportion of all whose property, rank, and interest would lead them to preserve the peace of the nation and the connection with Great Britain.

II. This was a barbarous doctrine, which could never be supported by any principle either of justice or of policy. The principle of concession which actuated the Parliament in these relaxations, proved that the light of justice and reason had broken in upon them, and excited reasonable expectations of further grants and general toleration.

The wealth of the Catholics multiplied, their numbers increased. The first chain of intolerance was loosened, and permitted them to take a view of that total emancipation which by unremitting struggles they were certain of attaining.

III. The paroxysms of ardent patriotism having somewhat abated in the Irish Parliament, distinctions and shades of distinctions were rising and re-opening into party, and into jealousies. Some men conceived that

Ireland had obtained every thing, others argued that she had acquired no securities, that enthusiastic unanimity which had so proudly signalized their first movements was gradually degenerating, the old courtiers, who had wandered from their standards, seized greedily upon every pretence to re-assume their stations; and many of that body, who a moment before had been unanimous, and supposed to be incorruptible, now began to remember themselves, and forget their country; but the people were staunch, their spirit was invincible, the voice of the volunteers was raised it was loud and clear, and echoed through the Parliament. The Government was arrested in its corrupting progress; many were recalled to a sense of duty by a sense of danger, and the situation of the country seemed approaching to another *crisis*.

Mr. Grattan acted on the purest patriotic principles, but they were over moderated by Earl Charlemont, and occasionally neutralized by an honourable confidence in Whig sincerity. He still contended (because such was his conviction) that the Irish Nation should rest satisfied, and confide in the sincerity of the British Ministry, and the existing guarantees, for the permanence of their constitution. He was devoted to the Whigs, because they professed the purest principles of well-regulated liberty; and he would not doubt the integrity of those whose principles he had adopted, till at length Mr. Fox himself, wearied by a protracted course of slow deception, uncongenial either to the proud impetuosity of his great mind, or the natural feelings of his open temper, at once confirmed the opinions of the Irish people, and openly proclaimed to Ireland the inadequacy of all the measures that had theretofore been adopted. He took occasion in the British Parliament, on the repeal of the sixth of George the First, being there alluded to, to state, "that the repeal of that Statute could not stand *alone*, but must be accompanied by a final adjustment, and by a solid basis of permanent connection." He said "that some plans of that nature would be laid before the Irish Parliament by the Irish Ministers, and a *treaty* entered upon, which *treaty*, when proceeded on, might be adopted by both Parliaments and finally become an *irrevocable* arrangement between the two countries."

By that short, but most important speech, the Irish delusion of a final adjustment was in a moment dissipated, the Viceroy's duplicity became indisputably proved; His Majesty's reply to the Irish Parliament was renounced by the very minister who had written it. The Irish address to the Duke of Portland appeared to have been premature and inconsiderate; and his reply could no longer be defended on the grounds either of its truth or its sincerity. Mr. Fox himself, with the true candour of an able statesman, avowed the insufficiency of the existing arrangement; and thus, by easy inferences, decided against the adequacy of the simple repeal for general purposes. His declaration, that "a further treaty was in contemplation," was prospective and ambiguous, and gave not only plausible but justifiable grounds, for an alarming uneasiness amongst the Irish people.

Notwithstanding this avowal, Mr. Flood was still but feebly supported in the House of Commons. The Volunteers, rather than the Parliament, had now the preponderance in public estimation, and their activity increased as difficulties augmented.

In England public matters were sinking into a state of languor and torpidity. The Marquis of Rockingham, in a fatally declining state of health, and his friend Lord Charlemont, in an habitually complaining one, carried on a well-bred, superficial, whining correspondence, as to the affairs of Ireland, every thing that was courteous, but nothing that was statesmanlike; and even if death had not unfortunately for the Whigs, snatched away Lord Rockingham, he and the Earl of Charlemont were not likely to effect the consummation of the political arrangements between the two nations. The latter nobleman could see wide, but he could not see deep. The former could neither see very wide, nor very deep, but he could see very distinctly; in cultivating moderation, they lost sight of energy, and their conduct at this moment was shallow and insipid.

Mr. Burke might have been sincere towards Ireland; but he had a game to play at for himself; and his talents, however great in their extent, were not found so consistent in their application. And though his fame never can be eclipsed, his abilities never depreciated; though his lessons will be ever instructive, and the vigour of his intellect could not be vanquished, still he had his trances, his visions, and his theories; and though always in the first line of general admiration, he stood not in the front rank of public confidence. He took no distinguished part in those transactions, appearing as if he were repugnant to commit himself in an imperfect treaty.

Whilst affairs remained in this precarious state, a debate occurred, more embarrassing than any that had preceded it, and which gave new features to the close of this, the most remarkable session of Irish Parliaments.

IV. The question of simple repeal had now been so often canvassed, so often argued, and had caught so strong a hold of the Irish people, that it was obvious it could not rest where it was, and that something further must be done to satisfy the Irish Nation; but what that something should be, was more embarrassing to the Government of both countries than any consideration which had theretofore occurred to them.

After the address of the Irish Commons to his Majesty, moved by Mr. Grattan, England could not be again so strongly applied to for further concession. She had promptly acceded to every thing that was *then* required of her, and was told by that address, that nothing remained further to be done as to a constitution between the two countries; she might, therefore, plausibly decline further demands upon the same subject. That address had in plain language, renounced all further constitutional claims by the Irish Parliament; and Mr. Grattan could not recede from such his own reiterated declarations. Mr. Flood, however, remained unshaken and firm in his opinion of the insufficiency of the arrangement, and determined to increase their security, through an unequivocal act of the Irish Legislature; and on the twenty-ninth day of July, he moved for leave to bring in a Bill, " to affirm the sole exclusive right of the Irish Parliament to make laws affecting that country, in all concerns *external* and *internal* whatsoever."

A most animated, and even virulent debate, took place on that motion. It was debated with great ability, but ill-placed confidence or ill-timed moderation still guided the majority of the Commons; and even the introduction of the Bill was negatived without a division.

Mr. Grattan heated by the language of his rival, blinded by an unlimited confidence in the integrity of the Whig Ministry, and for a moment losing sight of the first principle of constitutional liberty, then proposed a motion, equally singular for the language of its exordium, and the extravagance of its matter. He moved, "that the Legislature of Ireland was independent; and that any person who should propagate in *writing*, or *otherwise*, an *opinion* that any right whatsoever, whether external or internal, existed in any other Parliament, or *could* be *revived*, was inimical to both kingdoms."

The ingenuity of man could scarcely have formed a more objectionable precedent or dangerous resolution. It was too great an opportunity not to be taken immediate advantage of by Mr. Flood; his reply was equally severe and able; he represented the resolution as "placing Ireland in a state of tyranny worse than Russia; prohibiting both the Lords and Commons of Ireland, under a denunciation of being enemies to their country, from the common rights of every British citizen, to discuss the same constitutional question which had been so often before, and was at that very moment, debating in the House of Parliament, depriving every Irish subject of his natural liberty, either of speech or of writing: a proscription against all who differed with the honourable gentleman on a vital question respecting his own country, or who should presume to publish or even to whisper that difference, a resolution which would be scoffed at in Ireland, ridiculed in Great Britain, and be contemptible in both, a resolution which could have no operation as a law, no justification as a principle, and which could have no character to support it, but those of folly and of tyranny." He therefore moved an adjournment. The tide, however, flowed too strong against Mr. Flood personally. It was the great object of the Government to conquer him first, and then neutralize his adversary; and even those who were determined to negative Mr. Grattan's motion, also determined to negative the motion of adjournment, because it was Mr. Flood's; and a considerable majority decided against it.* Mr. Grattan then proposed another declaratory resolution, stretching away from the real facts as to any political application of those that existed, but unaccompanied by most of the former objections; and, at all events, leaving both his own and Mr. Flood's principles nearly where it found them at the commencement of the altercation. Mr. Grattan moved, that leave was " refused to bring in the (Mr. Flood's) Bill, because the sole and exclusive right to legislate for Ireland in all cases whatsoever, internally and externally, had been asserted by the Parliament of Ireland, and had been fully, finally, and irrevocably acknowledged by the British Parliament."

This resolution obviously stated some facts which did not exist. No final irrevocable acknowledgment ever had been made by the British Parliament. On the contrary, acts had been done, and declarations made by the Minister himself, that a future treaty would be necessary to render the arrangement full, final, or irrevocable.

Mr. Flood saw the weak point, and he possessed himself of it. He altered his language, became satiric, and ridiculed the resolution as the " innocent child of fiction and of fancy." He congratulated Mr. Grattan on changing his tone, and declared " that he would willingly leave him in the full enjoyment of this new production of his lively imagination." Mr. Grattan's motion then passed without further observation, and the House adjourned.

V. No further proceedings of importance took place in the House of Commons during the session, except two motions of Mr. Montgomery, of Cavan County, for leave to bring in a Bill to build Irish men of war for the protection of the trade of Ireland. This motion appeared too

---

* The division was ninety-nine to thirteen against Mr. Flood's motion, though the whole House saw clearly that Mr. Grattan's resolution could not possibly pass; yet so strong was the opposition to *any thing* proposed by Mr. Flood, that an adjournment was rejected. This debate, so near the termination of the session, appeared at first very disagreeable; but in the event it had great effect; and the embarrassments which Mr. Grattan's resolution, if *carried*, must necessarily have created, was a very strong ingredient amongst those considerations which induced the British Parliament voluntarily to pass an Act of *Renunciation*, which Mr. Grattan had thought unnecessary, before the Irish Parliament could meet again to discuss the subject, when the accumulating dissatisfaction of the nation might have given rise to more distracting measures.

distinct, and was of course negatived. He also moved for an address to the King, to reinstate Mr. Flood in his office of Vice Treasurer, from which he had been dismissed for supporting his country. This would have been just, but it was not eligible. Mr. Fitzpatrick received it in civility, but it was also negatived, as encroaching on the prerogative; and on the 27th of July, the Duke of Portland prorogued the Parliament, with a speech detailing all the advantages Ireland had received under his paternal administration; and thus ended the public transactions of his Grace the Duke of Portland's first viceroyalty to the Irish nation.

VI. This session of the Irish Parliament was the most interesting and important its history records; important, not to Ireland only, but to the best interests of Great Britain; illustrative of the first and finest principles of civil liberty; and a lecture on the rights and foundations of rights, by the establishment of which alone the independence of nations can be attainable, or, being attained, preserved. It displayed a scene of loyalty and of forbearance in the Irish nation, unequalled in the history of any armed people. It proved the possibility of an irresistible democratic power, roused without commotion; the entire population of an extensive country converted into a disciplined and independent army, to assert its liberties, yet, in the pursuit of that most animating of all objects, preserving perfect peace and substantial loyalty. It showed an independent and patriotic army, able in one day to crush or to drive every relic of usurpation from its shores for ever, with a moderation almost incredible; accepting, as a kind concession, those natural rights which it had the power of commanding; and, with a liberal and generous confidence, peculiar to its character, honourably, but fatally, insisting on no further guarantee for her constitution, than the faith of a government which had never before omitted an opportunity of deceiving her.

The Duke of Portland's proroguing speech to the Irish Parliament, July 27, 1782, is in itself the most unsophisticated tissue of hypocrisy on record, totally unparalleled in the history of the British Empire, or of any Minister who regarded either the law of nations, or the character of the sovereign. It was emphatically delivered by a

Viceroy, who, a few years afterwards, in 1800, in his place in Parliament, unblushingly declared, that he *never* considered the treaty between England and Ireland (consummated by himself) as *final*. His Grace's speech, addressed, in the name of the King, to the assembled Peers and Commons of Ireland, on the prorogation of that Parliament, is of the greatest importance, as connected with the events of 1799 and 1800; and when that speech is compared with a subsequent speech of the same nobleman in the Peers of England, not only an Irish subject, but even a disinterested citizen of the world, would draw conclusions in no way favourable to his Grace's political integrity. It was, however a useful lesson to all people, to trust their statesmen just so far and so long as their interest or their party called for their consistence. His Grace was pleased to speak as follows:

" The great and constitutional advantages you have secured to your country, and the wise and magnanimous conduct of Great Britain, in contributing to the success of your steady and temperate exertions, call for my congratulations, on the close of a session which must ever reflect the highest honour on the national character of both kingdoms.

" It must be a most pleasing consideration to you, to recollect, that in the advances you made towards the settlement of your constitution, no acts of violence or impatience have marked their progress. A religious adherence to the laws, confined your endeavours within the strictest bounds of loyalty and good order; *your* claims were directed by the *same* spirit that gave rise and stability to the *liberty* of Great Britain, and could not fail of success, as soon as the councils of that kingdom were influenced by the avowed friends of the constitution.

" Many, and great national objects, must present themselves to your consideration during the recess from parliamentary business; but what I would most earnestly press upon you, as that on which your domestic peace and happiness, and the prosperity of the Empire at this moment, most immediately depend, is to cultivate and diffuse those sentiments of affection and confidence which are now happily restored between the two kingdoms; convince the people in your several districts, as you are yourselves convinced, that every cause of past jealousies and discontents *is finally removed;* that both countries have *pledged* their *good faith* to each other, and that their best security will be an *inviolable* adherence to *that compact;* that the implicit reliance which Great Britain has reposed on the honour, generosity, and candour of Ireland, engages your national character to a return of sentiments equally liberal and enlarged; convince them that the two kingdoms are *now one*, indissolubly connected in unity of *constitution*, and unity of interests; and that the danger and security, the prosperity and calamity of the one, must equally affect the other, that they must stand and fall together."

CHAPTER XVI.

Insufficiency of Mr. Grattan's measures—Death of the Marquis of Rockingham and its consequences—Earl Temple Lord Lieutenant—Mr. Grenville Secretary—His Character—Lord Temple—Not unpopular—Mr. Corry a principal instrument of Lord Temple—Proceedings of the Volunteers—Strong resolutions to oppose English Laws—Bad effects of the dissension between Grattan and Flood—Sir George Young—Effect of Sir George Young's speech—Lord Mansfield's conduct accounted for—Consequence of these speeches—British Parliament belie their own Act—Lord Abingdon denies the King's right to pass the Bill—England by Statute admitted her usurpation, and relinquished for ever her right to legislate for Ireland—Renunciation Act—Mr. Grattan still perversely opposes Mr. Flood—The renunciation Act confirmed Mr. Flood's doctrine.

I. BILLS to carry into effect the concessions of England had been passed through the British Parliament with unusual expedition. The sixth of George the First, declaratory of the dependence of Ireland, had been repealed; and the arbitrary dictum of Blackstone, that favourite Druid of modern Britain, had been abandoned by his countrymen. But it quickly became obvious, that though Mr. Grattan's declaration of grievances had left to the Irish Parliament a certain latitude for reclaiming their constitutional rights in detail, he had not foreseen to what lengths those details might extend, or the danger of attempting to conclude on narrow discussions on that intricate subject. His address to the King now appeared to have so contracted in its tenor the claims which the declaration of grievances, if not specifically, had virtually alluded to, that many of the most important of Irish constitutional rights had been thereby altogether passed over; and concessions of England had been accepted of, without those guarantees which the invariable practices and principles of British government therefore, rendered absolutely indispensable to the permanence and security of Irish independence.

Had the constitutional arrangement been complete and

final, and the concessions of Great Britain as sincere as they appeared to be liberal, and without any view to ulterior revocation, never would two nations have been placed in an attitude more powerful and imposing, or pregnant with happier consequences to the interests and prosperity of both; they would have been firmly united by indissoluble ties, and bound to each other by a Gordian knot, which nothing but the scythe of time could have divided. But unfortunately, England was not sincere. Her cabinet remained mentally intolerant; and Ireland, after ten years of unexampled prosperity, was again destined to future miseries, equally unforeseen and unmerited.

It was for a moment supposed that commercial jealousies towards Ireland, those eternal enemies to every thing generous or cordial, had been at least partially excluded from British councils, to make room for a more just, liberal, and enlightened policy. Had it been so, the interests of both nations would have found their common level in their mutual prosperity; the moral and physical powers of both would have been invigorated and embarked in the same cause, attracting and consolidating their united strength into one impenetrable mass, which would have defied all the enmities, the machinations, and the powers of united Europe.

Arrangements of such a nature, founded on so strong and broad a basis, might have been durable as the ancient towers of Ireland, of which even tradition cannot trace the origin, but which neither time nor the elements have as yet had the power to dilapidate. Ireland was disposed, for a time, to be contented with her Parliament: suspicion is not one of her characteristic feelings; she looked at every object through the sunny medium of her own bright and warm generosity, and threw herself at once into the arms of her sister country. She did not, or she would not, till forced by its glare upon her vision, see the false and fatal artifices by which her independence was surrounded. She disdained to suspect those on whom she had already lavished a noble confidence; and she fancied she beheld all her better fortunes circling, like a glory, round the brow of her new-born freedom.

A phenomenon so novel and captivating, absorbed for a time the reflection of the people, and concealed from them that treacherous reservation, which subsequent events have proved to have then lurked behind the faithless, but specious language of the yielding country.

However, the matter was suddenly brought to a decisive issue. After a lingering indisposition, the Marquis of Rockingham the only link which bound the Whig ministry together, ceased to exist. This loss was irreparable, the cabinet became incomplete, and could not be recruited; its members suspected each other, and the nation suspected them, and, but a short period had elapsed, when the most unnatural and corrupt ministerial coalition in the annals of British Government, between Mr. Fox and Lord North, justified the suspicions of both the people and the parties, and taught Ireland what she might expect from the consistency of British Ministers.

II. A temporary confusion was the consequence of the Marquis of Rockingham's death. However, an entire new ministry was formed, and public affairs in England appeared to be acquiring at least a semblance of some stability.

In Ireland, the scene entirely changed. The Marquis of Rockingham no more, the administration of England remodelled without being improved; and Earl Temple sent over to supersede the Duke of Portland, and to take his chance of governing and tranquilizing the Irish people, as circumstances might warrant.

His Excellency was accompanied to Ireland by his brother, Mr. (now Lord) Grenville, in the office of Chief Secretary; a person not adapted to the habits of that people, the temper of the times, or the circumstances of the country; a proud English gentleman, deficient in that modulation and flexibility of character so useful to a minister, at times when he cannot control, and so peculiarly serviceable at all periods to the temporary rulers of the Irish nation; and as he and his family assumed a leading part, eighteen years afterwards, in the suppression of that constitution which he then came over professedly to complete, it becomes necessary to allude to some of those public qualities which have distinguished that personage in his political capacities on both occasions.

Mr. Grenville had improved by unremitting assiduity, whatever talents nature had entrusted him with: and so far as they could be extended, he worked them up into very considerable reputation, and never failed to exercise them with firmness, though not always with discretion, and occasionally with inconsistency.

He commenced his public course in an Irish office, and he pursued it till he arrived at the British Cabinet. In both he was efficient; but in the first he was mistaken, and in the latter he was overrated. Too unbending for the crown, and too aristocratic for the people, he sought influence from both, without attaching himself to either; and like the coffin of Mahomet, he was suspended between attraction. The popularity of the man was circumscribed by the austerity of the courtier; and the ambition of the courtier, counteracted by the inflexibility of the statesman. His powers were inferior to domination, but his pride superior to subserviency; his party therefore have been placed in a long abeyance, but which certainly could not be well justified, either by the policy of the state, or by the gratitude of the ruler.

The Viceroy, though a grander person was a very inferior statesman. He was a man of business; not less proud, yet rather more accessible than his brother, and would have worked his way better had he been aided by a more elastic secretary. They both mistook their course; they began where they should have concluded; and acted upon the vain idea of diverting away the attention of an ardent people from an animating object, by the novel purity of pecuniary retrenchments. On this erroneous principle, they passed over more important concerns, and proceeded to the detection of official peculations with unprecedented activity; they even sacrificed to this delusive, and comparatively frivolous object, one of the highest officers, and one of the most extensive political connections in Ireland. Earl Temple and his brother thus setting to work steadily, as men of business, laboured to gain a confidence amongst the people by financial reforms, before they had established a foundation for deserving it by constitutional services.

III. However, few acts of the first Temple administration gave the Irish nation any important grounds for complaint or for suspicion. Every day discovered and exposed some new official delinquency, and every day brought its dismissals or its punishments. In other times, and under other circumstances, this meritorious exertion would have had its full weight, and received adequate approbation; but that moment was not an ordinary one; a financial reform was but a secondary object, and was soon considered rather as an interruption to the view of constitutional arrangement, and leading away the attention of the nation from great measures, by those of comparatively unimportant consequence. This system failed in all its objects; the nation saw and despised the principle, they were not in a humour to relish naked financial arrangements, the idea of national indedependence had filled their minds, and popular tranquillity should have preceded financial retrenchment, then it would have been grateful, now it was contemptible.

The Viceroy, however, persevered in his official reformations; and though he obtained no credit from the body of the people, he appeared to make considerable progress amongst the aristocracy of the patriots.

Amongst those whom Lord Temple selected to aid him in this plausible reformation of public abuses, was a person, who, from that period, continued an active and on some occasions, a distinguished member of the Irish Parliament. On the question of an Union, he made himself particularly remarkable, and had nearly ended his mortal career in supporting the minister.

Mr. Isaac Corry, the son of an eminent merchant in Newry, had been elected representative in Parliament for his native town, and commenced his public life under the patronage of that dignified Irishman, Mr. John O'Neil, with great advantages. His figure and address were those of a gentleman, rather graceful and prepossessing; and though not regularly educated, he was not badly informed. He was a man of business, and a man of pleasure; he had glided over the surface of general politics, and collected the idioms of superficial literature; he possessed about a third rate public talent; his class of elocution in Parliament was sometimes useful and always agreeable, but on momentous subjects he was not efficient. In facing great questions, he frequently shrunk back, in facing great men, he was sufficiently assuming. His public principles were naturally patriotic; but his interest lost no time in adapting them to his purposes. He sought to acquire the character of an accomplished financier, but he was totally unequal to the mazes of financial speculation, and there he altogether failed. His private habits and qualities were friendly and engaging, his public ones as correct as his interest would admit of.

As a reward for his fidelity to the Irish Minister of 1799, he succeeded in the first object of his life, the supplanting of Sir John Parnell in the Chancellorship of the Irish Exchequer. But it added little to his emolument, and nothing to his reputation. He wrangled through the Irish Union as a ministerial partisan, and exposed himself as a financier in the Imperial Parliament. His influence was neutralized when he lost his country, his pride was extinguished when he lost his office, and he was defeated at Newry, in which he thought himself established. Like others of his repenting countrymen, he withdrew from public life, upon the purchase of his integrity, regretting past scenes, and disgusted with the passing ones. He lingered out his latter days in an inglorious retirement, the prey of chagrin, and the victim of unimportance. As a private friend, it is impossible but to regret him; as a public character he has left but little of celebrity.

Lord Charlemont and Mr. Grattan, dazzled by specious appearances, placed much confidence in, and formed somewhat of a political connection with the new Lord Lieutenant. But they soon found that it had become imperatively necessary to change the tone of their representations to Government; and during the recess of Parliament, they adopted language very different from and much stronger than that which they had conceived to be sufficient during the last administration. The interval between the prorogation and the meeting of a new Parliament, comprised a period of great importance in Irish history, and merits considerable attention, as bearing strongly on the subsequent transactions which extinguished its constitution.

IV. The armed Volunteers had now assumed a deliberative capacity. Political subjects became topics of regular organized discussion in every district of Ireland, and amongst every class and description of its population.

They paraded as soldiers, and they debated as citizens; and but few days passed over, in which they did not exercise in both capacities. More than 150,000 Volunteers now appeared upon their regimental muster-rolls; prepared to join their standards the moment their country demanded their exertions; an army so constituted must have been strong, an army so animated must have been invincible.

The Catholics now became also practically active in the same cause, considerable bodies of that body now took up arms, formed regiments in several districts, and placed themselves entirely under the command and control of their Protestant officers and fellow subjects. All was unanimity in the armed bodies; but a general discontent and suspicion, as to the conduct of Great Britain, appeared in rapid progress, and proceedings more than usually alarming were occurring every moment throughout the whole nation.

Many collateral and important constitutional points now successively appeared to have been omitted in the claim of rights; and many remained unaffected by the repeal of the English statute, but which sooner or later must necessarily give rise to new and great collisions. The debates of the last session inconclusive in their results, had, without remedying these difficulties, inflamed the people; and a new paroxysm of discontent actually seized upon the entire population. The Volunteers, however, soon placed the matter beyond all doubt or argument; they again entered into decisive resolutions, no longer to obey, or suffer to be obeyed, any statute or law *theretofore* enacted in England, and to oppose their execution with their lives and fortunes.* The magistrates refused to act under them, the judges were greatly embarrassed, no legal causes could be proceeded on, under the authority of the British statutes,† though naming Ireland, no counsel

---

* A few resolutions of the Volunteer corps will serve to show the spirit and temper of the whole; the most important will be detailed in the Appendix.

† *Resolutions, County of Monaghan.* "We, the High Sheriff, Foreman, and Grand Jury of the County of Monaghan, assembled, *Lent Assizes*, 1782:

"Thinking it now peculiarly necessary to declare our sentiments respecting the fundamental and undoubted rights of this nation, we do

would plead them, no juries would find for them, the operation of many important laws, theretofore in force, was necessarily suspended; and matters seemed verging towards great perplexity. The general dissatisfaction made rapid progress, assumed a more decisive attitude, and every discreet person became alarmed for the consequences.

The discussion and arrangement of those numerous constitutional and legal difficulties, though complicated and irritating, appeared absolutely indispensable. It became impossible longer to support the terms of the address to his Majesty, or to argue that "all constitutional questions between the two nations were at an end for ever;" the fact was practically negatived, and all reasoning on the sufficiency of the simple repeal, daily lost its weight amongst the people.

V. Whilst these important subjects were in agitation, and many men's opinions remained undecided in Ireland, the conduct of the British Parliament and of the British Ministry justly confirmed all the suspicions which had been entertained as to the sincerity of Great Britain.

unanimously declare, that we will, in every situation of life, and with all the means in our power, assert and maintain the constitutional rights of this kingdom, to be governed by such laws only as are enacted by the King, Lords, and Commons of Ireland, and that we will in every instance, uniformly and strenuously oppose the execution of any statutes, except such as derive authority from said Parliament, pledging ourselves to our country, and to each other, to support, with our lives and fortunes, this our solemn declaration; and further, we bind ourselves, that we will yearly renew this necessary vindication of our rights, until such time as they shall be explicitly acknowledged, and firmly established.

"Thomas Corry, Sheriff,
"Samuel Madden, Foreman, and Fellows."

Resolutions entered into by the Corps of Dublin Volunteers, on Friday, the 1st of March, 1782, His Grace the Duke of Leinster in the Chair.

"Resolved, That Great Britain and Ireland are, and ought to be, inseparably connected, by being under the dominion of the same King, and enjoying equal liberty, and similar constitutions.

"That the King, Lords, and Commons of Ireland only, are competent to make laws, binding the subjects of this realm; and that we will not obey or give operation to any laws, save only those enacted by the King, Lords, and Commons of Ireland, whose rights and privileges, jointly and severally, we are determined to support with our lives and fortunes."

"Signed (by order), John Williams, Sec."

Every day during the session of Parliament discord had been augmenting: Mr. Flood was frequently victorious in the argument; but Mr. Grattan was always victorious in the majority. Their contests were, at first moderate: but at length, discretion was abandoned on both sides and gave way to altercations, abounding in eloquence, but too personal and too acrimonious to be recorded in these memoirs.

This violent difference of opinion between those two great men, of course communicated its effects, more or less, amongst all their supporters, and became injurious to the general cause of the country. Mr. Grattan firmly believed that he was right; and he would not recede. His pertinacity formed a rallying station for some of the old courtiers, who hated both men, but Mr. Flood most, and gave them a pretence for their re-embodying against the country. Strong parties in Parliament had assailed Mr. Flood, he stood at bay, and no local statesman ever showed more talent, more judgment, more constitutional knowledge, and effective firmness, than he did in this memorable contest.

This divided state of the Irish nation was exactly what the Ministry were desirous to bring about. It somewhat discredited all the Irish parties, gave breathing time to the British Cabinet; and if disunion had extended itself materially to the people, it would have given the Government an opportunity of making arrangements entirely conformable to their own objects. This dividing system however, became entirely defeated by the injudicious conduct of some Members of the British Parliament, who could not restrain their chagrin at concessions which they disapproved of; but carried by their zeal beyond their discretion, their injudicious conduct united parties in Ireland, as against a common enemy.

Events now rapidly succeeded each other, to impress the Irish nation with a thorough conviction that they had to deal with a Government, from whom, neither political sincerity nor cordial concession could be further expected.

VI. Sir George Young, a member of the British Parliament, neither a native nor a resident of Ireland, had been placed in the office of Vice-Treasurer of Ireland, as a sinecure reward for his Parliamentary support of the British Government.

It was an office during *pleasure* only; and therefore no person holding that office could act *contrary* to the desire of the Government which appointed him. Yet so circumstanced, Sir George Young, in his place in Parliament, did *oppose* the Bills of *Concession* to Ireland, and the *repeal* of 6th George I. which had been brought in by the British *Ministers* themselves; he also *protested* against the *power* of passing such Bills by the English Parliament, and disclaimed the power of the King himself to relinquish the inherent rights of the British Legislature to *legislate* for Ireland.

No person, therefore, could suppose, that Sir George Young, a *dependent* placeman, and partisan of the British Ministers, *durst* have so acted, or have ostensibly opposed the King and his *Government*, without the express desire or implied concurrence of the Ministers themselves.

The effect of such a speech, by such a person, at such a moment, was almost electrical; but a much weightier authority against the independence of Ireland soon succeeded it. Lord Mansfield (though one of the greatest, was an arbitrary, and, in some points, one of the most mischievous judges that ever sat upon the English Bench,) notwithstanding the repeal of the 6th of George the First by the British Parliament, proceeded to entertain, in the Court of King's Bench, at Westminster, an Appeal from the Court of King's Bench of Ireland; observing, that " he knew of no law depriving the *British* Court of its vested jurisdiction."

The interest of money in England was only *five* per cent., in Ireland it was *six;* and Lord Mansfield had placed very large sums on Irish mortgages, to gain the additional one per cent. His Lordship well knew that such Irish investments were, in their nature, a troublesome species of security; but that they were not likely to gain any additional facilities by the appellant's jurisdiction being taken from the British Courts and transferred to Ireland herself: hence his Lordship's reluctance to part with it.

These considerations were not concealed by his Lordship. He was forced however to yield to circumstances; but he never did it with a good grace.

VII. The effect of this proceeding was sufficiently alarming; but another exciting circumstance immediately took place, of still higher order. The English Parliament passed an Act, regulating the importation of sugars from St. Domingo to all His Majesty's dominions in Europe. Ireland was a part of His Majesty's dominions in Europe; and this statute was construed as of course embracing Ireland, and thereby constituting an act of external legislation over Irish concerns, by the King of England, and Parliament of Great Britain, without the concurrence of the Irish legislature. This, however, was rather a refinement of construction; but the conduct of Lord Abingdon, in the British Lords, rendered all further confidence in the state of the arrangement between the two countries, as it then stood, totally inadmissible: it was too explicit to be mistaken.

Lord Abingdon, equally adverse to the rights of Ireland, followed, in the House of Peers, the example of Sir George Young in the House of Commons; and totally denying the authority of the King and the Parliament of England to emancipate Ireland, he moved for leave to bring in a declaratory Bill to re-assert the right of England to legislate externally in the *concerns* of Ireland. This remarkable Bill stated, "that the Kings of England being masters of the British Seas for eighteen centuries, and the Western Sea, which surrounded Ireland, belonging to the Kings of England, the British Parliament had the sole right to make laws to regulate the commerce of Ireland, &c."

It was impossible now for the Irish nation longer to remain silent. The aggregate of all these circumstances went clearly to a simultaneous attack upon the new independence of Ireland, and a decisive proof of what might occur when Great Britain acquired sufficient vigour to re-assert, with any prospect of enforcing, her supremacy.

Lord Abingdon's attempt was candid and direct, and, above all others, alarmed the Irish people. The Volunteers beat to arms throughout the whole kingdom; above 120,000 paraded. The Volunteers March was played by every band, and sung by every voice the war hymn of Ireland. All confidence in the sincerity of the British Ministry, its Cabinet, its Officers, its Parliament, was dissipated; and there were not wanting persons who believed and disseminated their opinion, that the rights of Ireland were actually betrayed. The danger and confusion of the times hourly increased; Mr. Flood preserved his firmness and his dignity, and gained much ground amongst the people. The repeal of the 6th George I. could no longer be urged by Mr. Grattan as a guarantee; the sincerity of England could no longer be relied upon; the people began to act for themselves; and the Anglo Irish Government was driven back to its old practices, and endeavoured, by every means within its power to diminish the number and overwhelming weight of their Parliamentary opponents. But the Volunteers were in line: the people cried to arms; the British Cabinet now trembled for the consequences of their own duplicity; yet they had neither honour to relinquish their system, nor courage to support it: they reluctantly perceived it was totally inoperative; and at length became sensible to the imminent dangers of their own situation. They felt the impossibility of either evasion or resistance; and early in the ensuing Session the British Ministry and the British Parliament, without any stimulating debate, and without waiting for further and peremptory remonstrances from Ireland, passed the most important statute that ever had been enacted as to the affairs of Ireland, a statute unequivocally and explicitly renouncing all *future* right to legislate for Ireland. They thereby appeared to have abrogated for ever that principle of legislative usurpation which they had for so many ages pertinaciously and unjustly exercised.

Anno vicessimo tertio.

GEORGII III REGIS.

CHAP. XXVIII. An act for removing and preventing all doubts which have arisen, or might arise, concerning the exclusive Rights of the Parliament and Courts of Ireland, in matters of legislation and judicature; and for preventing any writ of error or appeal from any of His Majesty's Courts in that kingdom from being received, heard, and adjudged in any of His Majesty's Courts in the Kingdom of Great Britain. Whereas, by an Act of the last Session of this present Parliament, (intituled An Act to repeal an Act, made in the Sixth Year of the Reign of his Late Majesty King George the First, intituled An Act for the better securing the Dependency of the Kingdom of Ireland upon the Crown of Great Britain,) it was enacted, that the said last mentioned Act, and all matters and things therein contained, should be *repealed:* And whereas, doubts have arisen whether the provisions of the said Act are sufficient to secure to the people of Ireland the Rights claimed by them, to be bound only by laws enacted by His Majesty and the Parliament of *that* Kingdom, in all cases whatever, and to have all actions and suits at law, or in equity, which may be instituted in that Kingdom, decided in His Majesty's Courts therein finally, and without apppeal from thence. Therefore, for *removing all doubts* respecting the same, may it please your Majesty that it may be declared and enacted, and be it declared and enacted by the King's Most Excellent Majesty, by and with the advice and consent of the Lords spiritual and temporal, and Commons, in this present Parliament assembled, and by the authority of the same, that the said right claimed by the *people of Ireland,* to be bound only by laws enacted by His Majesty and the Parliament of *that* Kingdom, in *all* cases whatever, and to have all actions and suits at law or in equity, which may be instituted in that Kingdom, decided in His Majesty's Courts therein finally, and without appeal from thence, shall be, and it is hereby declared to be *established* and *ascertained for ever,* and *shall,* at *no time hereafter be questioned* or *questionable.*

2*nd.* And be it further enacted, by the authority aforesaid, that no writ of error or appeal shall be received or adjudged, or any other proceeding be had by or in any of His Majesty's Courts in this Kingdom, in any action or suit at law or in equity, instituted in any of His Majesty's Courts in the Kingdom of Ireland; and that all such writs, appeals, or proceedings shall be, and they are hereby declared null and void to all intents and purposes; and that all records, transcripts of records, or proceedings, which have been transmitted from Ireland to Great Britain, by virtue of any writ of error or appeal, and upon which no judgment has been given or decree pronounced, before the first day of June, one thousand seven hundred and eighty-two, shall, upon application made by or in behalf of the party in whose favour judgment was given, or decree pronounced in Ireland, be delivered to such party, or any person by him authorised to apply for and receive the same.

VII. This most important measure was brought into the British House of Commons by Mr. Townshend, passed through both Houses, and received the Royal assent without debate and with very little observation. In England it was cautiously held out neither in the light of a new concession to Ireland, nor of a relinquishment of any then existing supremacy of Great Britain; but as a consequential *declaratory* part of a general constitutional arrangement entered into between the two nations.

In Ireland it was represented as not presuming to create a new, but merely to define a pre-existing constitution. These were wise constructions, and in these points of view gave no alarm nor jealousy to either country; while it seemed to *consummate* the desires and objects of the Irish nation. England had now surrendered all the interests and concerns, constitutional and commercial, external and internal, which Ireland claimed, into the hands and guardianship of her own legislature. To many, this great and finishing concession appeared a conclusive, magnanimous, and sapient measure of the British Ministry. Irish freedom appeared complete; her independence as a nation legislatively acknowledged for *ever*. The great outline of her constitution appeared to have been drawn irrevocably, the possibility of reassumption was regarded as chimerical, and nothing but commercial arrangements remained to be adjusted by the mutual good will, and according to the reciprocal interests of the two nations. For a moment, general happiness, great cordiality, and invincible strength, seemed to be in store for the British Empire, as the result and reward of this wise and honourable confederacy of two independent nations. A union of powers and of interests more dignified, substantial, and invigorating to a people, and more ennobling to an empire, never had existed. And it is grievous to contrast that moment of pride and strength with the desolating measure which in eighteen years afterwards sacrificed the pledged honour and good faith of one nation, to annihilate the independence and paralyze the prosperity of another.*

VIII. This legislative renunciation of British supremacy, however, appeared to some in a different point of view. Mr. Grattan, and many persons of great talent, considered that statute rather a confirmation than a relinquishment of British supremacy, and still adhered more strongly to the adequacy of simple repeal in preference to such a renunciation; and many considered that it did not go far enough. The arguments on both sides were carried on with great warmth and pertinacity; and the doubtful security of Irish independence was debated upon the construction of that very statute which was enacted to confirm it.

This Act of Renunciation, however, appeared to have a conclusive operation. It was conceived by many, that nothing further was necessary to be done, but such as the Irish Parliament was now in itself competent to enact. But though the measure tended to give a strong confidence in the good intentions of the British Parliament, it came too late to satisfy the Irish people as to the purity of their *own*. On the contrary, it convinced them of either its inefficiency or its corruption, or the Renunciation Act of the British Parliament would have been totally unnecessary. Mr. Flood's argument now appeared not only triumphant in Ireland, but fully acknowledged, and legislatively acted upon, even by Great Britain herself. The unfortunate opposition in the Irish Commons, and the still more unfortunate majorities of that House, which had scouted doctrines and measures thus subsequently admitted to be just and necessary, by the voluntary acts of England herself, made a deep impression on the Volunteers of Ireland.

It was true they had acquired their liberties, they had gained their independence; but they still had to *secure* it. The Renunciation Act of England had discredited the Irish Parliament with the Irish people. But it had its apology. It had been so long enfeebled and corrupted, so long within the iron trammels of usurpation,

* A full experience of thirty-two years has proved unanswerably the **truth** of this observation.

that the chain had become habitual, and therefore it was more to be dreaded that its broken links might be rivetted anew, and Ireland, in lapse of time, sink again under the same power which had originally enslaved it. The Irish Declaration of Rights had been one of those sudden events which ages might not again produce; it was the powerful struggle of an enslaved people, and the irresistible energy of an extraordinary man, uniting to command the acquiescence of a corrupt legislature.

Without the people, the Parliament would have been neutralized; and without the man, the people would have been unsupported : and it was indisputable, that whilst the work remained as yet unfinished, the Irish Parliament had slackened in its duties, and relapsed into its old habits of a corrupt and indolent confidence, contrary to every principle of prudence and foresight, and the opinion of the nation : the Irish people, therefore, as they gave credit to the British Parliament for voluntarily conceding what their own Parliament had refused, naturally lost all confidence in the future conduct and purity of their own legislature; a suspicion but too justly founded, and which has given rise to consequences deeply interesting to the fate of that country.

CHAPTER XVII.

Lord Charlemont's courtly propensities—Comparison of Grattan and Flood—Consequences of their jealousy to the country—The people enlightened, learn the true state of their situation—Discussion—And Arguments—Inefficiency of the measures as a future security—A Reform of Parliament indispensable to public security—Mr. Pitt—His duplicity and corruption—Constitutional reasons for a Reform of Parliament—Deduction—Conclusion drawn by the Volunteers—Proved by incontrovertible fact—State of Electors and Representatives compared—Mr. Curran—His character.

I. THESE historic incidents have been anticipated, to give a clearer insight into the interesting and important debates which immediately succeeded them. During the Marquis of Rockingham's lifetime, Earl Charlemont, always virtuous but often feeble, had found something most congenial to himself in the refined habits and mild plaintive disposition of that nobleman; and was led, by his love of order, to conceive a visionary amalgamation of popular rights and ministerial generosity; and the fundamental object of all British Cabinets—disunion amongst patriots—seemed likely to gain much ground through so debilitating a doctrine. Those who were guided by Lord Charlemont's tranquil credulity and courtly moderation, had been disposed to be content with simple repeal. But Mr. Flood had seen the crisis, and had boldly thrown down the gauntlet. Mr. Grattan had as boldly taken it up; direct hostilities commenced; and the same Parliament, which for a moment had been all confidence and unanimity, arrayed itself for combat under two powerful leaders.

Mr. Flood had become most prominent amongst the Irish patriots. He was a man of profound abilities, high manners, and great experience in the affairs of Ireland. He had deep information, an extensive capacity, and a solid judgment. His experience made him sceptical—Mr. Grattan's honesty made him credulous. Mr. Grattan was a great patriot—Mr. Flood was a great statesman. The first was qualified to achieve the liberties of a country—the latter to untangle a complicated constitution. Grattan was the more brilliant man—Flood the able senator. Flood was the wiser politician—Grattan was the purer. The one used more logic—the other made more proselytes. Unrivalled, save by each other, they were equal in their fortitude; but Grattan was the more impetuous. Flood had qualities for a great prince—Grattan for a virtuous one; and a combination of both would have made a glorious monarch. They were great enough to be in contest; but they were not great enough to be in harmony: both were too proud; but neither had sufficient magnanimity to merge his jealousies in the cause of his country.

It was deeply lamented, that at a moment, critical and vital to Ireland beyond all former precedent, an inveterate and almost vulgar hostility should have prevented the cooperation of men, whose counsels and talents would have secured its independence. But that jealous lust for undivided honour, the eternal enemy of patriots and of liberty, led them away even beyond the ordinary limits of Parliamentary decorum. The old courtiers fanned the flame—the new ones added fuel to it—and the independence of Ireland was eventually lost by the distracting result of their animosities, which in a few years was used as an instrument to annihilate that very legislature, the preservation of which had been the theme of their hostilities.

This irreconcileable difference of opinion between two of the ablest men of Ireland, generated the most ruinous consequences for that ill-fated country. Both had their adherents, as pertinacious as themselves. The simple repeal had contented Mr. Grattan and Earl Charlemont; the Renunciation Act was enforced by the perseverance of Mr. Flood and the people, and still considered inconclusive. Both parties adhered to their own conviction; nothing could warp the opinions of either; and to the day of their death their opinions remained unaltered, and events proved that *both* were mistaken.

II. By those two statutes, by daily political discussions amongst the Volunteers, and by a multitude of literary publications, circulated with activity, the people were at length informed of the plain, true facts of their own case and situation. They were reminded, as at their first formation, that Great Britain had long usurped the power of binding Ireland by acts of their own Parliament, and that Ireland had thereby been reduced to a state of constitutional slavery ; that the British Government, intending to carry its usual usurpation to an extraordinary length, had passed an Act in " the British Parliament," during the reign of George I., " binding Ireland by British statutes," cutting off at once every branch of Irish liberty ;* that this statute did not affect to originate any new power by England, but declared peremptorily, that such a right had always existed in the English Parliament, and always would be acted on when it suited the convenience of the British Ministry. They were reminded, that when the Irish nation became too wise and too powerful to be longer retained in subjection, England (in order to pacify the Irish nation) had herself voluntarily repealed that statute declaratory of her pre-existing power ; but did not, by that repeal, renounce the right which she had so long exercised, nor did she in any way declare that she would never *re-enact it:* that the same right remained, in abeyance ; nor had England admitted in any way that she had been *originally* erroneous in enacting it.

III. These being the plain and undisputed facts of the

* When the author uses the term liberty, as connected with Ireland, lest his application of that term might be *misconceived*, he thinks it right to state that he applies the term " liberty," *previous to* 1782, in contradistinction to the *then* existing constitutional subserviency of that country. From 1782 to 1800, he uses it as a constitutional quality, *actually* and fully *enjoyed* by Ireland; and *after* 1800, as a constitutional quality actually *relinquished;* because he thinks, and always has thought, and that in unison with the avowed opinion of many of the King's present law officers and judges of Ireland, that no *detached* distinct nation can be said to possess the attributes of a *constitutional liberty* without a *resident legislature* of her own to regulate her own concerns ; and because he conceives the Union between Great Britain and Ireland, considered *abstractedly* as a *union*, has too much of the "*imperium in imperio*" remaining, to be a *perfect* union of two nations, and too little of it to be a *federal compact;* and he considers that the tie of connection between England and Ireland, as it stood on the 1st *day of January*, 1800, was the most *perfect*, firm, and advantageous union (illustrating the term " liberty") that human wisdom could have devised.

case, it was thence argued that the mere repeal of the declaratory statute, so far from definitively renouncing the existing right of legislation over Ireland, confirmed it; and, by repealing, only enacted the expediency of discontinuing its exercise under existing circumstances. The statute which had *declared* that there existed such a pre-existing right in England to bind Ireland, was indeed repealed by England; but still, though the declaration was repealed, the right was not renounced, and remained only dormant till it might be advisable, under a change of circumstances, to re-declare it by a new statute.

The simple repeal of any statute certainly leaves the original jurisdiction untouched, exactly in the same situation as before the repeal of it, and with an undiminished right to re-enact it as might be convenient: and the 6th of George I., its enactments and repeal, stood exactly in the same situation as any enactment and repeal of any ordinary statute of the same monarch. It was therefore argued, that it had become indispensably necessary, for the security of Ireland, that the British Parliament should, by statutes of their own, not only repeal the Act declaratory of Irish dependence, but also expressly and for ever renounce the *existence* of any such legislative *authority* over Ireland, or future renewal of such usurpation, without which renunciation Ireland had no guarantee for her constitution.

Had the statute of George I. been an assumption of a new authority to legislate for Ireland, its simple repeal would have at once admitted the usurpation of such modern assumption; but as that statute was the recognition and declaration of pre-existing authority, coeval with the British Parliament itself, a repeal could not be binding on any future Parliament, which might at any future time be disposed to re-enact it.

But a statute of the British Parliament and the King of England, by his royal assent, directly renouncing the *pre-existence* of such assumed right by England, pledged all future Parliaments (as far as Parliaments can be pledged) to the same principle, and also definitively pledged all future Kings of England against any future re-assumption or exercise of such power over the Kingdom of Ireland; and though the Kings of England and Ireland must always be the same individual, the realms were totally distinct, their crowns were distinct, though on the same head; and Ireland, possessing her own independent legislature any such future attempt by a King of England would then be a direct breach of the law of nations, and a dereliction of his Irish office by the King of Ireland.

These arguments* became a universal subject of discussion; and were rendered of still greater interest by debates, which every day arose on other points interwoven with the arrangements. Numerous British statutes had been enacted, expressly naming and legislating for Ireland, as if enacted by its own Parliaments. All these remained still in activity, and great inconvenience must necessarily have arisen from an immediate and indiscriminate suspension of their operation. None were enacted in Ireland to supply their places; and great difficulties were occurring. Modern England could not be humiliated by generously declaring that her ancestors had exceeded their constitutional authority as to Ireland. On the contrary, it should have been her proudest boast to have done justice by avowing it. This was not humiliation—it was true glory: and when England, shortly afterwards, actually renounced for ever, by the act of her own legislature, her domination over Ireland, she could not have been much gratified by the temporizing complaisance of the Irish Parliament.

IV. It is also very remarkable, that though Mr. Walshe and the Recorder alone divided against the address of Mr. Grattan, in a very short time afterwards there was scarcely a member of Parliament, or a man in Ireland,

* The arguments used by Mr. Flood and Mr. Grattan on this intricate point, and which finally decided the fate of Ireland, branched out into so many parts, were debated with such ability by both parties, that though the arguments may be compressed, the strength and beauty of the language never can be given in any publication. At all events, those arguments have been published by a number of persons, and partly appear in Mr. Grattan's speeches, published by his son. The author, however, never being on that point of the same opinion as Mr. Grattan, mentioned to him his dissent and his difficulty as to the terms in which he should publish the points and issue of those arguments; and the author has no mode so authentic as by Mr. Grattan's letter to himself on that subject, obviously not a private one, but rather intended, in point of subject, to be made public.

who did not concur decidedly in their opinions; and even the British ministry and the British legislature, by their own voluntary act, confirmed their doctrine. Public discussions on one great subject seldom fail to involve reflections upon others, and these naturally brought the Irish people to discuss the imperfections of their own Commons House of Parliament, and to perceive, that without a comprehensive reform of that department, there was no security against the instability of events and the duplicity of England.

The following letter, however, from Mr. Grattan to the author, appears to throw new and material light upon the subject, and to develop the individual views and politics of Mr. Grattan himself, more clearly than any speech or document heretofore published.

This letter also proves, more than volumes, the insincerity of the Duke of Portland and the English Government: their distinction between the words " recognised" and " established," leaves their political *reservation* beyond the reach of scepticism.

This letter shows palpably the ruin that a want of *co-operation* between two great men brought upon the country; and, above all, it incidentally exposes the courtly, credulous, and feeble politics of Earl Charlemont, so injurious to the public cause, and so depressing to the vigour and energies of its greatest advocate.

To Mr. Ponsonby's chance *remissness* on a future crisis, is attributable the ultimate loss of the Irish legislature, as Lord Charlemont's political courtesy was, on this, fatal to its security. Patriots without energy, as bees without stings, may buz in sunshine, but can neither defend their hive, nor assail their enemy.

" *House of Commons, London,*
" *March,* 2*nd.*

" My dear Barrington,

" I am excessively sorry that your health has been impaired, and I hope it will soon be restored.

" I will get you the *Whig*-Club resolution. They proposed to obtain an internal reform of Parliament, in which they partly succeeded: they proposed to *prevent an union*, in which they failed.

"The address that declared no political question remained between the two countries, had in view to stop the growth of demand, and preserve entire the annexation of the Crown. It was, to us, an object to prevent any future political discussion touching the relative state of the two countries; because we might not be so strong as in that moment. And it was an object to us, and to the English Minister, to guard against any discussion that might shake the connection to which we were equally attached. Fox wished sincerely for the liberty of Ireland without reserve. He was an enemy to an union, and wished the freedom to be annexed to his name.

"The Act of repeal was a part of a treaty with England. A declaratory Act of title is the affirmance of the existence of a former title: the repeal is a disaffirmance of any such former title; the more so when accompanied by a transfer of the possession, *viz.* the transfer of the final judicature and the legislation for the colony-trade of the new-acquired islands, made in consequence of a protest by Ireland against the claim of England.

"The repeal was not any confession of usurpation—it was a disclaimer of any right. You must suppose what I have said, *unsaid*. A man of spirit may say *that;* but he will hesitate to unsay *word by word.* That was the case of England. She would not in so many words *confess* her usurpation, nor did she; on the contrary, when they pressed her, she exercised the power, and said, 'The constitution of Ireland is established and ascertained in future by the authority of the British Parliament.' It was proposed in the House of Commons to change the words, and say 'recognised for ever.' They agreed to the words 'for ever,' and refused the word 'recognised,' and kept in the word 'established.' This, I call making Ireland free with a vengeance.

"I wish, in your History, you would put down the argument on both sides. I can get you Flood's published by his authority.

"I am excessively thankful for the many handsome things you have said of me.

"Your's most truly,
"HENRY GRATTAN.

"*Chevalier Barrington,*
  "*Boulogne, près Paris.*"

V. Their late constitutional acquirements, though apparently confirmed beyond the power of revocation, might be yet a precarious tenure, whilst Ireland had a House of Commons, so framed and elected as to be susceptible of relapse into its former degradation; and though their constitution was not in any state of present danger, future insecurity must be the necessary consequence of a feeble or corrupt representation.

Over the Lords and over the Crown, the control of the people was insufficient and uncertain. It was just, therefore, that they should have a counterpoise, by a House of Commons of their own free selection; and events have since proved that the suspicions were prophetic.

These, and such like reflections, led the Irish people gradually according to their capacities, into a train of constitutional deductions; and suggested topics as to the reform and purity of Parliament, which they had never before thought of.

The great body of a people can never be capable of that cool and discriminating course of reasoning, which individuals or limited delegations are capable of exercising, hence they too frequently, in great general assemblies, follow, whether right or wrong, the sentiments of those who reason more plausibly than themselves, or whose elocution grasps at their feelings, and gives them a factitious superiority over ordinary understandings.

It was impossible that the great body of the Irish Volunteers, which had now assumed the guardianship of Ireland, could be capable of methodical, deep, systematic reasoning, or of unerring political deduction from arguments of enthusiastic and heated orators; but a great proportion of them reasoned by that instinctive power which nature confers on shrewd uncultivated capacities, and on none more than the humble orders of the Irish people; they caught the strong features of their case and their constitution: they knew that they had contributed by their arms and by their energy, to the common cause of their country, they felt that they had been victorious, they listened attentively to their officers, who, more learned than the soldiers, endeavoured to adapt their explanations to the strong, coarse minds which they sought to enlighten, they instructed them as to existing circumstances, and to future possibilities, and thus endeavoured to teach those whom they commanded, not only how to act, but why that principle of action was demanded by their country.

At this time, the visionary and impracticable theories of more modern days had no place amongst the objects of the armed societies of Ireland; but the naturally shrewd and intelligent capacities of the Irish people were easily convinced, that without some constitutional reform in the mode of electing the Commons House of Parliament, they could have no adequate security for permanent independence. They learned that paroxysms of liberty which give rise to revolutions, do not endure for ever, and that the spirit of Irish freedom, which had effected the liberation of their country, might expire, that the independence of the constitution, unless protected by a free parliament, never could be secure, that the enemy might attempt to regain her position, and that the battle would then be fought again under multiplied disadvantages.

Such a reform, therefore, as might insure the uninfluenced election and individual independence of the Irish representatives, appeared to be indispensable, not as a theoretical innovation, nor of a revolutionary complexion, but as a practical recurrence to the first and finest elements of the constitution as it then existed, without any deviation from the principles on which it had been with so much wisdom originally constructed. This species of reformation, and none other, was that which the Irish nation so judiciously sought for; nor were they without high authority and precedent to countenance that requisition. Mr. Pitt, that great, but mischievous and mistaken statesman, at that time professed himself to be a reforming patriot, but it was profession only, his deep and solid intellect was soon perverted by the pride of his successes, and confidence in his omnipotence. He reigned at an unexampled era, his fertile and aspiring, but arrogant genius, led him into a series of grand and magnificent delusions, generating systems and measures which, while professing to save, sapped the outworks of the British constitution, and accelerated, if not caused, the financial ruin in which he left his country. He, however, lived long enough to rule as a minister by that system of corruption which, as a patriot, he had reprobated; and to extinguish the Irish Parliament, by the loyalty and attachment of which his government had been uniformly supported.

The Irish people coincided with Mr. Pitt as to the necessity of a reform; nor did the leading reformers of Ireland materially differ with him in the details of that reformation: the principle was admitted by both nations, but Mr. Flood was undisguised, and Mr. Pitt was in masquerade.

The course of reasoning which led the armed associations of Ireland at that period to decide upon the imperative necessity of a reform of Parliament, was of that sober and convincing nature, which without sophism or declamation, proves itself by the force of uncontrovertible premises, and of plain and simple deductions.

VI. 1st. It could not be denied that the fundamental principle of the British constitution is a perfect relative equipoise and distinctiveness of its three component estates, the King, the Lords, and the representatives of the people.

2nd. It could not be denied, that any deviation from that equipoise and distinctiveness necessarily altered the political symmetry of the whole, and destroyed that counteracting quality of the three estates, on the preservation of which public liberty entirely depended.

3d. It could not be denied that the Members of the House of Commons, forming the third estate, should, by the theory of the constitution, be persons freely selected by the people themselves, to guard above all things against any coalition of the other estates, (the Crown and the Peers), which coalition must endanger the liberties of the people, by extending the prerogatives and powers of the Executive Government beyond the limits the constitution restrains them to.

4th. It could not be denied, that any one individual, arrogating to himself, and actually exercising a power to nominate, and by his own sole will elect and return representatives to the Commons House of Parliament, sent them into that assembly, not to speak the sentiments of the people, but the sentiments of the individual who nominated them, and caused an immediate deviation from

the fundamental principles of the British constitution; but where members of the House of Peers so nominated and returned persons to sit and vote as members in the House of Commons, it was, in fact, the House of Peers voting by proxy in the House of Commons; thereby at once destroying the independence and distinctiveness of the third estate, and enabling the Crown and the Peers, by coalition, to control the Commons, and establish a despotic throne and an arbitrary aristocracy.

The power, therefore, constitutionally conferred on the King by his royal prerogative of creating Peers, coupled with the power unconstitutionally practised by Peers, of creating Commoners, left the people no sufficiently counteracting constitutional protection for their liberties.

5th. It could not be denied, that purchasing the representation of the people in the Commons House of Parliament for money, and selling the exercise of that representation for office, was a constitutional crime of great magnitude; and that when such a practice was publicly countenanced, it of course destroyed the purity of Parliament, the principle of representation, and safeguard of the constitution.

But if these purchases were made by servants of the Executive Government, in trust, for the uses and purposes of its ministers to enable them to carry measures through the legislature, which their naked strength, official character, or the merits of the measure, might be unable to effect, it was unequivocal that such practices put an end totally to all security in the constitution, and that the people must owe the enjoyment of their liberties only to the timidity, the forbearance, or the possible wisdom of an official oligarchy.

The Volunteers now examined existing matters of fact in Ireland as applicable to these premises, and comparing the one with the other, the conclusion became so plain and obvious to the humblest capacities, that the necessity of reform or modification in the mode of electing members for the Parliament of Ireland, required no further argument.

To ascertain the relative matters of fact, as applicable to these premises, the Volunteers caused to be printed and published, lists of their House of Commons, designating the mode of election of every individual; the individual by whose personal influence each representative was elected; the number of persons who nominally returned the member; and, as far as could be ascertained, the money or valuable consideration, paid for such unconstitutional representation. The result of the inquiry left no room to doubt the applicability of those inquiries to a great proportion of the Commons House of Parliament. The Earl of Ely nominated nine members to the House of Commons. The Earl of Shannon nominated seven; and above twenty other members of the House of Lords nominated and elected members for the House of Commons. Many individuals openly sold their patronage, for money, to the best bidder, others returned members at the nomination of the Viceroy or his secretary; and it appeared that the number of representatives elected freely by the people, upon constitutional principles, did not compose one-fourth of the Irish Commons.

VII. An internal reform of Parliament was, on full consideration, deemed quite incompetent to meet the danger. Numerous statutes had been passed to punish, as a public crime, the bribery of an elector; but no law reached the individual who possessed and exercised an influence over electors, and then secretly sold that influence for money or for title. The elector who corruptly voted, was considered as a criminal; but the man who corruptly bought and sold his vote, was tolerated. On the fullest investigation, therefore, it appeared that in Ireland the third estate was, in a considerable degree, nominated by the second estate; that both the second and third estates were influenced by the first estate; and that the whole symmetry and equipoise of the constitution were theoretic, but had no solid or permanent existence.

The Volunteers at length determined to demand a reform of Parliament, and to bring the measure before the existing Commons in a garb which they conceived would render it irresistible; and from that determination arose the formation of a national representative convention of patriotic delegates selected from the armed regiments, the most extraordinary, animating, but unprecedented assembly ever yet beheld in the midst of a people, at the moment enjoying an ascertained constitution.

Had this assembly been conducted with discriminating caution and unflinching firmness, it might have attained all its objects, and have effected a complete renovation of the British constitution, through the Irish people. England would not long have delayed acting on the successful precedent of Ireland. This extraordinary meeting, however, though its objects were not effectuated, brought forward a great mass of talent and of patriotism which had theretofore lain dormant.

During the progress of all political reforms and revolutions, men have been frequently found pressing themselves forward into public notice, solely by the strength of their talents and the power of their energies; springing at once from the humblest ranks of obscurity, to the highest class of reputation.

One of these luminaries was about this period seen arising in Ireland, whose celebrity in that country had no competitor.

John Philpot Curran, a person of humble origin, of careless habits, and contemptible exterior, rose at once to give new lustre and spirit to an already highly enlightened and spirited profession. He had passed through the University of Dublin unsignalised by any very peculiar honours; and was admitted to the Irish bar, scarcely known, and totally unpatronised. With the higher orders, he had no intercourse, and had contracted manners, and adopted a kind of society, tending rather to disqualify him for advancement: but whatever disadvantages he suffered from humble birth, were soon lost sight of amidst the brilliancy of his talent, and a comparison of what he had been, with what he rose to, rendered the attainments of his genius the more justly celebrated. Never did eloquence appear in so many luminous forms, or so many affecting modulations, as in that gifted personage. Every quality which could form a popular orator was in him combined; and it seemed as if nature had stolen some splendid attribute from all former declaimers to deck out and embellish her adopted favourite. On ordinary occasions, his language was copious, frequently eloquent, yet generally unequal, but, on great ones, the variety of his elocution, its luxuriance, its effect, were quite unrivalled, solemn, ludicrous, dramatic, argumentative, humourous, sublime, in irony, invincible, in pathos, overwhelming, in the alternations of bitter invective and of splendid eulogy, totally unparalleled; wit relieved the monotony of narrative, and classic imagery elevated the rank of forensic declamation. The wise, the weak, the vulgar, the elevated, the ignorant, the learned, heard and were affected, he had language for them all. He commanded, alternately, the tear or the laugh; and at all times acquired a despotic ascendency over the most varied auditory.

These were the endowments of early Curran; and these were the qualities which, united to an extraordinary professional versatility, enabled him to shoot like a meteor beyond the sphere of all his contemporaries.

In private and convivial society, many of his public qualities accompanied him in their fullest vigour. His wit was infinite and indefatigable. A dramatic eye anticipated the flights of an unbounded fancy; but the flashes of his wit never wounded the feelings of his society; except, perhaps, those minds of contracted jealousy, which shrink up from the reluctant consciousness of inferiority. He was, however, at times, very unequal. As in a great metropolis (to use one of his own illustrations,) " the palace and the hovel, splendour and squalidness, magnificence and misery, are seen grouped and contrasting within the same precincts:" there were occasions when his wit sunk into ribaldry, his sublimity degenerated to grossness, and his eloquence to vulgarity; yet his strength was evident even in his weakness. Hercules, spinning as a concubine, still was Hercules; and, probably, had Curran been devoid of these singular contrarieties, he might have glided into a brilliant sameness; and, like his great contemporary, Burgh, though a more admired man, he would probably have been a less celebrated personage.

The innumerable difficulties he had to encounter in early life, were not easy to conquer; but once conquered, they added an impetus to his progress. His ordinary, mean, and trifling person; his culpable negligence of dress, and all those disadvantageous attributes of early indigence, were imperceptible or forgotten amidst his talents, which seldom failed to gain a decided victory over the prejudices even of those who were predetermined to condemn him.

His political life was unvaried: from the moment he became a Member of the Irish Parliament his temperature never changed. He pursued the same course, founded on the same principles. He had closely connected himself in party and in friendship with Mr. George Ponsonby; but he more than equalled that gentleman in the sincerity of his politics. From the commencement to the conclusion of his public life, he was the invariable advocate of the Irish people; he never for a moment deserted their interest or abandoned their defence. He started from obscurity with the love of Ireland in his heart; and while that heart beat, it was his ruling passion.

As a mere lawyer, he was in no estimation; but, as an able advocate, he had no rival; and, in his skill and powers of interrogation, he vastly excelled all his rivals. He never failed to uphold the rights and independence of the Irish bar, on every occasion where its privileges were trenched upon; and the Bench trembled before him when it merited his animadversions. None ever assailed him publicly, who was not overthrown in the contest; and even the haughty arrogance of Fitzgibbon seldom hazarded an attack, being certain of discomfiture.*

Mr. Curran was appointed Master of the Rolls (Mr. Ponsonby then Lord Chancellor.) He was disappointed in not obtaining a legal situation more adapted to his description of talents. He was also chagrined at not having obtained a seat in the Imperial Parliament, and at length resigned his office, upon a pension of 2,700l. per annum. He died at Brompton, on the 14th of October, 1817, after a short illness, and now " not a stone tells where he lies." His funeral was private, and he was buried in the yard of Paddington Church. The Author knew him. He had too much talent to last, every thing is worn out by incessant action. He was never fond of show, and in his latter days he both sought and obtained obscurity. Of the close of his life I have heard much, and credit little.

* Mr. Curran and Lord Clare, whilst the latter was Attorney General, had on one occasion a controversy which could only be terminated by a personal battle. The combatants fired two cases of very long pistols at each other, but certainly with very bad success and very little *eclat;* for they were neither killed, wounded, satisfied, nor reconciled; nor did either of them express the slightest disposition to continue the engagement.

CHAPTER XVIII.

Volunteers received by the King—Happy state of Ireland—Progressively prosperous—Untoward consequences of the collision between Flood and Grattan—A second Dungannon meeting of delegated Volunteers—Mr. Flood gains ground—Arguments—A National Convention decided on—Their first meeting—Interesting procession of the Delegates described—Entrance of the Delegates—Extraordinary coincidence of localities—Embarrassing situation—The Delegates meet at the Rotunda.

I. That unparalleled army, the Irish Volunteers, had now ascended to the zenith of their character and prosperity. They had liberated their country from a thraldom of seven centuries, their numbers, their attitude, and respectability, had conquered their independence from a more powerful nation, without bloodshed. The King received at his court, and his levees, with apparent cordiality, Volunteer officers and soldiers who without his authority, formed an army unconnected with his Crown, and independent of his Government: they acted without pay, and submitted to discipline without coercion.

The regular forces paid them military honours; the Parliament repeatedly thanked them for supporting a constitution upon which their establishment had undoubtedly encroached. They were adored by the people, dreaded by the Minister, honoured by the King, and celebrated through Europe. They had raised their country from slavery, and they supported their Monarch against his enemies. They were loyal, but determined to be free; and if their Parliament had been honest, Ireland would have kept her rank, and the nation preserved its tranquillity. The rise and progress of that institution have been already traced; its decline and fall must now be recorded.

At this period, Ireland appeared to have nothing to desire but capital and industry. She was free, she was independent, populous, powerful and patriotic; her debt did not exceed her means of payment; but of trading capital she had insufficient means, and her industry was cramped by the narrowness of her resources. All the materials and elements of industry were within her own realm, and the freedom of trade she had acquired, now promised a stimulus to her commerce which she had never before experienced. The people were united; Catholic and Protestant were on the most cordial terms; the voice of patriotism had exorcised the spirit of discord, the Catholic for the moment forgot his chains, and the Protestant no longer recollected his ascendency; peace, order, and security, extended over the whole Island; no army was required to defend the coasts, no police was wanted to preserve tranquillity, neither foreign nor domestic enemies could succeed against a prospering and united people.

Had the ardent nature of Ireland been then tempered by calm and persevering judgment, had ordinary foresight controlled or guided her zeal, and had rational *scepticism* moderated her enthusiasm, one short session of her own Parliament might have intrenched her independence, and established her constitution, beyond the power or the influence of all her enemies.

Untoward destiny, however, had decreed that unfortunate and ever mal-governed Island to fall into the error by which individuals so often meet their ruin. Having obtained successes beyond their expectation, a mist obscures their vision; they know not where to stop, they rush blindly to the dangers that surround them, and lose by indiscretion what they had achieved by fortitude.

It was justly feared that the too sensitive, credulous, and enthusiastic Irish, in a fallacious paroxysm of gratitude, might raise the drawbridge of their fortress for the admission of their enemies, and, amidst the dissensions of the most able and honest of their warders,* those who sought their overthrow might again penetrate into her citadel.

II. The unfortunate difference of sentiments between Mr. Flood and Mr. Grattan, by enfeebling the authority

---

* The jealousies, the adverse feelings, and discordant proceedings of Mr. Flood and Mr. Grattan, and their partisans, prevented the adoption of measures which might have secured the country against any attempt at union or annexation. See the speech of Lord Castlereagh, on 15th January, 1800.

of both, had diminished the security of the nation. Mr. Flood's diffidence of government was most congenial to the prospective interests of a people long enslaved. The energy of patriots had achieved, but it required the wisdom of statesmen to secure, their newly-acquired constitution. Both, however, united in opinion as to the necessity of a free and independent Parliament to protect that constitution; but no unanimity existed between them or throughout the country, as to the details of that measure.

By this unfortunate collision, the old courtiers obtained breathing time, and the Minister acquired hope. The hundred eyes of the British Argus were keen to discover the failings and frailties of the Irish patriots; nor did they watch long in vain; for a measure, which forms one of the most remarkable incidents of Irish History, soon gave the English Government an opportunity of resuming its operations against that devoted country.

The line of reasoning already described, as to the state of the Parliament, and the necessity for its reform, made a deep and general impression, and was indefatigably circulated throughout the whole nation. Discontent quickly sprang up amongst the people, and their meetings increased. At length delegates from several Volunteer regiments again assembled at Dungannon, to consider the expediency and means of an immediate reform of Parliament. Hence originated one of the most extraordinary scenes in the annals of any country.

III. Mr. Flood was now considered the most able leader of the Irish patriots. Those who supported his opinions still pertinaciously contended, that the measures already conceded were not, in themselves, guarantees for the constitution which had been acquired, or in any respect sufficient for the preservation of independence; that confidence in the existing state of her Parliament, would lull the nation into a fatal slumber, from which she might be awakened only by a new assault upon her freedom; and that no arrangement, without an explicit, formal, and unequivocal recantation by England, of her original usurpations, ought to have been accepted. They urged that such an avowal would certainly have been obtained, if the Parliament had not been corrupted or deceived. They contended, that if England should refuse such a declaration, that, in itself, would be positive proof of her general insincerity; and that if she haughtily persisted in retaining the theory of her usurpation, after the practice of it had been relinquished, it was evident she would watch the first favourable moment to impose still stronger chains than those that she had loosened.

This strong language had already been freely used to rouse the friends of Ireland to a conviction of the versatility which her Representatives had given such practical proofs of. It was most assiduously disseminated, and not without foundation, that the Irish Parliament, in its recent proceedings, had clearly evinced more talent than prudence, and less wisdom than declamation; that whilst patriots were debating in the House, the Secretary was negociating in the corridor; and therefore it was necessary to the public safety to strangle corruption in its cradle, and give the people a due confidence in the integrity of their Representatives.

It was considered, by many men of influence and fortune, that a reform of the Commons House of Parliament was attainable, and should be then attained. The national arrangements daily appeared more imperfect, for they had not been conducted with the sound principles of cautious statesmen, nor had satisfactory guarantees been established for their future security. As Parliament was then returned, no well-founded confidence could be placed in its *permanent* protection; and it was most judiciously stated by Mr. Flood, that *the speech of a puzzled Minister, put into the mouth of an embarrassed Monarch*, was at that moment the only security for the continuance of Ireland as an independent nation; that such independence might rest solely upon a single word of two syllables,* on which every future Minister might found fallacious reasoning, and place his own equivocal construction. This was, in truth, prophetic.

It was also more than insinuated, by men of clear and dispassionate judgment, that the struggles in Parliament were becoming rather for the supremacy of men and party, than for the preservation of the Constitution; that they were blind, rancorous, and ill-timed individual contests, dangerous to the state, and irritating to the people. They

* The word *Final*

argued, that the piercing eye of the British Minister would not fail to watch for the moment when, the Irish being enfeebled by their dissensions, he might destroy that independence which the architects of 1782 had attempted to establish, without guarding against the insecurity of the foundation. So far these arguments were true, but men stopped not here. It was suggested that a requisition to the Parliament, to reform itself, urged by the people, in their civil capacities only, might not have sufficient weight to command attention. If, however, 300 delegates were chosen by Volunteer regiments, from men of fortune, influence, and character, it would prove to the Parliament that a reform was required by those who had a right to require it, and could enforce it. They might send the heads of a Bill to Parliament through the hands of their own members; such a mode of presentation could create no cavil; and, above all, the very same men who would deliberate as volunteer delegates, and prepare such a bill, would be, in a great measure, those who, in their civil capacities, composed the several grand juries of the nation, many of them being members of the Legislature. The measure was almost unanimously determined upon.

IV. Three hundred delegates were now chosen by different corps, and the 10th of November (1783) was proclaimed for the first sitting of the Grand National Convention of Ireland, within the precincts of the two Houses of Parliament, the members of which were at the same period exercising their legislative functions. Never was any country placed in a more extraordinary or critical situation.

This state of affairs in Ireland was then seriously felt by the English Cabinet, it became alarmed. Ireland now stood in a high station. No longer (in the language of Mr. Gibbon) a remote and obscure Island, she formed a new feature on the face of Europe, and might assert her rank amongst the second order of European nations. In constitution and in laws, municipal and international, she was fundamentally the same as England; her legislature was, in theory, altogether independent. The individuality of their joint Monarch constituted the indefeasible basis of their federative connection; but their respective Parliaments alone could make laws to bind their respective people, to regulate their own commerce, and to pay their own armies. Ireland had wisely and magnanimously recorded her loyalty, and proclaimed her determination, that "*whilst* she shared the *liberty*, she would share the fate of the British nation;" but the compact was *reciprocal*, and she had bound herself *no further*.

England could not with apathy regard a military Convention, meeting and operating on political subjects, in the centre of the Irish Metropolis.

The attention of England was by the adoption of these extraordinary proceedings naturally roused to a more detailed review of the statistical circumstances of Ireland By the acquisition of a free commerce, and of unshackled manufactures, the revenue and resources of Ireland consequently became susceptible of extraordinary improvement, and might soon have equalled those of many continental nations, and solely at her own disposal and appropriation.

In the capability of military power also she had few rivals; at that period she contained, (and continues to contain) more fighting men, or men who *love fighting*, and who might be collected in a week, than any other state in Europe. The powerful and elevated position she was then about to occupy, and the unprecedented steps by which she had mounted to that eminence, could not be regarded without strong feelings of solicitude by the sister country.

The example of Ireland had afforded a grave and instructive lesson to an oppressed and vassal people, and a wholesome lecture to griping and monopolising governments. Of all the extraordinary circumstances which the state of Ireland then displayed, none was beheld, at that critical period, with such mingled wonder and alarm by England, as the rapid progress of the Volunteer associations. And the bold step of a delegated convention, the increasing numbers, discipline, and energy of that military institution, had no precedent, nor in the changed state of Europe, can the phenomenon ever appear in any country.

The Volunteers, now actually *armed and disciplined*, and whose delegates were now to be assembled were said to exceed 150,000 organzied men. But whatever the force then was, the Volunteer recruits, if called on, would have comprised the male inhabitants of nearly the whole island, including every rank, religion, and occupation.

Such a force, though self-levied, self-officered, and utterly independent of any control or subjection, save to their own chosen chiefs, still remained in perfect harmony amongst themselves, in entire obedience to the municipal laws of the country, holding the most friendly and intimate intercourse with the regular forces, and by their activity and local knowledge, preserving their country in a state of general and unprecedented tranquillity.

This extraordinary military body, equally ready to shed their blood in opposing a foreign enemy, supporting their own liberties, or defending those of England, combining the moral and physical powers, and nearly the entire wealth, of an immense population, nothing could have resisted; and whatever ground of alarm the British Government might then have felt, had ministers been mad enough, at that period, to have attempted its direct or compulsory suppression, instead of its attachment to the sister country, the result would inevitably have been a prompt separation of the two islands.

Ireland was in this state at the first meeting of the National Convention, and the Parliament assembled about the same time. The Volunteer elections were quickly ended without tumult or opposition, and their 300 delegates, each escorted by small detachments of Volunteers from their respective counties, entered the metropolis, and were universally received with a respect and cordiality impossible to be depicted; yet, all was harmony and peace. Many men of large fortune, many of great talent, and many members of the Lords and Commons, had been elected delegates *by the Volunteers*, and took upon themselves the double functions of Parliament and of the Convention.

The Royal Exchange of Dublin was first selected for the meeting of the Volunteer delegates. Whoever has seen the metropolis of Ireland must admire the external architecture of that building; but it was found inadequate to the accommodation of a very large deliberative assembly. It was therefore determined that the Rotunda (being then the finest room in Ireland) was best adapted for the meeting of the National Convention. This was, and continues to be, the great assembly-room of Dublin. It consists of a circular saloon of very large dimensions, connected with numerous and very spacious chambers, and terminates Sackville street, the finest of the Irish metropolis. It is surmounted by a dome, exceeding in diameter the Irish House of Commons, and was perfectly adapted to the accommodation of a popular assembly.

This saloon and the connected chambers had been fitted up for the important purpose to which they were to be appropriated. But little did the Irish people conceive, that what they then considered as the proudest day their nation had ever seen, only preceded a little time her national dissolution, and even prepared the grave in which her new-gained independence was to be inhumated. Every measure, however, had been previously taken to prepare that splendid chamber for this unparalleled assembly, and to receive the delegates and their escorts with every possible mark of respect and dignity. Volunteer grenadiers were ordered to attend on the Convention as a guard of honour during their sittings, and to mount an officer's guard at the house of the President; whilst Volunteer dragoons patrolled during the sittings, in the utmost tranquillity, throughout the entire city. The detachments of country corps, who had escorted their delegates, having a great emulation as to their appearance and acquipments on this grand occasion, had new dresses and accoutrements, and it was agreeable to see the noble hunters on which a great proportion of the cavalry were mounted. The horse had entered Dublin in very small detachments, from exceedingly numerous corps, and when occasionally formed into line, the great variety of their dresses, ensigns and equipments, presented a splendid, but very striking and singular appearance.*

* The author had been sent to town with a detachment of his father's cavalry corps, the "Cullenagh Rangers;" their undress was white, with black velvet facings, the full dress, scarlet. At the head of these few men, the author felt prouder than an Emperor, it made an impression on his youthful mind, which, even in the chill of age, is still vivid and animating, a glowing patriotism, a military feeling, and an instinctive, though a senseless lust for *actual service*, arose within him, a sensation which is certainly inherent in a great proportion of the Irish people, and which seldom forsakes them but with their lives.

The citizens of Dublin excelled in their hospitality, they appeared in crowds every where, forcing their invitations on the country Volunteers, every soldier had numerous billets pressed into his hand, every householder who could afford it, vied in entertaining his guests with zeal and cordiality. Every thing was secure and tranquil, but when it was considered that 300 members had virtually proclaimed a concurrent Parliament, under the title of a National Convention, and were about to lead a splendid procession through the body of the city, to hold its sittings within view of the Houses of Legislature, the affairs of Ireland seemed drawing fast to some decisive catastrophe. But it was also considered, that the Convention was an assembly of men of rank, of fortune, and of talent. The Convention, therefore, possessed an importance and a consistence that seemed to render some momentous consequence absolutely inevitable; the crisis did arrive, but it was unfortunate; Ireland tottered, retrograded and has fallen.

The firing of twenty-one cannon announced the first movement of the delegates from the Royal Exchange to the Rotunda, a troop of the Rathdown cavalry, commanded by Colonel Edwards, of Old Court, County of Wicklow, commenced the procession; the Liberty Brigade of artillery,* commanded by Napper Tandy, with a band, succeeded. A company of the Barristers' grenadiers, headed by Colonel Pedder, with a national standard for Ireland, borne by a captain of grenadiers, and surrounded by a company of the finest men of the regiment came after, their muskets slung, and bright battle-axes borne on their shoulders. A battalion of infantry, with a band, followed, and then the delegates, two and two, with side-arms, carrying banners with motto and in their respective uniforms, broad green ribbands were worn across their shoulders. Another band followed playing the special air alluded to. The chaplains of the different regiments in their cassocks,

* Some of the musicians of Dublin in 1780, had been employed to compose a march for the general adoption of the Volunteer corps throughout the kingdom, that all might be accustomed to march to the same air at their reviews, &c. They composed a simple-noted march, now obsolete, but of which the author retained a copy, still interesting, as connected with a recollection of the times, and of that unparalleled Institution.

marched each with his respective corps, giving solemnity to the procession, and as if invoking the blessing of Heaven on their efforts, which had a wonderful effect on the surrounding multitude. Several standards and colours were borne by the different corps of horse and foot, and another brigade of artillery, commanded by Counsellor Calbeck, with labels on the cannons' mouths,* was escorted by the Barristers' corps in scarlet and gold (the full dress uniform of the King's Guards:) the motto on their buttons being " *Vox populi suprema lex est.*"

The procession in itself was interesting, but the surrounding scene was still more affecting. Their line of march, from the Exchange to the Rotunda, was through the most spacious streets and quays of the city, open on both sides to the river, and capable of containing a vastly larger assemblage of people than any part of the metropolis of England. An immense body of spectators, crowding every window and house-top, would be but an ordinary occurrence, and might be seen and described without novelty or interest, but, on this occasion, every countenance spoke zeal, every eye expressed solicitude, and every action proclaimed triumph, green ribands and handkerchiefs were waved from every window, by the enthusiasm of its fair occupants; crowds seemed to move on the house-tops, ribands were flung upon the delegates as they passed; yet it was not a loud or boisterous, but a firm enthusiasm. It was not the effervescence of a heated crowd, it was not the fiery ebullition of a glowing people, it was not sedition, it was liberty that inspired them, the heart bounded though the tongue was motionless, those who did not see, or who do not recollect that splendid day, must have the mortification of reflecting that (under all its circumstances) no man did before, and no man ever will "behold its like again."

V. The entrance of the delegates into the Rotunda was more than interesting, it was awful. Each doffed his helmet or his hat, as if he felt the influence of that sacred place where he was about to sacrifice at the Shrine of Freedom. Every man knew he was, in some respect, overstepping the boundaries of the Constitution, but he

* Their motto was, " Oh Lord, open thou our lips, and our mouths shall sound forth thy praise!"

considered that his trespass was for the purpose only of adding security to that Constitution which he seemed to transgress.

Such a state of things never existed in any other country, consistent with perfect tranquillity. Ireland, however, proved on that occasion her superior loyalty, and gave the retort courteous to all her calumniators. It was a matter of fact that the independence of Ireland had been achieved, that it had been proclaimed in Ireland and in England, that it had been solemnly ratified and confirmed for ever by his Majesty from his throne, as monarch of both countries. That compact was therefore firm, because it was federal and final, and the delegates sought what their own Parliament alone was competent to discuss, and over which England had no control. A partial reform of the representation was a measure which the British Minister himself had the duplicity of proposing in England, yet of undermining in the sister country, even in the face of his own renunciation of all innovation and acknowledgment of the former usurpation.

VI. These would at any other time, have been subjects for deliberate consideration, but it was too late to reflect, the die was thrown, and, as if every thing conspired to increase the peculiarity of the scene, even the site of the Rotunda, where the Convention assembled, exactly terminated the street and fronted the river, on the other side of which, in a direct line, was seen the magnificent dome of the Commons House of Parliament, were 300 members, returned as representatives of the Irish people, according to the practice of the Constitution, were also deliberating.

Those localities excited, in every rational mind, something like a dread of possible collision, it was also a grave and curious consideration, that the avowed object of the Volunteer delegation was, in fact to degrade the character of the Parliamentary delegates, and, under the name of reform, convict them of corruption.

It was impossible not to perceive, that both were placed in a situation, which must necessarily terminate in the humiliation of one of them.

It was also remarkable that the Volunteers, who had thus sent their delegates to reform the Commons House of Parliament, had been themselves solemnly thanked the preceding session, for their support to the Constitution, by the very same House of Commons which they now determined to reorganize and reform.

It is impossible not to contrast this national convention of Ireland with the democratic assemblies which, in later days overwhelmed so many thrones and countries. With what pride must an Irishman call to his recollection the concentration of rank and fortune, and patriotism and loyalty, which composed that convention of the Irish people! With what pride must the few survivors remember the 300 Irish nobles and gentlemen, assembling peaceably and loyally to demand a reform, an object of all others the nearest to their hearts, and the most necessary to their independence!

Yet the recollection of that assembly must also cast a dark shade over the History of Ireland, by transferring a reflection on its proud birth to its humble termination.

A delineation of those scenes may appear, to modern readers, an exaggerated episode. That generation which beheld, or acted in those days, is drawing fast to a close; and whilst a few contemporaries exist, it would be unpardonable to leave the scenes altogether to future historians, who could convey but an imperfect recital of actions they had never seen, and frigid ideas of feelings they had never experienced. The results of that extraordinary measure may enable posterity to do some justice to calumniated Ireland, where loyalty appears to have wonderfully retained its influence over a powerful, proud, and patriotic assembly, and over an armed and irresistible population, under circumstances the most dangerous and irritating that had ever terminated with tranquillity in any nation.

The Artillery had scarcely announced the entry of the delegates into the Rotunda, when that silent respect which had pervaded the entire population, during the procession, yielded to more lively feelings; no longer could the people restrain their joy. At first, a low murmur seemed to proceed from different quarters, which, soon increasing in its fervour, at length burst into a universal cheer of triumph, like distant thunder, gradually rolling on, till one great and continued peal burst upon the senses; the loud and incessant cheering of the people soon reverberated from street to street, contributing the whole powers of acclamation to glorify an assembly which they vainly conceived must be omnipotent, it was an acclamation, long, sincere, and unanimous, and occasionally died away, only to be renewed with redoubled energy. The vivid interest excited by this extraordinary and affecting scene can never be conceived, save by those who were present, and participated in its feelings, nor can time or age obliterate it from the memory.

It is not unworthy of remark, that a wonderful proportion of female voices was distinguishable amidst these plaudits. A general illumination took place throughout the city, bands of music were heard every where, and never did a day and night of rejoicing so truly express the unsophisticated gratification of an entire population. The Government was astounded, the Privy Council had sat, but were far from unanimous, and had separated without decision. The old courtiers called the scene frantic, but it was not the frenzy of a mob, it was the triumph of a nation, incomprehensible to the vulgar meetings of another country.

The scene within was still more novel and impressive. The varied uniforms of the delegates had a very singular appearance; sent from different regiments, no two of them were dressed or armed alike; cavalry, infantry, grenadiers, artillery, generals, colonels, serjeants, privates; in fine, all possible varieties of military dress and rank were collected in one general body, destined to act solely in a civil capacity.

The cheers, the cannon, the music, the musketry, combined to prevent any procedure that day, save that of the members giving in their delegations, and nominating some officers to act during the session.

CHAPTER XIX.

The Bishop of Derry takes his seat at the Convention—His splendour—And pageantry—Procession—Popularity—Extraordinary Visit to the House of Lords—A Guard of Honour mounted at his house—Entirely devoted to the Irish people—His great qualities and acquirements—Opposes Charlemont and Grattan—First treacherous Scheme of the British Government again to enslave Ireland—The spirit of the Irish Parliament declines—Reasons for Reform in Parliament—Absolutely essential to her prosperity—Further traits of Lord Charlemont's Character—His inefficiency—His views—Opposes the Bishop of Derry's Election for the Presidency of the National Convention—Many Members of Parliament attend the Convention also -Earl Charlemont's dilemma—Proceedings of the Convention—The Bishop and Mr. Flood acquired the ascendency—The Parliament and Convention—Desperate step of Government—Fitzgibbon's Philippic—Most violent Debates—Bill rejected—Extraordinary coincidence of facts—Mr. Connolly's motion—Feeble and insidious resolution of Lord Charlemont—Fatal adjournment—Called a meeting of his partisans—Breaks his trust—Inexcusable conduct—False statement—Virtually dissolves the Convention before the full meeting—Lord Charlemont justly reprobated—Volunteers beat to arms—Lord Charlemont's intolerance—Opposed by the Bishop of Derry.

I. PREVIOUS to the meeting of the delegates, the Bishop of Derry had determined to convince the Irish people, that he was no lukewarm professor of adherence to their interest; his character, already given, is confirmed by every act of his life when in Ireland. He took his seat amongst the Irish delegates, at the Rotunda, with the greatest splendour; and, to prove that he preferred the claims of the Irish Volunteers to both his English rank as Earl of Bristol and his Irish rank as a spiritual noble, he entered Dublin in royal state, drew up his equipage at the entrance to the House of Lords, as if he halted to teach the Peers their duty to their country, and then moved forward to take his seat at the Rotunda, as an Irish Delegate in the National Convention. Such a circumstance can be scarcely credited in England; but had not Lord Charlemont's temporizing neutralized his spirit, it is probable that the Convention might have succeeded in its object. It is not, therefore, wonderful, that a British Peer, an Englishman, and above all, a Bishop, taking so decided a part in the cause of Ireland, should gain a popularity that few before him ever had so fully, or perhaps, more justly, experienced. He certainly was sincere; his proceedings on this occasion were extraordinary, and not unworthy of a special notice.

The Lords had taken their seats in the House of Peers when the Bishop of Derry began his procession to take his seat in the Convention. He had several carriages in his suite, and sat in an open landau, drawn by six beautiful horses, caparisoned with purple ribands. He was dressed in purple, his horses, equipages, and servants being in the most splendid trappings and liveries. He had brought to Dublin, as his escort, a troop of light cavalry, raised by his unfortunate and guilty nephew, George Robert Fitzgerald; they were splendidly dressed and accoutred, and were mounted on the finest chargers that the Bishop or their Commander could procure. A part of these dragoons led the procession, another closed it, and some rode on each side of his Lordship's carriage. Trumpets announced his approach, and detachments from several Volunteer corps of Dublin joined his Lordship's calvacade. He never ceased making dignified obeisances to the multitude: his salutations were enthusiastically returned on every side; "Long live the Bishop," echoed from every window; yet all was peace and harmony, and never did there appear so extraordinary a procession within the realm of Ireland.

This calvacade marched slowly through the different streets, till it arrived at the portico of the house of Lords, which adjoined that of the Commons. A short halt was then made, the trumpets sounded, the sudden and unexpected clangor of which echoed throughout the long corridors. Both Houses had just finished prayers, and were proceeding to business, and, totally unconscious of the cause, several members rushed to the entrance. The Bishop saluted all with royal dignity, the Volunteers presented arms, and the bands played the Volunteer's march. Of a sudden another clangor of trumpets was heard; the astonished Lords and Commons, unable to divine what was to ensue, or the reason of the extraordinary appearance of the Bishop, retired to their respective chambers, and with great solicitude awaited the result.

The Bishop, however, had done what he intended ; he had astonished both Houses, and had proved to them his principles and his determination ; amidst the shouts and cheers of thousands, he proceeded to the Rotunda, where, in point of dignity and importance, he certainly appeared to surpass the whole of his brother delegates. He entered the chamber in the greatest form, presented his credentials, took his seat, conversed a few moments with all the ceremony of a temporal prince, and then, with the excess of that dignified courtesy of which he was a perfect master, he retired as he had entered, and drove away in the same majestic style, and amidst reiterated applauses, to his house, where the Volunteers had previously mounted a guard of honour. He entertained a great number of persons of rank at a magnificent dinner, and the ensuing day began his course amongst the Delegates, as an ordinary man of business.

The personal appearance of the Bishop was extremely prepossessing ; rather under the middle size, he was peculiarly well made, his countenance fair, handsome, and intelligent, but rather expressive of a rapidity of thought than of the deliberation of judgment ; his hair, receding from his forehead, gave a peculiar trait of respectability to his appearance.

His manner appeared zealous and earnest, and rather more quick than is consistent with perfect dignity ; but he seemed to be particularly well bred and courteous ; and altogether, he could not be viewed without an impression that he was a person of talent and of eminence.

He appeared always dressed with peculiar care and neatness ; in general, entirely in purple, and he wore diamond knee and shoe buckles. But what I most observed in his dress was, that he wore white gloves, with gold fringe round the wrists, and large gold tassels hanging from them.

The Author was then too young, and too unimportant, to have the honour of any personal acquaintance with that distinguished prelate : but the singularity of his habits, his patriotic conduct, popular character, and impressive appearance, excited a satisfaction in beholding him, and impressed him strongly on my recollection.

The Bishop, in devoting himself to the service of the Irish people, could have no personal object but popularity. He could be greater in title; he was rich, and in health, vigour, and spirits; his learning was rare, his talents very considerable—in all respects he was an able man. From the moment he became an Irish Bishop he adopted Ireland, built an immense palace in a remote and singular situation, and did numerous acts which nobody could account for. He had many of those qualities in an eminent degree, which our more ancient histories have attributed to the proudest churchmen; but they were in him so blended with liberality, so tempered by enlightened principles, that they excited a very different mode of conduct from his episcopal predecessors. However, his ambition for popularity obviously knew no bounds, and his efforts to gain that popularity found no limits. His great failing was a portion of natural versatility, which frequently enfeebled the confidence of his adherents. It was supposed that the gentle, lambient flame of Charlemont, would soon be quenched in the rolling, rapid torrent of the Bishop's popularity, and that the epigrammatic eloquence of Grattan, cramped or overpowered by the influence of his splendour, would probably be withdrawn from the scene of action. The Bishop soon adopted his course; he paid his whole attention to Mr. Flood. In this he was right. It is not too much to say, that Mr. Flood was, at least, the best educated and deepest statesman, and the most able partisan, in the Irish Senate.

II. Whilst these extraordinary and brilliant scenes were proceeding in Ireland, the embarrassment of the British Ministers must necessarily be on the increase, if possible. They well knew, that if the Convention succeeded in reforming the Commons House of Parliament, the British Government would lose the use of the only instrument through which they ever could hope to regain their ascendency; and with this view, and at this critical period, the plot was suggested and the conspiracy formed, to replace Ireland within the trammels of the sister country, whenever a feasible opportunity should offer. The sequence of Irish events leaves no doubt of the truth of this observation.

These collisions were, to England a golden opportunity: plans against the Volunteer Associations were deeply laid, and with considerable prospect of eventually succeeding, first by working upon the courtly moderation and courteous feebleness of the short-sighted Charlemont, and credulity of Grattan, to dismiss the Convention, and thereby divide and dispirit the Volunteers. And next, by corrupting Parliament and seducing the Irish gentlemen, under pretence of upholding the British Constitution, to recapture the Irish independence. Whoever reads the political history of those realms from 1782 to 1800, cannot doubt that this object, from that period to the completion of the legislative Union, was never lost sight of.

The British Minister had also reasons nearer home for determining to undermine the reforming spirit of the Irish Volunteers. He knew that if a reform of Parliament were effected in Ireland, though the same reasons did not exist, yet the same measure could not be long withheld from the English nation; and as the Parliament of England was at that era supposed to be ruled absolutely by the influence of the Crown, the control of the Minister would receive a vital blow, which it never could recover.

The commercial system of England, also, whilst without external rivalship, had no necessity for a special protection. But now she had a rival in the free trade of Ireland, a subject which soon after came under full discussion. The jealousy of England was proved by her commercial propositions, and the Irish Parliament had yet sufficient honesty to resist that inroad.

But as a body that had laboured long and much, a lassitude and relaxation were obviously commencing in the Irish Senate, how long that spirit, which had acquired their rights, might retain its vigour to protect them, depended on the purity of the representatives, and this was the true reason for considering a reform imperative in Ireland.

Whilst, therefore, the subject of Reform is under discussion, it may be proper to see how far the then existing state of Ireland substantially required that measure, or warranted that conclusion. She was to commence as a trading country, and her situation on the map of the world seemed to combine many defects and many advantages. She appears partially secluded from that general intercourse which other states of Europe enjoy from their localities. England, on the east, intervenes between her and the British Channel and German Ocean; Scotland intercepts the Northern Seas; and though the most western point of Europe, and of course well situated for the western commerce, the enterprise and great capital, or jealousy, of England, could have excluded her at pleasure, if unprotected by her own Parliament, from any proportional participation in the colonial trade.* On a view of the whole, her position might have entitled her to have become a considerable emporium, but jealousy is natural to commercial nations, and Ireland would probably have possessed the same lust for monopoly, had she been circumstanced as Great Britain. But the non-importation resolutions of Ireland had alarmed Great Britain, and proved to her to what a zeal of retaliation the Irish people might be urged by any future measures of injustice.

The situation of Ireland places her comparatively out of the pale of busy Europe, by the absence of that political interest which the Powers of Europe take in the commerce of other and inferior countries. This was a deprivation which nothing could ever remedy or counteract, but a local legislature, constantly resident, and constantly alive to the foreign and domestic interests of their country.†

These were some of the causes which rendered a pure and independent Parliament more necessary to Ireland than to her sister country. Ireland never had been a

* It could not be very gratifying to the Irish traders or people, to see the immense colonial and general trade of Liverpool necessarily pass by the ports of Waterford and Dublin. The author has seen a fleet of seventy West Indiamen sail proudly down the Irish Channel to the merchants at Liverpool, and one solitary vessel separate from the fleet, and steer into the port of Dublin, with sugar and molasses, for home consumption.

† See ante Sir Lucius O'Brien's Speech on the conduct of Portugal. He proposed merely a declaration of war by Ireland against her, and in the end Portugal was obliged to redress her, notwithstanding the duplicity of the British minister and Mr. Eden.

nation of extensive commerce, yet even the narrow channels of her trade were ever contracted by the jealousies and monopoly of England; and this in public opinion, rendered a pure parliament indispensable, as the only ample security against such interference.*

To constitute an Irish Parliament, therefore, as much as possible free from every tinge of English commercial or political influence, was plausibly considered essential to the security of the former country. The necessity, in point of fact, can only be judged of by this view of the external state of Ireland at the crisis, when a military convention to discuss Reform surprised every nation of Europe, that would condescend or take the trouble to think about an island so secluded.

III. The public characters of the Bishop of Derry and his more moderate rival, were so extremely dissimilar, and their composition so totally repugnant, that any amalgamation of sentiment was utterly impossible. A cautious attachment to regularity and order, a sincere love for the people, a polished, courtly respect for the aristocracy, with a degree of popular ambition and a proportion of individual vanity, were the governing principles of Lord Charlemont during the whole of his political conduct. But, unfortunntely, these were accompanied by a strong taint of that religious intolerance which has since proved the interruption of Irish tranquillity.

No man in Ireland could do the honours of a review better; and though his personal courage was undoubted, no man in Ireland was likely to do the duties of a battle worse than Lord Charlemont. He guessed the extent of his own powers, and sedulously avoided any situation to which they might prove inadequate. If the people had not respected his virtues, they would not have submitted to his weakness; and if he had not loved the people, he would not have sacrificed his tranquillity to command them. He was an excellent *nurse*, tender of the consti-

* *Vide* King William's reply to the British Parliament; and in 1484 the great manufacturing towns of England and Scotland fully displayed the same attachment to their monopolies, even to the ruin of Irish commerce. They have become better informed since that period, and are, of course more liberal.

tution, but dreading every effective remedy prescribed for its disorders.

Lord Charlemont saw clearly that the Presidency of the National Convention was of vital consequence to the country, and the master-key of his own importance. He had his little as well as his great feelings, and both were set into action by this dilemma. He knew full well that if the bold and enterprising Prelate were at the head of that Convention, he would lose all weight with the Government, and all influence with the people. The measure was altogether too strong for the character of Lord Charlemont, he knew he should be incapable of governing that body, if it once got into any leading-strings but his own, and it was obvious that if his Lordship should get one step beyond his depth, he never could regain his position. His friends, therefore, anticipated every means to ensure his nomination to the Presidency, and the Bishop of Derry, before he was aware that there would be any effectual opposition to himself, found Lord Charlemont actually placed in that situation, where he might restrain, if not counteract the ultra energies of the reforming party. This was the very step the Government desired; Earl Charlemont might be managed, but the Bishop of Derry would have been intractable. Lord Charlemont involuntarily became the tool of Government, whilst he fancied he was labouring in the service of the people. From this moment the neutralizing system by which its President wished to conduct that assembly became obvious. Every body might foresee that not only the Convention, but perhaps the Volunteer associations were likely to droop.

Many sensible men had apprehended that the Bishop's politics might be too strong; the very act of his attaching himself to Ireland proved at once their vigour and eccentricity; and hence the Presidency of the Convention, in every point of view, became a measure of extreme importance.

IV. A few of the members of the House of Commons had declined their election to the Convention,* but some of the ablest and most respectable members performed

* The state of Parliament may be imagined from Mr. George Molineux's apologising to the House of Commons for being unable to bring forward a motion of which he had given notice—" As the close atten-

their duties alternately in both assemblies. The Lord Lieutenant and his Privy Council at the same time held their sittings at the Castle, exactly midway between the two Parliaments, they received alternate reports from each, and undecided whether the strong or the passive system were least, or rather most, fraught with danger, they at length wisely adopted their accustomed course, and determined to take advantage of the chances of division, and of the moderation, ductility, and pride of Lord Charlemont.

It was artfully insinuated to Lord Charlemont, by the friends of Government, that the peace of the country was considered to be in his hands, that he had accepted a situation of the most responsible nature, and that if he did not possess sufficient influence to curb the Convention, he ought at once to resign the trust, and thereby give the Parliament a ground of requiring the immediate dissolution of its unconstitutional rival.

Lord Charlemont found himself in a situation of great embarrassment. If he held the Presidency, he was responsible for its proceedings, if he resigned it, he would still be responsible for having countenanced the organization of the assembly, the Bishop would succeed him in his chair—and he would still be considered the inceptive promoter of whatever might be adopted by his successor. Lord Charlemont's pride resisted his resignation. He was too high to be commanded, he was too feeble to control, and he found himself in a state of great perplexity. After much deliberation, he adopted the suggestions of the courtiers, and was led blindfold to that deceptious course, which might answer his tranquil objects for the moment, but was beneath his character, and which must eventually have extinguished all the popular influence of the Volunteers, and have destroyed that of the country. In fine he lost himself; he sacrificed his country, and determined on a line of proceeding entirely unworthy of his former

tion he had been obliged to give to the National Convention, did not leave him time to prepare himself on Parliamentary subjects."

The members trying the petition on the Cork election, adjourned the trial, though the expense was daily very great, as there were some of the Committee who were obliged to attend their duty in the National Convention.

conduct; if he could not govern, he resolved to temporize, divide, neutralize, and dissolve the assembly.

This fatal system was eventually successful, and his Lordship effected the dissolution of that body whose confidence had raised him to so glorious an eminence, by which the British Government now foresaw the possibility of recapturing Irish independence. Lord Charlemont had been seized with a nervous dread of that very institution he had originally been so active in creating; and entirely, though unconsciously, surrendered himself to the darling objects of a deep and treacherous administration.

And here let it be remarked, that the independence of Ireland, which certainly was first achieved by the exertions of the Whigs, was now left unguarded, and afterwards destroyed by the corrupt tergiversation of many members of that *same party*. The inconsistent conduct of some of the Whigs, and their Place Bill in 1794,* were the proximate means through which the Union was ultimately effected.

V. The proceedings of the Convention were carried on for some time with the utmost regularity. The rules and orders, and customs of Parliament were adopted, and the meetings were held and continued without any material interruption. But when such an assembly had been delegated for the purpose of requiring the Parliament to purify itself, and remodel its constitution, it could not be expected that every member could possess similar views or similar feelings, or perhaps observe the most uninterrupted order and discipline in discussions. But the decorum and regularity of the Convention may be best exemplified by observing that there was not any meeting or discussion of the National Convention of Ireland, from its first to its last sitting, more confused or boisterous than what has very frequently been witnessed in the Commons House of the Imperial Parliament.

* The *Place Bill*, perseveringly forced by the Whigs upon the Government by admitting the vacating of seats by nominal officers (Escheatorship of Munster), enabled Lord Castlereagh to *pack* the Parliament in 1800, with a degree of undisguised effrontery never before attempted by any Minister. See hereafter, Mr. Crow's Letter to Lord Belvidere, in which the high crimes and misdemeanours of Lord Castlereagh are apparent beyond the power of refutal.

A strong opposition soon arose to the imbecile system of Lord Charlemont. Superior public characters at length assumed their stations, and effectively overwhelmed that childish affectation of delicacy, so utterly incompatible with the circumstances of the times, and the spirit of the patriots. Yet unfortunately Lord Charlemont was elected, and took the chair as President.

The Bishop, disappointed of the chair, lost no time in rendering it a seat of thorns. He took to his council, the man of all others best adapted to give weight and dignity to the measure of Parliamentary reform. Lord Charlemont supported reform most sincerely. Mr. Grattan was also a sincere and honest friend to a purification of Parliament: but his favourite scheme, as he said, to begin with, was an *internal* reform. He partially accomplished that object by the Place Bill, whilst, by one of its clauses, he most certainly lost both the Parliament and the Constitution.*

VI. The Bishop and Mr. Flood soon gained a full ascendency in the Convention, and many men of the very first rank, fortune, and influence, took part in its deliberations. Numerous plans were proposed, and reform, of all others the most difficult of political measures, was sought to be too promptly decided in a heated and impatient assembly.

By the imprudence of both parties, the Convention and the Parliament were driven into a direct collision. After much deliberation, a plan of reform, framed by Mr. Flood and approved by the Convention, was directed by them to be presented to Parliament forthwith, and the sittings of the Convention were made permanent till Parliament had decided the question. Mr. Flood obeyed his instructions, and moved for leave to bring in a Bill to reform the Parliament.

The Government felt that a collision of the two assemblies was unavoidable. The crisis, however, afforded no

---

* The Author, when a member of the Irish Parliament, clearly foresaw the use that any minister might make of the *vacating clause* and strongly opposed that clause in his place, though conceded by Government. The title of a Place Bill was so agreeable to the Opposition, that very few of them ever gave themselves the trouble of considering the details of it.

opportunity for mature consideration, and it was not long before the danger of so hasty a proceeding was fatally experienced. Government had yielded to the Volunteers when it could not resist them; but it was not probable that the Parliament would quietly capitulate to the Convention; whilst the triumph of the Parliament implied not only the destruction of the Convention but of the Volunteers.

The measure of reform, patriotic and noble, blinded the nation to every consideration but its attainment, actual and prompt; yet so many persons of character, fortune, and influence, were in both assemblies, that a discreet and prudent deliberation might possibly have devised means of averting so dangerous a crisis.

The Government resolved to risk a direct assault upon the Volunteers, by refusing leave to bring in Mr. Flood's Bill, because it had originated from *their* deliberations Strong language was used, but with some precaution, even by Mr. Yelverton, who had been a zealous Volunteer, but was now the Attorney General. His eloquence was splendid; but the bold, restless, arrogant spirit of Fitzgibbon, ever prone to offend, to irritate, and to pervert, in a speech replete with the most unnecessary invective, unwarrantable fury and abuse, assailed the Convention, the Volunteers, and the Bill, with every epithet and allusion that could bring the Government and the Volunteers into a state of direct hostility. Had his efforts been crowned with success, British connection would probably not have been of three months duration.

The House felt the danger of his conduct, and he was not supported in his philippics. Mr. Curran called Mr. Fitzgibbon a maniac and an incendiary; Mr. D. Daley termed Mr. Flood a demagogue. The debate became quite unprecedented in point of violence and party recrimination, but the good sense of some members endeavoured to moderate the partisans. The Bill, after a dreadful uproar, was rejected by 158 to 49;* 138 of the majority were placemen, and the very *persons on whom the reform was intended to operate.* It is very remarkable, that it was 138 placemen that rejected the Reform Bill in 1783, and that it was the same number of

* Ninety-three members were absent.

placemen who carried the Union Bill in 1800, which, if the reform had succeeded, never could have been passed.

Upon this very decision ultimately depended the existence of Irish independence. The Volunteers were insulted, their Bill was rejected without a hearing, their intentions were calumniated, even their name was reprobated; their services were forgotten, and that very corruption which they sought to reform thus had its full revenge.

Mr. Connolly—that weak, obstinate, and most inconsistent of the Irish Whigs, whom family and fortune alone could have raised from obscurity, endeavoured to give a finishing blow to that virtuous association,* which, in the same place, he had so often eulogised. He now explicitly denounced the Volunteers as enemies to that Constitution which they had obtained for their country, and which he afterwards surrendered to the Ministers, against whose measures he had arrayed himself on every important occasion.

This too great confidence of the Volunteers, in the success of their measures had thus led them too rapidly into a proceeding that required the most deliberate consideration. The refusal of Parliament to receive their Bill created a sensation which, for a moment, left the peace of Ireland on the very brink of a precipice. Lord Charlemont mistook his *fears* for his *prudence*, the Volunteers mistook their resentment for their patriotism, both were disposed to extremities, and some decisive crisis appeared absolutely inevitable. That great and patriotic army, which had the year before received the unanimous thanks of the Parliament, were, by the motion of a Whig, nearly denounced as rebels and little less than a declaration of war against them was voted, even without a division in the Parliament.

VII. By this fatal dilemma, resistance or dissolution

---

* After the division, Mr. Connolly moved, "That an humble address be presented to his Majesty, to declare the perfect satisfaction we feel, and the blessings we enjoy under his Majesty's most auspicious Government, and our present happy constitution." "And that, at *this time*, we feel it peculiarly incumbent on us to declare our resolution to support the same with our lives and fortunes."

This was an unequivocal attack upon the Volunteers: it was carried.

alone remained to the Convention. The most intelligent of that body determined that a day or two should be taken to reflect on the best course of proceeding. But Lord Charlemont dreaded the consequence of discussion, and decided rather to betray his trust than hazard insurrection, and to adopt the safer step of dissolving the Convention.

It is not easy to describe the uneasiness and deep solicitude of the Convention pending that debate. Reporters were perpetually passing and repassing between the two assemblies; the impatience of the Volunteers was rising into a storm; Earl Charlemont, overwhelmed by his apprehension, saw no course but to induce them to adjourn; they, however, waited till long after midnight, in a state between anger and anxiety. Lord Charlemont did not oppose, but he duped them. He received a note from the House of Commons, which he said left no hopes of a speedy decision, and he had the address and influence to induce the Convention to adjourn till Monday morning at the usual hour, then to decide upon ulterior measures, if their Bill should be rejected. But his Lordship had secretly determined that they should meet no more; the death of the Convention was pronounced by their adjournment; and the honest, patriotic, but feeble Charlemont, on the Monday morning began to extinguish that institution to which he owed his celebrity, and to paralyze that proud popular spirit to which alone Ireland was indebted for its constitution and independence.

VIII. Sunday was passed between his indecision and his timidity. In his weak and virtuous mind, pride and patriotism were ranged on the one side; but imbecility and a sense of incapacity to meet the crisis, blinded him to the nature of that insidious conduct, which on this, and perhaps the only occasion of his life, he meditated against his benefactors.

He had a meeting of a few of his friends, most of whom had the same sensations as himself. The Bishop of Derry and Mr. Flood appeared like daring spectres to his imagination; he dreaded to meet them at the Convention, and after much deliberation, he decided on a course which detracted from his reputation, and for which even the critical situation of the country could not allow him one point of justification.

On the Monday morning he repaired to the Rotunda, before the usual hour of sitting. None but his own immediate partisans were aware of his intention; the meeting was expected to be most important, and the Delegates had no suspicion of his Lordship's early attendance.

On his taking the chair, a Delegate immediately arose to expatiate on the insults which the Convention had received during the debate of Saturday. His Lordship became alarmed; a protracted statement might give time for the arrival of Delegates, when all his objects would surely be frustrated. He at once took a step which had scarcely a parallel for duplicity, and which, though of the shallowest nature, proved the most effectual.

He instantly silenced the member, as being out of order, on the ground that one House of Parliament never could take notice of what passed in another; and that the Convention had adopted the rules and orders of Parliament.

Thus by collecting every ray of *feebleness* and *absurdity* into one focus, he prevented any continuation of the subject; and whilst he declared the Convention a House of Parliament, resolved to terminate its existence.

IX. After some conversation, a farewell address was rapidly passed to his Majesty, and his Lordship boldly adjourned the Convention—*sine die*. The Rotunda was quickly vacated, and when the residue of the Delegates, the ardent friends of the Volunteer body, came to take their places, they found the doors closed, the Chairman withdrawn, and that body upon which the nation relied for its independence dissolved for ever.

The Delegates mortified and abashed, returned to their homes; many friends of Earl Charlemont were soon ashamed of their conduct; and his Lordship's want of sincerity, for the first time was indisputably proved, and underwent well-merited animadversions.

The Volunteer Delegates having returned to their constituents, could give but a puerile account either of their proceedings or of their Chairman. Every eye now turned on the Earl of Bristol, who became the idol of the people. Whilst Lord Charlemont gently desc nded into the placid ranks of order and of courtesy, the Bishop rose like a phœnix from the ashes of the Convention. The Volunteer Corps in many districts beat to arms; they paraded, they deliberated, but their bond of union was enfeebled or dissevered.

Amongst the weaknesses of Lord Charlemont, he had an odious tinge of bigotry, and was decidedly opposed to the admission of Catholics to the full enjoyment of the Constitution. The Bishop, with more zeal and much greater abilities was their warmest advocate.

Exclusion on the one side, and toleration on the other became the theme of both. The dispute ran high; partisans were not wanting, the people began to separate; and this unfortunate controversy gradually terminated in that fatal dissension which never ceased to divide the Irish nation, and at length effected all the objects of mischief that the most ruthless enemies of the Irish could have expected, or have even wished.

CHAPTER XX.

Celebrated Address of the Volunteers to the Bishop—Reply of the Bishop—Some thought the Bishop's answer too strong—A new Bill suggested—New measures of Earl Charlemont—Decline of the Volunteers—Insincerity of the concessions—Cupidity of English traders —Sordid interest absorbed her justice—Commercial treaty and tariff proposed—Commercial propositions—Mr. Pitt's duplicity—Magnificence of the Irish Court—The Propositions rejected—Mr. Brownlow opposes the eleven propositions—Passed the Commons—Mr. Pitt proposes twenty propositions—Embarrassment of the Secretary—Most violent debates in the Irish Parliament—The Minister virtually defeated—The treaty ended—Defeat of the treaty effected by the country gentlemen—Mr. Forbes a leading member of the House of Commons—Mr. Hardy—Mr. Carleton, Solicitor General—His singular character.

I. AFTER this fatal event, the Volunteers became less calm and more unguarded. The address of one regiment to the Bishop of Derry, forms an interesting feature of Irish history, and it gave rise to a reply, such as had not been ventured upon by any public character in either country.

A northern corps, of considerable strength, had adopted the patriotic title of the "Bill of Rights Battalion," and had entered into resolutions to "support their constitution, or be buried under its ruins." A large detachment of that corps marched from their county, determined to uphold the Bishop's principles, and support his measures, with their lives and fortunes. The address and the answer are strongly illustrative of the spirit of the times, and the embarrassment of the Cabinet.

This declaration ran like wild fire throughout the nation. The last sentence was the boldest and most unequivocal, the most daring and decisive, used in Ireland. A British Earl and Irish Bishop, of great wealth, learning, abilities, and of unbounded popular influence, risking his fortune, and perhaps his life, in support of Ireland, was in every respect a phenomenon.

26*

His Lordship's desire to put himself at the head of the Irish nation was no longer doubtful, and well was he calculated to lead it to every extremity. All men were now convinced that, had his Lordship been President of the National Convention, the moderate and courtly Charlemont must either have submitted to his standard, or have sunk into nihility.

"BILL OF RIGHTS BATTALION.

" Resolved—That the following Address be presented from this Battalion, *under arms*, to the Earl of Bristol, Lord Bishop of Derry, for his truly patriotic exertions in support of our rights and liberties :—

" *To the Right Honourable the Earl of Bristol, Lord Bishop of Derry. The Address of the Bill of Rights Battalion of Volunteers.*

" My Lord,—Having, with the eye of silent approbation, viewed your conduct, in every stage of its progress, at the Grand National Convention of Volunteer Delegates, we are impelled, by those generous sentiments that actuate the breasts of Irishmen, to offer your Lordship this Address, as a mark of affection and of gratitude.

" We see, with indignation and concern, the treatment which the wise, spirited, and salutary Resolutions of the Volunteer Convention have received; but we trust the virtuous efforts of a united people, under the auspices of your Lordship, will cleanse the Augean stable—the noisome stalls of venality and corruption.

"'The gloomy clouds of superstition and *bigotry*, those *engines of disunion*, being fled the realm, the intrests of Ireland can no longer suffer by a diversity of *religious persuasions*. All are united in the pursuit of one great object—the extermination of corruption from our Constitution; nor can your Lordship and your virtuous coadjutors, in promoting civil and *religious* liberty, be destitute of the aid of *all* professions.

" Permit us to assure you, that. as freemen, freeholders, and as Volunteers, our exertions to effectuate the grand work of reformation, shall be as strenuous as the aim is

important: and that we are, with unfeigned gratitude and attachment, your Lordship's most faithful friends.
"Signed, by order of the Battalion,
"JOHN ORR, *Sec.*"

A detachment from the Battalion, consisting of eighty rank and file, headed by their lieutenant-colonel, waited on his Lordship, on the 14th instant, at Downhill, and presented, *under arms*, their Address: to which his Lordship was pleased to give the subsequent reply:—

"GENTLEMEN.—When you acknowledged the services of your fellow-citizens, in the County of Antrim, in the late struggle for *liberty*, you rewarded their toils in that coin most valuable to *virtuous* men; and your approbation of their efforts, in some measure, consoled them for their want of success.

"But, when you step forth from your *own* county, to hail the individual of another, unknown to you but by his honest endeavours, and unconnected, except by that kindred spirit which seems now, at length, to pervade the whole body of Irishmen, and, like a Promethean fire, to animate a hitherto lifeless mass, the satisfaction excited in his mind, by the applauses of men who have a right to approve what they *dare to support*, can be known only to those who are conscious of deserving what they are fortunate enough to receive.

"When the *conscience* of a *patriot* bears testimony to the *truth* of the panegyric, and the sincerity of the panegyrists' praise ceases to be adulation, then they become the wholesome food of a manly mind, and *nourish* that *virtue* they were, at first, intended only to approve.

"But, gentlemen, those who dare assert their own rights, should rise above the mean policy of violating the rights of others.

"There is, in this island, a class of citizens equally respectable, and infinitely more numerous than those who have hitherto oppressed them—

"Men who have long crouched under the *iron rod* of their *oppressors*, not from any dastardly insensibility to their shackles—not from any unmanly indifference to the inalienable rights of men; but from a pious dread of wounding our common country through the sides of its *tyrants*—

"Men, in whose hearts beats at this instant as high a pulse for liberty, and through whose veins pours a tide of as pure blood, and as noble too, as any that animates the proudest citizen in Ireland—

"Men, whose ancestors, at the hazard of their property, and with the loss of their lives, obtained the first great Bill of Rights, and upon which every other must be founded—the Magna Charta of Ireland—

"Men, whose ancestors, in the midst of ignorance, could distinguish between the duties of a religionist and the rights of a citizen, and who enacted those elementary and never obsolete statutes of præmunire, which, for centuries, have been an irrefragable monument of their sagacity in distinguishing, and their fortitude in severing, their duty to *the Church of Rome from their dependence on its Court*—

"Men, the undegenerate progeny of such virtuous ancestors, who, with a firmness worthy of our imitation, and still more worthy of our gratitude, have endured those very outrages from their *country* which their forefathers spurned at from its *sovereign*, and who, under a series of accumulated wrongs, which would heighten the disgrace of human policy if they could be paralleled in its annals, have with a fortitude as unexampled as their oppression, allowed every thing dear to the human heart to be wrecked, except their religion and their patriotism, except their acquiescence to the will of an inscrutable God, and their affection for a mistaken and deluded country.

"But, Gentlemen, the hour is now come, when sound policy, as well as irresistible justice will compel those who demand their own rights, to support their claim by a restitution of those of their fellow citizens.

"When Ireland must necessarily avail herself of her whole internal force to ward off foreign encroachments, or once more acquiesce under those encroachments, the better to exercise anew the tyranny of a *part* of the community over the dearest and inalienable rights of *others*.

"For one million of *divided Protestants* can never, in the scale of human government, be a counterpoise against three millions of united *Catholics*. But, Gentlemen of the Bill of Rights Battalion, I appeal to yourselves, and summon you to consistency—TYRANNY is not GOVERNMENT, and ALLEGIANCE IS DUE ONLY TO PROTECTION.

"BRISTOL."
" 14*th January*, 1784."

II. The Government now became seriously alarmed. Never was any government in greater difficulty. Various were its advisers at this important moment; those in council, whose arrogance and arbitrary feelings generally outweighed their prudence, strongly enforced the most dangerous of all measures, the immediate arrest of the Bishop. They contended that, by such energy, and by at once depriving the Volunteers of so enthusiastic a partisan, they might check their progress; but they never reflected on the utter inability of Government to enforce that resolution.

The daring and dangerous strength of the Bishop's language, the glaring light which by the last sentence, was thrown upon the conditional terms of allegiance, as settled under the precedent of 1680, though totally inapplicable to the Irish nation, or to the state of its connection with Great Britain, astounded all men. But the Government soon perceived the inevitable convulsion which must have attended so violent a step as Fitzgibbon had recommended. It would have been the signal for 100,000 Volunteers rushing to the rescue, and one week would have produced an insurrection, the smallest spark would now have inflamed the nation.

The Government resolved to watch the progress of events over which control might be impossible. This course fully corresponded with their utmost expectations.

Many of the most patriotic Volunteers thought the address of the Bishop true in principle, but too strong in terms, particularly as it was addressed to an armed corps, in the centre of thousands who could not fail to kindle at the Promethean fire with which his Lordship had so classically animated his oration.

The idea of coercing the Parliament very rapidly lost ground, and in a short time it became the general opinion, that Mr. Flood's Reform Bill had been opposed by many upon the principle, that it was rather a command than a solicitation; and that it would be prudent to give the Parliament a fair trial before they absolutely condemned them. It was thought that the objection being removed, by the dissolution of the National Convention, a new bill should be presented in the ordinary course of parliamentary proceedings, by members solely in their civil character, and the disposition of the House and the resolves of Government be thus fairly ascertained.

The people were severed, but the Government remained compact; the Parliament was corrupted, the Volunteers were paralyzed, and the high spirit of the nation exhibited a rapid declension. *The jealousy of patriots is always destructive of liberty.*

III. A new event, however, soon proved the weak delusions of Earl Charlemont. At the dissolution of the Convention, he recommended a Reform Bill to be presented to Parliament, as emanating solely from civil bodies, unconnected with military character.* Every experiment is silly, where its failure can be clearly anticipated, and almost every man in Ireland well knew, that such a bill would be lost in such a Parliament. Mr. Flood, however, tried the experiment, and it failed; he attempted it without spirit, because he was without confidence. Mr. Grattan supported it with languor, because it was the measure of his rival. The military bill had been scouted, because it was military, and the civil bill was rejected because it was popular. A corrupt senate never wants a vicious apology.

The Volunteers now drooped, yet their resolutions were published, their meetings were not suspended, and their reviews continued; but these appeared only as boyish shows, to amuse the languid vanity of their *deluded general.* He passed their lines in military state; he received their salutes with grace and condescension, and recommended them to be tranquil and obedient; and, after a peaceable campaign of four hours duration, composed his mild and grammatical despatches, and returned

* The decided opinion of the *whole Bar*, after a long and solemn discussion, was that the Volunteers, as an armed body, had *not* divested themselves of any civil right political or personal.

to his Marino, and to the enjoyment of the more congenial elegancies of literature and of private friendships.

The temperate system now gained ground; some patriots lost their energy, others lost their influence, and the Government experienced the wisdom of their negative measures.

That noble institution, the Volunteers of Ireland, survived, however, these blows some years. This only luminary of her sphere was, by the devices of the Government, gradually obscured, and, at length extinguished !!

IV. It was not supposed that the concessions to Ireland had been voluntary on the part of Great Britain. They were only a sacrifice to circumstances, with the mental reservation of acting upon the original principle, as often as events might facilitate such a proceeding. The egotistical character of the English trader, the avarice inseparable from mercantile education, and the national impatience, under even an ideal rivalship, united in exciting every effort to neutralize the concessions; and it soon became palpable to both nations, that the free trade of Ireland might prove a sore impediment to the gratifications of the English monopoly. England could not so suddenly renounce the force of ancient habit, and of engrafted prejudices, and become, at once, liberal, enlightened, and magnanimous. No person conversant with the ruling principles of mankind, could suppose that her very nature could change in a day, and that she could be sincere towards Ireland, as long as it was imagined that the two countries had repugnant interests.

The insatiable cupidity of British capitalists, and the necessities of the British Government, had commenced their coalition even against the prosperity of England. The extravagance of the Government was supplied with facility, by the usuries of the monied interest, and a rein was given to that boundless waste of public money, which terminated in an overwhelming debt, and which nearly exhausted financial ingenuity, having not unfrequently assailed the principles and safeguards of her own Constitution.

These concessions were likewise rendered peculiarly unpalatable, by political circumstances. England, at that gloomy epoch, had not been able to retain one disinterested friend or sincere ally in Europe. She had subsidized German *mendicants*, and she had purchased human blood, she had hired military slaves from beggarly principalities; but these were not alliances for the honour of Great Britain.

The character which England had justly acquired previously to the year 1780, had raised her reputation above that of all the powers of Europe. The new attempt on Ireland, proclaimed that her sordid interests now absorbed every other consideration.

V. The minister's only excuse for his schemes, was the pecuniary wants of Government. But Mr. Pitt feared that Ireland would murmur at paying her portion of his profuse extravagance. Taxation commenced on luxuries, proceeded to comforts, to necessaries, and, at length, extended its grasp to justice and morality. A treaty for a commercial tariff between the two nations was now proceeded on, and exposed that duplicity which had been scarcely suspected. The Irish, unaccustomed to receive any concession or favour, and little versed in the schemes of commercial polity, gave a giddy confidence to the dignified terms in which their claims had been acknowledged. Some able men, however, reasoned that the very composition of British Cabinets, the means of getting into power, and of keeping it; their private interests, and public object, were decidedly adverse to any liberal participation of commercial advantages with Ireland. Upon the English monopolists alone, ministers could depend for replenishing their Exchequer, and for their retaining their power. Men also reasoned, that, if England and Ireland should clash on any point of commerce, a British Parliament could not serve two conflicting interests, and an Irish Parliament was not likely to surrender rights she had obtained with so much difficulty and danger.

It was, therefore, palpable (as Mr. Fox had mysteriously declared) that some further international measures were absolutely necessary, and as Ireland could now legislate for her own commerce with all the world, it seemed advisable, that a commercial treaty should be contracted by the two countries, which might provide against any collision, and secure to both nations the advantages of the federal compact.

Nothing could be more plausible than the theory of this measure, and few things more difficult to carry into execution.

VI. The detailed debates, on these commercial propositions are beyond the range of this compact history.* But it is essential to remark upon them with reference to the conduct of Great Britain, and it may be proper to allude to the state of Ireland, at the moment selected by the minister for making the first indirect attempt to recapture the independence of that devoted country.

The Irish nation was rapidly advancing to eminence and prosperity, her commerce improving, her debt light, the taxes inconsiderable, emigration had ceased, and population was augmenting, nearly two hundred nobles, and nearly all the commoners, resided on their demesnes and expended their rents amidst those who paid them. The Parliament seemed to have been awakened to a more sedulous attention to the wishes of the people. Mr. Pitt took advantage of the moment he saw that the nation was in good humour and grateful, and he determined, whilst he flattered their vanity to invade their constitution. The state of the Irish court and aristocracy, at this period, seemed particularly favourable to the experiment. The constant residence of the landed proprietors was an incalculable benefit; and their influence, in mitigating the avarice of the clergy and the irritating tyranny of the tithing system, was most grateful to the people.

The vice-regal establishment was at that period much more brilliant and hospitable than that of the monarch; the utmost magnificence signalized the entertainments of the Duke and Duchess of Rutland, and their luxury gave a powerful impulse to manufactures and industry. It was to be regretted however, that this magnificence was accompanied by circumstances which formed a new epoch

* The debates of the Irish Parliament upon these propositions, were taken with very considerable accuracy by Woodfall, and published by Byrne, in Dublin. They are valuable for disclosing the political characters and talents of nearly all the men of note, then members of the Irish Commons. Scarcely any other document better depicts the arrogant and decided character of Mr. Fitzgibbon which distinguished him through all the subsequent concerns of Ireland, until, in a characteristic attempt to lord it over the British Peerage, he was politically slain by the Duke of Bedford.

in the habits of Irish society: a laxity of decorum in both sexes of the fashionable aristocracy, had commenced, and though the voluptuous brilliancy of the Court was dazzling to the country, it was deficient in that proud, elevated dignity which had generally distinguished that society in former vice-royalties. Nothing could be more honourable than the conduct of the Duke of Rutland; but the sudden relaxation of manners at his Court, was by no means gratifying to those who had been accustomed to the undeviating strictness of decorum amongst the Irish ladies.*

This paroxysm of joy throughout the country, confidence amongst the gentry, and absence of suspicion in the Parliament, was judged by the British Government the opportunity most favourable, under colour of her commerce to undermine her Constitution. This proposition for a treaty of commerce between England and Ireland, as two *independent* countries, necessarily required a deeper consideration than any other event of her history. No decisive *international* overt act had, as yet, taken place between the two countries. But Mr. Pitt, in his anxiety to encroach upon the independent spirit of the compact, unintentionally confirmed it upon a clear international principle.

Mr. Orde, the Secretary of the Viceroy, on the 7th of February, 1785, proposed to the Irish Parliament eleven resolutions, as a distinct commercial treaty between two *independent* states. As such they were received, but the treaty was at length utterly rejected by the Irish Parliament.

Mr. Brownlow, one of the first country gentlemen of Ireland, most zealously opposed it as a badge of slavery, and an attempt to encroach on the independence of his country. It was, however, conditionally accepted, after much discussion; during which a manœuvre was practised by the Secretary, which would have disgraced the lowest trader. Mr. Orde expatiated with great plausibility upon the kind concessions of the English Government,

* Before this period, there had been but two actions of crim. con. in Ireland, in both of which noblemen were the plaintiffs; Lord Belvidere against his brother Captain Rochfort, and Lord Lisle against Dennis M'Carthy, his own postillion. There had, however, been several hundreds tried in England.

and the extraordinary advantages likely to result to Ireland; and urged the House to come to a hasty decision in their favour, "lest the *English monopolist* should pour in applications to the English Parliament to stop their progress, as too partial to Ireland." The bait took, and the resolutions were approved, and sent back with some alterations.

His artifice, however, was defeated, and Mr. Orde was left in a situation of excessive embarrassment and appeared equally ridiculous to both countries. Mr. Pitt having gained his first point, conceived it possible to assail more openly the independence of Ireland, by attaching her finances and commerce to Great Britain, so that her own Parliament should become, if not impotent, at least contemptible.

Instead, therefore of rediscussing the eleven resolutions as approved by Ireland, he brought twenty propositions before the English Parliament, incorporated in a Bill, framed with such consummate artifice, that it affected to confer favours, whilst it rendered the Irish Parliament only the register of all English statutes relating to commerce; and, by a perpetual money bill, appropriated a proportion of her hereditary revenue to the uses of the British Navy.

VII. Mr. Orde* himself was utterly uncertain how to proceed, and after many adjournments, on the 12th of August, 1785, he moved for leave to bring in a Bill pursuant to Mr Pitt's twenty propositions. The country gentlemen of Ireland, though they did not understand the commercial details of the subject, perceived the design of the minister. A storm arose in Parliament, the landed interests of the country were alarmed, the country gentlemen grew boisterous, the law officers were arrogant, the patriots retorted, and rendered the debate one of the most inflammatory that had for some years been witnessed.

* Mr. Orde, the Secretary, a cold, cautious, slow, and sententious man, tolerably well informed, but not at all talented, had a mind neither powerful nor feeble; as a public man he could not be despised, as an English Factor, he could plausibly enhance the property he was entrusted to dispose of, though he well knew there was a rent within its folds. He had much to gain, for of political reputation he had nothing to be deprived. He certainly did as much as could be effected on the subject, and a British peerage consoled him for his Irish discomfiture.

Long and furious was that remarkable contest. Fitzgibbon the Attorney General, exhibited an arrogance which more than equalled any of his former exhibitions; he insulted many, and used the most overbearing language to all who opposed him. The debate continued all night, and, at nine o'clock next morning, the violence was undiminished, and it was difficult to put the question: at length a division at once announced the equivocal victory of the Minister. The numbers for Government were 127, against the Minister 108, leaving only a majority of 19. As the motion was only for leave to bring in the Bill, it was obvious that on a second reading it would have been disgracefully rejected. Mr. Flood then moved a declaration of rights; another division still less favourable to the Minister succeeded; an adjournment, therefore, and a prorogation took place, and the subject was never renewed.

Mr. Pitt never would have brought in his Bill, had he not been assured of success by the Irish Secretary; this defeat, therefore, was the more galling, and it confirmed, in his persevering and inflexible mind, a determination, if he could not rule the Irish Parliament, to annihilate the independence of Ireland. Mr. Pitt never was scrupulous as to means, and a much more important point shortly confirmed his determination by proving that, upon vital subjects he had not yet sufficiently humbled the people, or been able sufficiently to seduce their representatives.

These propositions were in fact defeated by the honest obstinacy of the country gentlemen, and by the influence and talents of Mr. Grattan and Mr. Flood, who, upon this subject alone, were perfectly in unison. It is worthy of observation, that the zeal and honesty of Mr. Connolly, in supporting the independence of his country against the agency of Mr. Orde, were utterly reversed by his subsequently supporting the still more destructive measures of his corrupt and unfortunate relative.

VIII. During these scenes, some men, who, though not of the highest order of talent, were in considerable reputation and of untainted integrity, exerted themselves in defence of their country; amongst them, the most active was Mr. Forbes, the Member for Drogheda. Without any very distinguished natural abilities, and but moderately acquainted with literature, by his zealous attachment to Mr. Grattan, his public principles, and attention to business, he received much respect, and acquired some influence in the House of Commons. He had practised at the bar with a probability of success; but he mistook his course, and became a statesman, as which he never could rise to any great distinction. As a lawyer, he undervalued himself and was modest; as a stateman, he over-rated himse f, and was presumptuous He benefitted his party by his indefatigable zeal, and reflected honour upon it by his character; he was a good Irishman, and to the last undeviating in his public principles. He died in honourable exile, as Governor of the Bahama Isles.

In a class lower as a politician, but higher as a man of letters, and equal in integrity, stood Mr. Hardy, the biographer of Earl Charlemont. He had been returned to Parliament by the interest of Earl Granard, and faithfully followed the fortunes of that nobleman and his relative, Earl Moira, throughout all the political vicissitudes of Ireland.

His mind was too calm, and his habits too refined, for the rugged drudgery of the bar—he was not sufficiently profound for a statesman, and was too mild for a political wrangler—his ambition was languid, and he had no love of lucre—he therefore was not eminent either as a politician or a lawyer. Like many other modest and accomplished men he was universally esteemed. He had sufficient talents, had he possessed energy, and his interest was always the last of his considerations; his means were narrow, and his exertions inconsiderable.

IX. Mr. (afterwards Viscount) Carleton, was, during a part of this important period, Solicitor General of Ireland, and no man was less adequate to the parliamentary duties of that office. He was, of course, but little noticed by the recorders of that epoch; and is almost a dead letter in the memoirs of Ireland. His conduct on the Union, however, was remarkable.

Viscount Carleton was the son of a respectable merchant of Cork, and was created Solicitor General when the superior law offices were considered as stations of very considerable weight, and of much official dignity

At the bar he was efficient; on the bench he was exemplary. With a plain and exclusively forensic talent, cultivated by an assiduity nothing could surpass, he attained very considerable professional eminence: his whole capacity seemed to have been formed into points of law, regularly numbered, and always ready for use. His limited genius seldom wandered beyond the natural boundary; but whenever it chanced to stray to general subjects, it appeared always to return to its symmetrical technicalities with great gratification.

Habit and application had made him a singular proficient in that methodical hair-splitting of legal distinctions, and in reconciling the incongruity of conflicting precedents, which generally beget the reputation of an able lawyer. The government were glad to get him out of Parliament, and without intending it, did an essential service to the due administration of justice.

As Chief Justice of the Common Pleas, his naturally gentle manners and affability, his legal knowledge, and the rectitude of his decisions, procured him the unanimous approbation of his profession. He had no enemies. But, even in his prime, he was a most feeble and inefficient legislator and statesman; his capacity was not sufficiently comprehensive to embrace subjects of constitutional polity. He brought the attributes of his trade into Parliament, and appeared either blind or indifferent to those varied and luxuriant labyrinths which the principles of civil liberty eternally disclose, and which the enlightened legislator never fails to discover, and never ceases to enjoy.

When men shall read the childish, contemptible, and strained attempts at reasoning, which were pronounced by him upon the discussion of the Union, and reflect upon the duplicity of his professions, and his predetermined emigration, it must be regretted, that a judge so competent and independent, and a man so respected, should have yielded his country against his conviction, and lent his fair fame to the corrupting Minister.*

---

* After Lord Carleton had supported the Union, he was suffered to retire, *on the ground of declining health*, on a magnificent pension. He immediately emigrated to London, and lived in excellent health and spirits *for four-and-twenty years*.

CHAPTER XXI.

Death of tne Duke of Rutland—Marquis of Buckingham's second Government—The question of a Regency—Mr. Pitt's conduct—The Prince submitted to the restraints—The Irish resisted, and refused to restrain him—Unprecedented case—Collision between the two Parliaments—Round Robin—Irish address to the Prince—Sketch of the Arguments on the Regency question in Ireland—Constitutional state of both nations—Conduct of the nations contrasted—Reasons for the Irish Parliament proceeding by Address, and not by Statute, to appoint a Regent—Question whether the Parliaments of England or Ireland had committed a breach of the Constitution—Threats of the Viceroy—The Round Robin—Viceroy determined to retire—Reception of the Irish delegates by the Prince—Address of the Irish Parliament to the Prince—Reply of the Prince, eulogizing the Irish legislature—Afterwards neglected.

I. THE British Government, for a short time, affected to relinquish the idea of opposing the commercial interests of Ireland. It was determined to let the Irish take their own course, and patiently to await, till circumstances might enable them to act more decisively against their independence.

Mr. Pitt was obliged to rest upon his oars: his own bark was tempest tossed, whilst that of Ireland was running rapidly before a prosperous wind. This was the state of Ireland after the proposition-tempest had subsided, when the Duke of Rutland's incessant conviviality deprived (October, 1787) the British Peerage of an honourable, generous, and high-minded nobleman, and Ireland of a Viceroy, whose government did nothing, or worse than nothing, for the Irish people. With the aristocracy, the Duke was singularly popular, and he was not disliked by any class of the community; but his advisers were profligate, and his measures were corrupt. His Grace and the Duchess were reckoned the handsomest couple in Ireland.

The Marquis of Buckingham was sent, a second time, to govern Ireland. As a moderate, hard-working Viceroy, with a Catholic wife, he was selected, as not unlikely to be agreeable to the Irish.

Little, however, was it supposed, that the most important and embarrassing of all constitutional questions between the two countries was likely to occur during his administration. Unfortunately, however, such did arise, through the necessity of appointing a Regent during the Monarch's aberration of intellect.

This great question, and its influence on the federative compact of the two nations, now entirely occupied the attention of both Parliaments. The Prince, at that period, held a line of politics, and employed a class of servants, different from those he afterwards adopted. Mr. Pitt well knew that his own reign, and that of the Cabinet he commanded, were in danger—that they could endure no longer than some tatters of the royal prerogative and restraints on the Regent should remain in his hands as minister, by which he could curb the Regency, which might otherwise be fatal to his ambition and his cabinet.

He therefore resisted, with all his energy, the heir-apparent's right to the prerogatives of his father, and struggled to restrain the Prince from many of those essential powers of the executive authority.

The Prince acted with that dignity of which he was so much a master, but, through a state necessity, submitted reluctantly to the restraints prescribed by his own servants; and, from a delicacy to the feeling of his mother, retained in his service a minister whom, on every other ground, he would have been more than justified in dismissing with indignation.

The Irish nation had nothing to do with this private circumstance, and the Parliament would not obey the minister, or submit to the mandates of the British Government. They decided that the Prince was their Regent, in virtue of the federative compact; and they also determined that he should have all the regal prerogatives connected with the monarchy of Ireland.

Upon this subject debates arose, more embarrassing than any that had ever taken place in the Irish Parliament. It was a *casus omissus*, both in the British Revolution of 1688, and in the Irish Constitution of 1782.

The question was, whether the Parliament of Ireland were competent, by address or otherwise, to invest the Regent with more extensive privileges, as to Ireland, than the British Parliament had thought fit to entrust to him in England.

II. This point was without precedent; but it was argued, that if an act of Parliament were necessary, no Regent could be appointed, for an act implied the existence of the third estate, and the proper proceeding was, therefore, by address. The probability of His Majesty's recovery had a powerful influence on placemen and official connections. The Marquis of Buckingham took a decisive part against the Prince, and made bold and hazardous attempts upon the rights of the Irish Parliament. That body was indignant at his presumption, and he found it impossible to govern or control even the habitual supporters of every administration. Fitzgibbon, the Attorney General, was promised the seals, if he succeeded for Mr. Pitt, and he even announced that every opponent should be made the victim of his suffrage. Lord Buckingham even threatened those who would not coincide with the British Parliament; the then powerful family of Ponsonby, decided supporters of Government, on this occasion seceded from the Marquis, and which gave rise to the famous and spirited Round Robin.* Many however, may be induced to ask, why it was expedient to be honest in a circle.

After long and ardent debates, an address of the Irish Parliament was voted to the Prince, declaring him Regent of the Kingdom of Ireland, *in as full, ample*, and *unqualified* a manner as was enjoyed by his Royal Father.

The words, though simple, were as comprehensive as the English language could make them. The terms are: " Under the style and title of Prince Regent of Ireland, in the name and on behalf of his Majesty, to exercise and administer, according to the laws and constitution of this Kingdom, *all* regal powers, jurisdiction, and prerogatives to the Crown *and Government thereof belonging*."

In the Commons, the Address was moved by Mr. Grattan, and was carried without a division. It was

* That Round Robin was so *decisive*, that it was brought forward in 1800, as the most powerful argument in favour of a union.

moved in the Lords by the Earl of Charlemont, and was carried by a majority of only 19. Contents 45—Non-contents 26.

In the Commons, the number upon Mr. Grattan's Motion, for thus *transmitting* the Address were—for the Motion, 130: against it, 74.

The Address having passed both the Lords and Commons, it was sent to the Viceroy to be transmitted to His Royal Highness. The Marquis of Buckingham peremptorily refused acquiescence, and an embassy of two Lords and four Commoners,* was immediately appointed to humbly present the Address, in the name of the nation, to the Prince. A severe resolution of censure was then moved against the Lord Lieutenant, for a breach of official duty. It passed both Houses, and obliged him to quit the country. Though his extensive patronage was craftily applied and had procured him many adherents, he never afterwards could make any head in the Irish Parliament. The Address was the boldest step yet taken by the Irish nation, and it brought the independence of Ireland to a practical issue.

III. The vital importance of the Regency Question, in consolidating the independence of the Irish Nation, and the fallacious influence which it afterwards afforded to the arguments for extinguishing that independence, offer considerations more grave and more comprehensive than any that have occurred since England, by the Renunciation Act, admitted her usurpation.

The facts and reasoning on that subject are beyond the range of this volume—they are therefore here necessarily epitomised. However somewhat more than superficial detail is indispensable, to dispel that mist of mingled prejudice and ignorance of the English people, which has never ceased to obscure from their view every *clear* prospect of the true state of Ireland, when she evinced her unqualified adherence to the genuine spirit of the constitution.

In 1789 two branches of the legislature, the Peers and the Commons of Great Britain and of Ireland, were by common law originally, and by statute law, subsequently,

---

* The Lords were, the Duke of Leinster and Lord Charlemont. The Commons, Messrs. Connolly, J. O'Neil, W. B. Ponsonby, and J. Stewart

as distinct as those of any other independent nation. The third estate, the king, was common Monarch of both; the two crowns placed on the same brow were, by the common constitution, entailed for ever on the same dynasty: the executive power was united; the other branches utterly separate.

IV. The King of both countries having become incapable of executing his functions for either—his eldest son and heir apparent to the throne, in the full vigour of health and intellect, by the incapacity of his father, became the proper guardian of those two realms to the throne of which he was constitutionally to succeed.

So circumstanced, the British minister who as such had no constitutional right to interfere with Ireland, thought proper, through the British Parliament, to shackle the Regency with restrictions, that deprived the executive power in England of its constitutional prerogatives; such a measure, if adopted by Ireland, would have left her king incompetent, and her Regency imperfect, during the necessary suspension of the monarch's capacity to govern.

The Viceroy of Ireland, under the dictation of the British minister, resisted the legislature of Ireland in its own course of appointing the same Regent; and a collision ensued: the Irish supporting, and the English curtailing, the constitutional prerogative of the executive branch of the constitution, in the office of Regent.

V. In this state of things, the session was opened on the 5th February by the Marquis of Buckingham, who, in his speech from the throne, informed the two houses of the severe indisposition with which the King was afflicted, and at the same time, acquainted them that he had directed all the documents respecting his Majesty's health which could assist their deliberations to be laid before them.

Mr. Fitzherbert, the secretary, then moved the house, that it should resolve itself into a committee on the *Monday sen'night*, to take into consideration the state of his Majesty's health.

As the evident design of this delay was to prevent the Irish Parliament from coming to any resolutions relative to a Regency before the determinations of the British

Parliament could be proposed to them for their concurrence, it was opposed as derogatory to the *independence* of that Kingdom, and to the dignity and credit of its Parliament. Mr. Grattan therefore proposed that—"the House should meet on the *next* Wednesday." His amendment, after a long and warm debate, was carried by a majority of 128 to 74. A motion made by the Chancellor of the Exchequer for proceeding immediately upon the business of *supply*, was negatived.

VI. On Wednesday the 11th, Mr. Connolly moved, that "an address should be presented to the Prince of Wales, requesting him to take on himself the Government of Ireland, as Regent thereof during his Majesty's incapacity," (without any restriction.)

This motion gave rise to a long and violent debate, in which the Attorney General, Mr. Fitzgibbon (afterwards Chancellor of Ireland) eminently distinguished himself in opposition to the motion. It was supported by Mr. Grattan, Mr. Ponsonby, Mr. Curran, and other eminent speakers, and was ultimately carried without a division.

On Monday the 16th, the House of Lords being met, the Earl of Charlemont moved for an address to the Prince of Wales similar to that voted by the Commons, which, after some debate, was carried by a majority of nineteen. A protest was entered signed by seventeen Lords.

On Thursday the 19th, both houses waited upon the Lord Lieutenant with their address, and requested him to transmit the same, with this request his Excellency refused to comply, returning for answer that under the impressions he felt of his official duty and of the oath he had taken, he did not consider himself warranted to lay before the Prince an address, purporting to invest his Royal Highness with powers to take upon him the Government of the realm, before he *should* be enabled by law so to do; and therefore he declined transmitting their address to Great Britain.

Upon the return of the Commons to their own House, and the answer of the Lord Lieutenant being reported to them, Mr. Grattan observed, that in a case so extremely new it would be highly improper to proceed with hurry or precipitation : the House was called upon to act with dignity, firmness and decision; and therefore that due time might be had for deliberation, he would move the question of adjournment to the following day. The question was put and carried without opposition.

VII. On the next day he moved, That his Excellency the Lord Lieutenant, having thought proper to decline to transmit to his Royal Highness George, Prince of Wales, the address of both Houses of Parliament, a competent number of members be appointed to present the said address to his Royal Highness.

Mr. Grattan's motion was passed without any division, whereupon he moved, "That Mr. Connolly do attend the Lords with the said resolution, and acquaint them that this House requests them to appoint members of their own body to join with the members of the Commons in presenting the said address." This also passed without any division, and Mr. Connolly went up to the Lords accordingly. The message received in reply was, that the Lords had concurred in the resolution of the Commons, and had appointed his Grace the Duke of Leinster, and the Earl of Charlemont, to join with such members as the Commons should appoint to present the address of both Houses to his Royal Highness, the Prince of Wales.

Mr. Grattan then moved that the Right Hon. Thomas Connolly, Right Hon. J. O'Neil, Right Hon. W. Ponsonby, and J. Stewart, Esq. should be appointed commissioners on the part of the Commons, for the purpose of presenting the Address to his Royal Highness, the Prince of Wales, and they were appointed accordingly.

These motions having passed, Mr. Grattan then moved, that the two Houses of Parliament had discharged an indispensable duty in providing for the third estate of the Irish Constitution (rendered incomplete through the King's incapacity) by appointing the Prince of Wales, Regent of Ireland. This motion was carried after a long debate. Ayes 150, Noes 71.

Mr. Grattan then moved that it is the opinion of this House, "That the answer of his Excellency the Lord Lieutenant to both Houses, in refusing to transmit the said address, is *ill advised*, and tends to convey an unwarrantable and *unconstitutional censure on the conduct of both Houses.*"

Mr. Grattan's motion of *censure* was then put, on which the House divided, and there appeared for the motion 115 against it 83.

On the 25th, resolutions of the committee of supply (which provides for the payment of the interest of the national debt, the annuities and establishments,) being read, Mr. Grattan moved "That the words for TWO MONTHS, only ending the 26th of May, 1789, be added." On the question being put, there appeared, Ayes 104, Noes 85.

Mr. Grattan then moved that the *army* be provided for to the 25th of May only, which motion was carried. Ayes 102, Noes 77.

VIII. This determination of the Irish legislature in asserting their constitutional independence, and their entire rejection of all subserviency to the views or dictates of the British Parliament, was founded not only on the nature of their federative compact, but on the very principles of that constitution which it was their mutual duty to preserve in its full integrity.

By that constitution it was indispensable that every statute should receive its consummation only by the express assent of the King, as the third estate of that constitution.

In this case no third estate existed in a capacity to assent to or consummate any statute, and no *express* provision had been made by the constitution for such an emergency. The Irish legislature therefore, having no *competent* third estate to consummate a statute, adopted the next step admitted by the Constitution, of proceeding by address, for which they had the English precedent of 1688.

The British Minister however, determined to proceed by statute, and this difference therefore arose between the two legislatures, England proceeded by means which could not be constitutionally consummated, Ireland proceeded by means which constitutionally could. The Viceroy surrendered himself to the minister; the Irish legislature adhered to the Prince, and asserted their independence by an overt act, which England never since forgave; and, on the Union, used that act of Irish constitutionality as an argument for annihilating that legislature, which had dared to support the rights of their Prince against the ambition of his Minister.

IX. International controversies are frequently referred to the arbitration of foreign states, disinterested on the subject, and had the question been submitted to such an arbitrator, "Whether the British legislature abetting the conspiracy of Mr. Pitt, to abridge the executive power of its inherent rights, or that of Ireland supporting the royal prerogatives of their common Regent, and had committed a crime, should be extinguished for its inroad on the constitution," the awful sentence must have been pronounced against Great Britain; and even the dignified language of the Prince himself, evinced nothing adverse to the principle of so just a condemnation.*

Previous to the departure of the Delegates to present the address to the Prince of Wales, a declaration by the Viceroy had been made public, which threatened to visit with his displeasure, or reward by his favours, every member of the legislature who could either be deprived of office for his resistance, or induced to accept one for his desertion.

This declaration gave rise to the then celebrated Round Robin, which was subscribed by a great number of the highest and most leading characters of both Houses of Parliament, pledging themselves as a body and as individuals, against every attempt by Government either to seduce or to intimidate them. This was a fatal blow to all further struggles of the Viceroy. The tide ran too strongly to be resisted; the rank and influence of those who signed that document could no longer be opposed, and proved to the Viceroy the impossibility of his continuing the Government of Ireland, upon such a principle, and of course he determined to retire from the Viceroyalty.

X. The Delegates now proceeded to London to deliver to the Prince the joint address of both Houses of the Irish Parliament. The first nobles and commoners of that kingdom investing him with all those royal rights and prerogatives which had been refused to him by his British subjects, was too grand and gratifying an embassy not to receive the highest honours and attention his Royal

* See his letter to Mr Pitt, and his replies to the addresses

Highness and his friends could bestow. Nothing could exceed the dignified cordiality and splendour with which they were received by the Regent on that occasion. He felt all the importance of such a grant, and if gratitude has any permanent station in the hearts of monarchs, the Irish people had reason to expect every favour that future power could confer, on a nation whose firmness and fidelity had given him so imperishable a proof of their attachment.

The words of the address bespeak the independence and loyalty of the Irish legislature, and fix the constitutional limitation to the power conferred by them; they prayed:—

"We, his Majesty's most dutiful and loyal subjects, the lords spiritual and temporal and the Commons of Ireland in Parliament assembled, beg leave to approach your Royal Highness with hearts full of the most loyal and affectionate attachment to the person and government of your Royal Father, to express the deepest and most grateful sense of the numerous blessings which we have enjoyed under his illustrious House, and at the same time to condole with your Royal Highness upon the grievous malady with which it has pleased Heaven to afflict the best of sovereigns.

"We beg leave humbly to request that your Royal Highness will be pleased to take upon you the government of this realm, during the continuance of his Majesty's present indisposition, and no longer; and under the style and title of Prince Regent of Ireland, in the name and on behalf of his Majesty, to exercise and administer, according to the laws and constitution of this kingdom, all regal powers, jurisdictions, and prerogatives to the crown and government thereof belonging."

XI. The reply of his Royal Highness to this embassy from Ireland, is a document of most intrinsic value to the character, and ought to have been so to the interests of that calumniated and ruined island.

That royal document expressly upheld and for ever records the loyal, consistent, and constitutional principles, and conduct which guided the Irish legislature in that unprecedented proceeding, therein, not only explicitly, but most ardently eulogised by the heir apparent.

Yet it is unfortunate for the character and consistency of British Governments, to find seated high in the cabinet of George the Fourth, the very minister who, in the Irish Parliament, in 1799, gave the retort courteous to every word so uttered by that monarch, as Regent in 1789, and stigmatized as treason that just eulogium uttered but ten years before upon their loyalty.

Posterity, however, will read with disgust that, within so short a period, the very act which elicited those just and florid praises of devoted Ireland, was converted into a libel, and made a leading argument to effect the annihilation of the very legislature they had so ardently applauded.

It is a remarkable coincidence in Irish annals, that Providence was pleased to diminish her visitation on the King's capacity on the very day first appointed by the Prince to receive his investiture as Regent of Ireland, through the hands of the Irish Delegates; the object of this mission therefore could have no ulterior operation, and they returned to their country with every public honour and private estimation which their embassy and their characters so justly merited. The Prince therefore had no power previous to the Union of exemplifying his declaration of gratitude to Ireland. After the Union, when *Imperial* Regent, his British ministers showed no disposition to give his Royal Highness that power or opportunity; his energies seemed to retire as his powers were advancing, and when he became actual monarch of both countries, events proved that the Regencies were forgotten, and that gratitude was not a record.

CHAPTER XXII.

Ireland acted on her independence—Prosperous state of Ireland at that Period—The Rise of the Irish Nation consummated by the withdrawal of the Viceroy—Particularly important observation—Lord Westmoreland—Major Hobart—His character—State of Ireland on his accession to office—Concessions by Government—Delusion and negligence of the Opposition—Catholic emancipation commenced—Arguments of the Catholics—Catholic petition rejected by a great majority—Deep designs of Mr. Pitt—Mr. Pitt proceeds with his measures to promote a union—Lord Fitzwilliam appointed Lord Lieutenant—His character—Deceived and calumniated by Mr. Pitt—Great popularity of the Lord Lieutenant—Earl Fitzwilliam recalled—Fatal consequences—Ireland given up to Lord Clare, and insurrection excited—Lord Camden—United Irishmen—Unprecedented Organization—Lord Camden's character—Despotic conduct of Lord Clare—Earl Carhampton commander-in-chief—Disobeys Lord Camden—Again disobeys—The King's sign-manuel commands him to obey—He resigns.

I. UPON the return of the Delegates to Ireland, the first epocha which gives a title to this epitome of her history was consummated; her *Rise*. She had arisen from servitude to freedom, from a subservient to an independent Nation; the acquirement of that independence was a revolution, but it was a revolution without bloodshed. It was rather a regeneration, accomplished by the almost unanimous exertion of all the rank, the wealth, the character and the honesty of a vast population; the highest of the Aristocracy, and the humblest of the people joined hand in hand to regain their independence; and it may well be termed a loyal revolution, because the English legislature, by their own voluntary act, admitted their own previous usurpation, and denounced all further pretensions to dominate over Ireland; and the King of Great Britain on his throne, received and acknowledged his Irish subjects altogether legislatively unconnected with the rest of England. From that day Ireland rose in wealth, in trade, and in manufactures, agriculture, and every branch of industry that could enhance her value or render a people rich and prosperous. She had acquired her seat amongst the nations of the world, she had asserted her independence against the insolence of Portugal, she had suggested an Irish navy to protect her shores, she had declared a perpetual league of mutual amity and aid with Great Britain. The court of her Viceroy appeared as splendid as her monarch's. Her nobles resided and expended their great fortunes amongst the Irish people, the Commons all resided on their own demesnes, supported and fostered a laborious and tranquil tenantry. The peace of the country was perfect, no standing army, no militia, no police were wanting for its preservation; the activity of the Volunteers had suppressed crime in every district, religious prejudices were gradually diminishing; every means of amelioration were in contemplation or in progress. The distinctness of Ireland had been proclaimed to the world by overt acts of herself, and of her monarch and the King of England. The Irish sceptre in the hands of her King had touched the charter of her independence, on the faith of nations, before God and man its eternal freedom had been declared, and should have been inviolable. But by some inscrutable will of heaven, it was decreed that she should soon be again erased from the list of nations, punished without a crime, and laid prostrate at the feet of a jealous ally.

II. The spirit and independence of the conjoint Peers and Commons of Ireland, and their reception by the heir apparent, convinced the Viceroy of the impossibility of his retaining office; his declaration of departure being again repeated, was greeted in Dublin as a measure of the highest gratification to the Whigs and Patriots, and of the deepest regret to the adherents of the minister.

However, though the recovery of the King rendered the appointment of their Regent, at the time, unnecessary, it sufficiently asserted their constitutional and national independence, and as we have already mentioned, consummated that epoch which is termed the *Rise* of Ireland.

One observation is here not out of place, and it is rather a remarkable occurrence, that it was during the short interval which occurred between the first and second announcement of the entire incapacity of King George the Third, that he was induced by the same ministers who had resisted the regent, to forego his own Royal acts, rescind his own constitutional assent—melt down his Irish Crown, and place his Irish subjects under the guardianship of a mutilated and absent representation. It is therefore not easy to reconcile to ordinary reason the probability that a conscientious and moral monarch, during the interval of a disease so deep-seated and enfeebling to the human intellect, could calmly or judicially reflect on a measure so comprehensive in its results, and so corrupt in its attainment, as the legislative Union.

It was under all these circumstances, and the departure of the Viceroy, that the Earl of Westmoreland came over as his successor. But the line of his politics or government had not preceded him.

III. Mr. Pitt felt that he had made but slight progress towards his scheme of a union with Ireland; his projects had turned against himself; and the Irish Parliament, on the subject of the Regency, had taught him a lesson he had but little expectation of learning. However, the spirit of the Irish confirmed that austere and pertinacious statesman in his resolution to rule Ireland in Great Britain, and to leave her no power to impede the course of his ambition.

The Earl of Westmoreland was by no means ill adapted to the Irish people. He was sufficiently reserved to command respect, and dignified enough to uphold his station. His splendid conviviality procured him many rational partisans, and his extreme hospitality engendered at least, temporary friendships. He was honourable and good-natured, and, among the higher orders and his intimate associates, he was a popular Viceroy.

His Secretary, Major Hobart (Lord Buckinghamshire), was more a man of the world, and was admirably calculated for the higher classes of the Irish.

A perfect gentleman, cheerful, convivial, and conciliating, though decided; liberal, yet crafty; kind-hearted, but cautious; and with a mixture of pride and affability in his manner, he particularly adapted himself to his official purposes by occasionally altering the proportion of each, as persons or circumstances required their application. With an open, prepossessing, countenance he gained wonderfully upon every gentleman with whom he associated.* The period of Lord Westmoreland's government was certainly the summit of Irish prosperity. From the epoch of his departure she may date the commencement of her downfall. Lord Westmoreland's was charged with being a jobbing Government, but it was less so than that of any of his predecessors; and if he did not diminish, he certainly did not aggravate the burthens of the people.

IV. When Lord Westmoreland arrived, Ireland was in a state of great prosperity. He met a strong opposition in Parliament, but it was an honest opposition, the guardian of public liberty, and not a faction. It was constitutional in principle, and formidable in talent; it was rather a party to effect wholesome measures, than a systematic opposition to the Government. Only two subjects of vital importance were introduced during his administration; most of the others being plausible demands, calculated rather to gratify the people than to produce any radical change in the system of the Government. A Place Bill, a Pension Bill, and a Responsibility Bill, an inquiry into the sale of Peerages, and into the Police of Dublin, were amongst the most material measures pressed by the opposition during his viceroyalty. The Place Bill, however, supposed to be remedial, eventually became the most important that had ever been passed by an independent Irish Parliament.

The perseverance of the able men who formed the opposition, at length gave a pretence to the Minister to purchase an armistice, by conceding some of the measures they had so long and pertinaciously resisted.

It could not have been flattering however, to the warm supporters of Government, to be required by the Secretary

---

* The Board of Green Cloth (the Lord Lieutenant's second table), never was supported with more splendour than during Lord Westmoreland's Government. It was, at least, as good as his own, the class of society the same, the conviviality superior. *Economy* had not crept into *that* department, and every shilling that was granted to that establishment was expended upon it.

Major Hobart saved nothing in Ireland; he expended in the metropolis all he received; and the entire of the grants, then made by the Irish Parliament to support the Vice-regal establishment, was actually laid out on it, and the citizens of Dublin, in fact, reaped the profits of their taxation.

to become absolutely inconsistent, and to change their language without a change of circumstances, and recant opinions they had so frequently declared in conjunction with the minister.

Some of the most active supporters of Government, therefore, determined not to interfere in these concessions, and the opposition, on the other hand, was so keen at the chase, and so gratified at the concession of their long-sought measures, that they but superficially regarded the details or the mode of conceding, and never reflected, as legislators or as statesmen, that one of those measures might prove a deadly weapon, by which the executive Government might destroy the Parliament under pretence of purifying it. A Bill was brought in to vacate the seats of members accepting offices under Government, omitting the term of *bona fide* offices; thereby leaving the minister a power of packing the Parliament.

The opposition, blinded by their honest zeal, considered this ruinous Bill a species of reform, and were astonished at the concession of a measure at once so popular, and which they conceived to be so destructive of ministerial corruption.

The sagacity of Mr. Pitt, however, clearly showed him, that measure would put the Irish Parliament eventually into his hands; and the sequel proved, that, without that Bill, worded as it was, the corruption by the Ministers, the rebellion, force and terror combined, could not have effected the Union.

The Place, Pension, and Responsibility Bills, were proposed by Mr. Grattan, *acceded to by the Viceroy*, passed into laws, and considered as a triumph of the opposition over the venality of the Government.*

Mr. Grattan was certainly the most incorruptible public character on the records of the Irish Parliament. He worshipped popularity, yet there was a tinge of aristocracy in his devotion, which whilst it qualified its enthusiasm, still added to its purity.

* The Author was requested by Government to give his assent, in the House, to the Place Bill: but he had, at their original request, as well as on his own opinion, for some years opposed it; he therefore positively refused, and stood nearly alone in his opposition. Mr. Newenham and Sir John M'Cartney only supported him He foresaw its possible operation.

Such men may occasionally err in judgment, or may be misled by their ardour; and this was the case with Mr. Grattan, on this armistice with the Government.

Mr. Grattan did not always foresee the remote operation of his projects.

He was little adapted to labour on the details of measures; he had laid the broad foundation of the constitution, but sometimes regarded lightly the out-buildings that were occasionally attached to it. On this occasion, the Ministers were too subtle for him, and he heeded not that fatal clause which made no distinction between real and nominal offices. He considered not, that though offices of real emolument could not be so frequently vacated and transferred, as to give the Minister any very important advantage, those of nominal value might be daily given and resigned, without observation, and that, as the House was then constituted, the Minister might almost form the Commons at his pleasure.*

By comparing the Irish Parliament at the epochs of the Proposition and the Regency Bills, and at that of 1800, the fatal operation of the Place Bill can be no longer questionable. In one word—it carried the Union.†

V. During the administration of Lord Westmoreland, the first question (which so deeply affected the subsequent events of Ireland) was the partial emancipation of the Irish Catholics. Though the question did not, when introduced, appear to involve the consideration of a legislative union, its results communicated a powerful influence to that measure.

The national annihilation of Ireland was, in a considerable degree promoted by the impolitic mismanagement of the Catholic population.

Though many of the penal and restrictive statutes, by

* There are four nominal offices in Ireland—the Escheatorships of Leinster, Munster, Connaught, and Ulster, which are obsolete: their emoluments are 30s *per annum.* By means of these offices, Lord Castlereagh packed the parliament in 1800.

The Chiltern Hundreds in England are of the same nature; but the large number of the British Commons renders any thing like packing Parliament for occasional purposes, by that means, impossible. Nor durst a British minister practice that artifice, except to a very limited extent.

† See hereafter Mr Crow's Letter to Lord Belvidere.

which the Catholics had been so long excluded from all the most valuable rights, not only of British subjects, but of freemen, were repealed; and though the power of taking freeholds, and possessing landed property, was restored to them, these concessions were but a stimulus to further claims, and for which they created a most rational expectation.

The Catholics argued, that if they were allowed to purchase freeholds, and to receive, by descent, lands in fee, it must consequently be an injustice, an absurdity, and an insult, to debar them from the elective franchise, and the privileges which were by law attached to the possession of the same species of property by their Protestant fellow-subjects.

They said, that noblemen and commoners of great fortune, of their persuasion, who had been deprived of their rights by their attachment to hereditary monarchy, notwithstanding those partial concessions, still remained loaded with many attributes of actual slavery, in the midst of a free people; that after a century of loyal and peaceable demeanour towards a Protestant dynasty, they were still to be stigmatized as neither trustworthy nor loyal. Their language, firm and decided, was rational, and eventually successful. Government were now alarmed, and affected to take a liberal view of the subject; but were by no means unanimous as to the extent of the concessions. They conceived that tranquillity might be attained by mere religious toleration. This may be true, where but a small portion of the people are claimants: far different, however, where those excluded form the bulk, and the exclusionists a small minority of the people. However, the concessions were important, and greater than could have been credible before Lord Westmoreland's administration. The grant to Catholics of the elective franchise was the act more of Major Hobart and of his government than of himself. The forty shilling franchise was then granted to the poorest and most dependent peasantry of Europe, who might one day be influenced by one motive, and the next by its reverse. It is easier to grant than to recall, and strong doubts were fairly entertained as to the wisdom of that part of it.

The first important debates, on granting the elective franchise to Irish Catholics, were in 1792, on a petition, presented in their favour. It was then looked upon as a most daring step; intolerance was then in full vigour, and Mr. Latouche moved to reject the petition without entering on its merits.

The prejudice against the Catholics was then so powerful, that their petition was rejected with indignation, by a division of 208 to 23.

The Government, by this majority, hoped to render similar applications hopeless; but, a few months after, it was found necessary that the measure should be recommended from the Throne, and supported by Government, and was carried in the same House by a large majority. The strange proceeding of the Irish Parliament on this subject, may be accounted for by their dread of reclamation by the Catholics (should they be admitted to power) of their forfeited estates, held by Peers and Commoners, by grants of Elizabeth, Cromwell, and William; but which, on more mature reflection, they found to be chimerical.

The Legislature, however, by granting the elective franchise to the Irish Catholics, conceded to them the very essence of the British Constitution.

Mr. Pitt's ulterior views as to Ireland solve the enigma, that *the virulent enemies of the Catholics, who opposed the slightest concession, should directly after vote them the elective franchise.* Mr. Pitt's object was to reciprocally exasperate the two parties against each other. The indignant rejection of the petition of 1792, inflamed the Catholic with resentment, and elated the Protestant with triumph. The concession of 1793 reversed these passions; and both parties felt equally disgusted. The Minister took every advantage of the unpopularity of the Parliament.

A very remarkable incident of inconsistency occurred in the House of Lords upon this occasion. Lord Clare, the most unqualified enemy the Catholics ever had, and the most virulent against them, on the debate in 1793 spoke and voted for giving them the elective franchise, which he had previously asserted would be a breach of the Coronation Oath, and destructive to the Church and

State. On the other hand, Lord Charlemont, always the most zealous friend of the Irish *people*, and the most distinguished of the gentle breed of patriots, on the same debate spoke in favour of the Catholics, yet voted against any concession whatsoever.

Lord Clare wished to do mischief on Mr. Pitt's system, even at his own expense. Lord Charlemont wished to do good, but was too shallow to see the designs of the Chancellor, or even to mix policy with his candour.*

Though Lord Westmoreland was powerfully opposed in Parliament, during the whole of his government, the country was in peace, and he was zealously supported. Had he not been recalled, under pretence of making way for a general pacification, the nation had no reason to suppose his place would be much better filled. His recall, and the appointment and deposition of Lord Fitzwilliam, his successor, within three months, completed the train which Mr. Pitt had laid for the explosion. Having divided the country, and obtained the means of packing the Parliament, through the Place Bill, he suffered some men to disseminate the French revolutionary mania; and having proceeded so far, recalled Lord Westmoreland, and encouraged others to raise their loyalty into the region of madness.

His Lordship had not completed the usual term of residence, nor had he failed in his duties; and his appearing not to feel hurt at his abrupt recall was mysterious, and seemed to forbode some important scheme or deception.

VI. The appointment of Lord Fitzwilliam, who had previously opposed the administration, was, perhaps, the most deep and treacherous design ever contemplated by any minister. But Mr. Pitt had never been in Ireland, and experienced difficulties he did not anticipate. He fancied he might excite and suppress commotion at his convenience; but, in deciding upon forcing a premature

---

* The ablest of the Catholic leaders, at that time, was Mr. Keogh. he possessed a very strong intellect, and had more intelligence and more influence with that body, than any man of that persuasion; he was a leader at all their early meetings, and of very great use in forwarding their measures. After their attainment of the elective franchise, he still urged their claims with talent, vigour, and perseverance.

insurrection for a particular object, he did not calculate on the torrent of blood that would be shed, and the inveterate hatred that might be perpetuated against the British Government. His resolution was taken, and he prevailed upon one of the most pure and respected of the Whig leaders to become Viceroy of Ireland, under a supposition that he was selected to tranquilize and to foster that country. The Minister wanted only a high-minded victim, as an instrument to agitate the Irish. His Lordship had great estates in Ireland—was one of its most kind and indulgent landlords, and was extremely popular. His manners were, perhaps, too mild, but he had enlarged principles of political liberty, and of religious toleration. Mr. Pitt had assured him he should have the gratification of fully emancipating the Irish Catholics. Lord Fitzwilliam accepted the office only on that consideration, and with this entire conviction he repaired to Dublin, to carry into immediate execution what he conceived would for ever tranquilize that country. Mr. Pitt intended to inflame the country—throw upon the Viceroy the insinuation of disobedience—and openly charge him with a precipitancy, of which he himself was the real author.

Never was a scheme conducted with more address and secrecy. Lord Fitzwilliam was received with open arms by the people—he immediately commenced his arrangements—and Mr. Pitt began as closely to counteract them. In every act of his government, Lord Fitzwilliam was either deceived or circumvented.

Mr. Pitt's end was answered: he thus raised the Catholics to the height of expectation, and, by suddenly recalling their favourite Viceroy, he inflamed them to the degree of generating the commotions he meditated, which would throw the Protestants into the arms of England for protection, whilst the horrors would be aggravated by the mingled conflicts of parties, royalists and republicans.

By this measure, too, Mr. Pitt had the gratification of humbling Earl Fitzwilliam, disgracing the Whigs, overwhelming the Opposition, turning the Irish into fanatics, and thereby preparing the gentry of that country for the project that was immediately to succeed it.

The conduct of the Duke of Portland must have been either culpable or imbecile—he must either have betrayed Lord Fitzwilliam to Mr. Pitt, or Mr. Pitt must have made him a blind instrument of treachery to his friend. The first is most probable, as he remained in office after his friend had been disgraced, and, in direct contradiction to his own declaration, aided in the fatal project which was effected by that treachery.

The limits of this volume do not admit of stating in detail all the important facts which constituted the treachery of the Premier, and the fraud on Earl Fitzwilliam. His Lordship's letters to Lord Carlisle cannot be abridged; every line is material; in those letters only can the deception practised on that nobleman be found with that weight and accuracy which so remarkable an incident in both English and Irish history requires.

In those letters will be found, as in a glare of light, on the one side, that high-minded, pure, virtuous dignity of mind and action, and on the other, that intrepid, able, crafty, inflexible, and unprincipled conduct, which marked indelibly the characters of those remarkable personages.

Mr. Pitt having sent Lord Fitzwilliam to Ireland with unlimited powers to satisfy the nation, permitted him to proceed until he had unavoidably committed himself both to the Catholics and country, when he suddenly recalled him, leaving it in a state of excitation and dismay.

The day Lord Fitzwilliam arrived, peace was proclaimed throughout all Ireland. The day he quitted it, she prepared for insurrection.

The Beresfords and the Ponsonbys were arrayed against each other—and, in one week more the Beresfords would have been prostrate. Mr. Pitt, however, terminated the question, by dethroning Lord Fitzwilliam; the Whigs were defeated—and Ireland was surrendered at discretion to Lord Clare and his connection. Within three months after Lord Fitzwilliam's dismissal, Lord Clare had got the nation into full training for *military execution*.

VII. The arrival of Lord Camden to succeed Earl Fitzwilliam, was attended by almost insurrectionary outrage. The Beresfords were the ostensible cause of the people's favourite being overthrown: on that family, therefore, they conceived they should signalize their vengeance; and their determination was nearly carried into execution.

The Chancellor, in his carriage, was assailed; he received the blow of a stone on his forehead, which, with somewhat more force, would have rid the people of their enemy. His house was attacked; the populace were determined to destroy him, and were proceeding to execute their intentions. At that moment their rage was, most fortunately, diverted by the address of his sister, Mrs. Jeffries, who, unknown and at great risk, had mingled in the crowd: she misled them as to the place of his concealment. Disappointed of their object, they then attacked the Custom House, where Mr. Beresford, first commissioner of the revenue resided. Dreadful results were with reason apprehended.

Such was the inauspicious beginning of Lord Camden's government. From the day of his arrival the spirit of insurrection increased, and, in a short period, during his Lordship's Government, more blood was shed, as much of outrage and cruelty was perpetrated on *both sides*, and as many military executions took place, as in ten times the same period during the sanguinary reign of Elizabeth, or the usurpations of Cromwell or King William.*

VIII. The conspiracy of united Irishmen—never profoundly secret, soon became public; its members avowed themselves; but the extent of its objects was unknown, and its civil arrangements and military organization far exceeded those of any association in history. Constituents knew not their representatives, and the soldiers knew not the names of those by whom they were to be commanded. Even the members of their executive *Directory* were utterly unknown to some hundred thousand men, who had sworn obedience to their orders. Mr. Pitt was sur-

* I have always considered, and still consider William the Third as an usurper in *Ireland*, until the flight of James, and the Articles of Limerick, capitulated for the whole nation; *after* that, he was to be considered king *de facto*, by *conquest*. At all events, it was the result of a rebellion in England and of loyalty in Ireland; and it should be recollected, that the Irish people, *after* that capitulation, never did rise or rebel against his government, or that of his successors, as they did in Scotland twice, and partially in England.

The insurrection of 1798 was excited by the artifices of Mr. Pitt to promote a Union.

prised, and found the conspiracy becoming rather too extensive and dangerous for his purposes; for a moment he felt he might possibly get beyond his depth, and he conceived the necessity of forcing a premature explosion, by which he might excite sufficient horrors throughout the country to serve his purpose, and be able to suppress the conspiracy in the bud, which might be beyond his power should it arrive at its maturity.

Individually Lord Camden was an excellent man, and, in ordinary times, would have been an acquisition to the country, but he was made a cruel instrument in the hands of Mr. Pitt, and seemed to have no will of his own.

Earl Camden was of a high mind, and of unblemished reputation; his principles were good, but his talent was not eminent; he intended right but was led wrong; he wished to govern with moderation, but was driven by his council into most violent proceedings; to the arrogant dictum of Lord Clare he had not a power of resistance, and he yielded to cruelties that his mind must have revolted at.

His Lordship became extremely popular amongst the armed associations which were raised in Ireland under the title of Yeomen. He was considered the guardian of that institution. He did what justice he was permitted to do; and a single false act of his *own*, during his residence in Ireland, never was complained of. His Secretary, Earl Chichester (Mr. Pelham), held up the reputation of the Government to its proper standard. Without great talents, he had good sense, good manners, a frank address, with humane, honourable, and just intentions; but, at a critical moment he was obliged to return to England for his health, and Lord Camden filled up the vacancy by his nephew. This relative became one of the most celebrated persons of his day, and is the principal hero in the sequel of Irish history, and in England proved himself a most destructive minister to the finances and character of the British Empire.

However, with all his good qualities as Viceroy, Lord Camden's Government was by its consequences, the most ruinous, and most unfortunate, that Ireland ever experienced.

Lord Clare and his connections, intoxicated by their

victory over the late Viceroy, set no bounds to their triumph; they treated the people as their vassals, the country as their demesne, and its patronage as their private property.

IX. On a review of the state of Ireland at that period, it must be obvious to every deliberate observer, that the design of Mr. Pitt, to effect some mysterious measure in Ireland, was now, through the unaccountable conduct of the Irish Government, beginning to develope itself. The seeds of insurrection, which had manifested themselves in Scotland and in England, were by the vigour and promptitude of the British Government, rapidly crushed; and by the reports of Parliament, Lord Melville had obtained and published prints of the different pikes manufactured in Scotland, long before that weapon had been manufactured by the Irish peasantry. But in Ireland, though it appeared, from public documents, that Government had full and accurate information of the Irish United Societies, and that their leaders and chiefs were well known to the British Ministry, at the same period, and by the same means that England and Scotland were kept tranquil, so might have been Ireland.

Mr. Pitt, however, found he had temporized to the extremity of prudence; the disaffected had not yet appeared as a collected army, but a succession of partial outrages convinced him that prompt and decisive measures became absolutely indispensable. The Earl of Carhampton, Commander-in-Chief in Ireland, first expressed his dissatisfaction at Mr, Pitt's inexplicable proceedings. His Lordship had but little military experience, but he was a man of the world, of courage, and decision, ardent, and obstinate; he determined right or wrong, to annihilate the conspiracy. Without the consent of the Irish Government, he commanded the troops, that, on all symptoms of insurrectionary movements, they should act without waiting for the presence of any civil power. Martial law had not then been proclaimed. He went, therefore, a length, which could not possibly be supported; his orders were countermanded by the Lord Lieutenant; but he refused to obey the Viceroy, under colour that he had no rank in the army.

Lord Carhampton found that the troops in the garrison

of Dublin were daily corrupted by the United Irishmen; he therefore withdrew them, and formed two distinct camps on the south and north, some miles from the capital, and thereby, as he conceived, prevented all intercourse of the army with the disaffected of the metropolis. Both measures were disapproved of by the Lord Lieutenant, whom Lord Carhampton again refused to obey.

The King's sign manual was at length procured, ordering him to break up his camps, and bring back the garrison; this he obeyed, and marched the troops into Dublin barracks. He then resigned his command, and publicly declared, that some deep and insidious scheme of the Minister was in agitation: for, instead of suppressing, the Irish Government was obviously disposed to excite an insurrection.

Mr. Pitt counted on the expertness of the Irish Government to effect a premature explosion. Free Quarters* were now ordered, to irritate the Irish population; SLOW TORTURES were inflicted under the pretence of forcing confessions; the people were goaded and driven to madness.

General Abercromby, who succeeded as Commander-in-Chief, was not permitted to abate these enormities, and therefore resigned with disgust.† Ireland was by these means reduced to a state of anarchy, and exposed to crime and cruelties to which no nation had ever been subject. The people could no longer bear their miseries. Mr. Pitt's object was now effected, and an insurrection was excited.

* *Free Quarters* is a term not yet practically known in England Free Quarters rendered officers and soldiers despotic masters of the peasantry, their houses, food, property, and, occasionally, their *families* This measure was resorted, with all its attendant horrors, throughout some of the best parts of Ireland, previous to the insurrection, and for the purpose of exciting it.

† General Abercromby, in general orders, stated that the army placed under his command, from their state of disorganization, would soon be much more formidable to their friends than to their enemies; and that he would not countenance or admit Free Quarters.

CHAPTER XXIII.

Insurrection—Topography of Wexford County—Persecutions and cruelties of the Wexford Gentry—Commencement of Hostilities—State of the Insurgents—And their number—Expected attack on Dublin—Excellent plan of the Insurgents—Executions in cold blood, and barbarous exhibition in the Castle yard—Major Bacon executed without trial—Major Foot defeated—Col. Walpole defeated and killed—General Fawcett defeated—General Dundas and the Cavalry defeated by the Pikemen—Captain Armstrong's treachery—Henry and John Shears—The execution of the two brothers—Progress of the insurrection—Different Battles—Important Battle of Arklow—Spirited reply of Colonel Skerrit—Battle of Ross—Bagenal Harvey—Death of Lord Mountjoy—Unprecedented instance of Heroism in a Boy—The Royal Army driven out of the town—Description of Vinegar Hill—Details of the Engagement—General Lake's horse shot under him—Enniscorthy twice stormed—Wounded peasants burned—Mr. Grogan tried by Court Martial—His witness shot by the military—Bill of attainder—Ten thousand pounds costs to the Attorney General—Barbarous execution of Sir Edward Crosby and Mr. Grogan, under colour of a Court Martial.

I. THESE sanguinary transactions will, in the opinions of posterity, be placed to the account of those who might have prevented them. The success of the illiterate insurgents at the commencement, nearly confirmed them in the idea of their cause being divine: they were led to hope, that, by their numbers, impetuosity, and perseverance, they could obtain their liberation from an oppressive Government and a tyrannical aristocracy. The ignorance or indiscretion of many of the king's officers who had encountered them, excited their contempt, while their own natural habits and instinctive tact led them to a system of ambuscade and stratagem, which, in many instances proved disastrous to the king's forces. The pike, at the commencement, very frequently succeeded against the regular, and always against the yeoman cavalry; and, in close combat with even the infantry, it proved in some instances irresistible.*

* The extreme expertness with which the Irish handled the pike was

Almost all countries possess some national weapon, in the use of which the inhabitants are more expert than at any other, and their superiority at which is evinced in every insurrection. The Highland broadsword and target, in the rebellions of Scotland, were eminently successful; the Polish lances, the American rifle, and the Indian tomahawk, were often as successful against regular troops.

II. Wexford, though so near the metropolis, is not a frequented county, as it is not a direct thoroughfare to any other part of the kingdom: the towns of Gorey, Arklow, and Wicklow intervene between Wexford and Dublin. The king's troops were in possession of Arklow, and the country to the metropolis, through Wicklow. They interrupted the communication between Wexford and the Wicklow mountains; and, on that side, left the Wexford insurgents almost isolated in their original position.

In the interior of the county, however, the insurgents had many strong positions; and, on the south side, the town of New Ross was the only impediment to their making themselves masters of Waterford, where they were certain of being immediately joined by the Munster insurgents, particularly by the Waterford and Tipperary men, the most numerous and efficient in the kingdom; and this possession of New Ross gave rise to one of the most bloody and most protracted battles ever fought in Ireland.

The reckless ferocity, so natural to men resisting oppression, here had full scope for its terrific development. The peasantry of that country were, in a great proportion, of English descent; they had been taught that it was right to separate themselves from England; and they

surprising; by withdrawing, they could shorten it to little more than the length of a dagger, and, in a second, dart it out to its full extent. At Old Kilcullen, they entirely repulsed General Dundas, and the heavy cavalry, in a regular charge, killing two captains and many soldiers: the General escaped with great difficulty, by the fleetness of his horse. At New Ross, they entirely broke the heavy horse by their pikes. A solid mass, or deep column of determined pikemen, could only be broken by artillery, or a heavy fire of musketry: well-served artillery they could not withstand, if not close enough to be rushed upon. Colonel Foot's detachment of infantry was nearly annihilated by the pike at Oulart: only the major and two others escaped.

were filled with that dreadful doctrine, that, " if the object be good, the means are immaterial."

Upon this doctrine, however, many of the higher orders had unequivocally acted. A portion of the gentry of the county of Wexford were boisterous, overbearing, and devoid of judgment; their Christian principles were merged in their Protestant ascendency. The frenzy of an exterminating principle seemed to have taken root amongst them; and they acted as if under the impression, that burning every cottage, and torturing every cottager, were a meritorious proof of their faith and loyalty. Great and most unwarrantable excesses had been practised by some of the Protestant gentry on the lower orders: some of them were nearly as savage, and certainly as sanguinary as the most vicious of the insurgents. Those men committed their loyal brutalities without calculating that a single victory might enable the insurgents to retaliate.

The conduct of the Wexford gentry was held out, by insurgent leaders, to the inflamed population, as a system to be retaliated; nor is it possible to deny, that natural justice gave some colour to that sanguinary doctrine. The lower orders uninstructed in the distinction between the rights of Government and the mad excesses of the bigoted gentry or tyrannical functionaries, naturally mistook retaliation for justice, and followed exactly the course of devastation which had been inflicted upon themselves. The mansions of the gentry experienced the same fate which the gentry had inflicted on the cottages. The insurgents considered every Protestant a tyrant; the Protestants proclaimed every Catholic a rebel; reason was banished, mercy was denounced, and the reciprocal thirst for blood became insatiable.

III. Actual hostilities now commenced by skirmishes round the city of Dublin, and several simultaneous attacks were made by the insurgents, upon various posts and garrisons, with surprising pertinacity. They had neither officers, regular arms, nor discipline; their plans, therefore, though acutely devised, could have no certainty of regular or punctual execution; yet a masterly system of tactics, of combinations, and of offensive warfare had been originally determined upon. Though these, in a great measure, had been frustrated by the death of Lord

Edward Fitzgerald, and the arrest of the Directory, they were executed sufficiently to prove that there had been the plan of an effectual resistance to the Government.

The number of the insurgents is utterly impossible to be stated with accuracy. There then existed in Ireland at least 125,000 effective men at arms, who, from the smallness of the island, could be collected and marshalled in a week throughout the entire kingdom.*

The insurgents were unpaid—many of them nearly unclothed, few of them well armed, all of them undisciplined, with scarcely any artillery, no cavalry, their powder and ammunition mostly prepared by themselves, no tents or covering, no money, no certainty of provisions, obedience to their chiefs, and adherence to their cause, were altogether voluntary. Under these circumstances, their condition must have been precarious, and their numbers variable. No one leader amongst them had sufficient power to control or counteract their propensities, yet they fought with wonderful perseverance, address, and intrepidity.†

---

* Some of the returns stated that above four hundred thousand men had been sworn, and privately drilled; but little faith can be placed in any document on the subject. Had the cause continued to succeed, the numbers would have been double. In 1782, above one hundred thousand Independent Volunteers were well clothed, armed, and disciplined, and about fifty thousand more of an inferior description, were assembled.

† One of the insurgents in the town of Wexford, with whom I was well acquainted, gave me much information, and a great insight into the transactions of that county. He was a rational man, and disgusted with both parties, he would have been neutral, but neutrality was impossible; and Mr. Taylor, a Royalist, and a man of truth and integrity, whom the insurgents, on pain of death, had forced to print their proclamation, gave me many of their documents, and a great deal of intelligence. I collected, on all hands, that, on the first rising, there were not five thousand insurgents to attack the town of Wexford; but that the King's troops having evacuated the place, with a considerable force, and without any effort to defend it, and being harassed on their retreat, this first and most important success had its immediate effect, and before noon the next day more than twenty thousand Wexford men had flocked to their standards, and they hourly increased in number while success was possible. At the battle of New Ross, I was assured that Bagenal Harvey had thirty thousand, at the battle of Arklow there were more than 20,000: and, as the most unequivocal proof of their formidable numbers, at the engagement of Vinegar Hill, General Lake did not think it advisable to attack them with less than twenty thousand regular troops and

IV. A night attack on the metropolis had been long meditated by the united Irishmen, but its early execution had not been anticipated by the Government. The Lord Lieutenant ascertained that such an attempt was to be made on the 23d of May, 1798, by a large body of insurgents then collecting on the north of Swords and Santry, and on the south under the Rathfarnham mountains less than five miles from the city. Of their numbers, leaders, arms, or tactics, every body was ignorant, all was confusion and every report was extravagantly exaggerated. The regular garrison, and the yeomanry, prepared themselves with the utmost animation, but nobody knew his station, or could ascertain his duty. Orders were issued, and immediately revoked, positions were assigned and countermanded, more confused, indecisive, and unintelligible arrangements of a military nature never appeared.

No probable point of attack was signified, and the only principle of defence appeared to be comprised in one sentence, " every man for himself, and God for us all." Lord Clare appeared the most busy and active, as far as his tongue extended. Confidence and bravery were recommended in all quarters ; but a very serious uneasiness was perceptible throughout the metropolis ; his Lordship's activity was confined to the council chamber, and to the upper court of the castle.

As night approached, orders were given that the yeo-

---

a considerable artillery. Cavalry and mortars were brought to force their line, and even against such an attack they made a long and desperate resistance, and retreated from that large and disciplined army with very little (comparative) loss.

I had every reason to believe (and I omitted no means of ascertaining the reality), that above thirty-five thousand men had risen in the county of Wexford alone. This species of computation may, therefore, be indulged in as theory, certainly not as a true criterion. Wexford is only one of thirty-two counties, by no means the most populous, and far from the most extensive. Had the rising been general, the northern counties might have furnished as many, the southern counties more, and the midland less than Wexford. A rough (but no doubt uncertain) average, may be drawn from these data, as to what the possible or probable amount of insurgents might have been, throughout the entire kingdom, if the struggle had been protracted. It is equally clear, that had the insurgents possessed arms, officers, and discipline, their numbers would soon have rendered them masters of the kingdom.

men, cavalry and infantry, should occupy Smithfield, which was, at length, considered as the probable point of attack from Santry, where the peasantry were reported to have collected in the greatest numbers. The yeomen, amongst whom were nearly eight hundred attorneys, horse and foot, turned out. Their infantry was effective, and their cavalry excellent. The gradations of their discipline and enthusiasm were, however, extremely amusing; those who had imbibed their full quantum of generous fluids, were the most fierce and enthusiastic: others who had dined on substantial matters, were as steady as posts. But those who had been paraded before dinner, after standing under arms for some hours, could endure it no longer, and a forced loan of cheese, tongues, and bottled porter, from a Mr. Murray, of Great George's-street, was unanimously decided upon, and immediately carried into execution. The barristers, commanded by Captain Saurin, were from their position likely to sustain the first onset of the pikemen; and as night closed, such a scene of military array never was, and probably never will be witnessed. Smithfield is a long and very wide street, open at both ends, one of which is terminated by the quays and river. It is intersected by narrow streets, and formed altogether one of the most disagreeable positions in which an immense body of demi-disciplined men and horses ever were stationed in solid mass, without any other order than, "*if you are attacked, defend yourselves to the last extremity.*"

The cavalry and infantry were, in some places, so compactly interwoven, that a dragoon could not wield his sword without cutting down a foot soldier, nor a foot soldier discharge his musket without knocking down a trooper. The cavalry being elevated, could breathe freely in the crowd; but the infantry could scarcely avoid suffocation. A few hundred insurgents, with long pikes, coming on rapidly in the dark, might, without difficulty, have assailed the yeomen at once from five different points. The Barristers and Attorneys' corps occupied three of those points. So much for General Craig's tactics.

The danger was considered imminent, the defence impracticable; yet there was a cheerful, thoughtless jocularity with which the English nation, under grave circumstances, are totally unacquainted; and plain matter of fact men can scarcely conceive that renovating levity which carries an Irish heart buoyantly over every wave, which would swamp, or at least water-log, their more steady fellow-subjects. All the barristers, attorneys, merchants, bankers, revenue officers, shopkeepers, students of the University, doctors, apothecaries, and corporators, of an immense metropolis, in red coats, with a sprinkling of parsons, all doubled up together, awaiting in profound darkness (not with impatience), for invisible executioners to dispatch them without mercy, was not (abstractedly) a situation to engender much hilarity. Scouts now and then came, only to report their ignorance, a running buzz occasionally went round, that the videts were driven in—and the reports of distant musketry, like a twitch of electricity, gave a slight but perceptible movement to men's muscles. A few (faintly heard) shots on the north side also seemed to announce that the vanguard of the Santry men was approaching. In the mean time, no further orders came from the general, and if there had, no orders could have been obeyed. It appeared, at break of day, that both the Santry and Rathfarnham men had adjourned their main assault till some other opportunity.

The different corps now got more regular, the bands struck up "God save the King"—the danger of the night, in all its ramifications, re-occupied the tongue of every soldier in Smithfield; and at length an order came from General Craig (Lord Roden being victorious in a skirmish), to dismiss the troops, and to parade again in the evening. Never was an order obeyed with more alacrity, and never did insurgents lose so favourable an opportunity of covering a field of battle with more distinguished carcases.

The insurgents on the south intended to take the castle by surprise, whilst the Santry men assailed the barracks; but their plan was disconcerted by Lord Roden, at the head of his dragoons (called the fox hunters, from their noble horses). His Lordship marched rapidly upon them, and surprised the few who had collected; and, being supported by a small number of light infantry, the attack completely succeeded. A few were sabred, and some few made prisoners; but the body dispersed with little resistance. Lord Roden received a ball on his helmet, but was only bruised, and some dragoons were wounded; the other (county of Dublin) men retreated to join the Kildare men; the southern marched to unite themselves with those of Wicklow. Their plan had been excellent, had they acted steadily on it, success was not improbable; however, the metropolis for some time had no further dread of molestation.

A new, disgusting, and horrid scene was next morning publicly exhibited; after which military executions commenced, and continued with unabating activity. Some dead bodies of insurgents, sabred the night before by Lord Roden's dragoons, were brought in a cart to Dublin, with some prisoners tied together; the carcases were stretched out in the Castle yard, where the Viceroy then resided, and in full view of the Secretary's windows; they lay on the pavement as trophies of the first skirmish, during a hot day, cut and gashed in every part, covered with clotted blood and dust, the most frightful spectacle which ever disgraced a royal residence, save the seraglio. After several hours exposure, some appearance of life was perceived in one of the mutilated carcases. The man had been stabbed and gashed in various parts; his body was removed into the guard-room, and means were taken to restore animation; the efforts succeeded, he entirely recovered, and was pardoned by Lord Camden; he was an extraordinarily fine young man, above six feet high, the son of a Mr. Keough, an opulent landholder of Rathfarnham; he did not, however, change his principles, and was, ultimately, sent out of the country.

That morning, the yeomanry corps were called upon to attend the execution of Lord Roden's prisoners, who were ordered to be hanged from the lamp irons, or on the bridges. It was a service the respectable corps declined, several, however, went individually as spectators. The first victim to that arbitrary and ill-judged execution, was a Mr. Ledwitch, of Rathfarnham, the brother of a Catholic clergyman.*

* He was a remarkably large and heavy person, and was hanged on one of the bridges. By the inexperience of the executioner, Mr. Ledwitch suffered a prolonged and cruel death; the rope frequently slipped,

Others were executed at the same time; some of the lamplighters also paid with their lives for their former night's omission, and blood began to flow with but little mercy. Bacon (a Major of the old volunteers), was caught in a female garb, endeavouring to quit the city; and under a general order to execute, forthwith, all persons found in disguise, he was led to Carlisle Bridge, and hanged from the scaffolding. These species of executions became common, and habit soon reconciled men to what was not only disgusting, but horrible.

V. Martial law was now proclaimed, and the courts of justice closed, except on civil subjects. The barristers pleaded in their uniform, with their side-arms, one of the judges (Baron Medge) appeared on the bench in the same uniform, the names of the inmates of every house were pasted on every door, fabricated reports of massacres and poisonings were daily propagated, the city assumed, altogether, the appearance of one monstrous barrack, or slaughter-house. The attacks on the royal garrisons in Kildare and Dublin counties, were in many places unsuccessful; on other points the insurgents entirely succeeded, and no quarter was granted on either side. The town of Prosperous was taken, and the garrison were killed by the peasantry.

On the Wexford side the insurgents, at first, were almost uniformly successful; they took Wexford without resistance; the garrison retreated with much fighting and some loss. Enniscorthy was stormed by the peasantry, and, after a desperate conflict, most of the town was burned, and a great portion of the garrison cut to pieces; the residue escaped, with great difficulty, through the flames.* The victory was complete, and gave them the

and gave away; at length, his legs were tied up behind his back, and, after much struggling and dragging, he was dispatched with very considerable difficulty. It was a horrid sight.

* Captain Hay, of the light dragoons, had been taken prisoner some time before, and was accused of having acted as a commander of the peasantry in that attack, and at Arklow. This report acquired strength, from the circumstance that one of his brothers had been hanged as a rebel, and another of them had been an active insurgent during the occupation of Wexford. Captain Hay, however, was tried by a court-martial, and fully acquitted, on the ground of compulsion. He also appeared to have saved the lives of several loyalists at Enniscorthy, and particu-

possession of that fine position, Vinegar Hill, and the total command of an extensive country.

Major Foot, advancing too confidently with a detachment to Oulart, was totally defeated—only three of his corps escaped. Colonel Walpole, an inexperienced officer, solicited, and, as a court favour, obtained, a command to attack the insurgent army near Gorey; but he was surprised by them near that town; many of the troops were destroyed—the Colonel himself fell early in the action—the artillery was taken—and the whole corps were dispersed, or taken prisoners. The town of Gorey was sacked and burned. General Fawcett's detachment was as unfortunate. He marched from Duncannon fort, to unite with other corps collecting to attack Wexford: but he was himself attacked at the Three Rocks Mountain; all his artillery was captured; he was utterly routed, and with difficulty got back to Duncannon, with some relics of his corps.

In Kildare the success was alternate, but in most instances the regular troops had the advantage; torrents of blood were shed, and every idea of mercy seemed exploded; acts of ferocity, beyond belief, were committed on both sides.*

General Dundas confidently determined upon breaking a solid body of pikemen, by the impetuosity and weight of his heavy cavalry. The peasantry, in a deep close column, and under the ruined church of Old Kilcullen, received them on their pikes: two captains were killed, with many of the heavy cavalry, and the General escaped

larly a Mrs. Ogle's sister, whom he carried through the flames of a burning street, and a fire of musketry.

* It is a singular fact, that in all the ferocity of the conflict, the storming of towns and of villages, *women* were uniformly respected by the insurgents. Though numerous ladies fell occasionally into their power, they never experienced any incivility or misconduct. But the foreign troops in our service (Hompesch's) not only brutally ill-treated, but occasionally *shot* gentlewomen. A very respectable married woman in Enniscorthy (Mrs. Stringer, the wife of an attorney) was wantonly shot at her own window by a German, in cold blood. The rebels (though her husband was a royalist) a short time after this took some of those foreign soldiers prisoners, and piked them all, as they told them—"*just to teach them how to shoot ladies.*" Martial law always affects *both* sides; retaliation becomes the law of nature wherever municipal laws are not in operation; it is a remedy that should never be resorted to but in *extremis*.

with difficulty. The same body was attacked again the same day, with *artillery*, and quickly broken; but not till lanes had been repeatedly cut through them by round shot.

The removal of the troops into the camps of Laughlinston and the Naul, heretofore mentioned, gave rise to one of the most melancholy episodes of this history. At Laughlinston (seven miles from Dublin) some thousand men, mostly Irish militia, were encamped by Lord Carhampton. The United Irishmen sent emissaries to the camp; and disaffection was rapidly proceeding amongst troops. It was disclosed to Government by a Captain Armstrong, of the King's County Militia, who also did what every principle should have imperatively prohibited.

He was prevailed upon at the Castle, for a reward, to ingratiate himself, as a brother conspirator, amongst the higher classes; and to encourage their proceedings, so as to gain proofs of their guilt, through their implicit confidence in his fidelity. He then became an evidence even to death, against those whose culpability he had encouraged, and attended to execution the very gentlemen whom he made victims to their confidence in his integrity.

Captain Armstrong thus wormed himself into the confidence of the leaders, with the design of betraying them: his treachery was preorganized; and he proved himself a worse man and a more competent conspirator than those whom he made his victims. He had the honour of an officer, and the integrity of a gentleman to sustain; yet he deliberately sacrificed both, and saw two barristers executed through his treachery.

VI. Messrs. Henry and John Sheares were of the Irish bar, and of a respectable family, Henry, the elder, had a competent fortune, and was an excellent domestic person, with a most amiable family; he had received a university education, but was not possessed of talent—plain and friendly, occasionally warm, generally credulous, and always full of prejudices, his mind was never strong enough to resist his feelings, and though unexceptionable in private character, he had neither capacity, firmness, nor discretion for a public life. The younger brother, John, was tall, fair, handsome, and of gentlemanly address; his countenance was sensible, and, firm to inflexibility, with much more ta.ent than his brother, he guided him at his discretion. They were inseparable as brothers, and were united by an almost unparalleled attachment. Mr. John Sheares, upon the arrest of the others, became one of the executive directory of the United Irishmen, and, as a necessary consequence, Henry was a participator, and aided in procuring emissaries to seduce the troops at Laughlinston. There Captain Armstrong became acquainted with the two brothers, pledged to them his friendship, persuaded them that he would seduce his own regiment, gained their implicit confidence, faithfully fulfilled the counterplot, devised secret meetings, and worked up sufficient guilt to sacrifice the lives of both. They were arrested, tried, on his evidence convicted, and were hanged and beheaded in the front of Newgate. They came hand in hand to the scaffold: this was one of the most interesting trials in Ireland.

It is only justice to Lord Clare, to record an incident which proves that he was not insusceptible of humane feelings, and which often led me to believe that his nature might have been noble, had not every feeling of moderation been absorbed by that ambition, the fatal disappointment of which, at length hastened his dissolution.

By some unfortunate delay, a letter of Henry Sheares to me was not delivered till eleven o'clock of the morning after the trial. I immediately waited on Lord Clare, he read it with great attention; I saw he was moved; his heart yielded. I improved on the impression; he only said: "What a coward he is! but what can we do?"—he paused—"John Sheares cannot be spared. Do you think Henry can say any thing, or make any species of discovery, which may authorize the Lord Lieutenant to make a distinction between them? if so, Henry may be reprieved." He read the letter again, and was obviously affected. I had never seen him amiable before. "Go," said he, "to the prison; the execution will be deferred for one hour. See Henry Sheares, ask him this question and return to me at Cooke's office." I lost no time, but I found, on my arrival, that orders had been given that nobody should be admitted without a *written* permission. I instantly returned to the castle—they were all at council, Cooke was not in his office, I was delayed **several** minutes. At length the secretary returned, gave me the order to see them, and to the sheriff to delay the execution for one hour. I hastened to Newgate, and arrived at the very moment that the executioner was holding up the head of my old college friend, and saying, "*Here is the head of a traitor.*" I felt deeply affected.

VII. This insurrection, which commenced on the 23d of May, 1798, and concluded in a few months, produced a greater effusion of blood, more ferocity, and more devastation than ever were witnessed in Ireland within an equal period. Partial battles and skirmishes were incessant, but general engagements were not numerous.

It was generally in small bodies that the insurgents were successful. The principal battles were those of Arklow, Gorey, and Vinegar Hill, and the storming of Enniscorthy and Ross by the peasantry. At Arklow, in a regular line, the peasantry assailed a disciplined army in the field, and the result was a drawn battle. At Ross, after storming and gaining the town, after ten hours incessant fighting, they surrendered themselves to drunkenness and plunder, and were slaughtered in their inebriety.

At Vinegar Hill, the entrenchments were defended for several hours, though attacked by twenty thousand regular troops, with ordnance, and the loss of the insurgents was disproportionately small. They retired unpursued, and soon formed another army, and marched to the very heart of Ireland.

At Gorey, Carnew, the Three Rocks, and numerous places where they fought in ambuscades, they always succeeded; and had they confined themselves to desultory attacks and partisan warfare, they might soon have destroyed their local enemies the yeomen, and wearied and exhausted the regular troops. After the storming of Gorey, had they succeeded in taking Arklow, they might have marched to the metropolis in one day.

VIII. To protect Arklow, therefore, was imperatively necessary, yet it was but poorly garrisoned, and totally unprovided with ammunition or provisions. The garrison were considerably less than one thousand men, principally irregular troops, and not a field-work or other preparation had been made to defend the place. An old barrack, incapable of defence, was their only fortification, four pieces of field artillery their only ordnance, and a party of the Ancient Britons, commanded by Sir W. W. Wynn in person, and a few yeomen, their only cavalry. The insurgents had collected nearly thirty thousand men at the ruined town of Gorey, within a few miles of Arklow, which they boldly but indiscreetly declared they would storm the ensuing morning. The alarm of the metropolis at this intelligence, may be easily conceived. An immediate reinforcement of the garrison of Arklow could alone prevent an attack on Dublin, and an insurrection of the populace. The Cavan militia, commanded by the present Lord Farnham, were instantly despatched to succour General Needham, but the distance being more than thirty miles, they were hurried off in every sort of vehicle; and even the carriages of the nobility and gentry were seized or tendered for the occasion.

This was the most regular engagement throughout the whole of the insurrection. The pikemen amounted to many thousands—the king's troops were under fifteen hundred—the fire-arms on each side were nearly equal in number, but those of the insurgents were of every calibre and description, whilst their powder was carried in horns or in the pocket, and was but scantily supplied.

The Cavan regiment arrived at the critical minute. The conflict was in a level field at the extremity of the town; the royal infantry being in a line on open ground, with two pieces of cannon at each wing; the peasantry, with fire-arms, were drawn up in a line exactly parallel, with a very low ditch in front, and two pieces of artillery on each flank; small flags of green and yellow waved in every part of their position. The fire began as regularly as between disciplined armies—no movements were made on either side; the pikemen formed a crescent on a range of hills just over the royalists, and waited for any disorder to rush down and exterminate them. An uninterrupted fire was kept up by both parties for some hours, without any manœuvre, and with very little comparative execution. At length the insurgents dismounted one of the royal cannon, killed the gunners, and the battle was becoming doubtful. The left flank of the royal army was protected by some cavalry and houses, and the right by their barracks, and a piece of artillery which commanded the road. The peasantry had no pre-arranged plan of attack, and their immense body of pikemen remained inactive on the eminence, a few hundred yards from the scene of action. The royal officers became alarmed: had the insurgents' ammunition lasted, and the pikemen charged, the danger would have been realised. General Needham, and most of the officers were disposed to retire, as a matter of necessity; but Colonel Skerritt, of the Dumbarton fencibles, resolutely declared that his regiment never should retreat. A retrogade movement would have given an opportunity for a rush of the pikemen, which must have ended in the annihilation of the royal force. No quarter was expected upon either side. Had the royal troops advanced, they might have been easily surrounded; their alternative was, to succeed or perish. The ammunition of the royal army began to fail; but fortunately that of the peasantry was first exhausted. The firing gradually slackened, and, at length a very ferocious attack was made on the right wing, by a large body of pikemen, led by Father Murphy; a fourpounder opened its fire, and Father Murphy received a ball which tore him to pieces. The insurgents, thus dispirited, advanced no farther; and after an effort on the left, repulsed by some Ancient Britons, they began to retreat, but without precipitation. The royal army did not think it prudent to pursue, but retired to their barracks, whilst the peasantry fell back, unmolested, to Gorey. Thus concluded a battle by no means the most sanguinary, but, certainly, one of the most important of the insurrection. Had the peasantry succeeded, they would have been reinforced every mile of their march to Dublin, by the excited population of Wexford and Wicklow. Kildare, Meath, and Westmeath were in arms, and the capital itself had more than 30,000 organized United Irishmen within its walls; and, however intrepidly defended, must have yielded in a river of blood to the innumerable hosts of its enthusiastic assailants. Their failure, however, in the principal attacks in Kildare and Wicklow, had dispirited and disorganized a multitude without officers to direct them, and Ireland was thus saved. More than 30,000 peasantry were actually present at the battles of Ross and Arklow; and Wexford and Wicklow are by no means the most populous counties. At a very moderate computation, there were, in Wexford and Wicklow, at least 50,000 effective insurgents, either under arms, or prepared to take arms, had their measures continued to be successful. Their courage and perseverance may be estimated by the extraordinary incidents of the battle of Ross, which lasted ten hours with alternate success, and in which they were finally conquered, only by their insubordination, and the incapacity of their leaders.

IX. The battle of Ross, with respect to its incidents and extensive results, was one of the most important of the insurrection. Ross is surrounded on three sides by steep hills, and on the fourth by a river, dividing it from the southern counties, and having a long wooden bridge. The possession of Ross, therefore, would open a communication with the southern insurgents, who were prepared to rise, *en masse*, the moment their friends should occupy that town; and the city of Waterford, and probably the whole of the western and southern counties would have risen in their favor. Nearly 30,000 insurgents assembled on Corbet-Hill, near the town of Ross. Their General, Beauchamp Bagenal Harvey, was, of all men, probably the most unfit for so desperate an enterprise; his figure diminutive, his voice tremulous.

He was a Protestant barrister of fortune; good tempered, and of good private character; and was selected from being lord of Bragay Castle, and of considerable demesnes in the county of Wexford. Of individual courage he had sufficient, but of that manly heroic intrepidity which converts danger into enthusiasm, and is indispensable to the leader of such an army and such a cause, he was altogether unsusceptible. The other officers were little better than himself; and an army of 30,000 intrepid, persevering insurgents, could not produce one leader of sufficient tact or influence to guide and secure to them certain victory. Harvey and his aid-de-camp, Mr. Gray, a Protestant attorney, remained upon a neighbouring hill, inactive spectators during ten hours incessant *fighting*.

'The first attack commenced at six o'clock in the morning on only one entrance to the town, and that the most defensible by the garrison ; all the others were neglected, otherwise, the garrison not being sufficiently numerous to defend all, the town must have been entered from several quarters. A regiment of infantry and one of cavalry sallied out to distract the insurgents, and prevent their attack upon the other entrances. Both regiments were driven back with great loss, the cavalry by a charge of bullocks* and pikemen, the infantry by ambuscade and irregular attacks. Lord Mountjoy fell at the head of his regiment, the Dublin Militia, immediately at the gate; and the royalists and the peasantry entered Ross almost intermingled. The main street became the scene of a most sanguinary and protracted conflict; the royalists were forced back, and their artillery taken and turned on themselves. The market-house alone remained in possession of the troops; and after a long and bloody contest they retreated to the bridge, prepared, if necessary, to pass to the other side, and destroy the communication. Had they done this, they must have marched through the very heart of an insurgent country, and all would have been cut to pieces. There is scarcely a trait of individual courage which was not exemplified during that contest;†

* At this battle the insurgents practised a *ruse de guerre* used originally by the Romans. A regiment of heavy cavalry had marched out, to charge them on their first approach; they suspected the attack, and were prepared to receive them by a very unexpected salutation. They had cooped up in a field near two hundred bullocks. When these beasts are urged, and rush on in a body, nothing can stop them; a wall or even a house, they have been known to dash against, in their blind fury. When the heavy cavalry were in a proper position on the road, the rebels, with their pikes, goaded the bullocks; maddened by the smart, they rushed to the openings of the enclosure, which had been purposely made for them : nothing could withstand them; the cavalry were overwhelmed; man and horse were overthrown and trampled upon. Of such as could retreat through the gate, several met their death from the pikemen.

† The account of this battle I have had from many, but from none so accurately or circumstantially as from a gentlemen I have been long acquainted with, Counsellor Lundyfoot, son of the eminent person of that name. He had some property there, and curiosity led him to Ross, to see what was going forward; just as he got there he found he could not get away again, and was obliged to remain, and run his chance during the battle. He was a member of the barristers' infantry, and conceived that no soldier should on such occasions be inactive; he therefore

the battle occasionally slackened, but never ceased for a moment. The peasantry, certain of victory, lost all subordination; and, in their turn, were attacked by such of the garrison as had time to rally. Many were killed, almost without resistance; the town was set on fire, and in the midst of the flames the battle raged for hours most violently. The royalists recovered the main street. The insurgents were on the point of being finally repulsed, when a young gentleman of thirteen years of age, from the town of Wexford, of the respectable family of Lett, in that town, had stolen away from his mother, and joined General Harvey on Corbet Hill. The boy saw the disorder of the men, and the incapacity of their leaders, and with a boyish impulse he snatched up a standard, and calling out "Follow me who dare!" rushed down the hill, two or three thousand pikemen rapidly followed him in a tumultuous crowd, and uttering the most appalling cries. In a moment he was at the gate, rallied his party, and with his reinforcement rushed upon the garrison, who, fatigued and astonished at the renewed vigour of their enemy, were again borne down, and compelled with much loss, fighting step by step, to retire towards the bridge. For many hours the firing in the streets and houses was incessant; and the peasantry were very nearly in possession of the entire place, when again all subordination vanished, and again fortune forsook them. Some hundred houses were in a blaze; the horror was indescribable. The remaining body of the garrison, overcome by fatigue, became nearly unable to continue the contest.

The firing, however, continued till towards night, when the insurgents who had not entered the houses, having no officers to command them, retreated through the gate by which they had entered, half a mile to Corbet Hill, leaving some thousands of their comrades asleep in different houses, or in the streets to which the flames had not communicated. Of these, the garrison put hundreds to the sword, without any resistance; and more than 5000 were

armed, acted as a Volunteer, and was in the very midst of the battle during the ten hours it continued. He described to me the desperate valour of the peasantry, and confirmed to me a story, nearly incredible, of their ignorance; namely, an old man thrusting a wig into the mouth of an adverse cannon, to prevent its explosion.

either killed or consumed by the conflagration. The garrison, greatly diminished and exhausted by ten hours incessant fighting, without refreshments, lay down in the streets, slumbering amongst the dead; and had Harvey, at any hour before morning, returned with even 1000 fresh men, every soldier might have been slaughtered; resistance would have been impossible.

X. Vinegar Hill is a beautiful, verdant, low mountain; the river Slaney rolls smoothly at its foot on the one side, and the large town of Enniscorthy lies immediately under its base upon another; at one point the ascent is rather steep, on the others, gradual; the top is crowned by a dilapidated stone building. The hill is extensive, and completely commands the town and most of the approaches to it; the country around it is rich, sufficiently wooded, and studded with country seats and lodges. Few spots in Ireland, under all its circumstances, can at this moment be more interesting to a traveller. On the summit of this hill the insurgents had collected the remains of their Wexford army; the number may be conjectured, from General Lake deciding that 20,000 regular troops were necessary for the attack. The peasantry had dug a slight ditch around a large extent of the base; they had a very few pieces of small half-disabled cannon, some swivels, and not above two thousand fire-arms of all descriptions. But their situation was desperate; and General Lake considered that two thousand fire-arms, in the hands of infuriated and courageous men, supported by a multitude of pikemen, might be equal to ten times the number under other circumstances. A great many women mingled with their relatives, and fought with fury; several were found dead amongst the men, who had fallen in crowds by the bursting of shells.

The circumstantial details of that battle, however interesting, are too numerous for this volume, a few, however, are necessary.

General Lake, at the break of day, disposed his attack in four columns, whilst his cavalry were prepared to do execution on the fugitives. One of the columns (whether by accident or design is strongly debated) did not arrive in time at its station, by which the insurgents were enabled to retreat to Wexford, through a country where they could not be pursued by cavalry or cannon. It was astonishing with what fortitude the peasantry, uncovered, stood the tremendous fire opened upon the four sides of their position; a stream of shells and grape was poured on the multitude; the leaders encouraged them by exhortations, the women by their cries, and every shell that broke amongst the crowd was followed by shouts of defiance. General Lake's horse was shot, many officers wounded, some killed, and a few gentlemen became invisible during the heat of the battle. The troops advanced gradually but steadily up the hill; the peasantry kept up their fire, and maintained their ground, their cannon was nearly useless, their powder deficient, but they died fighting at their post. At length, enveloped in a torrent of fire, they broke, and sought their safety through the space that General Needham had left by the non-arrival of his column. They were partially charged by some cavalry, but with little execution; they retreated to Wexford, and that night occupied the town.

During the battle, the pike and blunderbuss were in constant exercise; both parties had committed great atrocities in cold blood, under the milder term of retaliation. Previous to that battle, Enniscorthy had been twice stormed; every street in it had streamed with blood; many hundred houses had been burned; and the combats had been hand to hand in the midst of flames and falling edifices. It is asserted that eighty-seven wounded peasants, whom the king's army had found on taking the town, in the market-house, used as an hospital, had been burned alive; and that in retaliation the insurgents burned above a hundred royalists in a barn at Scullabogue.

Amongst the remarkable and melancholy examples of the abuse of martial law, and the discretionary power given to military officers in Ireland, one which occurred on the taking of Wexford is a peculiarly fit subject for observation: Mr. Grogan, of Johnstown Castle, a man past seventy years of age, of very large fortune, irreproachable reputation, with the address, manners, and feelings of a gentleman. Overstreet and John, his two brothers, commanded yeomanry corps. The first of them was killed at the head of his corps (the Castletown Cavalry), at the battle of Arklow. The other was wounded at the head of his troop (the Heathfield Light Horse) during Major Maxwell's retreat from Wexford, and upon the recapture of Wexford. The semblance of a trial was thought expedient by General Lake, before he could execute a gentleman of so much importance and fortune. His case was afterwards brought before Parliament upon a Bill of attainder, and argued for three successive days, and nearly nights, and evidence was produced clearly exonerating him from any voluntary error. The only charge the Government (to excuse the culpability of General Lake) could prove, was his having been surrounded by the insurgent army, which placed him under surveillance, and who, to give importance to themselves, forced him one day into the town of Wexford, on horseback, a peasant of the name of Savage attending him, with a blunderbuss, and orders to shoot him if he refused to obey their commands; against his will, they nominated him a commissary, knowing that his numerous tenantry would be more willing in consequence to supply them. He used no weapon of any description, too feeble even to hold one in his hand.

A lady, of the name of Segrave, gave evidence that her family in the town were in want of food, and that she sent to Mr. Grogan to give her an order for some bread, which request, to save her family from starving, he reluctantly complied with. Through that order, she procured some loaves, and supplied her children; and for that act of benevolence, and on that lady's evidence, Mr. Grogan was sentenced to die as a traitor, and was immediately hanged and beheaded, when unable to walk to the place of execution, and already almost lifeless from age, imprisonment, pain and brutal treatment. It appeared before Parliament, upon interrogating the President of the Court, that the members of the Court Martial which tried him had not been sworn, that they were only seven instead of thirteen, the usual number, that his material witness was shot by the military, while on the road, between Johnstown Castle and Wexford, to give evidence of Mr. Grogan's entire innocence; and that, while General Lake was making merry at dinner (with his staff and some members of the Court that condemned him), one of the first gentlemen in the county (in every point far his superior), was hanged and mutilated before his windows. The author's intimate knowledge of Mr. Cornelius Grogan for many years enables him to assert most unequivocally, and it is but justice to his memory to do so, that, though a person of independent mind as well as fortune, and an opposition member of the Irish Parliament, he was no more a rebel than his brothers, who had signalized themselves in battle as royalists, and the survivor of whom was rewarded by the same Government, by an unprecedented Bill of attainder against that unfortunate gentleman, long after he was dead, by which his great estates were confiscated to the crown.

This Attainder Bill was one of the most illegal and unconstitutional acts ever promoted by any Government; but, after much more than ten thousand pounds, costs to crown officers and to Lord Norbury, as Attorney General, had been extracted from the property, the estates were restored to the surviving brother.

XI. These transactions are dreadful, even to the recollection: they were the ruin of the nation and its character, but are only mentioned to give some idea of that worst of all scourges, civil war, and of the most cruel of all tribunals, courts martial, a situation into which Mr. Pitt craftily permitted the Irish nation to fall, in order to promote his purpose of a union. The subsequent administration of Lord Cornwallis leaves no ground of scepticism upon this subject.

The infliction of torture was incessant, and acts of retaliation were as frequent. Gentlemen were executed, some with trials, others with worse than none. The execution of Sir Edward Crosby, was a murder; that of Mr. Grogan a butchery. The Viceroy had signed no warrants for their executions; he was seldom consulted respecting the prisoners, till their fate had been decided; his conduct was considerate, where he was not governed by his council.

The insurrection had been nearly exhausted, and Lord Camden, who was considered by Mr. Pitt an unfit person to employ for his ulterior objects, was recalled.

CHAPTER XXIV.

Appointment of Lord Cornwallis—His crafty conduct—French invade Ireland in a small number—British troops totally defeated, their artillery all taken—Races of Castlebar—Ninety militia men hanged by Lord Cornwallis—French outwit Lord Cornwallis—Lord Jocelyn taken prisoner—French surrendered—Mr. Pitt proceeds in his projects of a Union—The subserviency of the Lords—The Bishops—Bishops of Waterford and Down—Political characters of Lord Cornwallis and Lord Castlereagh—Unfortunate results of Lord Cornwallis's conduct in every quarter of the world—Lord Castlereagh—Union proposed—Great splendour of the Chancellor—Celebrated Bar Meeting—Mr. Saurin—Mr. Saint George Daly—Mr. Thomas Grady—Mr. Grady's curious harangue—Mr. Thomas Goold's speech—Thirty-two County Judges appointed by Lord Clare—Lord Clare opposes the Bar—Opening of the session of 1799—Lord Clare's great power—Lord Tyrone's character—Seconded by Mr. Fitzgerald—Mr. John Ball—His character.

I. Lord Cornwallis was now selected to complete the project of a union, and Lord Castlereagh was continued as Chief Secretary. His system was, of all others, the most artful and insidious; he affected impartially, whilst he was deceiving both parties; he encouraged the United Irishman, and he roused the royalist; one day he destroyed, the next day he was merciful. His system, however, had not exactly the anticpated effect. Every thing gave reason to expect a restoration of tranquillity; it was through the impression of horror alone that a union could be effected, and he had no time to lose, lest the country might recover its reason.

A portion of an armament, destined by France to aid the Irish insurgents, had escaped our cruisers, and landed about a thousand troops at Killala Bay. They entered Killala without opposition, surprising the bishop and a company of parsons who were on their visitation. Nothing could be better than their conduct, and the bishop, in a publication on this event, did them ample justice, at the expense of his own translation.

They were joined by a considerable number of peasantry, unarmed, unclothed, and undisciplined. But the

French did the best they could to render them efficient. After some stay at Killala, they determined to march into the country, and, even with that small force, they expressed but little doubt of reaching the metropolis.

Lord Hutchinson commanded the garrison of Castlebar a few miles from Killala. His force being pretty numerous, with a good train of artillery, he had no suspicion that a handful of French would presume to attack him.

II. General Lake with his staff had just arrived, and taken the command (as an elder officer), as Lord Hutchinson had determined to march the ensuing day, and end the question, by a capture of the French detachment. The repose of the generals was of short duration. Early in the morning they were roused by an account that the French and peasantry were in full march upon them. They immediately beat to arms, and the troops were moved to a position, about a mile from Castlebar, which, to an unskilled person, seemed unassailable. They had scarcely been posted, with nine pieces of cannon, when the French appeared on the opposite side of a small lake, descending a hill in columns, directly in front of the English. Our artillery played on them with effect. The French kept up a scattered fire of musketry, and took up the attention of our army by irregular movements. In half an hour, however, our troops were alarmed by a movement of small bodies to turn their left, which, being covered by walls, they had never apprehended. The orders given were either mistaken or misbelieved; the line wavered, and, in a few minutes, the whole of the royal army was completely routed, the flight of the infantry was as that of a mob, all the royal artillery was taken, our army fled to Castlebar, the heavy cavalry galloped amongst the infantry and Lord Jocelyn's light dragoons, and made the best of their way, through thick and thin, to Castlebar and towards Tuam, pursued by such of the French as could get horses to carry them.

About nine hundred French and some peasants took possession of Castlebar without resistance, except from a few Highlanders stationed in the town, who were soon destroyed.*

* The native character of the French never showed itself more strongly than after this action. When in full possession of the large town of

This battle has been generally called the *Races of Castlebar*. A considerable part of the Louth and Kilkenny regiments, not finding it convenient to retreat, thought the next best thing they could do would be to join the victors, which they immediately did, and in one hour were completely equipped as French riflemen. About ninety of those men were hanged by Lord Cornwallis afterwards at Ballynamuck. One of them defended himself by insisting, "that it was the army and not he who were deserters; that whilst he was fighting hard they all ran away, and left him to be murdered." Lord Jocelyn got him saved. The defeat of Castlebar, however, was a victory to the Viceroy; it revived all the horrors of the rebellion which had been subsiding, and the desertion of the militia regiments tended to impress the gentry with an idea, that England alone could protect the country.

Lord Cornwallis was supine, and the insurgents were active in profiting by this victory; 40,000 of them were preparing to assemble at the Crooked Wood, in Westmeath, only 42 miles from Dublin, ready to join the French and march upon the metropolis.

III. The French continued too long at Castlebar, and Lord Cornwallis at length collected 20,000 troops, with which he considered himself pretty certain of conquering 900 men. With above 20,000 men, he marched directly to the Shannon to prevent their passage, but he was outmanœuvered; the insurgents had led the French to the source of that river, and it was ten days before his Lordship, by the slowest possible marches, (which he did purposely to increase the public terror), reached his enemy. But he overdid the matter, and had not Colonel Vereker (Lord Gort) delayed them in a rather sanguinary skirmish in which he was defeated, it was possible that they might have slipped by his Lordship, and have been revelling in Dublin, whilst he was roaming about the Shannon: however, he at length overtook the enemy. Lord Jocelyn's

Castlebar, they immediately set about putting their persons in the best order, and the officers advertised a ball and supper that night, for the ladies of the town; this, it is said, was well attended; decorum in all points was strictly preserved; they paid ready money for every thing; in fact, the French army established the French character wherever they occupied.

fox-hunters were determined to retrieve their character, lost at Castlebar, and a squadron, led by his Lordship, made a bold charge upon the French; but the French opened, then closed on them, and they were beaten, and his Lordship was made prisoner.

The French corps, however, saw that ultimate success was impossible, having not more than nine hundred French troops, and they afterwards surrendered prisoners of war without further resistance, after having penetrated to the heart of the kingdom. They were sent to Dublin, and afterwards to France.

Horrors now were everywhere recommenced; executions were multiplied.* Lord Cornwallis marched against the peasantry, still masters of Killala; and after a sanguinary conflict in the streets, the town was taken: some were slaughtered, many hanged, and the whole district was on the point of being reduced to subjection, when Lord Cornwallis most unexpectedly proclaimed an armistice, and without any terms permitted the insurgents freely to disperse, and gave them thirty days, either to surrender their arms or be prepared for slaughter; leaving them to act as they thought proper in the interval. This interval was terrific to the loyalists; the thirty days of armistice were thirty days of new horror, and the Government had now achieved the very climax of public terror, on which they so much counted for inducing Ireland to throw herself into the arms of the protecting country. And the first step of Mr. Pitt's project was fully consummated.

IV. Mr. Pitt now conceived that the moment had arrived to try the effect of his previous measures to promote a legislative Union, and annihilate the Irish legislature. He conceived that he had already prepared inducements to suit every temper amongst the Irish Commons: in that he was partially mistaken. He believed that he had prepared the Irish Peers to accede to all his projects; in that he was successful.

The able, arrogant, ruthless bearing of Lord Clare upon the woolsack, had rendered him almost despotic in that imbecile assembly; forgetting their high rank, their

† His Lordship ordered above ninety of the militia to be immediately executed.

country, and themselves, they yielded unresistingly to the spell of his dictation, and as the fascinated bird, only watched his eye and dropt one by one into the power of the serpent.

The lure of translation neutralized the scruples of the Episcopacy. The Bishops yielded up their conscience to their interests, and but two of the spiritual Peers could be found to uphold the independence of their country, which had been so nobly attained, and so corruptly extinguished. Marly, bishop of Waterford, and Dixon, bishop of Down, immortalized their name, and their characters; they dared to oppose the dictator, and supported the rights of Ireland till she ceased to breathe longer under the title of a Nation.

This measure, of more vital importance than any that has ever yet been enacted by the British legislature, the fatal consequences of which are every day displaying, and still range far beyond the vision of short-sighted statesmen, was first proposed indirectly by a speech from the throne, on the 22d January, 1799.

The insidious object of that speech to entrap the House into a conciliatory reply was seen through, and resisted with a vigour which neither the English nor Irish Governments had ever suspected. The horrors of civil war, the barbarities practised on the one side, and sanctioned on the other, and the universal consternation of the whole kingdom, had, fortunately for Mr. Pitt, excited in many the fallacious idea that in the arms of England only Ireland could regain and secure tranquillity.

This shallow principle influenced or deluded many, but afforded to a greater number a specious pretence for supporting a measure which their individual or corrupt objects only induced them to sanction.

To do justice or to detail the speeches on this great subject, comprising as much eloquence as ever yet appeared in any legislative assembly, would be far too extensive a task for this volume. Short abstracts only can now be given here, and the leading arguments condensed, so as to bring the subject in all its important bearings before the capacity of every reader.

V. Ireland was now reduced to a state fitted to receive propositions for a Union. The loyalists were still struggling through the embers of a rebellion, scarcely extinguished by the torrents of blood which had been poured upon them; the insurgents were artfully distracted between the hopes of mercy and the fear of punishment; the Viceroy had seduced the Catholics by delusive hopes of emancipation, whilst the Protestants were equally assured of their ascendency, and every encouragement was held out to the sectarians. Lord Cornwallis and Lord Castlereagh seemed to have been created for such a crisis and for each other. An unremitting perseverance, an absence of all political compunctions, an unqualified contempt of public opinion, and a disregard of every constitutional principle, were common to both. They held that "the object justifies the means;" and, unfortunately, their private characters were calculated to screen their public conduct from popular suspicion.

Lord Cornwallis, with the exception of the Union, which renders him the most prominent person in Irish history, had never succeeded in any of his public measures. His failure in America had deprived England of her colonies, and her army of its reputation; his catastrophe at Yorktown gave a shock to the King's mind, from which, it is supposed, he never entirely recovered. In India he defeated Tippo Saib, but concluded a peace which only increased the necessity of future wars. Weary of the sword, he was sent as a diplomatist to conclude the peace of Amiens; but, out-manœuvered by Lucien Buonaparte, his Lordship's treaty involved all Europe in a war against England. He had thought to conciliate Lucien, by complimenting the First Consul, and sacrificed his sovereign's honorary title as King of France, which had been borne since the conquest of the Edwards and the Henrys, while he retained the title of Defender of the Faith, corruptly bestowed by the pope on a tyrant.* This was the instrument now employed by Mr. Pitt to effect the Union.

* The title of the King of England then was—"George III. King of Great Britain, France, and Ireland, Defender of the Faith," and so forth. It is very observable, that so *distinct* did the Kings of England consider the two nations, that in *three* royal titles *France* was made to *intervene* therein between England and Ireland. It was owing to the act of settlement, and not through any gift of heaven, that the House of Hanover mounted the throne of Great Britain.

VI. Lord Castlereagh had been more than seven years in the Irish Parliament, but was undistinguished. In private life, his honourable conduct, gentlemanly habits, and engaging demeanour, were exemplary. Of his public life, the commencement was patriotic, the progress corrupt, and the termination criminal. His first public essay was a motion to reform the Irish Parliament, and his last to annihilate it. It is impossible to deny a fact so notorious. History, tradition, or the fictions of romance, contain no instance of any minister who so fearlessly deviated from all the principles which ought to characterize the servant of a constitutional monarch, or the citizen of a free country. Incontestible facts prove the justice of this observation.

The rebellion had commenced on the 23d of May, 1798, and on the 22d of January, 1799, a union was proposed. The commercial propositions had taught Mr. Pitt that, in a period of tranquillity, nothing could be effected with the Irish Parliament by fraud or delusion. But for the terrors of the rebellion, the proposal of a Union might have united all parties against the Government; and Lord Cornwallis's unexampled warfare against nine hundred Frenchmen, was evidently intended more for terror than for victory.

Mr. Pitt's project was first decidedly announced by a pamphlet, written by Mr. Edward Cooke, the Under-Secretary, entitled, "Arguments for and against a Union considered." It was plausibly written, and it roused the people from their confidence that no English minister dared propose, or Irishman abet, a destruction of that independence which Ireland had possessed less than eighteen years. Mr. Cooke was promptly replied to, by a pamphlet, entitled, "Cease your Funning," a masterpiece of its kind, which, in the garb of wit and irony, conveyed the most skilful reasoning, and rendered Mr. Cooke's publication perfectly ridiculous. The author was then most deservedly high at the Irish bar, and is now its first law dignitary. It was sent to press five days after the first line was written. Above a hundred pamphlets were published on both sides of the question; but it was some time before the whole nation could believe such a measure durst be attempted.

VII. The Bar in Ireland was *formerly* not a working trade, but a proud profession, filled by gentlemen of birth and fortune, who were then residents in their country. The Government, the Parliament, every municipality then felt the influence of that profession, whose principal pride it always was to defend the Constitution. The number of offices connected with the law were then comparatively few. The estimable Lord Lifford, at his death, was succeeded on the woolsack by Lord Clare, who immediately gave the utmost latitude to his arbitrary temper and despotic principles as Chancellor.

He commenced his office with a splendour far exceeding all precedent. He expended four thousand guineas for a state carriage; his establishment was splendid, and his entertainments magnificent. His family connections absorbed the patronage of the State, and he became the most absolute subject that modern times had seen in the British islands. His only check was the Bar, which he resolved to corrupt. He doubled the number of the bankrupt commissioners; he revived some offices, created others, and, under pretence of furnishing each county with a local judge, in two months he established thirty-two new offices, of about six or seven hundred pounds per annum each. His arrogance in court intimidated many whom his patronage could not corrupt; and he had no doubt of overpowering the whole profession.

A meeting of the Bar, however, to discuss the Union, was called on the 9th of December, 1799, at the Exhibition Room, William-street, and Mr. Smith, as the father of the Bar, was voted in the chair. Among those who had called the meeting were fourteen of the King's counsel—E. Mayne, W. Saurin, W. C. Plunket, C. Bushe, W Sankey, B. Burton, J. Barrington, A. M'Cartney, G O'Farrell, J. O'Driscoll, J. Lloyd, P. Burrowes, R. Jebb, and H. Joy, Esquires.

Mr. Saurin opened the debate. His speech was vapid, and his resolution unpointed; but he had great influence in his profession. He was a moderate Huguenot, and grandson of the great preacher at the Hague; he was an excellent lawyer, and an amiable, pious Christian. He was followed by Captain Spencer, of the barristers cavalry.

Mr. Saint George Daly, a briefless barrister, was the first supporter of the Union. Of all men he was the least thought of for preferment; but it was wittily observed, " that the Union was the first brief Mr. Daly had spoken from." He moved an adjournment.

Mr. Thomas Grady was the Fitzgibbon spokesman— a gentleman of independent property, a tolerable lawyer, an amatory poet, a severe satirist, and an indefatigable quality-hunter. He had written the *" Flesh Brush,"* for Lady Clare; the " West Briton," for the Union; the " Barrister," for the Bar; and the " Nosegay," for a banker at Limerick, who sued him successfully for a libel.

" The Irish," said Mr. Grady, " are only the *rump of an aristocracy.* Shall I visit posterity with a system of *war, pestilence,* and *famine* ?* No! no! give me a Union. Unite me to that country where all is peace, and order, and prosperity. Without a Union we shall see embryo chief-judges, attorneys general in perspective, and *animalcula serjeants. All* the *cities* of the south and west are on the *Atlantic Ocean,* between the rest of the world and Great Britain; *they* are all for *it*—they must all become warehouses: the people are Catholics, and they are all for it," &c. &c. &c. Such an oration as Mr. Grady's had never before been heard at a meeting of lawyers of Europe.

Mr. John Beresford, Lord Clare's nephew and pursebearer, followed, as if for the charitable purpose of taking the laugh from Mr. Grady, in which he perfectly succeeded, by turning it on himself. Mr. Beresford afterwards became a parson, and is now Lord Decies.

Mr. Goold said—" There are 40,000 British troops in Ireland, and with 40,000 bayonets at my breast, the minister shall not plant another Sicily in the bosom of the Atlantic. I want not the assistance of divine inspi-

---

* Nothing could be more unfortunate than this crude observation of Mr. Grady, as the very three evils, war, pestilence, and famine, which he declared a union would avert, have since visited, and are still visiting the unioned country; which has received aid from England, to avert depopulation by that *famine* which the result of that Union was a leading cause of; and, inoculated with the late plague from Great Britain, they are now declared in a state of *war* by the British legislature.

ration to foretell, for I am enabled by the visible and unerring demonstrations of nature to assert, that Ireland was destined to be a free and independent nation. Our patent to be a state, not a shire, comes direct from heaven. The Almighty has, in majestic characters, signed the great charter of our independence. The great Creator of the world has given our beloved country the gigantic outlines of a kingdom. The God of nature never intended that Ireland should be a province, and *by G——she never shall.*"

The assembly burst into a tumult of applause; a repetition of the words came from many mouths, and many an able lawyer swore hard upon the subject. The division was—

  Against the Union, ... 166
  In favour of it, ... 32
          ———
    Majority, . . . 134

VIII. Thirty-two was the precise number of the county judges, and of this minority the following persons were afterwards rewarded for their adherence to Lord Clare:—

List of Barristers who supported the Union, and their respective rewards.

                  Per Annum.
1. Mr. Charles Osborn, appointed a Judge of the King's Bench, - - - - - - £3300
2. Mr. Saint John Daly, appointed a Judge of the King's Bench, - - - - - 3300
3. Mr. William Smith, appointed Baron of the Exchequer, 3300
4. Mr. M'Cleland, appointed Baron of the Exchequer, - 3300
5. Mr. Robert Johnson, appointed Judge of the Common Pleas, - - - - - 3300
6. Mr. William Johnson appointed Judge of the Common Pleas, - - - - - 3300
7. Mr. Torrens, appointed Judge of the Common Pleas, - 3300
8. Mr. Vandeleur, appointed a Judge of the King's Bench, - 3300
9. Mr. Thomas Maunsell, a County Judge, - - - 600
10. Mr. William Turner, a County Judge, - - - 600
11. Mr. John Scholes, a County Judge, - - - 600
12. Mr. Thomas Vickers, a County Judge - - - 600
13. Mr. J. Homan, a County Judge, - - - 600
14. Mr. Thomas Grady, a County Judge, - - - 600
15. Mr. John Dwyer, a County Judge, - - - 600

		Per Annum
16. Mr. George Leslie, a County Judge,	- - -	£600
17. Mr. Thomas Scott, a County Judge,	- - -	600
18. Mr. Henry Brook, a County Judge,	- - -	600
19. Mr. James Geraghty, a County Judge,	- - -	600
20. Mr. Richard Sharkey, a County Judge,	- - -	600
21. Mr. William Stokes, a County Judge,	- - -	600
22. Mr. William Roper, a County Judge,	- - -	600
23. Mr. C. Garnet, a County Judge,	. - -	600
24. Mr. Jemison, a Commissioner for the distribution of one million and a half Union compensation,	- -	1200
25. Mr. Fitzgibbon Henchy, Commissioner of Bankrupts,	-	400
26. Mr. J. Keller, Officer in the Court of Chancery,	- -	500
27. Mr. P. W. Fortescue, M. P. a *secret* pension,	- -	400
28. Mr. W. Longfield, an officer in the Custom House,	-	500
29. Mr. Arthur Brown, Commission of Inspector,	- -	800
30. Mr. Edmund Stanley, Commission of Inspector,	-	800
31. Mr. Charles Ormsby, Council to Commissioners Value,	-	5000
32. Mr. William Knott, M. P. Commission of Appeals,	-	800
33. Mr. Henry Deane Grady, Council to Commissioners Value,		5000
34. Mr. John Beresford, his father a title.		

Soon after this decision, Sir Jonah Barrington resigned his commission as an officer of the Barrister's Cavalry, and the corps shortly after ceased to act.

"*Letter from Sir Jonah Barrington to Captain Saurin Barristers' Cavalry.*"

"Merrion Square, January 20th, 1799.

"Permit me to resign, through you, the commission which I hold in the Lawyers' Cavalry; I resign it with the regret of a soldier, who knows his duty to his King, yet feels his duty to his country, and will depart from neither but with his life.

"That blind and fatal measure proposed by the Irish Government, to extinguish the political existence of Ireland to surrender its legislature, its trade, its dearest rights, and proudest prerogatives, into the hands of a British minister, and a British council, savours too much of that *foreign* principle, against the prevailing influence of which the united powers of Great Britain and Ireland are this moment combating, and as evidently throws open to the British empire the gate of that seductive political innovation, which has already proved the grave of half the governments of Europe.

"Consistent therefore, with my loyalty and my oath, I can no longer continue subject to the indefinite and unforeseen commands of a military government, which so madly hazards the integrity of the British empire, and existence of the British constitution, to crush a rising nation, and aggrandize a despotic minister.

"Blinded by my zealous and hereditary attachment to the established government and British connection, I saw not the absolute necessity of national unanimity, to secure constitutional freedom, I see it now, and trust it is not yet too late to establish both.

"I never will abet a now developed system, treacherous and ungrateful, stimulating two sects against each other, to enfeeble *both*, and then making religious feuds a pretext for political slavery.

"Rejecting the experiment of a reform, and recommending the experiment of a revolution.

"Kindling catholic expectation to a blaze, and then extinguishing it for ever.

"Alternately disgusting the rebel and the royalist, by indiscriminate pardon, and indiscriminate punishment.

"Suspending one code of laws, and adjudging by another without authority to do either; and when the country, wearied by her struggles for her King, slumbers to refresh and to regain her vigour, her liberty is treacherously attempted to be bound, and her pride, her security, and her independence, are to be buried alive in the tomb of national annihilation.

"Mechanical obedience is the duty of a soldier, but active uninfluenced integrity the indispensable attribute of a legislator, when the preservation of his country is in question, and as the same frantic authority, which meditates our *civil* annihilation, might in the same frenzy meditate *military* projects from which my feelings, my principles, and my honour might revolt, I feel it right to separate my civil and military functions; and, to secure the honest uninterrupted exercise of the one, I relinquish the indefinite subjection of the other.

"I return the arms I received from government—I received them pure, and restore them not dishonoured.

"I shall now resume my civil duties with zeal and with energy, elevated by the hope, that the Irish Parliament, true to itself, and honest to its country, will never assume a power extrinsic of its delegation, and will convince the British nation that we are a people equally impregnable to the attacks of intimidation, or the shameless practice of corruption.

" Yours, &c.
" JONAH BARRINGTON,
" *Lieut. L. Cavalry.*
" To WILLIAM SAURIN, Esq.
" *Commandant Lawyers' Corps.*"

The Right Honourable James Fitzgerald, then primeserjeant, was dissmissed from office, having peremptorily refused to vote for the Union. The office of prime-serjeant, unknown in England, in Ireland took precedence of the Attorney and Solicitor General. The emoluments were very great; Mr. Saint George Daly was immediately rewarded by that office, to the duties of which he was totally incompetent, never having been in any considerable practice at the bar.

A meeting was then called to express to Mr. Fitzgerald the thanks of his profession for his disinterested patriotism, never was there a more just and honourable tribute paid to an honest public character.

The bar had also determined, that the precedence in the courts should be continued to Mr. Fitzgerald; to this Lord Clare would not accede, and he treated the subject with great arrogance in his court. That session concluded without any other meeting of the profession.

The day after that debate, Mr. Saint George Daly drew up a protest of the minority, some of whom refused to sign it; he got some substitutes, so as to keep up his number of thirty-two, but not one person of professional eminence, of public character, or independence, appeared in the whole number; it was universally ridiculed, but Mr. Daly carried his object—his own promotion.

Five of the debates on the Union in the Irish Commons comprised every thing of the first importance upon the subject; of these, three took place in January, 1799, whilst men were impressed with the horrors of the rebellion and the fears of a French invasion. The debates of 1800 were after the Parliament had been packed through the Place Bill. The competence of Parliament to relinquish the Constitution, and their own existence, was discussed with extraordinary ability.

IX. The first debate took place on the 22nd January, 1799, and lasted till eleven o'clock in the morning of the 23rd, or twenty-two hours. The Government obtained a majority of only one and that by the palpable seduction of Mr. Fox. The second debate commenced at five o'clock on the same day, and continued till late in the morning of the 24th, when, the country being roused, the Treasury Bench was unexpectedly defeated.

The speech from the Viceroy, delivered on the opening of the session, which gave rise to the debate of 22nd January, recommended—" the unremitting industry with which our enemies persevere in their avowed design of endeavouring to effect a separation of this kingdom from Great Britain, must have engaged your particular attention, and His Majesty commands me to express his anxious hope that this consideration, joined to the sentiment of mutual affection and common interest, may dispose the Parliaments in both kingdoms to provide the most effectual means of maintaining and improving a connection essential to their common security, and of consolidating as far as possible into one firm and lasting fabric, the strength, the power and the resources of the British empire." The address to that speech, almost an echo, was moved by Lord Tyrone, who thus stamped for himself an eternal impression on the annals of Ireland. He was the eldest son of the Marquis of Waterford, a keen and haughty nobleman, possessed of that local influence which rank, extensive connections, unlimited patronage, and ostentatious establishments are almost certain to acquire: inflated with aristocratic pride and blinded by egotism, he became a powerful instrument of Lord Clare's ambition, whilst he conceived that he was only gratifying his own. Lord Clare, at that period, had covered the surface of the nation with the partisans of the Beresfords and himself, and no family ever possessed so many high and lucrative employments; they had no talent, no public services, no political honesty, which should have entitled them to the authority they exercised over their sovereign and country.

Lord Tyrone, an automaton of Lord Clare, possessed plain manners, an open countenance, a slothful uncultivated mind, unsusceptible of any refined impressions, or patriotic feelings; the example of his relatives gave him no stimulus beyond that of lucrative patronage. Whatever were his individual opinions upon the Union, his vapid, disingenuous, and arrogant speech evinced that he was not calculated to give weight to his family: his speech had been written by his friends, and, concealing it in the crown of his hat, he took a glance at it when at a loss: the exhibition, on such a subject, was too disgusting to be ridiculous: Lord Clare, on this occasion, exhibited the voracity of his ambition. The ancient and proud house of Beresford were, on that night, cringing as the vassals of an arrogant and splendid upstart.

The address was seconded by Mr. Robert Fitzgerald, of Corkbeg, an elderly country gentleman; he had an honest character, blunt, candid manners; and though he had not talent, he could deliver himself with some strength and with the appearance of sincerity. His speech on this occasion was short and feeble. He had been artfully seduced as a lure to the country gentlemen, by Lord Cornwallis's assuring him that, in the event of the Union, a royal dock-yard would be built near Cork, which would double the value of his estates.

In every debate upon that measure, it was insisted upon that the Parliament was incompetent, even to entertain the question of the Union; such was the opinion of Mr. Saurin, since Attorney General; Mr. Plunket, since Lord Chancellor; Serjeant Ball, the ablest lawyer of Ireland; Mr. Fitzgerald, Prime Sergeant of Ireland; Mr. Moore, since a Judge; Sir John Parnell, then Chancellor of the Exchequer; Mr. Bushe, since Chief Justice; and Lord Oriel, the then Speaker of the House of Commons. Nearly every unbribed or uninfluenced member of the learned profession adopted the doctrine of which these learned and able men were the unqualified organs. Lord Glenbervie, in his famous speech in favour of the Union, in the English House of Commons, in 1800, expressed his surprise that Messrs. Saurin, Plunket, and Barrington, *could* reason upon so untenable a position. He admitted their sincerity, but considered them not very clear in their intellects. His own speech was splendidly printed, but was miserably heavy. The Irish Union materially changed the representation of England, and altered the letter and spirit of the Scotch treaty; Ireland, however, was alone disfranchised.

Mr. John Ball, Member for Drogheda, who gave his unqualified opinion as to the legal and constitutional incapacity of the Commons to enact an Union, was the ablest lawyer of his day, and one of the purest characters, public and private, that had ever flourished in Ireland; amiable and consistent in every station and in every capacity, combining spirit and mildness, fortitude and moderation; he was cast in one of the finest moulds of firmness and patriotism. During his progress from comparative obscurity to the attachment and highest esteem of his profession, and of the public, he evinced an independence above all temptation. Though the ablest lawyer of his day, he was passed over in all Lord Clare's promotions.

CHAPTER XXV.

The three leading arguments used in Parliament in favour of a Union—Arguments of the Anti-Unionists—Not England which quelled the insurrection—English militia never acted in Ireland—Mr. William Smith supports the Union—Corrupt conduct of Mr. Trench and Mr. Fox—Mr. Trench palpably gained over—Mr. Trench recanted what he had a few moments before declared—The Place Bill and its unfortunate effects—Mr. Fox created a Judge of the Common Pleas for his tergiversation—Originally a Whig—Made a false declaration to avoid being counted—Effect of the Place Bill—His second deception—Conduct of Mr. Cooke and Admiral Pakenham—Mr. Marshall's disgraceful conduct—Debate commenced—Great popularity of the Speaker—Lord Castlereagh's policy—Sir John Parnell denied the competence of both the King and the Parliament to enact a Union—Mr. Tighe the same—Great effect of Mr. Ponsonby's speech—Remarkable agitation—Description of the scene—Lord Castlereagh's violent speech—Attack on Mr. Ponsonby—Mr. Ponsonby's sarcastic reply—Lord Castlereagh's desperation—Mr. John Egan attacks Mr. William Smith—Sir Laurence Parsons made a most able and eloquent speech—Mr. Frederick Falkiner nothing could corrupt—Prime Sergeant Fitzgerald dismissed—Mr. Plunket's speech—Spirited speech of Col. O'Donnell—Second shameful tergiversation of Mr. Trench, created Lord Ashtown—Most important incident in the annals of Ireland—State of the House of Commons—Mr. Fortescue's fatal speech—Mr. French and Lord Cole seceded—John Claudius Beresford—Extraordinary change in the feelings of the House—Sarcastic remark of Sir Henry Cavendish—Great popularity of the Speaker—Joy and exultation of the people—Singular anecdote of Mr. Martin—Meeting of the Lords—Their infatuation—Conduct of Lord Clare—Unpopularity of the Irish Peers—Two Bishops, Down and Limerick, opposed him—Character of the Bishop of Down—Commission of Compensation—Subsequent proceedings of the Viceroy and Lord Castlereagh—Ruinous consequence of Mr. Fortescue's conduct—Mistaken conduct of the Anti-Unionists—Their embarrassment—Bad effects of Mr. Fortescue's conduct—The Catholics—State of parties.

I. It would be impossible to do justice to the brilliant eloquence, and unanswerable reasoning, by which this measure was combated. Even a short abstract of the speeches delivered on that momentous question would swell this volume beyond its intended limits; those speeches will be the subject of a future publication.

At present, it must suffice to state the abstract points on which the arguments of Government for annexation were founded, and those by which they were so ably, and unanswerably refuted. First, the distracted state of the Irish Nation, its religious dissensions, and the consequent danger of a separation, unless protected from so imminent a peril, by the incorporation with Great Britain, and the incapacity of the Irish legislature alone to avert the dangers of the country, and preserve the constitution. Secondly, the great commercial advantages of a Union which must eventually enrich Ireland, by an extension of its commerce, the influx of British capital, and the confidence of England in the stability of its institutions, when guaranteed by the Union. Thirdly, the Government pressed with great zeal the example of Scotland, which had so improved, and become so rich and prosperous, after its annexation; a precedent which must convince the Irish of the incalculable advantages, which must ensue from a similar incorporation.

Many other arguments, but of a minor description, were urged by the purchased partisans of Government. But the leading points which elicited the splendid eloquence, the reasoning and the high spirit of its opponents, were exemplified by the argument of Mr. George Ponsonby.

II. Sir Lawrence Parsons, and many others in reply, not only animated, but convinced the assembly; the facts were too strong to be refuted, that the country had been worked up by the English minister to terrify the Irish gentry into a resubmission to whose shackles from which the spirit of the Volunteers, and of the nation, had but a few years before released them. They asked what could the Union do, which could not be done without it?

That there was no species of aid, no auxiliary power which England could afford to Ireland, either to restore or secure her tranquillity, that Ireland had not fully within her own reach and power. She had men—she had means—she had arms—she had spirit—she had loyalty—all in her domestic circle sufficient to restore her to peace, which had, for a moment, been interrupted by the machinations of those who would now take advantage of their own treachery. The Irish Parliament had within her own walls the power of reconciling religious differences, restoring peace or putting down insurrection, far more effectually than the English Government could pretend to possess.

It was argued that the insurrection, first organized and fostered by Mr. Pitt, and protracted by Lord Cornwallis, had been suppressed by the active zeal and measures of the Irish Parliament; and that the introduction of foreign and mercenary Germans, to immolate the Irish, instead of tending to extinguish, added fuel to the conflagration, and excited the strongest feelings of retaliation; nor could the people of independent Ireland brook the idea of being cut down by Welshmen.

III. It was not to the arms of England, but to the distinguished loyalty of the Irish Commons, and the prompt and vigorous measures of the Irish Parliament, that the speedy termination of that insurrection was to be attributed. The *English* Militia were brought over, after the contest had nearly ended, and never fired a shot in Ireland. They conducted themselves with decorum and due discipline, and returned to England with at least as good a character as they left it. The German mercenaries who were wantonly imported, as if to teach barbarity to the Irish insurgents, amply experienced by their own blood the expertness of their pupils, and only aggravated that people whom they had been brought to conquer.

The argument therefore, that the Irish legislature had not sufficient power to protect itself, was unfounded and fallacious, and only invented to keep up and augment the terrors of the Irish gentry.

The second ground of argument used by the supporters of the Union, great commercial advantages, appeared still more fallacious; its deception was too palpable to deceive the most ignorant of the people.

IV. The proposers of the Union were asked, what were the commercial advantages which Ireland could possibly gain by a Union, that she might not equally attain through her own Parliament without one? She was an independent nation, she had an independent legislature, she might regulate her own tariffs and conduct her commerce by her own statutes; the reciprocal connection of the two countries was an equal object to the commercial interests of both.

The non-importation and non-consumption resolutions of Ireland had once brought back the English monopolists to their reason; the same power remained with the Irish people. If she could resist commercial restraints in 1782, with tenfold more facility she could resist them in 1800; she could trade with more success, because she had since learned the rudiments of commerce, from a participation in which the avarice of monopolists and the unjust jealousies of Great Britain had theretofore excluded her.

The crafty prediction that English capital would flow into Ireland, when a Union was effected, was a visionary deception. For more capital would be annually withdrawn from Ireland by the emigration of the landed proprietors in conseqtence of Union, than could be gained by any accession of British capital. Ireland was an agricultural country; her natural fertility pointed out to her the true source of her internal employment and the proper subjects of her external commerce; and when the famine which the slightest stagnation of trade causes amongst the manufacturers of the first towns of England, the decrepitude of their meagre operatives, the wretched enervating slavery to which the necessity of the parents and the brutality of the manufacturer condemn the infants of that nation, are considered, it would make a sufficient reply to either the certainty or the consequence of British capital.

V. The third and most deceptious argument of the Union supporters, because the most plausible, was the precedent of Scotland, and the great advantages derived by her in consequence of her Union.

Of all the false reasoning, mis-stated facts, fallacious premises, and unfounded conclusions, that any position ever was attempted to be supported on, the arguments founded on the Scottish precedent were the most erroneous, and no deception ever was more completely and fully detected than by the speeches made in the Irish Parliament in 1799 and 1800, and by several able pamphlets, which, at that period, flowed in full tide upon the public.*

* Two pamphlets, and a speech of Mr. Goold at the Bar meeting published in 1799, go very ably into all those subjects.

These replies, being founded on matters of fact and attested by incontrovertible records, put at once a decisive conclusion to every argument deduced by the advocates of Union, from that subject.

First, as to matter of fact, Scotland and Ireland in their relation with England, stood on grounds diametrically opposite to each other on every point that could warrant a Union on the one side, or reject it on the other.

Scotland and England forming only one Island, divided by a frontier, many parts of which a man could step over, had ever been in a state of sanguinary warfare. The facility of invasion on both sides, left no moment of a certain undisturbed tranquillity to either. Their inroads were incessant, their reconciliations, only the forerunner of new contests, interrupted by short intervals of peace, until the accession of Mary. She had been Queen of France, and on her return to her native country, introduced a French connection with Scotland, which added to the excitement of both nations, and naturally increased the apprehensions of England from the power of a neighbour, so supported as Scotland then must have been.

The two crowns were united in the person of James the First; and in the reign of Charles, the Scottish army renounced their allegiance and sold their King, and surrendered him to his enemies, and eventually to the executioner. It was considered by King William III., when he usurped the British throne, that if they so acted by one King, they might do so by another, and his sanguinary conduct towards that country, still widened the breach between the two nations. At length the reign of Anne brought the question of Union forward, not as in Ireland, a mere voluntary discussion, but one of absolute necessity.

VI. Had Anne died childless, the crowns must have been severed, and that of Scotland, by descent, would have gone to the Scottish Duke of Hamilton, as Hanover was, on the demise of his late Majesty, separated from England. This important fact puts an end to all comparisons between the relative state of the two countries.

The Scottish Parliament, to put an end to all doubts on the subject of separation, passed an Act entitled the

Act of security. By that statute, the Scottish Parliament enacted that the crown of Scotland should *never be worn by the same Monarch as that of England.* By the Irish Parliament it was enacted that the two crowns should *" ever"* be *worn by the same Monarch* and never *disunited.*

VII. Thus it incontestibly appears by an Act of Scotland herself, that without a Scottish Union England and Scotland though the same island, *must* in a short space of time have been constitutionally severed, and governed by different and distinct monarchs for *ever*, whereas Ireland, though a different and distinct island, with a great intervening sea, had decided the very *reverse* of Scotland, and had united herself indissolubly and voluntarily to England, by a mutual federative compact, both crowns to be for *ever* worn by the *same* Monarch.

How the supporters of the Irish Union, therefore, could have the face to call in the Scottish Union as a precedent, to show the necessity of an Irish Union, can only be accounted for by that voluntary blindness, and premeditated absence of all candour and liberality, which are the inseparable companions of political delinquency.

But, in fact, the supporters of an Irish Union were themselves the greatest enemies to British connection, for this clear and obvious reason; the Scottish Union was a matter of state *necessity;* the connection of England and Ireland a mutual *international compact,* and as such equally binding, sacred, and inviolable, on *both* sides; and as the principle of all international as well as individual contracts, is binding just so long as the mutual compacts are adhered to. Such a mutual, sacred, and international compact, voluntarily, constitutionally, and legally guaranteed by both legislatures, confirmed by the King of both countries in his double capacity, and touched by his sceptre, had been enacted and did exist between England and Ireland long *previous* to the measure of a Union, so pressed on Ireland by England; such a Union was therefore a direct unequivocal infraction, of that international treaty, and federative compact, the mutual and inviolable adherence to which, in *all* its provisions, was the only valuable consideration to Ireland.

It was truly argued, that in this point of view, therefore no similarity existed between the position of Scotland and of Ireland, when the Irish nobles were cashiered of their hereditary honour, and the Irish people plundered of two thirds of their constitutional representation.

VIII. Another fact stated, and most ably reasoned on, during the debates on the Irish Union to prove the absurdity of the attempted comparison, was that the Scottish and Irish Parliaments, at that period, had in their organization and proceedings no similitude whatsoever; the Lords and Commons of Scotland formed but one chamber, the representatives of the people (such as they were) and the Peers called the hereditary counsellors of the crown sat mingled and voted together promiscuously; nothing like the British constitution even in theory existed in Scotland: church, state, and legislation had no analogy; two countries, therefore, possessing such incongruous materials of legislation, and a species of *imperium in imperio*, entirely inconsistent with the constitution of the superior nation, could not continue to exist in the same island, without the daily probability of collision, and the danger of hostilities, aided by the facility of invasion by either country; this condition imperatively required some means to avert so probable and imminent a danger to both countries.

No such dangers, however, existed as to Ireland; and if she had not been politically excited by the British minister, and by the example of England and Scotland, or even after that excitement had subsided, and put an end to, had she been permitted to rest, and regain her tranquillity and vigour, and proper measures had been then adopted to continue that tranquillity, no country on earth had more capabilities, and no country in Europe would have been more prosperous, tranquil, and happy, than misgoverned Ireland.

The grand and fundamental point, which was then urged, reasoned upon, and which never has, and never can be refuted, was the incompetence of Parliament to betray its trust. Whilst the first elements of the British constitution exist, that principle is its surest protection; the entire incompetence of representatives elected by the people, as their delegated trustees, to represent them in the great national inquest, and as such trustees, and guardians, to preserve the rights and constitution so entrusted to them, inviolate; and at the expiration of the term of that trust, deliver back their trust to their constituents, as they received it, to be replaced in their own hands, or of other trustees for another term. But they had, and could have no power to betray their trust, convert it to their own corrupt purposes, or transfer the most valuable of all funds, an independent constitution, the integrity of which they became trustees solely for the purpose of protecting.

This being a fundamental principle of British law, is placed under the protection of the Judges; and the very essence, first principle and element of British equity, is placed under the protection of the Chancellor. That high functionary, in his double capacity, of the first judge of the country, and also the adviser of the King in all cases within his jurisdiction, is bound to support by authorities, that principle which forms the only safeguard to the British Constitution.

IX. Many of the ablest lawyers of 1799 and 1800 justly estimated for their deep knowledge, great talents, and incorruptible integrity, gave both in and out of Parliament unqualified and decided opinions, which are too important not to be recorded; they entirely denied the competence of the Irish Commons, to pass or even to receive any act of Union extinguishing their own existence and betraying the trusts they were delegated to protect. When the names of Saurin, Ponsonby, Plunket, Ball, Bushe, Curran, Burrowes, Fitzgerald, A. Moore, &c. are found supporting that doctrine by their learning, their public character, and their legal reputation; and such men as Grattan, Parsons, Forbes, Parnel, O'Hara, &c. &c. united with Corry, Clements, Caulfield, Cole, Kingsborough, &c., and the flower of the young Irish nobles, in the Commons House of Parliament; it is impossible not to accede to a doctrine, supported by every principle of law, equity, and constitution.

This great fact, therefore (and the irrefragable authorities on which it rests are repeated, and spread over many parts of this short history), necessarily produces a deduction, more intrinsically important, and involving more grave considerations, than any other that can arise upon this subject. From these principles, it follows as a corollary, that the Act of Union carried by such means, was in itself a nullity *ab initio*, and a fraud upon the then existing constitution; and if a nullity in 1800, it is incontrovertible that nothing afterwards did, or possibly could, validate it in 1833.

No temporary assent, or in this case submission, could be deduced as an argument, no lapse of time, unless by proscription (beyond which the memory of man runneth not), can ever establish any Act originally illegal; no limitation through lapse of time, can bar the rights and claims of the crown, there is no limitation, through lapse of time, to the church, no limitation through lapse of time, can bar the chartered right of even a petty corporation; and *à fortiori*, no lapse of time can legalize any act hostile to the rights of a free people, or extinguish the legislature of an independent nation. In that point of view, therefore, no legislative union ever was constitutionally enacted between the two countries.

But considering that question in another point of view, it is the invariable principle of all international law, that the infraction of a solemn treaty, on the one side, dispenses with any adherence to the same treaty by the other, of course, annuls both, and leaves the contracting parties *in statu quo*, as they respectively stood before the treaty, and it was therefore argued by those able men, that the renunciation act of the 23d George III., "recognizing the unqualified independence of Ireland, and expressly stipulating and contracting that it should endure for ever," was the very essence, and consideration, of the international and federative treaty; and through its infraction by England, both countries stood in the very same state as at the period when England repealed her own statute of George I., and admitted its unconstitutionality, and her own usurpation, Ireland, of course, remained in the same position as she stood at that period.

X. From all these considerations it inevitably follows that if through force, or fraud, or fear, or corruption, in enacting it, the Union was null, then any act of the Imperial Parliament, repealing the Act of Union, would be in fact only repealing a nullity, and restoring to Ireland a legislature she never had been constitutionally deprived of. It was admitted that, had the infraction of the federative treaty been the act of Ireland, then this reasoning would have lost its validity; but the contrary is direct and indisputable.

The Union propositions came from England herself, they were rejected; she returned to the charge, and forced them upon Ireland, though at the same time the English Parliament had solemnly pledged the honour, both of themselves, and their sovereign, for the eternal support of its independence, and the federative treaty.

These arguments, and many more, were used both in and out of Parliament, to arrest the progress of that destructive and faithless measure, but in vain; however, two great events, so long and so violently resisted for more than a century, have lately been accomplished; which give rise to constitutional questions, and have materially changed the state both of the people and the legislature, roused Ireland from her torpor, and brought forward claims which had so long lain dormant. And it is by the late measures of England herself, that the Irish people have been led to consider that the nation was only in a slumber, and her legislature only in *abeyance*.

XI. These grave and embarrassing points of constitutional law, were by various speeches and pamphlets combated by Mr. William Smith (the present Baron,) who lent the whole power of his able, and indefatigable genius, to prove the omnipotence of Parliament, and combat all the reasoning of those distinguished men, who have been heretofore alluded to: particularly Mr. Foster, against whose doctrine he wrote a long and laboured pamphlet.

Baron Smith's ideas and reasoning are so metaphysically plaited and interwoven, that facts are lost sight of in the multiplicity and minuteness of theories and distinctions, and ordinary auditors, after a most learned, eloquent, and argumentative charge, or argument, are seldom able to recollect a single sentence of either, (the dogmas excepted,) after they are out of the Court House. In all his arguments, as to the omnipotence of the Irish Parliament to surrender its legislature, he manufactures his theories, as if the Irish Commons submitted willingly to prostitution, and argued in principle, that if members were purchased, it was in a market *overt*, and that th-unconstitutionality of the sale merged in the omnipotent majority of the purchaser.

It is to be regretted that the learned Baron, who is always able, and frequently four days in the week patriotic, should in 1800 have accepted a seat on the Bench, as a premium for his share of the omnipotency. The English people would have considered the Baron's reasoning, for the extinction of the Irish Parliament, in a very different point of view, if it had been used by him to prove the expediency of removing the British Parliament, to legislate in Dublin.

XII. A very remarkable incident during the first night's debate occurred in the conduct of Mr. Luke Fox and Mr. Trench, of Woodlawn, afterwards created Lord Ashtown. These were the most palpable, undisguised acts of public tergiversation and seduction ever exhibited in a popular assembly. They afterwards became the subject of many speeches and of many publications; and their consequences turned the majority of one in favour of the Minister.

It was suspected that Mr. Trench had been long in negociation with Lord Castlereagh, but it did not in the early part of that night appear to have been brought to any conclusion, his conditions were *supposed* to be too extravagant. Mr. Trench, after some preliminary observations, declared, in a speech, that he would vote against the Minister, and support Mr. Ponsonby's amendment. This appeared a stunning blow to Mr. Cooke, who had been previously in conversation with Mr. Trench. He was immediately observed sideling from his seat nearer to Lord Castlereagh. They whispered earnestly, and, as if restless and undecided, both looked wistfully towards Mr. Trench. At length the matter seemed to be determined on. Mr. Cooke retired to a back seat, and was obviously endeavouring to count the house, probably to guess if they could that night dispense with Mr. Trench's services. He returned to Lord Castlereagh, they whispered, again looked most affectionately at Mr. Trench, who seemed unconscious that he was the subject of their consideration. But there was no time to lose, the question was approaching, all shame was banished, they decided on the terms, and a significant and certain glance, obvious to every body, convinced Mr. Trench that his conditions were agreed to. Mr. Cooke then went and sat down by his side ; an earnest but very short conversation took place; a parting smile completely told the house that Mr. Trench was that moment satisfied. These surmises were soon verified. Mr. Cooke went back to Lord Castlereagh, a congratulatory nod announced his satisfaction. But could any man for one moment suppose that a Member of Par liament, a man of very large fortune, of respectable family, and good character, could be publicly, and without shame or compunction, actually seduced by Lord Castlereagh, in the very body of the house, and under the eye of two hundred and twenty gentlemen? Yet this was the fact. In a few minutes Mr. Trench rose, to apologize for having indiscreetly declared he would support the amendment. He added, that he had thought better of the subject since he had *unguardedly* expressed himself; that he had been *convinced* he was wrong, and would support the Minister.

Scarcely was there a member of any party who was not disgusted ; it had, however, the effect intended by the desperate purchaser, of proving that Ministers would stop at *nothing* to effect their objects, however shameless or corrupt. This purchase of Mr. Trench, had a much more fatal effect upon the destinies of Ireland. His change of sides, and the majority of *one* to which it contributed, were probably the remote causes of persevering in a Union. Mr. Trench's venality excited indignation in every friend of Ireland.*

Another circumstance that night proved by what means Lord Castlereagh's majority of even *one* was acquired.

The Place Bill, so long and so pertinaciously sought for, and so indiscreetly framed by Mr. Grattan and the Whigs of Ireland, now, for the first time, proved the very engine by which the Minister upset the opposition, and annihilated the Constitution.

That bill enacted, that members accepting offices, places, or pensions, during the pleasure of the Crown,

---

* Had Mr. Fox and Mr. Trench voted as they professed, a majority of three would have appeared in favour of Mr. Ponsonby's amendment; and Englishmen will scarcely credit that any Government could, with a majority against them, have presumed to persevere in their subversion of the Constitution.

should not sit in Parliament unless re-elected; but, unfortunately, the Bill made no distinction between valuable offices which might influence, and nominal offices, which might job, and the Chiltern Hundreds of England were, under the title of the Escheatorships of Munster, Leinster, Connaught, &c., transferred to Ireland, with salaries of forty shillings, to be used at pleasure by the Secretary. Occasional and temporary seats were thus bartered for by Government, and by the ensuing session, made the complete and fatal instrument of packing the Parliament and effecting a Union.

Mr. Luke Fox, a barrister of very humble origin, of vulgar manners, and of a coarse, harsh appearance, was endued with a clear, strong, and acute mind, and was possessed of much cunning. He had acquired very considerable legal information, and was an obstinate and persevering advocate; he had been the usher of a school, and a sizer in Dublin University; but neither politics nor the belles-lettres were his pursuit. On acquiring eminence at the bar, he married an obscure niece of the Earl of Ely's; he had originally professed what was called whiggism, merely, as people supposed, because his name was Fox. His progress was impeded by no political principles, but he kept his own secrets well, and being a man of no importance, it was perfectly indifferent to every body what side he took. Lord Ely, perceiving he was manageable, returned him to Parliament as one of his automata; and Mr. Fox played his part very much to the satisfaction of his manager.

When the Union was announced, Lord Ely had not made his terms, and remained long in abeyance; and as his Lordship had not issued his orders to Mr. Fox, he was very unwilling to commit himself until he could dive deeper into probabilities; but rather believing the opposition would have the majority, he remained in the body of the House with the Anti-Unionists, when the division took place. The doors were scarcely locked, when he became alarmed, and slunk, unperceived, into one of the dark corridors, where he concealed himself: he was, however, discovered, and the serjeant-at-arms was ordered to bring him forth, to be counted amongst the Anti-Unionists, his confusion was very great, and he seemed at his wit's end, at length he declared he had taken advantage of the Place Bill; had *actually accepted the Escheatorship of Munster,* and had thereby vacated his seat, and could not vote.

The fact was doubted, but, after much discussion, his excuse, *upon his honour,* was admitted, and he was allowed to return into the corridor. On the numbers being counted, there was a majority of ONE for Lord Castlereagh, and, exclusive of Mr. Trench's conduct ; but for that of Mr. Fox the numbers would have been equal; the measure would have been negatived by the Speaker's vote, and the renewal of it, the next day, have been prevented: this would have been a most important victory.

XIII. The mischief of the Place Bill now stared its framers in the face, and gave the Secretary a code of instruction how to arrange a Parliament against the ensuing session.

To render the circumstance still more extraordinary and unfortunate for Mr. Fox's reputation, it was subsequently discovered, by the public records, that Mr. Fox's assertion was false ; but the following day Lord Castle reagh purchased him outright ; and then, *and not before,* appointed him to the nominal office of Escheator of Mun ster, and left the seat of Lord Ely for another of his creatures.* This is mentioned, not only as one of the most reprehensible public acts committed during the discussion, but because it was the primary cause of the measure being persisted in.

The exultations of the public on this disappointment of the Minister knew no bounds; they reflected not, that, next day, a new debate must endanger their ambiguous triumph. The national character of the Irish, during both the 23rd and 24th, displayed itself in full vigour.

The debate upon the report of the address, and the pertinacity which urged the Government to a second combat, soon roused them from their dream of security.

Both parties now stood in a difficult and precarious

---

* This did not conclude the remarkable acts of Mr. Fox: after his seat had been so vacated, he got himself re-elected for a Borough under the influence of the Earl of Granard, a zealous Anti-Unionist ; here he once more betrayed the country, and was appointed a Judge when the subject was decided.

predicament: the Minister had not time to gain ground by the usual practices of the Secretary; and the question must have been either totally relinquished or again discussed. The Opposition were, as yet, uncertain how far the last debate might cause any numerical alteration in their favour; each party calculated on a small majority, and it was considered that a defeat would be equally ruinous to either.

It was supposed that the Minister would, according to all former precedent, withdraw from his situation, if left in a minority, whilst an increased majority, however small, against the Anti-Unionists, might give plausible grounds for future discussions.

The next day the people collected in vast multitudes around the House; a strong sensation was every where perceptible; immense numbers of ladies of distinction crowded at an early hour, into the galleries, and by their presence and their gestures animated that patriotic spirit, upon the prompt energy of which alone depended the fate of Ireland.

Secret messengers were dispatched in every direction, to bring in loitering or reluctant members—every emissary that Government could rely upon was busily employed the entire morning; and five and thirty minutes after four o'clock, in the afternoon of the 24th of January, 1799, the House met to decide, by the adoption or rejection of the Address, the question of national independence or annihilation. Within the corridors of the House, a shameless and unprecedented alacrity appeared among the friends of Government.

Mr. Cooke, the Under Secretary, who, throughout all the subsequent stages of the question, was the private and efficient actuary of the Parliamentary seduction, on this night exceeded even himself, both in his public and private exertions to gain over the wavering members. Admiral Pakenham, a naturally friendly and good-hearted gentleman, that night acted like the captain of a press-gang, and actually *hauled* in some members who were desirous of retiring. He had declared that he would act in *any* capacity, according to the exigencies of his party; and he did not shrink from his task.

A Mr. Marshall, of the Secretary's office (not a mem-her), forgot all decorum, and disgraced the cause by his exploits about the entrances of the House. Others acted as keepers in the coffee-room; and no member who could be seduced, intimidated, or deceived, could possibly escape the nets that were extended to secure him.

Nor did the leaders of Opposition remain inactive; but the attendance of their friends being voluntary, was, of course, precarious. The exertions of Mr. Bowes Daly and others, were, however, strenuous.

At length a hot and open canvass, by the friends of Government, was perceived, wherever an uncertain or reluctant member could be found, or his connections discovered.

XIV. The debate commenced about seven o'clock. Silence prevailed in the galleries; but an indecent confusion and noise ran through the corridors, and frequently excited surprise and alarm at its continuance: it was the momentous canvass—it was rude, sometimes boisterous, and altogether unsual.

The Speaker at length took his chair, and his cry of "Order! order!" obtained a profound silence. Dignified and peremptory, he was seldom disobeyed; and a chairman more despotic, from his wisdom and the respect and affection of the members of every side, never presided over a popular assembly.

When prayers commenced, all was in a moment gloomy and decorous, and a deep solemnity corresponded with the vital importance of the subject they were to determine.

This debate, in point of warmth, much exceeded the former. Lord Castlereagh was silent; his eye ran round the assembly, as if to ascertain his situation, and was often withdrawn with a look of uncertainty and disappointment. The numbers had a little increased since the last division, principally by members who had not declared themselves, and of whose opinions the Secretary was ignorant.

Lord Castlereagh, however, wincing under his negative castigation of the former evening, had now determined to act on the offensive, and give, by his example, more spirit, and zeal to his followers than they had hitherto exhibited It was his only course, and though inoperative, it was ably attempted.

The debate, however, had hardly commenced, when he was assailed as if by a storm. Several members rose at once to tell the Secretary their opinions of his merits— a personal hostility appeared palpable between the parties; the subject and arguments were the same as those of the preceding night, but they were accompanied much more by individual allusions.

Sir John Parnell, late Chancellor of the Exchequer, who had been dismissed for refusing to support a Union, opened the debate. He spoke with great ability; he plainly avowed his opinion that it was a revolutionary change of the Constitution, which the Parliament had no power to enact, and to which the King could not, consistently with his Coronation Oath, give the royal assent.

Mr. Tighe, of Wicklow, followed and delivered his sentiments against the measure in the same terms, and with equal decision. Mr. George Ponsonby arose to move an amendment, negativing the address as far as it alluded to a Union.

When Mr. George Ponsonby was roused, he had great debating powers: on minor subjects he was often vapid, but on this occasion he far exceeded himself in argument, elocution, and in fortitude. He was sincere—his blood warmed—he reasoned with a force, a boldness, and with an absence of all reserve, which he never before had so energetically exhibited. As a lawyer, a statesman, and a loyal Irish subject, he denied that either the Lords, or the Commons, or the King of Ireland, had the power of passing or assenting to a Legislative Union. He avowed his opinion that the measure was revolutionary, and would run the destructive lengths of endangering the compact between the crown and the subjects, and the connection of the two nations.

It is scarcely to be imagined what an effect such a speech, from a calm, discreet, and loyal man, a constitutional lawyer, and representative of a high aristocratic family, produced in that House. It was, in point of extent and powers, unexpected from so calm a character; and the impression therefore was proportionably greater.

The words, as he spoke them, were imbibed by every man who was a free agent in Parliament. In the course of his speech he assailed Lord Castlereagh with a strength and unreserved severity, which greatly exceeded the usual bounds of his philippics.

Cool and deliberate irony, ten times more piercing than the sharpest satire, flowed from his lips, in a slow rolling flood of indignant denunciation. His calm language never for one moment yielded to his warm impressions; and it was doubly formidable, from being restrained by prudence, and dictated by conviction.

During Mr. Ponsonby's oration, a very impressive scene was exhibiting on the treasury bench. Lord Castlereagh had been anticipated—he seemed to be astounded—he moved restlessly on his seat—he became obviously disconcerted, whispered to those who sat near him, and appeared more sensitive than he had ever been on any public occasion.

As Mr. Ponsonby advanced, the Secretary became more affected; occasionally he rose to interrupt; and when Mr. Ponsonby ceased, he appeared to be struggling with violent emotions: but he was unable to suppress the poignancy of his feelings, and he writhed under the castigation. His face flushed—his eyes kindled—and, for the first time in that House, he appeared to be rising into a high state of agitation. Mr. Ponsonby, who stood directly before him, formed an admirable contrast: not a feature moved—not a muscle was disturbed; his small grey eyes rivetted upon his adversary, expressed contempt and superiority more eloquently than language; and with these cool and scornful glances, which are altogether indescribable, Mr. Ponsonby, unperturbed, listened to a reply which raised Lord Castlereagh in the estimation of his adherents.

He had that morning decided on a course which the experience of the former evening had induced him to think might affect the debate in favour of the Government. He had resolved to act on the offensive, and, by an extravagant invective against the principles of the Anti-Unionists, to blind and detach some of the dullest of the country gentlemen from a party which he intended to represent as an anarchial faction; and by holding up to his supporters an exemplary contempt for all *public opinion*, diminish the effect of patriotic declamation, from the powerful effect of which the opponents of a Union

acquired so much strength and importance. On these grounds he had decided to act boldly himself, and to encourage and excite a simultaneous attack upon the principles and conduct of the leading members who opposed him.

XV. For this species of conflict the youthful Minister was admirably adapted. He had sufficient firmness to advance, and sufficient pertinacity to persist in any assertion. Never had he more occasion to exert all his powers; nor did he fail in his efforts. He had no qualms or compunction to arrest his progress. In his reply there was no assertion he did not risk—no circumstance he did not vouch for—no aspersion he did not cast; and he even went lengths which he afterwards repented. To the Bar he applied the term "pettifoggers;" to the Opposition, "cabal—combinators—desperate faction;" and to the nation itself, "barbarism—ignorance," and "insensibility to protection and paternal regards she had ever experienced from the British nation." His speech was severe beyond any thing he had ever uttered within the walls of Parliament, and far exceeded the powers he was supposed to possess. He raked up every act of Mr. Ponsonby's political career, and handled it with a masterly severity; but it was in the tone and in the manner of an angry gentleman. He had flown at the highest game, and his opponent (never off his guard) attended to his Lordship with a contemptuous and imperturbable placidity, which frequently gave Mr. Ponsonby a great advantage over warmer debaters. On this occasion he seemed not at all to feel the language of Lord Castlereagh; he knew that he had provoked it, and he saw that he had spoken effectually by the irritation of his opponent.

Lord Castlereagh was greatly exhausted, and Mr. Ponsonby, turning round, audibly observed, with a frigid smile, and an air of utter indifference—"the ravings of an irritated youth—it was natural."

This was one of the most important personal conflicts during the discussions of the Union, and it had a very powerful effect, at least, on the spirit of his Lordship's followers. Truth was unimportant to him: on personal attacks, his misrepresentation might honourably be re-

tracted at convenient opportunities. He had no public
character to forfeit; and a majority of his supporters
were similarly circumstanced. Prompt personal hostility,
therefore, was the line he had that morning decided on;
and it was the most politic step a minister so desperately
circumstanced could adopt. When vicious measures are
irrevocably adopted, obtrusive compunction must instantly be banished. He determined to reject every consideration, but that of increasing his majority; but he was
routed by the very course he had calculated on to ensure
a victory. The foresight of Mr. Ponsonby had penetrated through his policy, and showed him that, to counteract the enemy, he should become the assailant, seize
the very position his adversary had selected, and anticipate the very line on which he had determined to try the
battle. This line Mr. Ponsonby had acted upon, and in
this he had succeeded.

The discussion now proceeded with extraordinary asperity; but the influence of the Speaker, with a few exceptions, preserved the Members in tolerable order: it
was often difficult to determine which side transgressed
the most. Mr. Arthur Moore on this night took a decided part; and Mr. Egan trampled down the metaphori-
cal sophistries of Mr. William Smith, as to the competence of Parliament; such reasoning he called rubbish,
and such reasoners were scavengers; like a dray horse he
galloped over all his opponents, plunging and kicking,
and overthrowing all before him. No member on that
night pronounced a more sincere, clumsy, powerful oration—of matter he had abundance—of language he made
no selection; and he was aptly compared to the Trojan
horse, sounding as if he had armed men within him.

Never was there a more unfortunate quotation for the
Government than one made by Mr. Serjeant Stanly from
Judge Blackstone.

The dictum of a puisne Judge, in a British court of
law, was cited, to influence the opinion of 300 members
in the Irish Parliament on the subject of their own annihilation.

The debate continued with undiminished animation
and hostility until ten o'clock on the morning of the 24th,
when Sir Laurence Parsons (Lord Rosse) supported

Mr. Ponsonby in a speech luminous, and in some parts almost sublime. He had caught the flame which his colleague had but kindled, and blazed with an eloquence of which he had shown but few examples, the impression was powerful.

Mr. Frederick Falkiner, member for Dublin County, who immediately followed, was one of the most remarkable instances of inflexible public integrity in Ireland; he would have been a valuable acquisition to the Government, but nothing could corrupt him. Week after week he was ineffectually tempted, through his friends, by a peerage or aught he might desire; he replied: "I am poor, 'tis true; but no human power, no reward, no torture, no elevation, shall ever tempt me to betray my country, never mention to me again so infamous a proposal." He was, however, afterwards treated ungratefully by the very constituents whom he had obeyed, and died a victim to poverty and patriotism.

Mr. James Fitzgerald had been dismissed from the office of Prime Serjeant, the highest at the bar, for refusing to relinquish his independence. He scorned to retain it under circumstances of dishonour, and on this night spoke at great length, and with a train of reasoning which must have been decisive in an uncorrupted assembly; he refused every offer, and never returned to office.*

Colonel Maxwell, (Lord Farnham), Mr. Lee (Waterford), Mr. Barrington Judge of the High Court of Admiralty, and many others, pressed forward to deliver their sentiments against so fatal a project. Every moment the debate grew warmer, and the determination to oppose it became more obvious, the members of Government were staggered, the storm increased, but Lord Castlereagh was calm; he rose and spoke with a confident assurance

---

* No man in Ireland was more sincere in his opposition to a Union than Mr. Fitzgerald; he was the first who declared his intention of writing its history.

He afterwards relinquished the design, and urged me to commence it— he handed me the prospectus of what he intended, and no man in Ireland knew the occult details of that proceeding better than he. He is the Father of Mr. Vesey Fitzgerald; had a very good fortune, and was one of the most successful and persevering lawyers that ever practised in Ireland.

peculiar to himself; and particularly disavowed all corruption, though he had dismissed every man who would not promise to support him, and had near seventy subservient placemen at that moment on his side.

XVI. At length Mr. Plunket arose, and, in the ablest speech ever heard by any member in that Parliament, went at once to the grand and decisive point, the incompetence of Parliament, he could go no further on principle than Mr. Ponsonby, but his language was irresistible, and he left nothing to be urged. It was perfect in eloquence, and unanswerable in reasoning. Its effect was indescribable; and, for the first time, Lord Castlereagh, whom he personally assailed, seemed to shrink from the encounter. That speech was of great weight, and it proved the eloquence, the sincerity, and the fortitude of the speaker.

But a short speech on that night, which gave a new sensation, and excited novel observations, was a maiden speech by Colonel O'Donnell of Mayo County, the eldest son of Sir Neil O'Donnell, a man of very large fortune in that county; he was colonel of the Mayo regiment. He was a brave officer, and a well bred gentleman; and in all the situations of life he showed excellent qualities. On this night, roused by Lord Castlereagh's invectives, he could not contain his indignation; and by anticipation " disclaimed all future allegiance, if a Union were effected, he held it as a vicious revolution, and avowed that he would take the field at the head of his regiment to oppose its execution, and would resist rebels in rich clothes as he had done the rebels in rags." And for his speech in Parliament he was dismissed his regiment without further notice.

As a contrast to the language of Colonel O'Donnell, it is curious to observe the new exhibition of Mr. Trench, of Woodlawn. He was not satisfied with the disgusting exhibition of the preceding night, but again introduced himself to a notice which common modesty would have avoided. He now entered into a defence of his former tergiversation, and, most unfortunately for himself, contradicted distinctly the substance of both his former speeches. He thus solved all the doubts which might have arisen as to his former conduct, closed the mouth of every friend from any possibility of defending him, and delivered himself, without reserve, into the hands of his seducers. He said, " he had, since the night before, been fully convinced of the advantages of a Union, and would certainly support it." The Irish Peerage was soon *honoured* by his addition, as Lord Ashtown.

After the most stormy debate remembered in the Irish Parliament, the question was loudly called for by the Opposition, who were now tolerably secure of a majority, never did so much solicitude appear in any public assembly; at length above sixty members had spoken, the subject was exhausted, and all parties seemed impatient. The House divided, and the Oppositton withdrew to the Court of Requests. It is not easy to conceive, still less to describe, the anxiety of that moment; a considerable delay took place. Mr. Ponsonby and Sir Laurence Parsons were at length named tellers for the amendment; Mr. W. Smith and Lord Tyrone for the address. One hundred and eleven members had declared against the Union, and when the doors were opened, one hundred and five was discovered to be the total number of the Minister's adherents. The gratification of the Anti-Unionists was unbounded; and as they walked deliberately in, one by one, to be counted, the eager spectators, ladies as well as gentlemen, leaning over the galleries, ignorant of the result, were panting with expectation. Lady Castlereagh, then one of the finest women of the Court, appeared in the serjeant's box, palpitating for her husband's fate. The desponding appearance and fallen crests of the Ministerial benches, and the exulting air of the opposition members as they entered, were intelligible.* The murmurs of suppressed anxiety would have excited an interest even in the most unconnected

* Mr. Egan, Chairman of Dublin County, a coarse, large, bluff, red-faced Irishman, was the last who entered. His exultation knew no bounds; as No. 110 was announced, he stopped a moment at the Bar, flourished a great stick which he had in his hand over his head, and with the voice of a Stentor cried out, " *And I'm a hundred and eleven!*" He then sat quietly down, and burst out into an immoderate and almost convulsive fit of laughter; it was all heart. Never was there a finer picture of genuine patriotism. He was very far from being rich, and had an offer to be made a Baron of the Exchequer, with 3,500*l.* a year, if he would support the Union, but refused it with indignation. On any other subject he would have supported the Government.

stranger, who had known the objects and importance of the contest. How much more, therefore, must every Irish breast which panted in the galleries have experienced that thrilling enthusiasm which accompanies the achievement of patriotic actions, when the Minister's defeat was announced from the chair! A due sense of respect and decorum restrained the galleries within proper bounds; but a low cry of satisfaction from the female audience could not be prevented, and no sooner was the event made known out of doors, than the crowds that had waited during the entire night, with increasing impatience for the vote which was to decide upon the independence of their country, sent forth loud and reiterated shouts of exultation, which, resounding through the corridors and penetrating to the body of the House, added to the triumph of the conquerors, and to the misery of the adherents of the conquered Minister.

The numbers on this division were :—

For Mr. Ponsonby's Amendment	111
For Lord Tyrone's address	105
Majority against Government . .	6

On this debate, the members who voted were circumstanced as follows :—

Members holding offices during pleasure	69
Members rewarded by offices for their votes	19
Member openly seduced in the body of the House . .	1
Commoners created peers, or their wives peeresses, for their votes	18
	102
Supposed to be uninfluenced	3
The House composed of	300
Voted that night	216
Absent Members	84

Of these eighty-four absent members, twenty-four were kept away by absolute necessity, and of the residue there can be no doubt they were not friends to the Union, from this plain reason—that the Government had the power of enforcing the attendance of all the dependent members, and the Opposition had no power, they had none but voluntary supporters ; of which number Lord Castlereagh was enabled to seduce forty-three during the prorogation, and by that acquisition out-voted the Anti-Unionists on the 5th of February, 1800.

XVII. The members assembled in the lobby were preparing to separate, when Mr. Ponsonby requested they would return into the House and continue a very few minutes, as he had business of the utmost importance for their consideration ; this produced a profound silence ; Mr. Ponsonby then, in a few words, "congratulated the House and the country on the honest and patriotic assertion of their liberties ; but declared, that he considered there would be no security against future attempts to overthrow their independence, but by a direct and absolute declaration of the rights of Irishmen, recorded upon their journals, as the decided sense of the people, through their Parliament ; and he, therefore, without further preface, moved, " *That this House will ever maintain the undoubted birthright of Irishmen, by preserving an independent Parliament of Lords and Commons resident in this Kingdom*, as stated and approved by his Majesty and the British Parliament in 1782."

Lord Castlereagh, conceiving that further resistance was unavailing, only said, " that he considered such a motion of the most dangerous tendency ; however, if the House were determined on it, he begged to declare his entire dissent, and on their own heads be the consequences of so wrong and inconsidrate a measure." No further opposition was made by Government ; and the Speaker putting the question, a loud cry of approbation followed, with but two negatives, those of Lord Castlereagh and Mr. Toler (Lord Norbury); the motion was carried, and the members were rising to withdraw, when the Speaker wishing to be strictly correct, called to Mr. Ponsonby, to *write* down his motion accurately ; he, accordingly, walked to the table to write it down. This delay of a few moments, unimportant as it might seem in the common course of human occurrences, was an incident which, ultimately deranged the constitution of an empire, and annihilated the legislature of an independent nation, a single moment, the most critical that ever occurred in history; and of all the events of Ireland, the most fatal and irretrievable.

This may teach posterity, that the destinies of nations are governed by the same chances, subject to the same fatalities, and affected by the same misfortunes, as those of the humblest individual.

XVIII. Whilst Mr. Ponsonby was writing his motion, every member, in profound silence, was observing the sensations of the opposite party, and conjecturing the feelings and anticipating the conduct of their adversaries.

This motion involved, in one sentence, every thing which was sought after by the one party and dreaded by the other; its adoption must have ruined the Minister and dismissed the Irish Government. The Treasury Bench held a mournful silence, the Attorney General, Mr. Toler, alone appeared to bear his impending misfortune with a portion of that ease and playfulness which never forsook him.

On Mr. Ponsonby's handing up his motion, he stood firm and collected, and looked around him with the honest confidence of a man who had performed his duty and saved his country, the silence of death prevailed in the galleries, and the whole assembly displayed a spectacle as solemn and important as any country or any era had ever exhibited.

The Speaker repeated the question—"the ayes" burst forth into a loud peal, the gallery was in immediate motion, all was congratulation. On the question being put the second time (as was usual), a still louder and more reiterated cry of "aye, aye," resounded from every quarter; only the same two negatives were heard, feebly, from the ministerial side, Government had given up the contest, and the independence of Ireland was on the very verge of permanent security, when Mr. William Charles Fortescue, member for Louth County, requested to be heard before the final decision was announced.

He said, "that he was adverse to the measure of a legislative Union, and had given his decided vote against it, but he did not wish to bind himself for *ever; possible* circumstances might hereafter occur, which might render that measure expedient for the empire, and he did not approve of any determination which for *ever* closed the doors against any possibility of future discussion."

The Opposition were paralyzed, the Government were roused, a single sentence plausibly conceived, and (without reflecting on its destructive consequence) moderately uttered, by a respectable man, and an avowed Anti-Unionist, eventually decided the fate of the Irish nation. It offered a pretext for timidity, a precedent for caution, and a subterfuge for wavering venality.

XIX. Mr. French, of Roscommon, a country gentleman of high character, and Lord Cole, a young nobleman of an honest, inconsiderate mind, who had, on the last division, voted sincerely against the Minister, now, without a moment's reflection on the ruin which must necessarily attend every diversity of sentiment in a party associated by only one tie, and bound together only upon one subject, declared themselves of Mr. Fortescue's opinion. Mr. John Claudius Beresford,[*] who had only been restrained from adhesion to the Clare connection by being representative of the metropolis, avowed himself of the same determination; and thus that constitutional security, which a direct and peremptory declaration of indefeasible rights, one moment before, was on the point of permanently establishing, was, by the inconsiderate and temporising words of one feeble minded member, lost for ever. It is impossible to express the surprise and disappointment of the Anti-Unionists.

To be defeated by the effort of an enemy was to be borne, but to fall by the secession of a friend was insupportable. The narrow jealousies and unconnected materials of the Anti-Unionists were no longer to be concealed, either from friends or enemies. Mr. Ponsonby felt the critical situation of the country, the opposition had but a majority of five on the first division; three seceders would have given a majority to Government, and a division could not be risked.

Mr. Ponsonby's presence of mind instantly suggested

[*] Mr. John Claudius Beresford, though he could not vote against the instructions of the *City*, took every opportunity of expressing, incidentally, his *entire confidence* in the fair intentions of *Lord Castlereagh's government ;* and never appeared to be really sincere in his opposition to a Union. His speech is a fine specimen of temporizing.

the only remaining alternative. He lamented "that the smallest contrariety of opinion should have arisen amongst men who ought to be united by the most powerful of all inducements, the salvation of their independence. He perceived however, a wish that he should not press the motion, founded, he supposed, on a mistaken confidence in the engagements of the Noble Lord (Lord Castlereagh,) *that he would not again bring forward that ruinous measure without the decided approbation of the people, and of the Parliament.* Though he must doubt the sincerity of the Minister's engagements, he could not hesitate to acquiesce in the wishes of his friends, and he would therefore withdraw his motion."

XX. The sudden transition from exultation to despondency became instantly apparent, by the dead silence which followed Mr. Ponsonby's declaration, the change was so rapid and so unexpected, that from the galleries, which a moment before were full of congratulation and of pleasure, not a single word was heard, crest-fallen and humbled, many instantly withdrew from the scene, and though the people without knew of nothing but their victory, the retreat was a subject of the most serious solicitude to every friend of Irish independence.

Such an advantage could not escape the anxious eye of Government; chagrin and disappointment had changed sides, and the friends of the Union, who a moment before had considered their measure as nearly extinguished, rose upon their success, retorted in their turn, and opposed its being withdrawn. It was, however, too tender a ground for either party to insist upon a division, a debate was equally to be avoided, and the motion was suffered to be withdrawn. Sir Henry Cavendish keenly and sarcastically remarked, that "it was a retreat after a victory." After a day's and a night's debate without intermission, the House adjourned at eleven o'clock the ensuing morning.

Upon the rising of the House, the populace became tumultuous, and a violent disposition against those who had supported the Union was manifest, not only amongst the common people, but amongst those of a much higher class, who had been mingling with them.

On the Speaker's coming out of the House, the horses were taken from his carriage, and he was drawn in triumph through the streets by the people, who conceived the whimsical idea of tackling the Lord Chancellor to the coach, and (as a captive general in a Roman triumph) forcing him to tug at the chariot of his conqueror.

Had it been effected, it would have been a signal anecdote, and would, at least, have immortalized the classic genius of the Irish.

The populace closely pursued his Lordship for that extraordinary purpose; he escaped with great difficulty, and fled, with a pistol in his hand, to a receding door-way in Clarendon-street. But the people, who pursued him in sport, set up a loud laugh at him, as he stood terrified against the door; they offered him no personal violence, and returned in high glee to their more innocent amusement of drawing the Speaker.

XXI. A scene of joy and triumph appeared universal, every countenance had a smile, throughout all ranks and classes of the people, men shook their neighbours heartily by the hand, as if the Minister's defeat was an event of individual good fortune, the mob seemed as well disposed to joy as mischief, and that was saying much for a Dublin assemblage. But a view of their enemies, as they came skulking from behind the corridors, occasionally roused them to no very tranquil temperature. Some members had to try their speed, and others their intrepidity. Mr. Richard Martin, unable to get clear, turned on his hunters, and boldly faced a mob of many thousands, with a small pocket pistol in his hand. He swore most vehemently, that, if they advanced six inches on him, he would immediately " shoot *every mother's babe* of them as dead as that paving stone"—(kicking one.) The united spirit and fun of his declaration, and his little pocket pistol, aimed at ten thousand men, women, and children, were so entirely to the taste of our Irish populace, that all symptoms of hostility ceased; they gave him three cheers, and he regained his home without further molestation.

Mr. O'Driscol, a gentleman of the Irish Bar, one of the most sincere and active Anti-Unionists, used great and successful efforts to tranquilize the people; and to his persuasions was chiefly to be attributed their peaceable dispersion. In one particular instance, he certainly prevented a most atrocious mischief, if not a great crime, by his prompt and spirited interference.

The House of Lords met on the 22d of January, 1799, the same day as the Commons, to receive the speech of the Viceroy. Though the nation was not unprepared for any instance of its subserviency, some patriotic spirits might reasonably have been expected on so momentous a subject as the Union; in this expectation, however, it was but feebly gratified.

Never did a body of hereditary nobles, many of ancient family, and several of splendid fortune, so disgrace their ancestry.

After an ineffectual resistance by some, whose integrity was invincible, the Irish Lords recorded their own humiliation, and, in a state of absolute infatuation, perpetrated the most extraordinary act of legislative suicide which ever stained the records of a nation.

The reply of the Irish Lords, to the speech of the British Viceroy, coincided in his recommendation, and virtually consented to prostrate themselves and their posterity for ever. The prerogatives of rank, the pride of ancestry, the glory of the peerage, and the rights of the country, were equally sacrificed.

The facility with which the Irish Lords re-echoed their sentence of extinction was quite unexampled.

That stultified facility can only be elucidated by taking a brief statistical view of what was once considered an august assembly, but which the over-bearing influence of the absolute and vindictive Chancellor had for some years reduced to a mere instrument of his ambition.

In the hands of the Chancellor, Lord Clare, the House was powerless, his mere automaton or puppet, which he coerced or humoured, according to his ambition or caprice.

There were, however, amongst the Irish nobility, a few men of spirit, pride, talent, and integrity; but they were too few for resistance.

The education of the Irish noblemen of that day was little calculated for debate or Parliamentary duties; they very seldom took any active part in Parliamentary discussions, and more rarely attained to that confidence in public speaking, without which no effect can be produced. They could argue, or might declaim, but were unequal to what is termed debate; and being confirmed in their torpidity by an habitual abstinence from Parliamentary discussions, when the day of danger came, they were unequal to the contest.

Lord Clare, on the contrary, from his forensic habits, his dogmatic arrogance, and unrestrained invective, had an incalculable advantage over less practised reasoners. The modest were overwhelmed by flights of astounding rhapsody, the patriotic borne down by calumny, the diffident silenced by contemptuous irony; and nearly the whole of the Peerage, without being able to account for their pusillanimity, were either trampled under his feet, or were mere puppets in the grasp of this all-powerful Chancellor. Such was the state of the Irish Lords in 1799. The extent of Lord Clare's connections, and the energy of his conduct during the last insurrection, had contributed to render him nearly despotic over both the Government and the country. Dickson, Bishop of Down, and Marlay, Bishop of Limerick, were the only spiritual peers that ventured to oppose him, both were of invincible integrity and undeviating patriotism, his Grace of Limerick was the uncle of Mr. Grattan; and the Bishop of Down was the intimate friend of Mr. Fox: unfortunately, both were too mild, unassuming, and dignified, to contend successfully against so haughty and remorseless an opponent.

XXII. The Bishop of Down was a prelate of the most faultless character, the extreme beauty of his countenance, the gentleness of his manners, and the patriarchal dignity of his figure, rendered him one of the most interesting persons in society.

His talents were considerable, but they were neutralized by his modesty; and he seldom could be prevailed upon to rise in the House of Peers upon political subjects. On this night, however, stung to the quick by the invectives, and indignant at the designs of the Chancellor, he made a reply to him of which he was supposed incapable. Severity from the Bishop of Down was likewise so unusual, that the few sentences he pronounced, stunned the champion more than all the speeches of his more disciplined opponents.

Nothing, however, could overcome the influence of Lord Clare. The Irish Lords lay prostrate before the Government, but the leaders were not inattentive to their own interests. The defeat of Government in the Commons gave them an importance they had not expected.

The debates and conduct of the Irish peers bear a comparatively unimportant share in the transactions of that epoch, and have but little interest in the memoirs of those times; but the accounts of Lord Annesley, &c., record their corruption.*

It is not the object, therefore, of these anecdotes, to dilate more upon the proceedings of that degraded assembly, than incidentally to introduce, as episodes, their individual actions, and to state that a great proportion of the million and a half levied upon Ireland, and distributed by Lord Castlereagh's Commissioners of Compensation, went into the pockets of the Lords Spiritual and Temporal of Ireland.

XXIII. From the hour that Mr. Ponsonby's motion was withdrawn, Government gained strength, the standard of visionary honours and of corrupt emoluments was raised for recruits, a congratulatory, instead of a consolatory dispatch, had been instantly forwarded to Mr. Pitt, and another to the Duke of Portland; and it was not difficult to foresee, that the result of that night, though apparently a victory over the proposition for a Union, afforded so strong a point for the Minister in the subsequent negotiations, by which he had determined to achieve his measure. The arguments and divisions on succeeding debates proved, beyond the possibility of question, the overwhelming advantage which Mr. Fortescue's precedent had given to those who were determined to dispose of their consistency under colour of their moderation.

The bad consequences which were likely to result from this event, did not at first occur to many of the Opposition. Some of the leading members of that party, highly elated at the success of the last division, could see no-

---

* It is supposed that the important parts of those records have been suppressed at court; the writer could only trace them to the bureau of Lord Annesley, but never could procure authenticated extracts. It is therefore only from the payments at the Treasury, and the admission of the parties, that the corrupt payments can be substantiated. One volume of the reports made by the commissioners of compensation and distribution of £1,500,000 was given to the Author by Mr. Vesey Fitzgerald; some extracts are given from it; the rest have been suppressed.

thing but the prospect of an increasing majority and an ultimate triumph; these were numerous but short-sighted. Others regarded, with a wise solicitude, the palpable want of political connection in the party that opposed the Minister. However, Lord Castlereagh who had so confidently pressed forward a measure which Parliament had decidedly rejected, and the public universally reprobated, found his situation the most difficult imaginable. He had no just reason to expect support in minor measures, who had proved himself utterly unworthy of the confidence of Parliament on one of the first magnitude. His pride was humbled, but his firmness and perseverance overcame his difficulties, and the next important division on Lord Corry's motion clearly proved the consummate address with which he had trafficked with the members during the interval. All the weapons of seduction were in his hands; and, to acquire a majority, he had only to overcome the wavering and feeble. A motion of Lord Corry's, made a few days afterwards, in order to prevent any future scheme of a Union, after a long debate, was also negatived (by a majority of fifty-eight), and thus concluded all discussion on the Union for that session. The session, however, had scarcely closed, when his Lordship recommenced his warfare against his country. The treasury was in his hands, patronage in his note-book, and all the influence which the scourge or the pardon, reward or punishment could possibly produce on the trembling rebels, was openly resorted to. Lord Cornwallis determined to put Irish honesty to the test, and set out upon an experimental tour through those parts of the country where the nobility and gentry were most likely to entertain him. He artfully selected those places where he could best make his way with corporations at public dinners, and with the aristocracy, country gentlemen, and farmers, by visiting their mansions and cottages. Ireland was thus canvassed, and every gaol was converted to a hustings.

In reflecting, therefore, on the extraordinary fate of Mr. Ponsonby's declaratory motion just and not inconsiderate alarm must have been excited in the mind of every man who had determined boldly and unequivocally to support the freedom of his country.

It was not now difficult to perceive, that, to the cool and reasoning part of the nation, melancholy forebodings must naturally arise, from the decided absence of that cordial, unqualified co-operation amongst the members of the opposition, by whose undeviating unanimity alone the revival of the project, and the probable ruin of the country could be resisted.

It was evident that, by the thoughtless conduct of Mr. Fortescue, Lord Cole, and Mr. French, the conclusive rejection of the proposal was prevented, had they been even one moment silent, Ireland would have been a proud, prosperous, free, tranquil, and productive member of the British Empire. But their puerile inconsistency lost their country, gave a clue to the Secretary, and the Government, before plunged in a hopeless perplexity, and opened a wide door for future discussion, which Mr. Ponsonby's motion would have for ever prevented.

In a body composed as the Parliament of Ireland, though this misfortune must ever be deplored, and those gentlemen for ever censured, yet such an event was not a subject for astonishment. A great number of those who composed the House were most inexperienced statesmen—they meddled but little individually in any arrangement of debates, and voted according to their party or their sentiments, without the habit of any previous consultation.

Such men, therefore, after the last division against the Minister, could not suppose he would again revive the question, and they partook of the general satisfaction. *Moderation* was now recommended, as the proper course for a loyal opposition, and the proposal for a Union having been virtually negatived, it was observed by the *courtly* oppositionists to be at least unkind, if not indiscreet, to push Government further at a "*moment like the present.*"

On the other hand, those who wished to complete the victory, could not shut their eyes to the hazard of moderate proceedings, and their zeal led them to wish to improve their advantage, and, if possible, to remove Lord Cornwallis from the Government, as a finishing stroke to the measure. But the conduct of Mr. Fortescue and his supporters had miserably deceived them, and had con vinced the leaders of the Opposition that they were about to tread very uncertain ground, and that their first consideration should be, how far the possibility of attaining their ultimate object should be weighed against the probable event of losing their majority by another trial of strength.

Reasoning people without doors, saw the danger still more clearly than those who had individually to encounter it. Regardless of the solemn engagements he had made in the House, and by which he had imposed on many of the opposition, the Minister and his agents lost no opportunity, nor omitted any means, of making good their party amongst the Members who had not publicly declared themselves, and of endeavouring to pervert the principles and corrupt the consistency of those who had. Lord Castlereagh's ulterior efforts were extensive and indefatigable, his spirit revived and every hour gained ground on his opponents. He clearly perceived that the ranks of the Opposition were too open to be strong, and too mixed to be unanimous. The extraordinary fate of Mr. Ponsonby's declaration of rights, and the debate on a similar motion by Lord Corry, which so shortly afterwards met a more serious negative, proved the truth of these observations, and identified the persons through whom that truth was to be afterwards exemplified.

The disheartening effects of Mr. Fortescue's conduct (notwithstanding the general exultation of the country), appeared to make a very powerful impression on the public mind, it was assiduously circulated by Government as a triumph, and on all occasions reluctantly alluded to by the Anti-Unionists, it became apparent that the increasing majority against the minister, on the second division, if unaccompanied by that fatal circumstance, would have effectually established the progressive power of the opposition, and rapidly hastened the upset of Government.*
But the advantage of that majority was lost, and the

* It is observable, that in all debates of Parliament, "*a moment like the present*" or, "*this is not the time*," or, "*it would be highly inconvenient at this time*," &c. are invariably used as arguments by Ministers when they have no substantial reasons to give for their refusals, it is a **sweeping species** of reply of great utility, as it answers all subjects **and all reasoning**.

possibility of exciting division amongst the Anti-Unionists could no longer be questioned. This consideration had an immediate and extensive effect, the timid recommenced their fears, the wavering began to think of consequences the venal to negociate: and the public mind, particularly amongst the Catholics, who still smarted from the scourge, became so deeply affected, and so timorously doubtful, that some of the persons, assuming to themselves the title of *Catholic Leaders*,* sought an audience, in order to inquire from Marquis Cornwallis, "What would be the advantage to the Catholics, if a Union should happen to be effected in Ireland?"

However, great confidence in an ultimate crushing of the project kept its place in the Opposition. The Parliament, unaccustomed to see the Minister with a majority of only one, considered him as totally defeated. A rising party is sure to gain proselytes. Government, therefore, lost ground as the Opposition gained it; and for a few days it was generally supposed that the Viceroy and Secretary must resign. Many of their adherents shrunk from them. A large proportion of Parliament was far beyond the power either of fear or corruption, yet the impartial history of these times must throw a partial shade over the consistency of Ireland, and exhibit some of the once leading characters in both Houses in a course of the most humiliating, corrupt, and disgusting servility; contradicting by the last act of their political lives, the whole tenor of their former principles, from the first moment they had the power of declaring them to the nation. In another quarter, those who formed an Opposition to the Minister on the question of a Union, had been, and wished to continue, his avowed supporters on every other. The custom of the times, the venality of the court, even the excessive habits of convivial luxury, had combined gradually to blunt the poignancy of public spirit, and the activity of patriotic exertions, on *ordinary*

* Mr. Bellew (brother to Sir Patrick Bellew), Mr. Lynch, and some others, had several audiences with the Viceroy; the Catholic Bishops were generally deceived into the most disgusting subservience, rewards were not withheld, Mr. Bellew was to be appointed a County Judge, but that being found impracticable, he got a secret pension, which he has now enjoyed for thirty-two years.

subjects. The terrors of the rebellion, scarcely yet extinguished had induced many to cling for protection round a government whose principles they had condemned, and whose politics they had resisted. The subtle Viceroy knew full well how to make his advantage of the moment, and by keeping up the delusion, under the name of *loyalty and discretion*, he restrained within narrow limits the spirit of constitutional independence wherever he found he could not otherwise subdue it.*

---

* Mr. Curran, Mr. Grattan, and some other members of the Opposition, seceded from the new Parliament. Never was any step more indiscreet, more ill timed, or to themselves more injurious; that the cause of Ireland should lose two such advocates at the very moment she most required them, was truly unfortunate. Mr. Grattan returned to Parliament when too late, Mr. Curran, never; and h s fine talents were lost to himself and his country for ever

CHAPTER XXVI.

The different views of the Opposition—Opposition not sufficiently organized or connected—Disunion in consequence of the Catholic question—Catholics duped—Alternately oppressed and fostered—Lord Clare's great influence—Very important despatch from Mr. Pitt, to Lord Cornwallis—Unprecedented plan of Lord Castlereagh—Remarkable dinner—The plan or conspiracy—Acceded to—Rewards in Perspective—Meeting of Anti-Unionists at Lord Charlemont's—Opposition Lords meet—Lord Castlereagh's Plan laid before them—Counterplan proposed—Rejected—Earl Belmore—His motion to the same effect as Mr. Ponsonby's—Rejected—Very numerous addresses against the Union—Particularly Dublin—A Privy Council—Lord Clare's violence—Military execution—People killed and wounded—Inefficiently brought before Parliament—Anti-Union dinner—Mr. Handcock of Athlone, a conspicuous patriot—Corrupt state of the British Parliament—Compared with that of Ireland at the Union—Mr. Handcock bribed.

I. THE Members of the old Opposition who had been returned to the new Parliament in 1797, did not exceed fifty ; but several others, who had been connected (and some of them closely) with Government, showed a tendency, on the Union alone to sever themselves from their old attachment; accustomed to support administration, they formed no cordial co-operation with those who had professed a more extensive principle of opposition ; and though they wished to oppose the *Union*, they did not wish to oppose the *Minister*, and they acted without decisive effect, because they wrought on too contracted a foundation.

The opposition to Union were, in fact, united on no one question but that of the Union, even in the measure of that opposition they were not agreed, much less in the mode of securing a retreat or of profiting by a victory. But still the opposition to annexation brought them closely together. A view of the House at this period was quite unprecedented ; the friends of Catholic Emancipation were seen on the same benches with those of Protestant ascendency, the supporters of reform divided with the borough influence, a sense of common danger drew men together on this topic who were dissimilar in sentiment, adverse in opinion, jealous in interest, and antagonists in principle. They conjointly presented a formidable front to the enemy, but possessed within themselves neither subordination nor unqualified unanimity, qualities which were essentially necessary to preserve so heterogeneous a body from the destructive weapons which were provided for their overthrow.

There was no great leader whom they could collectively consult or obey, no systematic course determined on for their conduct, no pre-arranged plan of proceeding without doors, or practical arrangement for internal debate; their energies were personal, their enthusiasm graduated, and their exertions not gregarious. Every man formed his own line of procedure: the battle was hand to hand, the movements desultory; whether they clashed with the general interest, or injured the general cause, was hardly contemplated, and seldom perceived until the injury had happened.

II. The *talent* of Parliament principally existed amongst the members who had formed the general opposition to the Union. Some habitual friends of administration, therefore, who had on this single question seceded from the Court, and who wished to resume their old habits on the Union being disposed of, obviously felt a portion of narrow jealousy at being *led* by those whom they had been accustomed to *oppose*, and reluctantly joined in any *liberal* opposition to a Court which they had been in the habit of supporting. They desired to vote against the Union in the abstract, but to commit themselves no farther against the Minister. Many, upon this temporizing and ineffective principle, cautiously avoided any discussion, save upon the *direct* proposition; and this was remarkable, and felt to be ruinous in the succeeding session.*

But the strongest and most fatal cause of division amongst the Members of the opposition, was certainly

---

* It is worthy of observation, that Lord Castlereagh was so aware of that feeling amongst those who opposed the Union, that, in 1800, Lord Cornwallis's speech did not even hint at a revival of that measure Hence the diminished minority on Sir Laurence Parson's motion.

their radical difference of opinion on the Catholic question. Those who had determined to support the Catholic cause, as the surest mode of preventing any future attempts to attain a Union, were obliged to dissemble their intentions of proposing emancipation, lest they should disgust the Catholic opponents who acted with them solely against the Union. Those who were enemies to Catholic relaxation were also obliged to conceal their wishes, lest their determination to resist that measure should disgust the advocates of emancipation, who had united with them on the present occasion.

The Viceroy knew mankind too well to dismiss the Catholics without a comfortable conviction of their certain emancipation; he turned to them the honest side of his countenance: the priests bowed before the soldierly condescensions of a starred veteran. The titular Archbishop was led to believe he would instantly become a real prelate; and before the negociation concluded, Dr. Troy was consecrated a decided Unionist, and was directed to send pastoral letters to his colleagues to promote it. Never yet did any clergy so retrograde as the Catholic hierarchy, &c., on that occasion. It is true that they were deceived; but it was a corrupt deception, and they felt it during eight and twenty years. Most of them have since sojourned to the grave, simple titulars, and have left a double lesson to the world, that Priests and Governments can rely but little on each other, and that the people should in general be very sceptical in relying upon either.

Nothing could be more culpable than the conduct of a considerable portion of the Catholic clergy; the Catholic body were misled, or neutralized, throughout the entire of that unfortunate era. In 1798 they were hanged; in 1799 they were caressed; in 1800 they were cajoled; in 1801 they were discarded; and, after a lapse of twenty-six years, they were complaining louder than when they were in slavery. Nothing can now keep pace with their population but their poverty; *and no body of men ever gave a more helping hand to their own degradation and misery.*

Lord Castlereagh, in his nature decided and persevering, was stimulated still more by the spirit and arrogance of the restless and indefatigable Chancellor. Lord Clare had professed himself an enemy to the Union; but, deluded by his ambition, he conceived he might rule the British councils, as he had governed those of Ireland. The Union, rejected his power would be extinguished; if it were carried, his influence might be transferred to a larger field; he therefore determined that the measure should be achieved, whether by fraud, or force, or corruption, was to him a matter, if not of indifference, at least of no perplexing solicitude.

Lord Castlereagh enlisted him willingly under his banners, whilst the Marquis Cornwallis, pertinacious, yet plausible, cajoled men, whom the address of Fitzgibbon would have irritated, or the undisguised corruption of Castlereagh have disgusted or alarmed.

III. Mr. Pitt had, by a *private* despatch to Lord Cornwallis, desired that the measure should not be then pressed, unless he could be *certain* of a majority of *fifty*.* The Chancellor, on learning the import of that despatch, expostulated in the strongest terms at so pusillanimous a decision. His Lordship never knew the meaning of the word moderation in any public pursuit, and he cared not whether the Union were carried by a majority of one or one hundred.

Lord Castlereagh, though practically unskilled, was intuitively artful, he was cool, whilst Lord Clare was inflamed; and Lord Cornwallis, as a soldier, preferred stratagem to assault, and cautiously opened his trenches before every assailable member. Lord Castlereagh had reflected on an unfavourable circumstance, which he had the spirit and policy, as far as possible, to counteract.

In the former session, the opposition had derived con-

* The original despatch I saw and read; it was brought from Mr. Cooke's office *secretly*, and shown to me for a *particular* purpose, and completely deceived me, but I could not obtain possession of it. I afterwards discovered that it had not been replaced in the office. It was subscribed by Mr. Pitt himself, and the name of *Mr. Bankes* occurred more than once in it; it did not compliment him.

I have reason to believe that that despatch, with some other *important* papers, was afterwards accidentally dropped in College Green, and found by Doctor Kearney, then Provost of Dublin University. He told me he had found such papers, and promised to show them to me at a future day when the question was decided, but never did. Doctor Kearney was a grotesque figure, wonderfully short and droll, but a man of learning and of excellent character in every respect. He was afterwards made Bishop of Ossory, he was an *Anti-Unionist*.

siderable advantage from the spirit with which many of
the party had inclined towards personal hostilities; this,
in the ensuing session, was to be retaliated with interest;
but many of Lord Castlereagh's adherents, though engaged
to vote, might not be so well inclined to combat for a
Union. He was naturally of high spirit, but this was not
to be imparted to others, nor could he, prudently, exhibit
it himself: he had the command of money, but not the
creation of courage, and his cause was not calculated to
generate that feeling; he therefore devised a plan, unprecedented, and which never could have been thought
of in any other country than Ireland: it has not been the
subject of any publication.*

IV. He invited to dinner, at his house in Merrion Square,
above twenty of his most staunch supporters, consisting of
"tried men," and men of "fighting families," who might
feel an individual pride in resenting every personality of
the opposition, and in identifying their own honour with
the cause of Government. This dinner was sumptuous;
the Champagne and Madeira had their due effect: no
man could be more condescending than the noble host.
After due preparation, the point was skilfully introduced
by Sir John Blaquiere (since created Lord de Blaquiere,)
who, of all men, was best calculated to promote a gentlemanly, convivial, fighting conspiracy; he was of the old
school, an able diplomatist; and with the most polished
manners and imposing address, he combined a friendly
heart and decided spirit; in polite conviviality he was
unrivalled.

Having sent round many loyal, mingled with joyous
and exhilarating toasts, he stated, that he understood the
opposition were disposed to personal unkindness, or even
incivilities, towards His Majesty's best friends, the Unionists of Ireland. He was determined that no man should
advance upon him by degrading the party he had adopted,
and the measures he was pledged to support. A full
bumper proved his sincerity, the subject was discussed

---

* It was communicated to me on the morning *after* its development, by
a Member of Parliament, who was *himself* present and engaged in the
enterprise, but *whose real* principles were decidedly averse to a Union, to
which he had been induced to give his insincere support; but though he
had ample spirit, he had too much good sense to quarrel on the subject

with great glee, and some of the company began to feel a zeal for "*actual service.*"

Lord Castlereagh affected some coquetry, lest this idea should appear to have originated with him; but, when he perceived that many had made up their minds to act even on the offensive, he calmly observed, that some mode should, at all events, be taken to secure the constant presence of a sufficient number of the Government friends during the discussion, as subjects of the utmost importance were often totally lost for want of due attendance. Never did a sleight-of-hand man juggle more expertly.

One of his Lordship's prepared accessories (as if it were a new thought) proposed, humourously, to have a dinner for twenty or thirty every day, in one of the committee chambers, where they could be always at hand to make up a House, or for any *emergency* which should call for an unexpected reinforcement, during any part of the discussion.

The novel idea of such a detachment of legislators was considered whimsical and humourous, and, of course, was not rejected. Wit and puns began to accompany the bottle; Mr. Cooke, the Secretary, then, with significant nods and smirking inuendos, began to circulate his official rewards to the company. The hints and the claret united to raise visions of the most gratifying nature, every man became in a prosperous state of official pregnancy: embryo judges, counsel to boards, envoys to foreign courts, compensation pensioners, placemen at chance, and commissioners in assortments, all revelled in the anticipation of something *substantial* to be given to every Member who would do the Secretary the honour of accepting it.

The scheme was unanimously adopted, Sir John Blaquiere pleasantly observed that, at all events, they would be sure of a good *cook* at their dinners. After much wit, and many flashes of convivial bravery, the meeting separated after midnight, fully resolved to eat, drink, speak, and *fight* for Lord Castlereagh. They so far kept their words, that the supporters of the Union indisputably showed more personal spirit than their opponents during the session.

The house of Lord Charlemont was the place of meeting for the leading Members, opponents of the Union; the hereditary patriotism and honour of his son, the present Earl, pointed him out for general confidence. The next morning after Lord Castlereagh's extraordinary coterie, a meeting was held at Charlemont House, to consider of the best system to be pursued in the House of Commons, to preserve the country from the impending ruin.

No man in Ireland was more sincere than Lord Charlemont. Lord Corry was by far more ardent, and Lord Leitrim more reserved, in their manners: the Commoners who attended, were alike honest and honourable: their objects were the same, but their temperature was unequal; and this meeting, with very few exceptions, was exactly the reverse of that of the Minister: patriotic, disinterested, indedendent, and talented; but of a calm, gentle, and reflective character.

Lord Castlereagh's project against their courage was communicated to most of them; and three distinct proposals (it would, perhaps, be improper to state them now) were made on that occasion.

In the judgment of the proposer (who still retains the same opinion,) either of them, if adopted with spirit and adhered to with perseverance, would have defeated the Minister; but the great body of the meeting disapproved of them. Mr. Grattan, Lord Corry, Mr. John Ball, Colonel O'Donnell, Mr. O'Donnell, Mr. Egan, and some other gentlemen, zealously approved of by far the most decisive and spirited of the three expedients. The proposer well knew that no ordinary measures could be successful against the Government, and that by nothing but extremes could the Union be even suspended. The residue of the meeting were, perhaps, more discreet; and never was there seen a more decided predisposition to tranquillity, than in the majority of the distinguished men at that important assembly of Irish patriots.

However, on the very first debate, in 1800, it appeared indisputably that Lord Castlereagh had diffused his own spirit into many of his adherents, and it became equally apparent, that it was not met with corresponding ardour by the opposition: to this, however, there was one memorable exception, to Mr. Grattan alone was it reserved to support the spirit of his party, and to exemplify the gallantry he so strongly recommended to others. Roused by

Mr. Corry, the Chancellor of the Exchequer, he gave him no time for repentance ; and, considering the temper of the times, the propensity of the people, and the intense agitation upon the subject, it is marvellous, that this was the only instance of bloodshed during the contest. Mr. Grattan had shot him at day break, and the intelligence arrived whilst the House was yet sitting, its effect was singular. The project at Lord Castlereagh's well warranted reprisals.*

V. Lord Corry, now Earl Belmore, was one of the most zealous, unflinching, and respectable of the Anti-Unionists : a young nobleman of considerable talent and integrity, he felt sorely the ruin which the flippant imbecility and short vision of Mr. Fortescue and Lord Cole had brought upon the country. He could not believe but that all those who had composed the majority against the Union, would, on recovering their recollection, see the necessity of Mr. Ponsonby's motion, and he determined, by a declaration of a similar purport, to give them an opportunity of recovering from that error which they inadvertantly fell into.

In this, however, his Lordship was mistaken, the extreme impolicy of any pledge of eternal enmity to Union had, from the last day, been sedulously inculcated by the friends of Government, upon every feeble-minded or wavering member; and Lord Corry's motion, after an animated, long, and high-blooded debate, was definitively negatived by a considerable majority, and gave another handle to the Viceroy for ulterior efforts.

Though the fate of Lord Corry's motion was of a most distracting nature, it made but little impression on the confidence of the Anti-Unionists ; they could not bring themselves to suppose that a measure so vital, so conclusive, and so generally detested, being once negatived, could again be proposed by the (defeated ministers) to the same Parliament. Thousands of addresses were presented, and resolutions passed against any further discussion, and, for a time, rejoicing and confidence were the general subjects throughout the whole nation.

* Two of the three expedients proposed, at first view, might appear extravagant, and were called impracticable ; one was certainly easy, all were loyal, and either of them would have been effective.

VI. The rejoicings in the metropolis exceeded all others. Dublin was more than any other place interested in defeating a measure which must, by the consequent emigration of the nobles and commoners, deprive it of every advantage which their splendour and luxury of society, their grand and numerous establishments, influx of strangers, and expenditure of great fortunes amongst its citizens, must confer upon a city which was not commercial.

These ebullitions of joy and gratitude to their deliverers, and hostility to the Unionists, were excessive. Lord Castlereagh was hung in effigy and burnt facing the door of the author, in Merrion Square; but no disturbance occurred that could possibly justify military execution. The violent spirit, however, of the Chancellor, anticipated some attack on his partisans, which conscious culpability, a heated imagination, and his own terrors had raised up as a spectre before him, and led him to countenance one of the most unjustifiable. On the universality of the rejoicings and rather boisterous demonstrations of joy, at the defeat of Government, his alarmed Lordship under colour of taking precautions to preserve the peace, called a Privy Council to the Castle, which might screen himself under the authority of that body, from the individual imputation of those measures of severity, which he determined to put in force against the rejoicing population, should any feasible opportunity be given for the interference of the military. This is a matter of fact, but care was taken that any order which might be given, or the proximate authority through which any wanton violence might be committed amongst the people, should not be made public.

About nine at night, a party of the military stationed in the old Custom House, near Essex Bridge, silently sallied out with trailed arms, without any civil magistrate, and only a serjeant to command them; on arriving at Capel-street the populace were in the act of violently huzzaing for their friends, and, of course, with equal vehemence execrating their enemies; but no riot act was read, no magistrate appeared, and no disturbance or tumult existed to warrant military interference.

The soldiers, however, having taken a position a short

way down the street, without being in any way assailed, fired a volley of balls amongst the people; of course a few were killed and some wounded; amongst the former were a woman and a boy, a man fell dead at the feet of Mr. P. Hamilton, the King's Proctor of the Admiralty, who, as a mere spectator, was viewing the illumination. This is only mentioned to evince the violent spirit which guided the Government of that day, and the tyrannic means which were resorted to, to terrify the people from testifying their zeal at their deliverance, as they fancied, from the proposed annexation.

This outrage was made a subject of complaint to Parliament, but so well were the actors concealed, that nothing could be developed to lead to punishment. The rejoicings however, were neither ended nor checked by military execution, and, at the conclusion of the session, the same spirit of hostility to the Union remained not only as unsubdued, but still more decided than at its commencement.

A most remarkable proof of the shameless lengths, at that period, resorted to by the Viceroy and Minister to gain over a sufficient number of the Anti-Unionists against the ensuing sessions, occurred immediately after the close of the session of 1799.

VII. A public dinner of all the patriotic members was had in Dublin to commemorate the rescue of their country from so imminent a danger. One hundred and ten members of Parliament sat down to that splendid and triumphant entertainment.

Never was a more cordial, happy assemblage of men of rank, consideration, and of *proven* integrity, collected in one chamber, than upon that remarkable occasion. Every man's tried and avowed principles were supposed to be untaintable, and pledged to his own honour and his country's safety; and amongst others, Mr. Handcock, member for Athlone, appeared to be conspicuous; he spoke strongly, gave numerous Anti-Union toasts, vowed his eternal hostility to so infamous a measure, pledged himself to God and man to resist it to extremities, and, to finish and record his sentiments, he had composed an Anti-Union song of many stanzas, which he sung himself with a general chorus, to celebrate the spirit, the cause, and the patriotism of the meeting; this was encored more than once by the company, and he withdrew towards day with the reputation of being in 1799, the most pure, unflinching opponent of the measure he so cordially resisted.

From that day, Lords Cornwallis and Castlereagh wisely marked him out as one of their opponents who should be gained over on *any terms.*

Human nature is the same in every part of the globe; wherever ambition, vanity or avarice take root, and become ruling passions, their vegetation may be checked for a day, but the root is perennial: and Ireland had no reason to suppose nature would favour her by an unqualified exemption of her representatives from those alluring vices which she had so profusely lavished on and exemplified in the British Parliament, that at length it became so politically vicious and intolerably corrupt, that the remedy of a democratic reform, in the Commons, or more properly, a recurrence to the theory of the constitution, was found indispensable to secure the remains of that constitution against the overwhelming influence of the Peers and the oligarchy which menaced its annihilation.

It was, therefore, the very summit of British egotism and injustice, to pretend that the corrupt state of the Irish Parliament formed a leading and just ground for altogether extinguishing its existence, though it appears in full proof, that in proportion to their respective numbers, the British Commons at the period of the Irish Union contained one fourth more corrupt, corruptible, and influenced members than that of Ireland at *any period,* and that the British Minister on the regency question, intimidated, influenced, or corrupted the British House of Commons, when that of Ireland was found pure enough to resist all his efforts, and support the heir apparent.

The English people, therefore, from a recurrence to unequivocal facts, and from a sad experience of the infinite ease with which any minister corrupted and controlled at pleasure their own Parliament, will scarcely believe that all the arts, the money, the titles, the offices, the bribes, their minister could bestow, all the influence he possessed, all the patronage he could grant, all the promises he could make, all the threats he could use, all the terrors he could excite, all the deprivations he could inflict, could seduce or warp away scarcely more than a half of the members of the Irish Commons, from their duty to their country and that on the question of annexation by union, his utmost efforts could not influence more than eight above a moiety of their number; yet, with only 158 out of 300, which in England would be considered a defeat, he persevered and effected the extinguishment of the legislature, a majority, which, on any important question would have cashiered a British minister. Yet such was the fact in Ireland; and the division of the 5th and 6th February, 1800, on the Union, will remain an eternal record of the unrivalled incorruptible purity of 115 members of that Parliament. This observation is matter of absolute fact; it may be proper to give it even by anticipation, as an illustration, and a fact of which the English people seem to have been totally ignorant. For her own sake probably England will soon recur to Irish history, where she will find her long sufferings, and more unshaken loyalty to her English kings than in any other country or portion of her people.*

This not misplaced digression will be considered as a prelude to the sequel of Mr. Handcock, being a sample and a warning to England of what might be also the fate of their own representation.

The blandishments of the crafty Viceroy, were now unsparingly lavished on Mr. Handcock; simple money would not do, they endeavoured to persuade him that his principles were disloyal, his song was sedition, and that further opposition might end in treason; still he held out until title was added to the bribe, his own conscience was not strong enough to resist the charge, the vanity of his family lusted for nobility. He wavered, but he yielded; his vows, his declaration, his song, all vanished before vanity, and the year 1800 saw Mr. Handcock of Athlone Lord Castlemaine. But the reputation of a renegade was embodied with the honours of his family, and pecuniary compensation for a Parliamentary return could do no mischief to his public reputation; he became a strong supporter of the Union.

* *Vide ante*, page 225.

CHAPTER XXVII.

Felons in the gaols induced, by promise of pardon, to sign petitions in favour of the Union—Every means of corruption resorted to by the Viceroy—Viceroy doubtful of future support—Resorted to Place Bill—Unparalleled measure of public bribery avowed by Lord Castlereagh—Bill to raise £1,500,000, for bribes—Grave reflection on the King's assenting to an avowed act of corruption—A few bribes called Compensation—The British Parliament had anticipated the proposal—Lord Cornwallis's speech peculiarly artful—Lord Loftus moves the address—Lord Castlereagh's reason—Sir Laurence Parson's important motion and speech—Debate continued all night—Lord Castlereagh's plan put into execution—Mr. Bushe—Mr. Plunket—Mr. St. George Daly—His character—His attack on Mr. Bushe—On Mr. Plunket—Replied to by Mr. Barrington—Mr. Peter Burrows—Affecting appearance of Mr. Grattan in the House of Commons—Returned for Wicklow the preceding evening—The impediment laid by Government—Returned at midnight—Entered the house at seven in the morning in a debilitated state—Description of his entry—Powerful sensation caused by his splendid oration—Mr. Corry induced to reply—No effect on the House—The three Bagwells seceded from Government—Lord Ormond changed to the minister—Mr. Arthur Browne's tergiversation—Division—Mr. Foster's speech—Important incident—Bad conduct of the clergy—Very singular circumstance—Mr. Annesley chairman of the committee on the Union—Bishop of Clogher returns Mr. Annesley to Parliament—Messrs. Ball and King petition—Succeed—Mr. Annesley declared not duly elected—Left the chair and quitted the House—Not a legal chairman—Shameful and palpable act of corruption by Sir William Gladowe Newcomen—Bribe proved—Bribery of Mr. Knox and Mr. Crowe—Their speeches against the Union—The Earl of Belvidere most palpably bribed to change sides—His resolutions—Mr Knox and Mr. Crowe bribed—Mr. Usher bribed to secrecy—The corrupt agreement of Mr. Crowe and Mr. Knox to vacate their seats for Union members, in presence of Mr. Usher, a Parson—The terms with Lord Castlereagh—Mr. Charles Ball's affecting conduct—The Anti-Union members, despairing, withdraw in a body—Last sitting of the Irish Parliament—The House surrounded by military—Most affecting scene—Bad consequences to England—Unhappiness of the Speaker—Ireland extinguished.

1. It is not possible to comprise in a single volume a tithe of the means and measures of every description, resorted to by the Viceroy and Secretary, not only to

seduce the members, but to procure addresses favourable to their views, from every or any rank or description of people, from the first rank to the very lowest order; beggars, cottagers, tradesmen, every individual who could be influenced, were tempted to put their names or marks to addresses, not one word of which they understood the intent, still less the ruinous result of. Even public instances were adduced, some mentioned in Parliament, and not denied, of felons in the gaols purchasing pardon, or transmutation, by signatures, or by forging names, to Union eulogiums.

English generals, who, at a moment when martial law existed, or a recollection of its execution was still fresh in every memory, could not fail to have their own influence over proclaimed districts and bleeding peasantry; of course, their success in procuring addresses to Parliament, was not limited either by their power, their disposition, or their instructions.

The Anti-Union addresses, innumerable and fervid, in their very nature voluntary, and the signatures of high consideration, were stigmatized by the title of seditious and disloyal; whilst those of the compelled, the bribed, and the culprit were printed and circulated by every means that the treasury, or the influence of the Government, could effect.

Mr. Darby, High Sheriff of King's County, and Major Rogers of the artillery, had gone so far as to place two six-pounders towards the doors of the Court House, where the gentlemen and freeholders of the county were assembling to address as Anti-Unionists; and it is not to be wondered at, that the dread of grape shot not only stopped those, but numerous meetings for similar purposes; yet this was one of the means taken to prevent the expression of public meetings without, and formed a proper comparison for the measures resorted to, within the walls of Parliament.

As this volume cannot detail the innumerable circumstances and episodes which a perfect history of those times would embody, it may be enough to say, that if the English readers of this work will imagine any act that an indefatigable, and, on this subject, the most corrupt of Governments could by possibility resort to, to carry a

measure they had determined on; such readers cannot
imagine acts more illegal, unconstitutional, and corrupt,
than those of the Viceroy of Ireland, his secretary and
under-secretary, employed, from the close of the session
of 1799 to that of 1800; in the last of the Irish Parliaments every thing therefore is passed over, or but slightly
touched on, till the opening of the last session.

II. Lords Cornwallis and Castlereagh, having made
good progress during the recess, now discarded all secrecy
and reserve. To recite the various acts of *simple metallic
corruption* which were practised without any reserve,
during the summer of 1799, are too numerous for this
volume. It will be sufficient to describe the proceedings,
without particularizing the individuals. Many of the
Peers, and several of the Commoners had the patronage
of boroughs, the control of which was essential to the
success of the Minister's project. These patrons Lord
Castlereagh assailed by every means which his power and
situation afforded. Lord Cornwallis was the remote, Lord
Castlereagh the intermediate, and Mr. Secretary Cooke,
the immediate agents on many of these bargains. Lord
Shannon, The Marquis of Ely, and several other Peers
commanding votes, after much coquetry, had been secured
during the first session; but the defeat of Government
rendered their future support uncertain. The parliamentary patrons had breathing time after the preceding
session, and began to tremble for their patronage and
importance; and some desperate step became necessary
to Government to insure a continuance of the support of
these personages. This object gave rise to a measure
which the British nation will scarcely believe possible,
its enormity is without parallel.

Lord Castlereagh's first object was to introduce into
the House, by means of the Place Bill, a sufficient number of dependents to balance all opposition. He then
boldly announced his intention to turn the scale, by bribes
to all who would accept them, under the name of *compensation* for the loss of patronage and interest. He publicly declared, *first*, that every nobleman who returned
members to Parliament should be paid, in cash 15,000*l.*
for every member so returned; *secondly*, that every
member who had *purchased* a seat in Parliament should

have his purchase-money repaid to him, by the Treasury of Ireland ; *thirdly*, that all members of Parliament, or others, who were losers by a Union, should be fully recompensed for their losses, and that 1,500,000*l.* should be devoted to this service : in other terms, all who supported his measure were, under some pretence or other, to share in this bank of corruption.

A declaration so flagitious and treasonable was never publicly made in any country ; but it had a powerful effect in his favour ; and, before the meeting of Paliament, he had secured a small majoriy, (as heretofore mentioned,) of eight above a moiety of the members, and ne courageously persisted.

After the debate on the Union in 1800, he performed his promise, and brought in a Bill to raise one million and a half of money upon the Irish people, nominally to compensate, but really to bribe their representatives, for betraying their honour and selling their country. This Bill was but feebly resisted ; the divisions of January and February (1800) had reduced the success of the Government to a certainty, and all further opposition was abandoned. It was unimportant to Lord Castlereagh, who received the plunder of the nation ; the taxes were levied, and a vicious partiality was effected in the partition.

The assent to the Bill by his Majesty, as King of Ireland, gives rise to perhaps the most grave consideration suggested in these Memoirs.

A king, bound by the principles of the British Constitution, giving his sacred and voluntary fiat to a Bill to levy taxes for the compensation of members of Parliament, for their loss of the opportunities of selling what it was criminal to sell or purchase, could scarcely be believed by the British people.

It may be curious to consider how the English would endure the proposal of such a measure in their own country, a British Premier who should advise his Majesty to give his assent to such a statute, would experience the utmost punishment that the severest law of England could inflict for that enormity. Nor should the Irish people be blamed for refusing to acquiesce in a measure which was carried in direct violation of the law, and infraction of the statutes against bribery and corruption, and in defiance of every precept moral and political.

There were times when Mr. Pitt would have lost his head for a tithe of his Government in Ireland: Stafford was an angel compared to that celebrated statesman.

When the compensation statute had received the royal assent, the Viceroy appointed four commissioners to carry its provisions into execution. Three were Members of Parliament, whose salaries of 1200*l.* a year each (with probable advantages) were a tolerable consideration for their former services. The Honourable Mr. Annesley, Secretary Hamilton, and Dr. Duigenan, were the principal commissioners of that extraordinary distribution.

It is however to be lamented, that the records of the proceedings have been *unaccountably disposed of*. A voluminous copy of claims, accepted and rejected, was published, and partially circulated; but the great and important grants, the *private* pensions, and *occult* compensations, have never been made public, further than by those who received them.* It is known that

	£	s.	d.
Lord Shannon received for his patronage in the Commons	45,000	0	0
The Marquis of Ely	45,000	0	0
Lord Clanmorris, besides a Peerage	23,000	0	0
Lord Belvidere, besides his *douceur*	15,000	0	0
Sir Hercules Langrishe	15,000	0	0

III. At length, the Parliament being sufficiently arranged to give Government a reasonable assurance of success, Lord Castlereagh determined to feel the pulse of the House of Commons distinctly before he proposed the measure of the Union.

* The extraordinary claims for compensation, and some extraordinary grants by the Commissioners, would, on any other occasion, be a fit subject for ridicule. But the application of *one million and a half sterling*, to purposes so public and so vile, renders it an eternal blot on the Government in Ireland, and on the minister and cabinet of England for permitting the King to give the royal assent to so indisputably corrupt a statute.

Amongst other curious claims for Union *Compensations*, in the Report *printed and circulated*, appear, one from the Lord Lieutenant's *ratcatcher* at the Castle, for decrease of employment; another from the *necessary woman* of the Privy Council of England, for increased trouble in her department; with numerous others of the same quality.

The British Parliament had already framed the terms on which the proposition was to be founded, giving to its own project the complexion of a favour, and triumphing by anticipation over the independence of Ireland.

This was a masterpiece of arrogance; and it was determined to try the feelings of the Commons by a negative measure, before the insulting one should be substantially propounded to them. The 15th day of January, 1800 (the last session of the Irish Parliament,) gave rise to a debate of the most acrimonious nature, and of great importance.

The speech of Lord Cornwallis from the throne was expected to avow candidly the determination of the Minister to propose, and if possible achieve, a Legislative Union. Every man came prepared to hear that proposal; but a more crafty course was taken by the Secretary.

To the surprise of the Anti-Unionists, the Viceroy's speech did not even hint at the measure, the suggestion of a Union was sedulously avoided. Lord Viscount Loftus (now Marquis of Ely)* moved the address, which was as vague as the speech was empty. Lord Loftus was another of those young noblemen who were emitted by their connections to mark their politics: but neither the cause nor his Lordship's oration conferred any honour on the author; and his speech would have answered any other subject just as well as that upon which it was uttered.

There was not a point in the Viceroy's speech intended to be debated. Lord Castlereagh, having judiciously collected his flock, was better enabled to decide on numbers; and to count with sufficient certainty on the result of his labours since the preceding session, without any hasty or premature disclosure of his definitive measure.

This negative and insidious mode of proceeding, however, could not be permitted by the opposition; and Sir Laurence Parsons, after one of the most able and luminous speeches he had ever uttered, moved an amendment, declaratory of the resolution of Parliament to preserve the Constitution as established in 1782, and to support the freedom and independence of the nation. This motion

---

* His Lordship, who took so prominent and invidious a part in the transaction, had been christened Lee Boo by the humourous party of the House, and was only selected to show the Commons that his father had been purchased.

was the touch-stone of the parties; the attendance of the Unionists in the House was compulsory, that of its opponents optional; and on counting the members, sixty-six (about a fifth of the whole) were absent, a most favourable circumstance for the Minister. Every mind was at its stretch, every talent was in its vigour: it was a momentous trial; and never was so general and so deep a sensation felt in any country. Numerous British noblemen and commoners were present at that and the succeeding debate, and they expressed opinions of Irish eloquence which they had never before conceived, nor ever after had an opportunity of appreciating. Every man on that night seemed to be inspired by the subject. Speeches more replete with talent and energy, on both sides, never were heard in the Irish Senate, it was a vital subject. The sublime, the eloquent, the figurative orator, the plain, the connected, the metaphysical reasoner, the classical, the learned, and the solemn declaimer, in a succession of speeches so full of energy and enthusiasm, so interesting in their nature, so important in their consequence, created a variety of sensations even in the bosom of a stranger, and could scarcely fail of exciting some sympathy with a nation which was doomed to close for ever that school of eloquence which had so long given character and celebrity to Irish talent.

The debate proceeded with increasing heat and interest till past ten o'clock the ensuing morning (16th.) Many members on both sides signalized themselves to an extent that never could have been expected. The result of the convivial resolution at Lord Castlereagh's house, already mentioned, was actually exemplified and clearly discernible; an unexampled zeal, an uncongenial energy, an uncalled for rancour, and an unusual animation broke out from several supporters of Government, to an extent which none but those who had known the system Lord Castlereagh had skilfully suggested to his followers, could in any way account for. This excess of ardour gave to this debate not only a new and extraordinary variety of language, but an acrimony of invective, and an absence of all moderation, never before so immoderately practised.

This violence was in unison with the pugnacious project of anticipating the Anti-Unionists in offensive operations, some remarkable instances of that project were actually put into practice, and are not unworthy of being recorded in the Irish chronicles.

Mr. Bushe, the late Chief Justice of Ireland, was as nearly devoid of private and public enemies as any man. Endowed with superior talents, he had met with a corresponding success in an ambitious profession and in a jealous country. His eloquence was of the purest kind; but the more delicate the edge, the deeper cuts the irony, and his rebukes were of that description; and when embellished by his ridicule, coarse minds might bear them, but the more sensitive ones could not. Mr. Plunket's satire was of a different nature, his weapon cut in every direction, and when once unsheathed, little quarter could be expected. His satire was, at times, of that corroding yet witty nature, that no patience could endure; yet, on this debate, both these gentlemen were assailed with intrepidity by a person whose talents were despised, and the price of whose seduction glared in an appointment to the highest office at the Irish bar—a barrister without professional practice or experience, and who was not considered susceptible of black letter. As a statesman he had no capacity, and as an orator he was below even mediocrity, from an embarrassed pronunciation which seemed to render any attempt at elocution a most hopeless experiment. Such was Mr. St. George Daly, appointed Prime Serjeant of Ireland in the place of Mr. Fitzgerald, raised over the heads of the Attorney and Solicitor General, and, from a simple briefless advocate elevated to the very highest rank of a talented and learned profession. Mr. Daly, however, was a gentleman of excellent family, and common sense, and, what was formerly highly esteemed in Ireland, of a "fighting family." He was the brother of Mr. Dennis Daly, of so much talent, and of so much reputation amongst the patriots of eighty-two. He was proud enough for his pretensions, and sufficiently conceited for his capacity: and a private gentleman he would have remained, had not Lord Castlereagh and the Union placed him in public situations where he had himself too much sense not to feel that he certainly was over-elevated. This gentleman is particularly noticed, as, on this night, he, in some points, over came the public opinion of his incapacity, and he surprised the House by one of the most clever and severe philippics which had been pronounced during the discussions upon the Union, more remarkable from being directed against two of the most pure and formidable orators in the country.

The contempt with which Mr. Daly conceived his capacity was viewed by the superior members of his profession, the inaptitude he himself felt for the ostensible situation he was placed in, the cutting sarcasms liberally lavished on his inexperience and infirmity, in lampoons and pamphlets, combined to excite an extraordinary exertion to extricate himself from the humiliating taunts that he had been so long experiencing. Mr. Daly's attack on Mr. Bushe was of a clever description, and had Mr. Bushe had one vulnerable point, his assailant might have prevailed. He next attacked Mr. Plunket, who sat immediately before him; but the materials of his vocabulary had been nearly exhausted; however, he was making some progress, when the keen visage of Mr. Plunket was seen to assume a curled sneer, which, like a legion offensive and defensive, was prepared for any enemy. No speech could equal his glance of contempt and ridicule, Mr. Daly received it like an arrow, it pierced him, he faltered like a wounded man, his vocal infirmity became more manifest, and after an embarrassed pause, he yielded, changed his ground, and attacked by wholesale every member of his own profession who had opposed a Union, and termed them a disaffected and dangerous faction. Here again he received a reply not calculated to please him, and at length he concluded one of the most remarkable speeches, because one of the most unexpected, that had been made during the discussion. Every member who had been in the habit of addressing the House, new ones who had never spoken, on that night made warm, and several of them eloquent, orations.

Mr. Peter Burrows, a veteran advocate for the rights of Ireland, wherever and whenever he had the power of declaring himself, on this night made an able effort to uphold his principles. He was a gentleman of the bar who had many friends, and justly; nothing could be more ungracious than the manner, nothing much better than the matter, of his orations. His mind had ever been too independent to cringe, and his opinions too intractable for an arbitrary minister: on this night he formed a noble and distinguished contrast to those of his own profession, who had sold themselves and the representation for a mess of pottage.

The House had nearly exhausted itself and the subject; when, about seven o'clock in the morning, an incident the most affecting and unexpected, occurred, and which is too precious a relic of Irish Parliamentary chronicles, not to be recorded.

IV. The animating presence of Mr. Grattan on this first night of the debate was considered of the utmost importance to the patriots, it was once more raising the standard of liberty in Parliament. He had achieved the independence of his country in 1782, and was the champion best calculated at this crisis to defend it, a union of spirit, of talent, and of honesty, gave him an influence above all his contemporaries. He had been ungratefully defamed by the people he had liberated, and taking the calumny to heart, his spirit had sunk within him, his health had declined, and he had most unwisely seceded in disgust from Parliament, at the very moment when he was most required to defend both himself and his country. He seemed fast approaching to the termination of all earthly objects, when he was induced once more to shed his influence over the political crisis.

At that time Mr. Tighe returned the members for the close borough of Wicklow, and a vacancy having occurred, it was tendered to Mr. Grattan, who would willingly have declined it but for the importunities of his friends.

The Lord Lieutenant and Lord Castlereagh, justly appreciating the effect his presence might have on the first debate, had withheld the writ of election till the last moment the law allowed, and till they conceived it might be too late to return Mr. Grattan in time for the discussion. It was not until the day of the meeting of Parliament that the writ was delivered to the returning officer. By extraordinary exertions, and perhaps by following the example of government in overstraining the law, the election was held immediately on the arrival of the writ, a sufficient number of voters were collected to return Mr.

Grattan before midnight. By one o'clock the return was on its road to Dublin; it arrived by five; a party of Mr. Grattan's friends repaired to the private house of the proper officer, and making him get out of bed, compelled him to present the writ to Parliament before seven in the morning, when the House was in warm debate on the Union. A whisper ran through every party that Mr. Grattan was elected, and would immediately take his seat. The Ministerialists smiled with incredulous derision, and the opposition thought the news too good to be true.

Mr. Egan was speaking strongly against the measure, when Mr. George Ponsonby and Mr. Arthur Moore (now Judge of the Common Pleas) walked out, and immediately returned, leading, or rather helping, Mr. Grattan, in a state of total feebleness and debility. The effect was electric. Mr. Grattan's illness and deep chagrin had reduced a form, never symmetrical, and a visage at all times thin, nearly to the appearance of a spectre. As he feebly tottered into the House, every member simultaneously rose from his seat. He moved slowly to the table; his languid countenance seemed to revive as he took those oaths that restored him to his pre-eminent station; the smile of inward satisfaction obviously illuminated his features, and reanimation and energy seemed to kindle by the labour of his mind. The House was silent, Mr. Egan did not resume his speech, Mr. Grattan, almost breathless, as if by instinct, attempted to rise, but was unable to stand, he paused and with difficulty requested permission of the House to deliver his sentiments without moving from his seat. This was acceded to by acclamation, and he who had left his bed of sickness to record, as he thought, his last words in the Parliament of his country, kindled gradually till his language glowed with an energy and feeling which he had seldom surpassed. After nearly two hours of the most powerful eloquence, he concluded with an undiminished vigour, miraculous to those who were unacquainted with his intellect.

Never did a speech make a more affecting impression, but it came too late. Fate had decreed the fall of Ireland, and her patriot came only to witness her overthrow. For two hours he recapitulated all the pledges that England had made and had broken, he went through the great events from 1780 to 1800, proved the more than treachery which had been practised towards the Irish people. He had concluded, and the question was loudly called for, when Lord Castlereagh was perceived earnestly to whisper to Mr. Corry, they for an instant looked round the House, whispered again, Mr. Corry nodded assent, and, amidst the cries of question, he began a speech, which, as far as it regarded Mr. Grattan, few persons in the House could have prevailed upon themselves to utter. Lord Castlereagh was not clear what impression Mr. Grattan's speech might have made upon a few hesitating members; he had, in the course of the debate, moved the question of adjournment; he did not like to meet Sir Laurence Parsons on his motion, and Mr. Corry commenced certainly an able, but, towards Mr. Grattan an ungenerous and an unfeeling personal assault, it was useless, it was like an act of a cruel disposition, and he knew it could not be replied to. At length the impatience of the House rendered a division necessary, and in half an hour the fate of Ireland was decided. The numbers were—

For an *Adjournment*, Lord Castlereagh had . . 138
For the *Amendment* 96

Majority 42*

* One of the most unexpected and flagitious acts of public corruption was that of Mr. Arthur Brown, member for the University of Dublin. He was by birth an American, of most gentlemanly manners, excellent character, and very considerable talents. He had by his learning become a senior fellow of the University, and was the law professor. From his entrance into Parliament he had been a steady, zealous, and able supporter of the rights of Ireland, he had never deviated; he would accept no office; he had attached himself to Mr. Ponsonby, and was supposed to be one of the truest and most unassailable supporters of Ireland.

In the session of 1799 he had taken a most unequivocal, decisive, and ardent part against the Union, and had spoken against it as a crime, and as the ruin of the country; ne was believed to be incorruptible. On this night he rose, but crest-fallen and abashed at his own tergiversation; he recanted every word he had ever uttered, deserted from the country, supported the Union, accepted a bribe from the Minister, was afterwards placed in office, but shame haunted him, hated himself: an amiable man fell a victim to corruption. He rankled, and pined, and died of a wretched mind and a broken constitution

This decision, undoubtedly, gave a death wound to the Irish nation. Many, however, still fostered the hope of success in the opposition; and Lord Castlereagh did not one moment relax his efforts to bribe, to seduce, and to terrify his opponents.

The Anti-Unionists, also, lost no opportunity of improving their minority; and the next division proved that they had not. The adjournment was to the 5th day of February; the Union propositions, as passed by the British Parliament, were, after a long speech, laid before the House of Commons by Lord Castlereagh : on that day Mr Bagwell, of Tipperary County, seceded from Government, the present Marquis of Ormond had also divided from it; and the minority appeared to have received numerous acquisitions. Mr. Saurin, Mr. Peter Burrows, and other eminent gentlemen of the bar, now appeared to make the last effort to rescue their country.

V. Lord Castlereagh, upheld by his last majority, now kept no bounds in his assertions and in his arrogance; and after a debate of the entire night, at eleven the ensuing morning the division took place. It appeared that the Anti-Unionists had gained ground since the former session, and that there existed 115 Members of the Irish Parliament, whom neither promotion, nor office, nor fear, nor reward, nor ambition, could procure to vote against the independence of their country, though nations fall, that opposition will remain immortal.

Lord Castlereagh's motion was artful in the extreme, he did not move expressly for any adoption of the propositions, but that they should be printed and circulated, with a view to their ultimate adoption.

This was opposed as a virtual acceptation of the subject; on this point the issue was joined, and the Irish nation was, on that night, laid prostrate. The division was—

Number of Members	300
For Lord Castlereagh's Motion	158
Against it	115
Of Members present, majority	43
Absent	27

By this division, it appears that the Government had

a majority of the House of only *eight*, by their utmost efforts, 27 were absent, of whom every man refused to vote for a Union, but did not vote at all, being kept away by different causes ; and of consequence *eight* above a moiety carried the Union ; and of the 158 who voted for it in 1800, 28 were notoriously bribed or influenced corruptly.

Although this was ominous to the ultimate fate of the nation, the contest still proceeded with unremitting ardour ; numerous debates and numerous divisions took place before the final catastrophe, in numbers, Government made no progress, and never could or did obtain a majority of fifty on the principle of a Union.

The details of the subsequent proceedings are not within the range of this desultory memoir. The speech of Mr. Foster, the Speaker, against the measure occupied four hours : a deference to his opinion, and a respect for his true patriotism, caused a dead silence throughout the entire of his oration, on any other occasion, that oration would have been overwhelming ; but the question was, in fact, decided before he had, in the committee, any opportunity of declaring his opinion ; and his speech was little more than recording his sentiments.

Some very serious facts occurred during the progress of the discussion which may be worth reciting. The House was surrounded by military, under pretence of keeping the peace, which was not in danger, but, in fact, to excite terror ; Lord Castlereagh also threatened to remove the Parliament to Cork, if its proceedings were interrupted. But, unfortunately, the Anti-Unionists had no efficient organization, no decided leader ; scattered and desponding, they* did not excite sufficient external exer-

* The fulsome address from the Catholic clergy and Bishop Lanigan from Kilkenny to Marquis Cornwallis, in favour of the Union, fortunately rendered the addresses perfectly *ridiculous*. One of his excellency's eyes, by some natural defect, appeared considerably diminished and, like the pendulum of a clock, was generally in a state of *motion* The Right Reverend Bishop and clergy having never before seen the Marquis, unfortunately commenced their address with the most *mal a propos* exordium of " your excellency has always kept a *steady eye* on the interests of Ireland." The address was presented at Levee. His excellency however was graciously pleased not to return any answer to that part of their compliment. Mr. Curran, on seeing the address,

tion; destiny seemed to resign the nation to its fate; their own brethren forsook them. The Bishops Troy, Lanigan and others, deluded by the Viceroy, sold their country, and basely betrayed their flocks, by promoting the Union, the great body of Catholics were true to their country, but the rebellion had terrified them from every overt act of opposition, all was confusion, nothing could be effected against Lord Castlereagh, who had one million and a half to bribe with, under pretence of compensation, besides, the secret-service money of England was at his command, and that was boundless. Had the proposal been made two years later, all the wealth and power of England could not have effected the annexation.

The subject is now ended, posterity will appreciate the injuries of Ireland. The only security England has for the permanence of the Union, is a radical change in the nature and genius of the people; or a total change of system in the mode of governing. How blind must those Governments be, which suppose that Ireland ever can be retained permanently by the coercive system! Eight millions of people, whose lives cannot be precious to them, never can be permanently yoked to any other nation, not much more physically powerful, and not near so warlike, save by a full participation of rights and industry; with employment, protection, and any means of subsistence, the Irish might be the easiest managed people on the face of Europe; naturally loyal, naturally tractable, naturally adapted to labour, it is a total ignorance of their character abroad, with a system of petty tyranny at home, that destroys this people, governing by executions has the very opposite effect from that intended, death is too common to have much terrors for a desperate peasantry, hang 100,000 every year, it would make no sensible diminution of the Irish population, and certainly would add nothing to the tranquillity of the country; on the contrary, every execution increases the number of the dissatisfied, who can be contented with the execution of his kindred? The only guardians of that devoted people, the only persons

said the only match for it he had ever read was the mayor of Coventry's speech to Queen Elizabeth: "When the Spanish Armada attacked your *Majesty*, ecod they got the *wrong sow by the ear*." The Queen desired them to go home and she would send an answer.

who could direct or guide them, are now, by the Union, for ever taken away from them; their landlords now reside in other countries; no labourers are now employed on the old demesnes that supported them. What are they to subsist upon? An idle population can never cease to be a disturbed one; and, if it be possible to convince the English people that the state of Ireland must soon influence their own condition, much will be effected; if England should be convinced that Ireland has been plundered by a British Minister, of the only certain means of ensuring her tranquillity (a resident Parliament,) that the plunder has been without any beneficial operation to England herself, great progress will be made toward some better system. Half the time of the Imperial Parliament is now occupied upon a subject of which nothing but local knowledge can give a competent idea; and it is the opinion of the wisest and most dispassionate people, that now reflect upon the state of the connection, that either the Union must be rendered closer and more operative for its professed objects, interests must be more amalgamated, and the nations dovetailed together, or the Union be altogether relinquished, the dilemma is momentous, but the alternative is inevitable.

This digression arises from the circumstances which have been mentioned just preceding it. To a true-hearted Irishman, it must be a subject of solicitude, but a reflection on 1800, never can arise without exciting emotions of disgust and feelings of indignation.

After a long, an ardent, but an ineffective struggle, the Anti-Unionists gave way entirely; and but little further resistance was offered to any thing.

During the progress of the Union bill through the committee, a circumstance took place, which, with reference to analagous subjects, is of the utmost legal and constitutional importance.

Mr. Richard Annesley (afterwards Lord Annesley) was called to the chair of the committee, on the motion of Lord Castlereagh, and sat as chairman nearly throughout the entire discussion.

Mr. R. Annesley and General Gardner, had been returned members for the city of Clogher by the Bishop, whose predecessors had exercised that patronage through the votes of four or five of their own domestics, or, perhaps of only their steward or chaplain, and in their own hall. On this occasion, however, the Bishop's nomination of Mr. Annesley and General Gardner was opposed by Mr. Charles Ball and Colonel King, as an experiment, at the suggestion of Mr. Plunket. On the election, these candidates tendered a number of the resident inhabitants of the district as legal constituents of that ancient city, over which the Bishops had, in despotic times, assumed a patronage, not only contrary to the inherent rights of franchise, but altogether unconstitutional, it being merely a nomination of Members of the Commons by a spiritual Lord. The Bishop's returning officer had, of course, rejected all lay interference, and Mr. Annesley and General Gardner were returned by five or six domestics of the prelate.

This election, however, was most vigorously contested by Mr. Ball and Colonel King; they canvassed the vicinity informed the landholders of their inherent rights, and of the Bishop's usurpation. A great number appeared, and tendered their votes for the new candidates, who, in their turn, objected to every voter received for those of the Bishop; and, thus circumstanced, the return came back to Parliament.

The Bishop's nominees took their seats, as lawful members of Parliament; and as such Mr. Annesley was named chairman to the committee of the whole House, which voted *all the details and articles of the Union.* Mr. Ball and Colonel King, however, petitioned against that return. A committee was appointed to decide the question: every possible delay was contrived by the Government, and every influence was attempted, even over the Members of the committee, nothing was too shameful for the arrogance of the Chancellor (who took a furious part) and the corruption of the Secretary.

VI. After a month of arduous and minute investigation, an old document was traced to the Paper Office at the Castle, which the Viceroy endeavoured to have suppressed by the keeper of the records. On its production, the usurpation of the Bishops was proved beyond all possibility of argument, and Mr. Annesley, through whose voice every clause of the Union had been put and carried, was declared by the House a usurper, and his election, and the return thereupon, was pronounced null and void. By this decision, the whole of the proceedings of the committee had been carried on, through the instrumentality and functions of a person not *de jure* a member of Parliament at the time he so acted. This point, if it had been then vigorously pushed, must have led to most serious and deep constitutional questions.

It was the *lex Parliamentaria* that, on an election for a Member of Parliament, all votes taken before a returning officer not legally qualified as such, were null and void.*

Mr. Charles Ball was excluded from voting against the Union the whole time of Mr. Annesley's so usurping the duties of a member, and voting in its favour. Whether his acts could be construed to be legal was a point rendered useless, by the certainty of the Union being effected.

Mr. Annesley was in his seat in the House when the report of the committee was read: the effect was considerable. Mr. Annesley and General Gardner instantly rose and left the House, and Mr. Charles Ball and Colonel King were as quickly introduced, dressed in the Anti-Union uniform, and took their seats in the place of the discarded members. A new chairman was substituted for Mr. Annesley.

Another curious instance of palpable corruption remains on record. Sir William Gladowe Newcomen, Bart., member for the county of Longford, in the course of the debate, declared he supported the Union, as he was not instructed to the contrary by his constituents. This avowal surprised many, as it was known that the county was nearly unanimous against the measure, and that he was well acquainted with the fact. However, he voted for Lord Castlereagh, and he asserted that conviction alone was his guide; his veracity was doubted, and in a few months some of his bribes were published. His wife was also created a peeress.

* It was contended by the constitutional lawyers, that the votes of a committee taken by a chairman who was not a member of the House, the journals he signed, and the reports he brought up, were void, and, *a fortiori*, every act of the committee.

One of his bribes has been discovered, registered in the Rolls office, a document which it was never supposed would be exposed, but which would have been grounds for impeachment against every member of Government who thus contributed his aid to plunder the public and corrupt Parliament.

The following is a copy, from the Rolls Office of Ireland:

By the Lord Lieutenant and General Governor of Ireland,

CORNWALLIS.

" Whereas Sir William Gladowe Newcomen, Bart., hath by his memorial laid before us, represented that, on the 25th day of June, 1785, John, late Earl of Mayo, then Lord Viscount Naas, Receiver General of Stamp Duties, together with Sir Thomas Newcomen, Bart., and Sir Barry Denny, Bart., both since deceased, as sureties for the said John, Earl of Mayo, executed a bond to his Majesty, conditioning to pay into the treasury the stamp duties received by him; that the said Earl of Mayo continued in the said office of Receiver General until the 30th day of July, 1786, when he resigned the same, at which time it is stated that he was indebted to his Majesty in the sum of *about* five thousand pounds, and died on the 7th of April, 1792; that the said sureties are dead, and the said Sir Thomas Newcomen, Bart., did by his last will appoint the memorialist executor of his estate; that the memorialist proposed to pay into his Majesty's Exchequer the sum of two thousand pounds, as a *composition* for *any* money that might be recovered thereon, upon the estate being released from any further charge on account of the said debt due to his Majesty. And the before-mentioned *Memorial* having been referred to his Majesty's *Attorney General,* for his opinion what would be *proper* to be done in this matter, and the said Attorney General having by his report unto us, dated the 20th day of August, 1800, advised that, under all the circumstances of the case, the sum of two thousand pounds should be accepted of the memorialist on the part of Government," &c. &c.

" J. TOLER."

By this abstract it now appears, even by the memorial of Sir William Gladowe, that he was indebted at least five thousand pounds, from the year 1786, to the public treasury and Revenue of Ireland; that, with the interest thereon, it amounted in 1800 to ten thousand pounds; that Sir William had assets in his hands, as executor, to pay that debt; and that, on the Union, when all such arrears must have been paid into the Treasury, the Attorney General, under a reference of Lords Cornwallis and Castlereagh, was induced to sanction the transaction as reported; "viz. " under *all its circumstances*," to forego the debt, except two thousand pounds. Every effort was made to find if any such sum as two thousand pounds was credited to the public, and none such was discovered. The fact is, that Lord Naas owed ten thousand pounds, consequently Sir William owed twenty thousand; that he never *bona fide* paid to the public one shilling, which, with a peerage, the patronage of his county, and the pecuniary pickings also received by himself, altogether formed a tolerably strong bribe, even for a more qualmish conscience than that of Sir William.

But all the individual instances of the corrupt influence which seduced so many members of the Irish Parliament to betray their trusts, and transmit their names to posterity as the most fatal enemies of that island where they drew their breath, would be a labour of too great an extent for a work of this description. But it will suffice to convince the British Empire, that the Union between England and Ireland was the corrupt work of the very minister who was afterwards called over, with his Irish flock to become the shepherd of the British nation.

VII. The few following authenticated examples of corrupt seduction by Lords Cornwallis and Castlereagh *individually*, may give some slight idea of the general system:—

Mr. Francis Knox and Mr. Crowe, two Irish barristers, were returned to Parliament for the close borough of Philipstown, under the patronage of Lord Belvidere. In the session of 1799 they violently opposed the Union. Mr. Knox said; " I am satisfied that in point of commerce, England has nothing to give to this country; but, were it otherwise, I would not condescend to argue the subject;

for I would not surrender the liberties of my country for the riches of the universe! I cannot find words to express the *horror* I feel at a proposition so extremely degrading. It is insulting to entertain it, even for a moment. What! shall we deliberate whether this kingdom shall cease to exist; whether this land shall be struck from the scale of nations; whether its very name is to be erased from the map of the world for ever? Shall it, I say, be a question whether we surrender to another separate country and to another separate legislature, the lives, liberties, and properties of five millions of people, who *delegated us* to defend, but not to destroy the constitution? It is a monstrous proposition, and should be considered, merely in order to mingle our disgust and execration with those of the people, and then to dash it from us, never to be resumed!" Mr. Crowe held similar language.

The Earl of Belvidere then called a meeting of the county of Westmeath, to enter into resolutions against the Union; and his proposed resolutions, in his own handwriting, declaratory of his resistance to that measure, are here inserted. Mr. Crowe termed its supporters "flagitious culprits," and boldly declaimed against the unexampled profligacy of the Viceroy and his Irish Secretary. It is fortunate for history that irrefragable proofs exist of this statement, and that Great Britain may peruse the mode by which Ireland has been united to her. Every line of such documents might well form a ground of prosecution or impeachment, for high crimes and misdemeanours, against both the Viceroy and the Secretary.

The Earl of Belvidere and his two friends had expressed themselves too strongly against the Union, and were of too much importance to be left untempted. The Marquis, therefore, undertook to manage the Peer, whilst Lord Castlereagh engaged to seduce the Commoners. Mr. Usher, the Earl's chaplain, wise man, and adviser, was also enlisted to effect the seduction of his patron and of his accessories. The negociation completely succeeded.

The English nation will scarcely believe the fact, that, within a few months, his Lordship with Mr. Knox and Mr. Crowe, were literally purchased; and, in four months after publishing the resolutions against the Union, new resolutions, in favour of the measure, were circulated by his Lordship among his tenantry. As soon as the bribe was fixed, as he conceived, the whole of his Lordship's former *principles were recanted*, and condemned as hasty, and against the general opinion of the people.

Lord Cornwallis had now gained his point, and turned round on the apostates, they were disgraced traitors: they were now helpless, they durst not again recant. The terms had been munificent, nothing required by Lord Belvidere had been refused by the Marquis; but after he had made their defection public and irrevocable, he gave his Lordship to understand that there was a misconception as to the *terms*, which, being matters of detail, could be more properly arranged by the Secretary; and thus he turned them over to the mercy of Lord Castlereagh. His Lordship, seeing they were entrapped beyond the power of escaping, soon convinced them that he also knew how to despise the instruments he had corrupted. Mr. Usher, the chaplain, was to be remunerated for soothing the conscience of Lord Belvidere, the clergy are seldom reluctant when good bargains are going forward: but a general dissatisfaction now arose among all the parties. Usher, however, was contented, he got a cure of souls for his political guilt, and, after having aided in corruption, went to preach purity to his parishioners!

VIII. The English people would scarcely credit the most accurate historian, did not the annexed letter prove the whole transaction, and leave them to ruminate upon the nefarious system to which they were themselves subject, under the same Minister. In England, an impeachment would have been the result of this disclosure; but, in Ireland, it was the *least* of Lord Castlereagh's malpractices.

Mr. Crowe's letter, shortly after Lord Belvidere was purchased by Lord Cornwallis.

October 4th, 1799.

My Dear Lord,

This moment yours of the 3d inst. has been delivered by the postman. I am heartily concerned that I am obliged to differ with your Lordship (for the first time during a three and twenty years' friendship) in point of fact: as to what passed between you and Lord Cornwallis, it has nothing to do with the present question, which is simply, "whether the agreement made by Mr. Knox with Lord Castlereagh is to be adhered to or violated." This agreement was two months subsequent to your conversation with Lord Cornwallis, and you will recollect you had two interviews with the Viceroy, the latter of which was, by no means, so flattering as the first, and was very far from holding out splendid expectations, but all prior discussions are always done away by a subsequent agreement; for otherwise it would be absurd ever to think of making one, which would be always open to be departed from by any of the parties, on a suggestion that in a prior conversation this thing was said or the other thing was offered. An agreement once made, nothing remains but to carry it into effect according to its terms as fast as possible. The business then comes to this, what was the agreement made by Mr. Knox with Lord Castlereagh, respecting the only point that has induced your Lordship to delay matters, all the rest being confessedly understood, namely, "the vacating Mr. Knox's seat and mine, in order to give the return of the two members to Government in our places."

This particular Mr. Knox stated distinctly and explicitly, that Lord Castlereagh, at the outset of the negociation, laid it down as a *sine qua non*, that we must vacate our seats in the present Parliament, and that he should have the nomination of the two new members." But such a distinction as your Lordship conceives of vacating for the question of Union, and in case Government should be defeated on that measure, that those two new members should vacate, and that you should have a power of nominating in their stead for the remainder of the Parliament, never in the slightest degree was made by Mr. Kox, nor even by your Lordship; but, on the contrary, your Lordship assented to that part as well as to every other part of the treaty with Lord Castlereagh, and from the instant you thus gave your assent, a full, complete, and perfect agreement took place. Mr. Usher was present at all this, and it is his duty to come forward and declare the fact.

On the 10th of July this negociation commenced, and from that period to this, I have been kept in town from my concerns in law, in constant expectation of having it concluded, and now, nearly at the end of three months, to have it all upset is very severe.

As to the engagement that your Lordship describes and that your burgesses signed, it is a direct contradiction to that part of the agreement it professes to be conformable to, and is so much trouble for nothing but what appears extraordinary to me, along with all the rest of this extraordinary business is, that your Lordship should prepare or get this engagement signed after you were apprised, both by Mr. Knox's letters and mine to you and Mr. Usher, that any thing short of the identical paper sent down by Mr. Knox, would not answer. I have nothing more to add than to request your Lordship will bring Mr. Usher up with you directly.

I am, my dear Lord,
Your's most sincerely,
ROB. CROWE.

To the Earl of Belvidere, &c., &c., &c.

[The Original of this letter is in the Author's possession.]

RESOLUTIONS

In the hand-writing of the Earl of Belvidere, prepared by him for the Freeholders of the County of Westmeath, against a Legislative Union in 1799. *His Lordship afterwards voted for and supported that measure warmly.*

Resolved, That the free and independent Legislature of Ireland having been unequivocally established, every measure that tends to encroach on it calls for our implicit disapprobation.

The depending project of a Union with Great Britain, the appearance of being merely a transfer of the Parliament is, in fact, a complete extinction of it; that it is the duty of Irishmen of every description to come forward, and by all constitutional means to resist a scheme so subversive of the real interest, prosperity and dignity of their country.

That we entertain too high an opinion of the integrity of our representatives, to suppose them capable of voting

away the rights of the people, had a power of such a nature been ever invested in them.
[The Original is in the Author's possession.]

This transaction between Lord Cornwallis and Castlereagh, and Lord Belvidere and Messrs. Knox and Crowe, ought to be one of the most useful lessons to the British nation; there will be seen, in the sad fate of Ireland, the means by which their own liberties may be destroyed.

Before the third reading of the Bill, when it was about to be reported, Mr. Charles Ball, Member for Clogher, rose, and, without speaking one word, looked round impressively, every eye was directed to him, he only pointed his hand significantly to the bar, and immediately walked forth, casting a parting look behind him, and turning his eyes to Heaven, as if to invoke vengeance on the enemies of his country. His example was contagious. Those Anti-Unionists who were in the House immediately followed his example, and never returned into that Senate which had been the glory, the guardian, and the protection of their country. There was but one scene more, and the curtain was to drop for ever.*

* One of those singular incidents which, though trivial, occasionally produce a great sensation, occurred in the progress of the Bill, on the debate respecting the local representation. From the nature of the subject and the strong feelings of every party, the slightest incident, the most immaterial word, or unimportant action, was construed into an indication of something momentous. Mr. Charles Ball, the new Member for Clogher, was a most ardent, impetuous, and even furious opponent of a Union, on any terms or under any circumstances. He was a very large, eager, boisterous, and determined man; he uttered whatever he thought, and there was no restraining his sentiments. In the midst of the crowded coffee-room he declared his astonishment, that whilst hundreds of wretched men every day sacrificed their lives in resisting those who openly attacked their liberty, there were none who did not at once rid their country of the monsters who were betraying it. "It could be easily done," said he, "by a few hand-grenades, or shells, thrown from the gallery when your ministerial gentlemen are locked up for a division."

The extravagance of the idea excited general merriment; but there were some who actually conceived the practicability of the scheme. Mr Ball, with affected gravity, added, that he had heard such a plan was intended; and this only increased the previous merriment. The House presently commenced its sitting, and Mr. Secretary Cooke had taken the chair of the Committee, when suddenly a voice like thunder burst from the gallery, which was crowded to excess; "*Now*" (roared the Stentor), "*now let the bloodiest assassin take the chair!—let the bloodiest assassin take the chair!*"

The day of extinguishing the liberties of Ireland had now arrived, and the sun took his last view of indepen dent Ireland, he rose no more over a proud and prosperous nation, she was now condemned, by the British Minister, to renounce her rank amongst the States of Europe, she was sentenced to cancel her constitution, to disband her Commons, and disfranchise her nobility, to proclaim her incapacity, and register her corruption in the records of the empire. On this fatal event, some, whose honesty the

Any attempt at description of the scene would be unavailing, the shells and hand-grenades of Mr. Ball presented themselves to every man's imagination. All was terror and confusion; many pressed towards the doors, but the door-keepers had fled, and turned the keys to prevent the escape of the culprit. A few hats fell by accident from the galleries, which were in a state of tumult. These appeared like bomb-shells to the terrified Members; pocket-pistols and swords were upon the point of being produced; every man seemed to expect the bloody assassins to rush in hundreds from the galleries. No explosion, however, took place; no assassins descended; and a scuffle in the gallery was succeeded by an exclamation, "We have secured him! We have secured him!" which restored some confidence to the senators. The serjeant-at-arms now ascended, sword in hand, and was followed by many of the Members, whose courage had been quiescent till there was a certainty of no danger. Mr. Denis Brown, as a forlorn hope, was the first to mount the gallery. After a valiant resistance, an Herculean gentleman was forced down into the body of the House, by a hundred hands. As soon as he was effectually secured, all the Members were most courageous; some pommelled, some kicked him, and at length he was thrown flat upon the floor, and firmly pinioned. The whole power of Parliament, however, could not protect them from his eloquence; and most powerfully did he use his tongue. The gigantic appearance of the man struck every body with awe, and none but the lawyers had the least conception that he was a Mr. Sinclair, one of the most quiet and well-behaved barristers of the whole profession. He was a respectable, independent, and idle member of the Irish Bar, but an enthusiast against a Union. He had dined with a party of the same opinions at the house of a friend who was undoubtedly a madman, but whose excellent wine and wild conversation had elevated Mr. Sinclair so very far above all dread, that he declared he would himself, that night, in spite of all the traitors, make a speech in the House, and give them his full opinion of the only measure that should be taken against them. He accordingly repaired to the gallery, and, on seeing the Secretary take the chair, he could no longer contain himself, and attempted to leap down among the Members; but being restrained by some friends who were with him, he determined to make his speech, and commenced with the most appalling expression of what he conceived should be the fate of the Unionists. He was committed to Newgate by the House, and remained there till the session ended

tempter could not destroy, some, whose honour he durst not assail, and many who could not control the useless language of indignation, prudently withdrew from a scene where they would have witnessed only the downfall of their country. Every precaution was taken by Lord Clare for the security, at least, of his own person. The Houses of Parliament were closely invested by the military no demonstration of popular feeling was permitted, a British regiment, near the entrance, patrolled through the Ionic colonades, the chaste architecture of that classic structure seemed as a monument to the falling Irish, to remind them of what they had been, and to tell them what they were. It was a heart-rending sight to those who loved their country, it was a sting to those who sold it, and to those who purchased it, a victory, but to none has it been a triumph. Thirty-three years of miserable experience should now convince the British people that they have gained neither strength, nor affection, nor tranquillity, by their acquisition ; and that if population be the " wealth of nations," Ireland is getting by far too rich to be governed much longer as a pauper.

The British people knew not the true history of the Union, that the brilliant promises, the predictions of rapid prosperity, and "consolidating resources,"* were but chimerical. Whilst the finest principles of the constitution were sapped to effect the measure, England, by the subjugation of her sister kingdom, gained only an accumulation of debt, an accession of venality to her Parliament, an embarrassment in her councils, and a prospective danger to the integrity of the empire. The name of Union has been acquired, but the attainment of the substance has been removed farther than ever.

The Commons House of Parliament, on the last evening afforded the most melancholy example of a fine independent people, betrayed, divided, sold, and, as a State, annihilated. British clerks and officers were smuggled into her Parliament to vote away the constitution of a country to which they were strangers, and in which they had neither interest nor connection. They were employed

* *" Consolidating the strength and resources of the Empire"* was Lord Castlereagh's *fundamental* argument on proposing that measure: but he lived long enough to see that it had the very contrary operation.

to cancel the royal charter of the Irish nation, guaranteed by the British Government, sanctioned by the British legislature, and unequivocally confirmed by the words, the signature, and the great seal of their monarch.

The situation of the Speaker, on that night, was of the most distressing nature; a sincere and ardent enemy of the measure, he headed its opponents; he resisted it with all the power of his mind, the resources of his experience, his influence and his eloquence.

It was, however, through his voice that it was to be proclaimed and consummated. His only alternative (resignation) would have been unavailing, and could have added nothing to his character. His expressive countenance, bespoke the inquietude of his feeling; solicitude was perceptible in every glance, and his embarrassment was obvious in every word he uttered.

The galleries were full, but the change was lamentable, they were no longer crowded with those who had been accustomed to witness the eloquence and to animate the debates of that devoted assembly. A monotonous and melancholy murmur ran through the benches, scarcely a word was exchanged amongst the members, nobody seemed at ease, no cheerfulness was apparent, and the ordinary business, for a short time, proceeded in the usual manner.

At length the expected moment arrived, the order of the day for the third reading of the Bill, for a "Legislative Union between Great Britain and Ireland," was moved by Lord Castlereagh, unvaried, tame, coldblooded, the words seemed frozen as they issued from his lips; and, as if a simple citizen of the world, he seemed to have no sensation on the subject.

At that moment he had no country, no god but his ambition; he made his motion, and resumed his seat, with the utmost composure and indifference.

Confused murmurs again ran through the House, it was visibly affected, every character, in a moment, seemed involuntarily rushing to its index, some pale, some flushed, some agitated; there were few countenances to which the heart did not despatch some messenger. Several Members withdrew before the question could be repeated, and an awful momentary silence succeeded their departure

The Speaker rose slowly from that chair which had been the proud source of his honours and of his high character; for a moment he resumed his seat, but the strength of his mind sustained him in his duty, though his struggle was apparent. With that dignity which never failed to signalize his official actions, he held up the Bill for a moment in silence; he looked steadily around him on the last agony of the expiring Parliament. He at length repeated, in an emphatic tone, "as many as are of opinion that THIS BILL do pass, say aye." The affirmative was languid but indisputable, another momentary pause ensued, again his lips seemed to decline their office: at length, with an eye averted from the object which he hated, he proclaimed, with a subdued voice, " *the* AYES *have it*." The fatal sentence was now pronounced, for an instant he stood statue-like; then indignantly, and with disgust, flung the Bill upon the table, and sunk into his chair with an exhausted spirit. An independent country was thus degraded into a province, Ireland, as a nation, was EXTINGUISHED.

ORIGINAL RED LIST,

Or the Members who voted against the Union in 1799, *and* 1800, *with observations.*

Those Names with a * affixed to them, are County Members; those with a †, City Members; and those with a §, Borough Members; those in *Italics* CHANGED SIDES, and got either Money or Offices.

OBSERVATIONS

1.* Honorable A. Acheson Son to Lord Gosford.
2.* William C. Alcock County Wexford.
3.* Mervyn Archdall . County Fermanagh.
4.§ W. H. Armstrong . . Refused *all* terms from Government.
5.* *Sir Richard Butler* Changed sides. See Black List.
6.* *John Bagwell* . . Changed sides TWICE. See Black List.
7.§ Peter Burrowes . . Now Judge of the Insolvent Court; a stea dy Anti-Unionist.
8.* *John Bagwell, Jun.* . Changed sides. See Black List.
9.† John Ball . . . Member for Drogheda—*incorruptible*
10.† Charles Ball . . Brother to the preceding.
11.† Sir Jonah Barrington . King's Counsel—Judge of the Admiralty— *refused all* terms.
12.§ Charles Bushe . . . Afterwards Solicitor General, and Chief Justice of Ireland—incorruptible.
13.† John C. Beresford . *Seceded* from Mr. Ponsonby in 1799, on his declaration of independence. That secession was fatal to Ireland.
14. *Arthur Brown* . Member for the University, *changed sides* in 1800; was appointed Prime Serjeant by Lord Castlereagh, through Mr. Cooke —of all others the most open and palpable case. See Black List.
15.§ William Blakeney . *A Pensioner*, but opposed Government.
16.* William Burton . Sold his *Borough*, Carlow, to a Unionist (Lord Tullamore,) but remained staunch himself.
17.* H. V. Brooke.
18.§ Blayney Balfour.
19.§ David Babbington . . Connected with Lord Belmore.
20.† Hon. James Butler . (Now Marquis of Ormonde) *voted in* 1800 *against a Union*, but with Government on Lord Corry's motion.
21.* Col. J. Maxwell Barry, (Now Lord Farnham) nephew to the Speaker.

OBSERVATIONS.

22.§ *William Bagwell*. Changed sides TWICE, concluded as a *Unionist*. See Black List.
23.* Viscount Corry . . (Now Lord Belmore) dismissed from his regiment by Lord Cornwallis—a zealous leader of the Opposition.
24.† *Robert Crowe* . . A Barrister, bribed by Lord Castlereagh See his Letter to Lord Belvidere.
25.* Lord Clements . (Now Lord Leitrim.)
26.* Lord Cole . . (Now Lord Enniskillen) *unfortunately* dissented from Mr. Ponsonby's Motion for a declaration of independence in 1799, *whereby* the Union was revived and *carried*.
27.§ Hon. Lowry Cole A General; brother to Lord Cole.
28.* R. Shapland Carew.
29.† Hon. A. Creighton . Changed sides, and became a Unionist. See Black List.
30.† Hon. J. Creighton . Changed sides. See Black List
31.* Joseph Edward Cooper.
32.† *James Cane* . . Changed sides. See Black List.
33.* Lord Caulfield . . (Now Earl Charlemont) son to Earl Charlemont, a principal Leader of the Opposition
34.† Henry Coddington.
35.§ George Crookshank A son of the Judge of the Common Pleas
36.* Dennis B. Daly Brother-in-law to Mr. Ponsonby; a most active Anti-Unionist.
37.† Noah Dalway.
38,* Richard Dawson.
39.* Arthur Dawson . Formerly a Banker, father to the late Under-Secretary.
40.* Francis Dobbs . . Famous for his Doctrine on the Millennium; an ENTHUSIASTIC Anti-Unionist.
41.† John Egan . . . King's Council, Chairman of Kilmainham; offered a Judge's seat, but could not be purchased, though far from rich.
42. R. L. Edgeworth.
43.† George Evans.
44.* Sir John Freke, Bart., (Now Lord Carberry.)
45.* Frederick Falkiner . Though a distressed person, could not be purchased.
46.§ Rt. Hon. J. Fitzgerald, Prime Sergeant of Ireland; could *not* be bought, and was dismissed from his high office by Lord Cornwallis; father to Mr. Vesey Fitzgerald.
47 * William C. Fortescue, One of the three who inconsiderately opposed Mr. Ponsonby, *and thereby carried the Union.*
(Poisoned by accident.)
48.* Rt. Hon. John Foster Speaker; the chief of the Opposition throughout the whole contest

OF THE IRISH NATION. 463

OBSERVATIONS

49.* Hon. Thomas Foster.
50.* Sir T. Fetherston, Bart Changed sides. See Black List.
51.* Arthur French . . Unfortunately coincided with Mr. Fortescue in 1799, against Mr. Ponsonby.
52.§ Chichester Fortescue . King at Arms; brought over in 1800, by Lord Castlereagh; voted both sides; ended a Unionist.
53.§ William Gore . . . Bought by Lord Castlereagh in 1800.
54.§ Hamilton Georges. A distressed man, but could not be purchased; father-in-law to Secretary Cooke.
55.§ Rt. Hon. H. Grattan.
56.§ Thomas Goold . . . Now Serjeant, brought into Parliament by the Anti-Unionists.
57.† Hans Hamilton . . Member for Dublin County.
58.† Edward Hardman . . City of Drogheda; the Speaker's friend.
59.§ Francis Hardy . . Author of the Life of Charlemont; brother-in-law to the Bishop of Down.
60.§ Sir Joseph Hoare.
61.* William Hoare Hume, Wicklow County.
62.§ Edward Hoare . . Though *very old*, and *stone blind*, attended all the debates, and sat up all the nights of debate.
63.§ Bartholomew Hoare . King's Counsel.
64.§ Alexander Hamilton King's Counsel; son to the Baron.
65.§ Hon. A. C. Hamilton.
66.§ Sir F. Hopkins, Bart. Prevailed on to take money to *vacate*, in 1800, and let in a Unionist.
67.† H. Irwin.
68.* Gilbert King
69.† Charles King.
70.* Hon. Robert King.
71.* Lord Kingsborough (Now Earl Kingston.)
72. Hon. George Knox Brother to Lord Northland; lukewarm.
73.† Francis Knox . Vacated his seat for Lord Castlereagh. See Mr. Crowe's Letter.
74.* Rt. Hon. Henry King.
75.† Major King . . . He opened the Bishop of Clogher's Borough in 1800.
76.§ Gustavus Lambert · Brother to Countess Talbot
77.* David Latouche, jun.. A Banker.
78.§ Robert Latouche . . Ditto.
79.§ John Latouche, sen. . Ditto.
80.§ John Latouche, junr. . Ditto.
81.* Charles Powell Leslie.
82.* Edward Lee . . Member for the County of Waterford; zealous.
83.† Sir Thomas Lighton, Bt. A Banker.
84.* Lord Maxwell . . . Died Lord Farnham
85.*Alexander Montgomery

OBSERVATIONS.

86.§ Sir J. M'Cartney, Bart. Much distressed, but could not be bribed; nephew, by affinity to the Speaker.
87.§ *William Thomas Mansel*, Actually *purchased* by Lord Castlereagh.
88.§ Stephen Moore . Changed sides on Lord Corry's Motion. See Debates.
89.§ John Moore.
90. Arthur Moore . . Now Judge of the Common Pleas; a staunch Anti-Unionist.
91.* Lord Mathew . . . (Now Earl Llandaff) Tipperary County.
92.§ Thomas Mahon.
93.§ John Metge . . . Brother to the Baron of the Exchequer.
94.§ Richard Neville Had been a dismissed treasury officer; sold his vote to be reinstated; *changed sides*. See Black List.
95.§ Thomas Newenham . The Author of various Works on Ireland; one of the steadiest Anti-Unionists.
96.* Charles O'Hara . . Sligo County.
97.* Sir Edward O'Brien . Clare County.
98.§ Col. Hugh O'Donnel . A most *ardent* Anti-Unionist; dismissed from his regiment of Mayo militia.
99.§ James Moore O'Donnel, Killed by Mr. Bingham in a duel.
100.§ Hon. W. O'Callaghan, Brother to Lord Lismore.
101 Henry Osborn . . Could not be bribed; his brother was.
102.* Right Hon. Geo. Ogle, Wexford County.
103.§ Joseph Preston An eccentric character could not be purchased.
104 * *John Preston* . Of Bellintor, was *purchased* by a title (Lord Tara,) and his brother, a Parson, got a living of £700 a-year.
105.* Rt. Hon. Sir J Parnell, Chancellor of the Exchequer, dismissed by Lord Castlereagh; incorruptible.
106.§ Henry Parnell.*
107.§ W. C. Plunket . . Now Lord Plunket. See his able speech.
108.* Right Hon. W. B. Ponsonby . . . Afterwards Lord Ponsonby.
109.§ J. B. Ponsonby . Afterwards Lord Ponsonby.
110.§ Major W. Ponsonby . A General, killed at Waterloo.
111.* Rt. Hon. G. Ponsonby, Afterwards Lord Chancellor; died of apoplexy.
112 * Sir Laurence Parsons, King's County; now Earl of Rosse; made a remarkably fine speech.
113 § Richard Power . . Nephew to the Baron of the Exchequer.
114.* Abal Ram . . . . *Changed sides*.
115.* Gustavus Rochfort County Westmeath; seduced by Government, and *changed sides* in 1800 See Black List.

* Sir John Parnell was one of the ablest supporters of Government of his day. His son has taken assiduously a more extensive and deeper field of business in finance, but in any other point, public or private, has no advantage over his father

OF THE IRISH NATION. 465

OBSERVATIONS.

116 § John S. Rochfort   Nephew to the Speaker.
117.   Sir Wm. Richardson
118.§ *John Reily* . . . . *Changed sides.* See Black List.
119.   William E. Reily.
120.§ Charles Ruxton.
121.§ William P. Ruxton.
122.* *Clotworthy Rowley*   *Changed sides.* See Black List.
123.§ *William Rowley* . . *Changed sides.* See Ditto.
124.§ *J. Rowley* . .   *Changed sides* See Ditto
125.* Francis Saunderson.
126.* William Smyth . . Westmeath
127.* James Stewart.
128.§ Hon. W. J. Skeffington.
129.* Francis Savage.
130.§ Francis Synge.
131.§ Henry Stewart.
132.§ Sir R. St. George, Bart.
133.§ *Hon. Benj. Stratford.* Now Lord Aldborough; gained by Lord Castlereagh; *changed sides.* See Black List.
134.* Nathaniel Sneyd.
135.* *Thomas Stannus*   *Changed sides,* Lord Portarlington's Member. See Black List.
136.§ Robert Shaw . . A Banker.
137.§ Rt. Hon. Wm. Saurin, Afterwards Attorney General; a steady but calm Anti-Unionist.
138.§ William Tighe.
139.§ Henry Tighe.
140.§ John Taylor.
141.§ Thomas Townshend.
142.* *Hon. Richard Trench,* Voted against the Union in 1799; was gained by Lord Castlereagh, whose relative he married, and voted for it in 1800; was created an Earl, and made an Ambassador to Holland; one of the Vienna Carvers; and a Dutch Marquess.
143.* Hon. R. Taylor.
144.§ Charles Vereker   . (Now Lord Gort) City Limerick
145.§ Owen Wynne.
146.* John Waller.
147.§ E. D. Wilson.
148 § *Thomas Whaley*   First voted *against* the Union; *purchased* by Lord Castlereagh; he was Lord Clare's brother-in-law. See Black List.
149.* Nicholas Westby.
150.* John Wolfe .   Member for the County Wicklow; Colonel of the Kildare Militia, refused to vote for Government, and was cashiered; could not be purchased.

By the Red and Black Lists (published at the time, the *originals* being now in the Author's possession) it is *evident*, beyond all contradiction, that of those who had, in 1799, successfully opposed the Union, or had *declared* against it, Lord Castlereagh, palpably purchased *twenty-five* before the *second* discussion in 1800, which made a difference of fifty votes in favour of government; and it is therefore equally evident, that, by the public and actual bribery of those twenty-five members, and not by any change of opinion in the country, or any fair or honest majority, Mr. Pitt and his instruments carried the Union in the Commons House of Parliament; and it is proper the English nation should know accurately *how* they have acquired the *incumbrance* of Ireland in its present form, and what little importance was set on every principle of the British Constitution, in the mind of the same Minister whom they immediately afterwards entrusted with their own liberties, their money, and their national reputation—every one of which was more or less sacrificed, or squandered, during his administration in England, and his negociations at Vienna.

The observations annexed to the names in these Lists were, at the time, either in actual proof, or sufficiently notorious to have been printed in various documents at that epoch. As to the House of Lords, the servile—almost miraculous—submission with which they surrendered their hereditary prerogatives, honours, rights, and dignities, into the hands of the Lords Clare and Castlereagh, is a subject unprecedented. But this being announced for discussion by the Imperial Parliament, in the ensuing session, through the interference of Lord Rossmore, &c. &c., no list of the Lords is here given, in order not to anticipate that parliamentary stricture, which will be, no doubt, more potent and elucidating than any which could with propriety be made in any other place than in that august assembly. As the capitulation was disgusting, the discussion must be severe.

ORIGINAL BLACK LIST.

<table>
<tr><td></td><td>OBSERVATIONS.</td></tr>
<tr><td>1. R. Aldridge</td><td>An English Clerk in the Secretary's office; no connection with Ireland.</td></tr>
<tr><td>2. Henry Alexander</td><td>Chairman of Ways and Means; cousin of Lord Caledon; his brother made a Bishop; himself Colonial Secretary at the Cape of Good Hope.</td></tr>
<tr><td>3. Richard Archdall</td><td>Commissioner of the Board of Works.</td></tr>
<tr><td>4. William Bailey</td><td>Commissioner of Ditto.</td></tr>
<tr><td>5. Rt. Hon. J. Beresford,</td><td>First Commissioner of Revenue; brother-in-law to Lord Clare.</td></tr>
<tr><td>6. J. Beresford, jun</td><td>Then Purse-bearer to Lord Clare, afterwards a Parson, and now Lord Decies.</td></tr>
<tr><td>7. Marcus Beresford</td><td>A Colonel in the Army, son to the Bishop, Lord Clare's nephew.</td></tr>
<tr><td>8. J. Bingham*</td><td>Created a Peer; got £8000 for two seats; and £15,000 compensation for Tuam. This gentleman first offered himself for sale to the Anti-Unionists; Lord Clanmorris.</td></tr>
<tr><td>9. Joseph H. Blake</td><td>Created a Peer—Lord Wallscourt, &c.</td></tr>
<tr><td>10. Sir J. G. Blackwood,</td><td>Created a Peer—Lord Dufferin.</td></tr>
<tr><td>11 Sir John Blaquiere,</td><td>Numerous Offices and Pensions, and created a Peer—Lord De Blaquiere.</td></tr>
<tr><td>12. Anthony Botet</td><td>Appointed Commissioner of the Barrack Board, £500 a-year.</td></tr>
<tr><td>13. Colonel Burton</td><td>Brother to Lord Conyngham; a Colonel in the Army.</td></tr>
<tr><td>14. Sir Richard Butler,</td><td>Purchased and changed sides; voted against the Union in 1799, and for it in 1800. Cash.</td></tr>
<tr><td>15. Lord Boyle</td><td>Son to Lord Shannon; they got an immense sum of money for their seats and Boroughs; at £15,000 each Borough.</td></tr>
<tr><td>16. Rt. Hon. D. Brown,</td><td>Brother to Lord Sligo.</td></tr>
<tr><td>17. Stewart Bruce</td><td>Gentleman Usher at Dublin Castle; now a Baronet.</td></tr>
<tr><td>18. George Burdet</td><td>Commissioner of a Public Board, £500 per annum.</td></tr>
<tr><td>19. George Bunbury</td><td>Ditto.</td></tr>
</table>

* The Author of this work was deputed to learn from Mr. Bingham what his expectations from Government for his seats were; he proposed to take from the Opposition £8000 for his two seats for Tuam, and oppose the Union. Government afterwards added a Peerage and £15,000 for the Borough

		OBSERVATIONS.
20	Arthur Brown	Changed sides and principles, and was appointed Serjeant; in 1799 opposed the Union, and supported it in 1800; he was Senior Fellow of Dublin University; lost his seat the ensuing election, and died.
21.	—— Bagwell, sen.	Changed twice; got half the patronage of Tipperary; his son a Dean, &c. &c.
22.	—— Bagwell, jun.	Ditto, got the Tipperary Regiment, &c.
23.	William Bagwell	His brother.
24.	Lord Castlereagh	The Irish Minister.
25.	George Cavendish	Secretary to the Treasury during pleasure; son to Sir Henry.
26.	Sir H. Cavendish	Receiver General during pleasure; deeply indebted to the Crown.
27.	Sir R. Chinnery	Placed in office after the Union
28.	James Cane	Renegaded, and got a pension.
29.	Thomas Casey	A Commission of Bankrupts under Lord Clare; made a City Magistrate.
30.	Colonel C. Cope	Renegaded; got a Regiment, and the patronage of his county.
31.	General Cradock	Returned by Government; much military rank; now Lord Howden.
32.	James Crosby	A regiment and the patronage of Kerry, jointly; seconded the Address.
33.	Edward Cooke	Under Secretary at the Castle.
34.	Charles H. Coote	Obtained a Regiment (which was taken from Colonel Wharburton) patronage of Queen's County, and a Peerage, (Lord Castlecoote) and £7,500 in cash for his interest at the Borough of Maryborough, in which, in fact, it was *proved* before the Commissioners that the Author of this work had more interest than his Lordship.
35.	Rt. Hon. I. Corry	Appointed Chancellor of the Exchequer, on dismissal of Sir John Parnell.
36.	Sir J. Cotter	Privately brought over by cash.
37.	Richard Cotter	
38.	Hon. H. Creighton	Renegaded (see Red List) privately purchased.
39.	Hon. J. Creighton	
40.	W. A. Crosbie	Comptroller to the Lord Lieutenant's Household.
41.	James Cuffe	Natural son to Mr. Cuffe of the Board of Works, his father created Lord Tyrawly.
42	General Dunne	Returned for Maryborough by the united influence of Lord Castlecoote and Government, to keep out Mr. Barrington; gained the election by only *one*.
43.	William Elliot	Secretary at the Castle
44	General Eustace	A Regiment.

OBSERVATIONS.

45. Lord C. Fitzgerald, Duke of Leinster's brother; a Pension and a Peerage; a Sea Officer of no repute.
46. Rt. Hon. W. Fitzgerald.
47. Sir C. Fortescue . Renegaded (see Red List) Officer, King at Arms.
48. A. Fergusson . . Got a place at the Barrack Board, £500 a year, and a Baronetcy.
49. Luke Fox . . Appointed Judge of Common Pleas; nephew by marriage to Lord Ely.
50. William Fortescue Got a secret Pension, out of a fund (£3,000 a year) entrusted by Parliament to the Irish Government, solely to reward Mr. Reynolds, Cope, &c. &c., and those who informed against rebels.
51. J. Galbraith . . Lord Abercorn's Attorney; got a Baronetage
52. Henry D. Grady* . First Counsel to the Commissioners.
53. Richard Hare Put two members into Parliament, and was created Lord Ennismore for their votes.
54. William Hare . . His son.
55. Col. B. Henniker . A regiment, and paid £3,500 for his Seat by the Commissioners of Compensation.
56. Peter Holmes . . A Commissioner of Stamps.
57. George Hatton . . Appointed Commissioner of Stamps.
58. Hon. J. Hutchinson, A General—Lord Hutchinson.
59. Hugh Howard . . Lord Wicklow's brother, made Postmaster General.
60. Wm. Handcock An extraordinary instance; he made and sang (Athlone) songs *against* the Union in 1799, at a public dinner of the Opposition, and made and sang songs for it in 1800; he got a Peerage.
61. John Hobson . . Appointed Storekeeper at the Castle Ordnance.
62. Col. G. Jackson A Regiment.
63. Denham Jephson Master of Horse to the Lord Lieutenant.
64. Hon. G. Jocelyn . Promotion in the Army, and his brother consecrated *Bishop of Lismore.*
65. William Jones.
66. Theophilus Jones . Collector of Dublin
67. Major Gen. Jackson, A Regiment.
68. William Johnson Returned to Parliament by Lord Castlereagh, as he himself declared, " to put an end to it;" appointed a Judge since.
69. Robert Johnson . . Seceded from his patron, Lord Downshire, and was appointed a Judge.

* This gentleman the Author knew to be entirely indisposed to a Union, but peculiar circumstances prevented him imperatively but honourably from following his own impression. The Author communicated to Mr. George Ponsonby these causes, as he thought it but justice to Mr. Grady, who, on some occasions, did not conceal his sentiments, and acted fairly.

OBSERVATIONS.

70. John Keane . . A Renegade; got a Pension; See Red List.
71. James Kearny . Returned by Lord Clifton being his Attorney· got an office.
72. Henry Kemmis . Son to the Crown Solicitor.
73. William Knot . . Appointed a Commissioner of Appeals £800 a year.
74. Andrew Knox.
75. Colonel Keatinge.
76. Right Hon. Sir H. Langrishe . A Commissioner of the Revenue, received £15,000 cash for his patronage at Knoctopher.
77. T. Lingray, sen. . Commissioner of Stamps, paid £1,500 for his patronage.
78. T. Lindsay, jun. Usher at the Castle, paid £1,500 for his patronage.
79. J. Longfield . . . Created a Peer; Lord Longueville.
80. Capt. J. Longfield . Appointed to the office of Ship Entries of Dublin taken from Sir Jonah Barrington.
81. Lord Loftus . . . Son to Lord Ely, Postmaster General; got £30,000 for their Boroughs, and created an English Marquis.
82. General Lake . An Englishman (no connection with Ireland;) returned by Lord Castlereagh, *solely* to vote for the Union.
83. Right. Hon. David Latouche.
84. General Loftus . . A General; got a Regiment; cousin to Lord Ely.
85. Francis M'Namara, Cash, and a private Pension, paid by Lord Castlereagh.
86. Ross Mahon . Several appointments and places by Government.
87. Richard Martin . Commissioner of Stamps.
88. Right Hon. Monk Mason . . . A Commissioner of Revenue.
89. H. D. Massy . . Received £4,000 cash.
90. Thomas Mahon.
91. A. E. M'Naghten . Appointed a Lord of the Treasury, &c.
92. Stephen Moore . A Postmaster at will.
93. N. M. Moore.
94. Right Hon. Lodge Morris . . . Created a Peer.
95. Sir R. Musgrave Appointed Receiver of the Customs £1,200 a year.
96. James M'Cleland . A Barrister—appointed Solicitor General, and then a Baron of the Exchequer.
97. Col C. M'Donnel . Commissioner of Imprest Accounts, £500 per annum.

OF THE IRISH NATION. 471

OBSERVATIONS.

98 Richard Magenness, Commissioner of Imprest Accounts, £500 per annum.
99. Thomas Nesbit . A Pensioner at will.
100. *Sir W. G. New- comen, Bart.* Bought (see Memoir *ante,*) and a Peerage for his wife.
101. Richard Neville . Renegaded ; reinstated as Teller of the Exchequer.
102. William Odell . A Regiment, and Lord of the Treasury.
103. Charles Osborne . A Barrister; appointed a Judge of the King's Bench.
104. C. M. Ormsby Appointed First Council Commissioner.
105. Adml. Pakenham, Master of the Ordinance.
106. Col. Pakenham . A Regiment; killed at New Orleans.
107. H. S. Prittie . . A Peerage—Lord Dunalley.
108. R. Pennefather.
109. T. Prendergast . An office in the Court of Chancery, £500 a year; his brother Crown Solicitor.
110. Sir Richard Quin, A Peerage.
111. Sir Boyle Roche . Gentleman Usher at the Castle.
112. R. Rutledge.
113. Hon. C. Rowley . Renegaded, and appointed to office by Lord Castlereagh.
114. Hon. H. Skeffington,Clerk of the Paper Office of the Castle, and £7.500 for his patronage
115. William Smith . A Barrister; appointed a Baron of Exchequer.
116. H. M. Sandford . Created a Peer; Lord Mount Sandford.
117. Edmond Stanley Appointed Commissioner of Accounts.
118. John Staples.
119. John Stewart . Appointed Attorney General, and created a Baronet.
120. John Stratton.
121. *Hon. B. Stratford,* Renegaded to get £7,500, his half of the compensation for Baltinglass.
122. *Hon. J. Stratford,* Paymaster of Foreign Forces, £1,300 a-year, and £7,500 for Baltinglass.
123. Richard Sharkey . An obscure Barrister; appointed a County Judge.
124. *Thomas Stannus,* Renegaded.
125. J. Savage.
126. Rt. Hon. J. Toler, Attorney General; his wife, an old woman, created a Peeress; himself made chief Justice, and a Peer.
127. Frederick Trench, Appointed a Commissioner of the Board of Works.
128. Hon. R. Trench . A Barrister; created a Peer, and made an Ambassador. See Red List.
129. Charles Trench . His brother; appointed Commissioner of Inland Navigation—a new office created by Lord Cornwallis, for rewards.

OBSERVATIONS

130. Richard Talbot.
131. P. Tottenham . Compensation for patronage; cousin, and politically connected with Lord Ely.
132. Lord Tyrone . 104 offices in the gift of his family; proposed the Union in Parliament, by a speech written in the crown of his hat.
133. Chas. Tottenham, In office.
134. —— Townsend . A Commissioner.
135 Robert Tighe . . Commissioner of Barracks.
136 Robert Uniack . A Commissioner; connected with Lord Clare.
137 James Verner . Called the Prince of Orange.
138 J. O. Vandeleur Commissioner of the Revenue; his brother a Judge.
139 Colonel Wemyss . Collector of Kilkenny.
140. Henry Westenraw, Father of Lord Rossmore, who is of the very reverse of his father's politics

THE END

www.ingramcontent.com/pod-product-compliance
Lightning Source LLC
Chambersburg PA
CBHW051850300426
44117CB00006B/332